THE CAMBRIDGE COMPANION TO
AMERICAN POE

This *Companion* shows that American poetry c
having important continuities with the poetry ...., takes
place in new modes and contexts that require new critical paradigms. Offering a
comprehensive introduction to studying the poetry of the new century, this
collection highlights the new, multiple centers of gravity that characterize
American poetry today. Chapters on African American, Asian American,
Latinx, and Indigenous poetries respond to the centrality of issues of race and
indigeneity in contemporary American discourse. Other chapters explore poetry
and feminism, poetry and disability, and queer poetics. The environment, capitalism, and war emerge as poetic preoccupations, alongside a range of styles from
the spoken word to the avant-garde, and an examination of poetry's place in the
creative writing era.

Timothy Yu is the author of *Race and the Avant-Garde: Experimental and Asian
American Poetry since 1965*, the editor of *Nests and Strangers: On Asian
American Women Poets*, and the author of a poetry collection, *100 Chinese
Silences*. He is Martha Meier Renk-Bascom Professor of Poetry and Professor of
English and Asian American Studies at the University of Wisconsin–Madison.

THE CAMBRIDGE
COMPANION TO
TWENTY-FIRST-CENTURY AMERICAN POETRY

EDITED BY
TIMOTHY YU
University of Wisconsin–Madison

CAMBRIDGE
UNIVERSITY PRESS

CAMBRIDGE
UNIVERSITY PRESS

University Printing House, Cambridge CB2 8BS, United Kingdom

One Liberty Plaza, 20th Floor, New York, NY 10006, USA

477 Williamstown Road, Port Melbourne, VIC 3207, Australia

314–321, 3rd Floor, Plot 3, Splendor Forum, Jasola District Centre,
New Delhi – 110025, India

79 Anson Road, #06–04/06, Singapore 079906

Cambridge University Press is part of the University of Cambridge.

It furthers the University's mission by disseminating knowledge in the pursuit of
education, learning, and research at the highest international levels of excellence.

www.cambridge.org
Information on this title: www.cambridge.org/9781108482097
DOI: 10.1017/9781108699518

First published 2021

A catalogue record for this publication is available from the British Library.

Library of Congress Cataloging-in-Publication Data
NAMES: Yu, Timothy (Professor of literature) editor.
TITLE: The Cambridge companion to twenty-first-century American poetry / Timothy Yu.
DESCRIPTION: Cambridge, United Kingdom ; New York, NY : Cambridge University
Press, 2020. | Series: Cambridge companions to literature | Includes
bibliographical references and index.
IDENTIFIERS: LCCN 2020026300 | ISBN 9781108482097 (hardback) | ISBN
9781108699518 (ebook)
SUBJECTS: LCSH: American poetry – 21st century.
CLASSIFICATION: LCC PS617 .C36 2020 | DDC 811/.608–dc23
LC record available at https://lccn.loc.gov/2020026300

ISBN 978-1-108-48209-7 Hardback
ISBN 978-1-108-74195-8 Paperback

CONTENTS

Contents

NOTES ON CONTRIBUTORS

KIMBERLY QUIOGUE ANDREWS is Assistant Professor of English and Creative Writing at Washington College. Her current research explores the interplay between literary-analytical modes of thinking and experimental poetic practice in and around the age of professionalized creative writing programs. Her scholarly work has appeared in *Textual Practice*, *Modernist Cultures*, *New Literary History*, and elsewhere. She is also the author of two volumes of poetry: *BETWEEN* (Finishing Line Press, 2018) and *A Brief History of Fruit* (University of Akron Press, 2020).

ANTHONY BLACKSHER is an assistant professor of sociology at San Bernardino Valley College. He is the associate editor of the *San Diego Poetry Annual* (Garden Oak Press).

STEPHANIE BURT is Professor of English at Harvard University. Her most recent books include *After Callimachus* (Princeton University Press, 2020); *Don't Read Poetry* (Basic Books, 2019); and *Advice from the Lights* (Graywolf, 2017), a National Endowment for the Arts Big Read selection.

DAVID A. COLÓN is Associate Professor of English and Comparative Race & Ethnic Studies at Texas Christian University. His anthology of Miguel González-Gerth's ambilingual poetry *Between Day and Night: New and Selected Poems, 1946–2010* (2013) was named an Outstanding Title by the Association of American University Presses. His essays on Latino/a poetry and poetics have appeared in *The Cambridge History of Latina/o American Literature*, *The Princeton Encyclopedia of Poetry & Poetics*, *American Poets in the 21st Century*, *Cultural Critique*, *Jacket2*, and many other volumes.

SARAH DOWLING is an assistant professor in the Centre for Comparative Literature and Victoria College at the University of Toronto. Dowling is the author of *Translingual Poetics: Writing Personhood under Settler Colonialism* (University of Iowa Press, 2018) and three poetry collections: *Entering Sappho* (Coach House, 2020), *DOWN* (Coach House, 2014), and *Security Posture* (Snare, 2009).

MISHUANA GOEMAN, Tonawanda Band of Seneca, is a professor of Gender Studies, American Indian Studies, affiliated faculty of Critical Race Studies in the Law School, and Special Advisor to the Chancellor on Native American and Indigenous Affairs at the University of California, Los Angeles (UCLA). She is the author of *Mark My Words: Native Women Mapping Our Nations* (University of Minnesota Press, 2013) and a co-PI on two community-based digital projects, *Mapping Indigenous L.A.* (2015) and *Carrying Our Ancestors Home* (2019).

DECLAN GOULD is Assistant Professor of Teaching Instruction in the Intellectual Heritage Program at Temple University. She is the author of the chapbooks *"Like" or "As"* (dancing girl press, 2017) and *Model Figure* (Shirt Pocket Press, 2015) and the co-editor of *(Dis)Integration: Buffalo Poets, Writers, Artists 2017*. Her writing appears or is forthcoming in the *Journal of Literary and Cultural Disability Studies, Amodern, Denver Quarterly, P-Queue, Full Stop, The Conversant, Jacket2,* and *Laura Hershey: On the Life & Work of an American Master*. She holds a PhD in English from the University at Buffalo and an MFA in poetry from Temple University.

CAROLINE HENSLEY is a PhD student in the Department of English at the University of Wisconsin–Madison studying postcolonial literatures and health humanities. She serves as a Mellon-Morgridge Graduate Fellow for an interdisciplinary program at UW–Madison titled "Health and Inequality."

JAVON JOHNSON is Assistant Professor and Director of African American and African Diaspora Studies at the University of Nevada, Las Vegas. He is the author of *Killing Poetry: Blackness and the Making of Spoken Word Communities* (Rutgers University Press, 2017) and the coeditor of *The End of Chiraq: A Literary Mixtape* (Northwestern University Press, 2018). Additionally, Johnson is a three-time national poetry slam champion who has appeared on HBO's *Def Poetry Jam* and TVOne's *Verses and Flow* and who is currently completing his first book of poems, *Ain't Never Not Been Black* (Button, 2020).

SUEYEUN JULIETTE LEE is the author of the poetry books *Solar Maximum* (Futurepoem, 2013), *No Comet, That Serpent in the Sky Means Noise* (Kore Press, 2017), and *Aerial Concave Without Cloud* (Nightboat Books, 2021). A former Pew Fellow in the Arts for Literature, she has held residencies in performance, video art, and dance in Iceland, Norway, and the United States. Her installation, video, and collaborative performance work *Peace Light* (2018) was commissioned by the Asian Arts Initiative in celebration of their twenty-fifth anniversary. She has served as an editorial consultant for the Asian American Writers' Workshop and the Smithsonian Institute's Asian Pacific American Center's inaugural Asian American literary festival.

KEITH D. LEONARD is Associate Professor of Literature at American University. He is the author of *Fettered Genius: The African American Bardic Poet from Slavery to Civil Rights* (University of Virginia Press, 2005).

MICHAEL LEONG'S recent publications include the poetry collection *Words on Edge* (Black Square Editions, 2018) and the critical monograph *Contested Records: The Turn to Documents in Contemporary North American Poetry* (University of Iowa Press, 2020). He teaches at California Institute of the Arts.

CHRISTOPHER NEALON teaches English at Johns Hopkins University. He is the author of two books of literary criticism, *Foundlings: Lesbian and Gay Historical Emotion before Stonewall* (Duke University Press, 2001) and *The Matter of Capital: Poetry and Crisis in the American Century* (Harvard University Press, 2011), and four books of poetry: *The Joyous Age* (Black Square Editions, 2004), *Plummet* (Edge Books, 2009), *Heteronomy* (Edge Books, 2014), and *The Shore* (Wave Books, 2020). He lives in Washington, DC.

JONATHAN SKINNER is Reader in English and Comparative Literary Studies at the University of Warwick. He founded the journal *ecopoetics* and is the author of numerous essays in ecocriticism, sound studies, geopoetics, and postwar and contemporary American poetry and poetics. His poetry collections include *Earth Shadow* (Ahsahta, 2020), *Birds of Tifft* (BlazeVOX, 2011), and *Political Cactus Poems* (Palm Press, 2005).

JACQULYN TEOH is a PhD candidate in the Department of English at the University of Wisconsin–Madison. Her work has appeared in *Modern Fiction Studies* and *The Wiley-Blackwell Encyclopedia of Postcolonial Studies* (Wiley-Blackwell, 2016).

ANN VICKERY is Associate Professor of Writing and Literature at Deakin University. She is the author of *Stressing the Modern: Cultural Politics in Australian Women's Poetry* (Salt Publishing, 2007) and *Leaving Lines of Gender: A Feminist Genealogy of Language Writing* (Wesleyan University Press, 2000). She is coauthor of *The Intimate Archive: Journeys through Private Papers* (National Library of Australia, 2009) and coeditor of *Poetry and the Trace* (Puncher and Wattmann, 2013) and *Manifesting Australian Literary Feminisms: Nexus and Faultlines* (Australian Literary Studies, 2009). She is also the author of two poetry collections, *Devious Intimacy* (Hunter Publishers, 2015) and *The Complete Pocketbook of Swoon* (Vagabond Press, 2014).

STEPHEN VOYCE is Associate Professor of English at the University of Iowa, where he also holds appointments in the Digital Studio and the Center for the Book. He is the author of *Poetic Community: Avant-Garde Activism and Cold War Culture* (University of Toronto Press, 2013), the editor of bpNichol's *a book of variations:*

love – zygal – art facts (Coach House Books, 2013), and the director of the Fluxus Digital Collection.

DOROTHY WANG is Professor of American Studies at Williams College. She is the author of *Thinking Its Presence: Form, Race, and Subjectivity in Contemporary Asian American Poetry* (Stanford University Press, 2013); the first national conference on race and creative writing was named after the monograph. She also conceived of and cofounded the Race and Poetry and Poetics in the UK (RAPAPUK) research collective, based in the UK.

TIMOTHY YU is Professor of English and Asian American studies at the University of Wisconsin–Madison. He is the author of *Race and the Avant-Garde: Experimental and Asian American Poetry since 1965* (Stanford University Press, 2009) and the editor of *Nests and Strangers: On Asian American Women Poets* (Kelsey Street Press, 2015). He is also the author of a poetry collection, *100 Chinese Silences* (Les Figues Press, 2016).

CHRONOLOGY

TIMOTHY YU AND JACQULYN TEOH

2000–2019

Date	Events/Awards	Publications
2000	Anthropocene popularized as a geological concept by atmospheric chemist Paul. J. Crutzen George W. Bush elected US president Pulitzer Prize: C. K. Williams, *Repair* National Book Award: Lucille Clifton, *Blessing the Boats: New and Selected Poems, 1988–2000* National Book Critics Circle Award: Judy Jordan, *Carolina Ghost Woods* Stanley Kunitz appointed Poet Laureate Consultant in Poetry to Library of Congress	
2001	George W. Bush sworn in as 43rd US president September 11 attacks on the United States; the United States invades Afghanistan Pulitzer Prize: Stephen Dunn, *Different Hours*	Alice Fulton, *Felt* Allen Grossman, *How to Do Things with Tears* Nada Gordon and Gary Sullivan, *Swoon* Rod Smith, *The Good House*

(cont.)

Date	Events/Awards	Publications
	National Book Award: Alan Dugan, *Poems Seven: New and Complete Poetry* National Book Critics Circle Award: Albert Goldbarth, *Saving Lives* Billy Collins appointed Poet Laureate	
2002	Lilly Pharmaceuticals heiress Ruth Lilly bequeaths $100 million to *Poetry: A Magazine of Verse* *Russell Simmons Presents Def Poetry Jam* begins airing on HBO Ron Silliman launches "Silliman's Blog" Pulitzer Prize: Carl Dennis, *Practical Gods* National Book Award: Ruth Stone, *In the Next Galaxy* National Book Critics Circle Award: B. H. Fairchild, *Early Occult Memory Systems of the Lower Midwest*	Rachel Blau DuPlessis, *Drafts 1–38* Myung Mi Kim, *Commons* Major Jackson, *Leaving Saturn* Robyn Schiff, *Worth* Harryette Mullen, *Sleeping with the Dictionary* Lyn Hejinian, *The Language of Inquiry*
2003	Establishment of the Poetry Foundation US war in Iraq begins Pulitzer Prize: Paul Muldoon, *Moy Sand and Gravel* National Book Award: C. K. Williams, *The Singing* National Book Critics Circle Award: Susan Stewart, *Columbarium* Louise Glück appointed Poet Laureate	Kenneth Goldsmith, *Day* K. Silem Mohammad, *Deer Head Nation* C. D. Wright, *One Big Self* *Poets Against the War*, ed. Sam Hamill Mei-mei Berssenbrugge, *Nest*
2004	Myspace and Facebook founded	Jen Bervin, *Nets* D. A. Powell, *Cocktails* Christine Pugh, *Rotary*

(*cont.*)

Date	Events/Awards	Publications
	Inaugural Kundiman Workshop Retreat held at the University of Virginia	Claudia Rankine, *Don't Let Me Be Lonely*
	MacArthur Fellowship: C. D. Wright	Srikanth Reddy, *Facts for Visitors*
	Pulitzer Prize: Franz Wright, *Walking to Martha's Vineyard*	Matthew Rohrer, *A Green Light*
	National Book Award: Jean Valentine, *Door in the Mountain: New and Collected Poems, 1965–2003*	Cole Swensen, *Goest*
	Ted Kooser appointed Poet Laureate	
2005	YouTube founded	Elizabeth Alexander, *American Sublime*
	Hurricane Katrina devastates areas of Louisiana and Florida, killing more than 1,800 people	Jennifer Moxley, *Often, Capital*
	Kyoto Protocol on climate change goes into effect	Juliana Spahr, *This Connection of Everyone with Lungs*
	Pulitzer Prize: Ted Kooser, *Delights and Shadows*	Kay Ryan, *The Niagara River*
	National Book Award: W. S. Merwin, *Migration: New and Selected Poems*	Anne Winters, *The Displaced of Capital*
	National Book Critics Circle Award: Jack Gilbert, *Refusing Heaven*	John Yau, *Ing Grish*
		Richard Siken, *Crush*
2006	Twitter founded	Joshua Clover, *The Totality for Kids*
	Tarana Burke creates the "Me Too" campaign for survivors of sexual assault	Noah Eli Gordon, *Inbox*
	Pulitzer Prize: Claudia Emerson, *Late Wife*	Terrance Hayes, *Wind in a Box*
	National Book Award: Nathaniel Mackey, *Splay Anthem*	Alice Notley, *Grave Light: New and Selected Poems, 1970–2005*
	National Book Critics Circle Award: Troy Jollimore, *Tom Thomson in Purgatory*	

(*cont.*)

Date	Events/Awards	Publications
	Donald Hall appointed Poet Laureate	
2007	First iPhone released	Rae Armantrout, *Next Life*
	Mass shooting at Virginia Tech kills thirty-two people	Matthea Harvey, *Modern Life*
	MacArthur Fellowship: Peter Cole	Susan Howe, *Souls of the Labadie Tract*
	National Book Award: Robert Hass, *Time and Materials*	Rod Smith, *Deed*
	National Book Critics Circle Award: Mary Jo Bang, *Elegy*	Aracelis Girmay, *Teeth*
	Charles Simic appointed Poet Laureate Consultant in Poetry to Library of Congress	
2008	Global financial crisis peaks; Bush administration sanctions Emergency Economic Stabilization Act of 2008	Anne Boyer, *The Romance of Happy Workers*
		Kevin Davies, *The Golden Age of Paraphernalia*
	Election of Barack Obama as US president	Rodrigo Toscano, *Collapsible Poetics Theater*
	Pulitzer Prize: Philip Schultz, *Failure*	
	National Book Award: Mark Doty, *Fire to Fire: New and Collected Poems*	Craig Santos Perez, *from unincorporated territory [hacha]*
	National Book Critics Circle Award: Juan Felipe Herrera, *Half the World in Light;* August Kleinzahler, *Sleeping If Off in Rapid City*	Petra Kuppers and Neil Marcus, *Cripple Poetics: A Love Story*
	Kay Ryan appointed Poet Laureate Consultant in Poetry to Library of Congress	
2009	Barack Obama sworn in as 44th US president	Rita Dove, *Sonata Mulattica*
	CantoMundo founded	Frank Bidart, *Watching the Spring Festival*
	Obama signs the Native American Apology Resolution	Carl Phillips, *Speak Low*

(*cont.*)

Date	Events/Awards	Publications
	Pulitzer Prize: W. S. Merwin, *The Shadow of Sirius*	
	National Books Critics Circle Award: Rae Armantrout, *Versed*	
2010	*Deepwater Horizon* oil spill occurs	Ben Lerner, *Mean Free Path*
	Asian American Literary Review and *Lantern Review* founded	Anne Carson, *Nox*
	Instagram launched	Timothy Donnelly, *The Cloud Corporation*
	First VIDA count highlights gender imbalances in publishing	Charles Bernstein, *All the Whiskey in Heaven: Selected Poems*
		John Koethe, *Ninety-Fifth Street*
		Valerie Martinez, *Each and Her*
2011	Eduardo C. Corral becomes first Latino poet to win the Yale Series of Younger Poets with *Slow Lightning*	Bhanu Kapil, *Schizophrene*
		Jean Valentine, *Break the Glass*
	Button Poetry founded by Sam Cook and Sierra DeMulder	Yusef Komunyakaa, *The Chameleon Couch*
	Occupy movement established with "Occupy Wall Street" protest in New York City	Adrienne Rich, *Tonight No Poetry Will Serve: Poems: 2007–2010*
	MacArthur Fellowship: Kay Ryan and A. E. Stallings	
	Pulitzer Prize: Kay Ryan, *The Best of It: New and Selected Poems*	
	National Book Award: Nikky Finney, *Head Off & Split: Poems*	
	National Book Critics Circle Award: Laura Kasischke, *Space, in Chains*	
	Philip Levine appointed Poet Laureate	
2012	Brooklyn Poets founded	Cathy Park Hong, *Engine Empire*

(*cont.*)

Date	Events/Awards	Publications
	Shooting of Trayvon Martin in Sanford, Florida	Eileen Myles, *Snowflake / Different Streets*
	Mass shooting at Sandy Hook Elementary in Connecticut kills twenty-six people	Brenda Shaughnessy, *Our Andromeda*
	"Superstorm" Sandy strikes the East Coast of the United States	Patricia Smith, *Shoulda Been Jimi Savannah*
	Pulitzer Prize: Tracy K. Smith, *Life on Mars*	
	National Book Award: David Ferry, *Bewilderment: New Poems and Translations*	
	National Book Critics Circle Award: D. A. Powell, *Useless Landscape, or A Guide for Boys*	
	Natasha Trethewey appointed Poet Laureate	
2013	Reelection of President Obama	Lucie Brock-Broido, *Stay, Illusion*
	Black Lives Matter movement founded	Adrian Matejka, *The Big Smoke*
	Pulitzer Prize: Sharon Olds, *Stag's Leap*	Brenda Hillman, *Seasonal Works with Letters on Fire*
	National Book Award: Mary Szybist, *Incarnadine*	
	National Book Critics Circle Award: Frank Bidart, *Metaphysical Dog*	
2014	Shooting of Michael Brown Jr. in Ferguson, Missouri; #BlackPoetsSpeakOut launched in response	Rupi Kaur, *Milk and Honey*
	Pulitzer Prize: Vijay Seshadri, *3 Sections*	Hugo Garcia Manriquez, *Anti-Humboldt*
	National Book Award: Louise Glück, *Faithful and Virtuous Night*	Dawn Lundy Martin, *Life in a Box Is a Pretty Life*
		Claudia Rankine, *Citizen: An American Lyric*

(*cont.*)

Date	Events/Awards	Publications
	Charles Wright appointed Poet Laureate	
2015	"Yi-Fen Chou" is revealed to be the pseudonym of Michael Derrick Hudson in a biographical note published as part of the 2015 edition of *The Best American Poetry*, edited by Sherman Alexie	Paolo Javier, *Court of the Dragon* Leah Lakshmi Piepzna-Samarasinha, *Bodymap* Philip Metres, *Sand Opera*
	Mongrel Coalition Against Gringpo established in response to Kenneth Goldsmith's poem "The Body of Michael Brown" and Vanessa Place's Twitter-based remix of *Gone with the Wind*	
	Obergefell v. Hodges legalizes gay marriage in all fifty states	
	Pulitzer Prize: Gregory Pardlo, *Digest*	
	National Book Award: Robin Coste Lewis, *Voyage of the Sable Venus*	
	National Book Critics Circle Award: Ross Gay, *Catalog of Unabashed Gratitude*	
	Juan Felipe Herrera appointed Poet Laureate	
2016	Bob Dylan awarded Nobel Prize in Literature for "having created new poetic expressions within the great American song tradition"	Solmaz Sharif, *Look* Brenda Shaughnessy, *So Much Synth* Douglas Kearney, *Buck Studies*
	Paris Agreement signed	
	Election of Donald Trump as US president	Stephen Collins, *Once in Blockadia*
	Protests against Dakota Access Pipeline led by Standing Rock Sioux	Allison Cobb, *After We All Died* Ocean Vuong, *Night Sky with Exit Wounds*

(*cont.*)

Date	Events/Awards	Publications
	Mass shooting at Pulse nightclub in Orlando, Florida kills forty-nine people	
	Pulitzer Prize: Peter Balakian, *Ozone Journal*	
	National Book Award: Daniel Borzutzky, *The Performance of Becoming Human*	
	National Book Critics Circle Award: Ishion Hutchinson, *House of Lords and Commons*	
2017	Donald Trump sworn in as 45th US president	Tommy Pico, *Nature Poem*
	Kevin Young named Poetry Editor of *The New Yorker*	Patricia Smith, *Incendiary Art*
	#MeToo movement rises to prominence in wake of sexual assault allegations against producer Harvey Weinstein	Divya Victor, *Kith*
		Bonafide Rojas, *Notes on the Return to the Island*
		Sueyeun Juliette Lee, *No Comet, That Serpent in the Sky Means Noise*
	"Unite the Right" white nationalist rally in Charlottesville, Virginia	John Yau, *Bijoux in the Dark*
	Mass shooting in Las Vegas, Nevada kills fifty-eight people	Danez Smith, *Don't Call Us Dead*
	Pulitzer Prize: Tyehimba Jess, *Olio*	Evie Shockley, *semiautomatic*
	National Book Award: Frank Bidart, *Half-Light: Collected Poems, 1965–2016*	Eve Ewing, *Electric Arches*
	National Book Critics Circle Award: Layli Long Soldier, *Whereas*	
	Tracy K. Smith appointed Poet Laureate	
2018	US government separates thousands of migrant children and parents at the Mexico border	Jos Charles, *feeld*
		Wendy Trevino, *Cruel Fiction*
	Dr. Christine Blasey Ford testifies in US Senate to sexual assault by	

(cont.)

Date	Events/Awards	Publications
	Brett Kavanaugh; Kavanaugh is later confirmed as a Supreme Court Justice Pulitzer Prize: Frank Bidart, *Half-Light: Collected Poems, 1965–2016* National Book Award: Justin Phillip Reed, *Indecency* National Book Critics Circle Award: Ada Limón, *The Carrying*	
2019	President Trump is impeached Pulitzer Prize: Forrest Gander, *Be With* National Book Award: Arthur Sze, *Sight Lines* Joy Harjo appointed Poet Laureate	Ilya Kaminsky, *Deaf Republic* Jericho Brown, *The Tradition*

TIMOTHY YU

Introduction

Any effort to characterize, much less comment critically upon, the literary production of a century of which less than a quarter has elapsed is a task that is more than usually humbling for the literary critic. The scholar cannot rely on established canons (or counter-canons) of major authors, or on a broad consensus about the era's characteristic aesthetic trends or styles that might become visible with greater historical distance. The events, debates, and controversies that consume the attention of writers and critics today may well be forgotten tomorrow, while writers and issues that might have seemed marginal at the time may come to seem to later readers like the most significant developments of that era. The scholar of poetry as it is happening *now* cannot even rely upon standardized historical narratives that might provide context for today's poetry, since we are as likely to debate what has actually *happened* in the twenty-first-century so far as we are to debate the work of the writers who are working within it. T. S. Eliot's lament, in his assessment of Joyce's *Ulysses*, that "contemporary history" is an "immense panorama of futility and anarchy" can perhaps be read (against the grain of Eliot's intention) less as a condemnation of modernity than as a description of the situation of any historian of "the contemporary" who would seek to impose structure on the welter of current events.

Yet the distinct challenges of writing twenty-first-century literary history may also have salutary effects. Shifting our attention away from individual, canonical writers and from dominant critical narratives is in fact very much in keeping with the multiple centers of gravity that increasingly characterize American poetry. The turn of the twenty-first-century provides an opportunity for critics to reevaluate, revise, and rewrite the frameworks that dominated the discussion of American poetry in the second half of the twentieth century, frameworks that often highlighted certain developments in poetry (and history) at the expense of others.

The increasingly broad scope of the term "contemporary American poetry" points to the need for such a reassessment of our scholarly frameworks for American poetry. Does a literary-historical narrative that begins in 1945 still provide the most useful context for understanding American poetry through 2020 and beyond? Standard scholarly accounts of post-1945 American poetry still often begin with Donald Allen's *The New American Poetry 1945–1960* (1960) and its ensuing binary setting the "new American poetry" of Charles Olson, Allen Ginsberg, Robert Creeley, or Frank O'Hara against the more traditional aesthetics of writers such as Robert Lowell, James Merrill, or Elizabeth Bishop. Whether this binary was characterized as the "raw" vs. the "cooked," the "academic" vs. the "outsider," or the "mainstream" vs. the "avant-garde," the face-off between such binaries has tended to structure most overviews of contemporary American poetry. Even when such binaries are not evoked, they can be glimpsed in a critic's choice to focus either on individual canonical authors or on groupings or movements.

The rise of a critical discourse around language writing in the later 1980s and 1990s can, in retrospect, be seen as replicating many of these binaries, with writers such as Charles Bernstein, Susan Howe, and Lyn Hejinian granted the mantle of the avant-garde in opposition to what Bernstein himself would call "official verse culture." Indeed, by the later 1990s and early 2000s, many poets seemed inclined to seek a truce or accommodation between these perceived binaries between the "mainstream" and the "experimental," visible in the titles of the self-consciously boundary-straddling journal *Fence* or the anthology *American Hybrid* (2009).

In questioning the continuing relevance of this particular critical binary for twenty-first-century American poetry, I am not arguing that this binary has somehow been transcended, or that "mainstream" and "avant-garde" have successfully fused. Indeed, as we shall see, the poetic "avant-garde" continues to be a topic of debate and controversy. Yet the terms of that debate are no longer what they were in the 1960s or even the 1990s. Perhaps the simplest way to characterize the way such discussions have shifted is that our understanding of "insiders" and "outsiders" in American poetry has changed significantly in the twenty-first-century, thanks in part to changing historical, social, and literary contexts.

From the critical perspective of the twenty-first-century, perhaps the most striking thing about both the post-1945 "new American poetry" and its supposed antagonists is their whiteness. The two anthologies often said to inaugurate the opposition between insider and outsider in contemporary poetry – Allen's *New American Poetry* and Donald Hall, Robert Pack, and Louis Simpson's *New Poets of England and America* (1957) – contain between them only a single poet of color: LeRoi Jones (later Amiri Baraka). The poetic avant-garde in particular has often seemed to be the exclusive province of white men; even in the 1980s, the group of poets associated with language writing was not only almost entirely white but so male-dominated that some of its practitioners felt compelled to ponder the question, "Why don't women do language-oriented writing?"[1]

While there is nothing new about the whiteness of dominant accounts of American poetry – or of American culture more generally – the first decades of the twenty-first-century have seen more vocal and activist efforts to diversify the main currents of American culture, whether through the contents of literary anthologies or the casts of Hollywood films. Yet part of the argument this collection hopes to make is that a late-twentieth-century narrative of the increasing diversification of an established poetic canon is inadequate to the task of describing the rapidly shifting landscape of American poetry. Such an additive, incremental approach arguably continues to position the canon of white male writers (both "establishment" and "avant-garde") at the center of the conversation, incorporating other writers in a tokenistic fashion insofar as they conform to the terms of an already-established poetics. Efforts to articulate categories such as "women's experimental writing" or "black experimental writing," particularly in the 1990s, existed in tension with what the poet Harryette Mullen, in her essay "Poetry and Identity," called "The assumption ... that 'avant-garde' poetry is not 'black' and that 'black' poetry, however singular its 'voice,' is not 'formally innovative'" (30).

Yet there have always been numerous traditions and communities within American poetry – a theme already well-established by the 1990s that scholarship has increasingly taken up since 2000. Much of this discourse has been driven by growing attention to African American poetry and poetics. Scholarship of the 1990s, such as the work of Aldon Lynn Nielsen and Nathaniel Mackey, established distinct and long-standing traditions of experimentation with African American poetry, laying the groundwork for an explosion of work on African American poetics in the early twenty-first-century by scholars such as Keith D. Leonard, Evie Shockley, Meta DuEwa Jones, Brent Hayes Edwards, and Anthony Reed. The past decade or so has also seen the appearance of the first full-length studies of Asian American poetry, from Josephine Park's *Apparitions of Asia* (2008) to Dorothy Wang's *Thinking Its Presence* (2013). The recent emergence of Latinx literature as a major category of US literature has also led to new scholarly work on Latinx poetics, such as Frederick Luis Aldama's *Formal Matters in Contemporary Latino Poetry* (2013), while poets and scholars such as Janice Gould, Robert Dale Parker, and Dean Rader have helped build a substantial critical discourse around Native American poetry.

At least three traits distinguish this new scholarship from earlier work in the field. The first might simply be thought of in terms of critical mass: for the first time, a substantial scholarly literature now exists on a diverse range of African American, Asian American, Latinx, and Native poets. Second, these shifts signal a shift in the makeup of the academy itself, as much of this work is *by* scholars of color and Native scholars in addition to examining work by such writers. Perhaps most importantly, twenty-first-century scholarship has made (or affirmed) the case for distinct poetic traditions informing the work of poets of color and Native poets. Rather than seeing the work of such writers as voices from the margins that have gradually been incorporated into a traditional poetic canon still defined by white writers, recent scholarship has increasingly argued for placing the work of African American, Asian American, Latinx, and Native poets at the center of discussions about contemporary American poetry.

Such shifts in scholarly discourse track shifts in the public profile of American poetry and its institutions. Two examples bookend this period: The premiere of *Def Poetry Jam* on HBO in 2002 opened the twenty-first-century by giving new mainstream prominence to the long-established culture of spoken word performance, often placing poets of color front and center; and, in the mid-2010s, Claudia Rankine's *Citizen* (2014) not only became one of the most widely discussed books of the decade within the poetry world but became a mainstream bestseller and even made a cameo appearance in the 2016 presidential campaign, when a woman was seen reading it as an act of protest at a Donald Trump rally.[2] *Citizen*, in particular, with its treatment of racist microaggressions in a wider history of violence against African Americans, resonated deeply with the Black Lives Matter movement and the centrality of contemporary debates about anti-black racism in US society.

What may be most characteristically new about twenty-first-century poetry is that such critical conversations about race and poetry have increasingly not been seen as "only" the province of writers of color but have shaped conversations about *all* American poetry – including by white poets. One of the most heated recent controversies in poetry focused on Kenneth Goldsmith's 2015 performance of "The Body of Michael Brown," in which Goldsmith read an edited version of the autopsy report of Brown, an unarmed young black man whose killing by police in Ferguson, Missouri in 2014 sparked widespread protest. Goldsmith, a prominent leader of the "conceptual poetry" movement who had read his work at the White House, faced fierce public backlash for what was seen as his exploitation of Brown's death, with the ensuing controversy reaching the pages of *The New Yorker* and *The Guardian*. As Sueyeun Juliette Lee discusses in more detail in Chapter 9 in this collection, the Goldsmith controversy represented a reckoning of sorts for the category of the poetic avant-garde, which, in seeking to comment upon race, unexpectedly found its own whiteness the subject of critique.

These episodes represent, among other things, a forceful challenge to the binary between poetic form and content, which has too often broken down along racialized lines; the work of writers of color has been more often read for its political or cultural "content" rather than its use of or experimentation with poetic form. Yet formal choices, of course, take place within social and political contexts as well. Spoken word, for instance, has still received relatively little scholarly attention and remains largely outside academic accounts of contemporary American poetry; however, it has, over the past several decades, developed distinct forms, aesthetics, styles, and institutions that are largely independent of traditional venues such as the university or elite publishing houses. Rankine's complex negotiations with form, from her deep investment in the lyric to the mixture of poetry, essayistic writing, and visual art that characterizes *Citizen*, reveal a poetics that approaches race *through* form, inquiring into the various forms the black body takes, and is seen through, in US public space.

The present collection acknowledges the centrality of race in twenty-first-century American poetry by opening with chapters on African American, Asian American, Latinx, and Native American poetry. While each of these chapters are grounded in the deeper histories of their respective poetic traditions, each focuses primarily on how writers of color and Native writers have responded to, critiqued, and advanced these traditions since the year 2000. Keith D. Leonard (Chapter 1) elucidates what has been called a "post–civil rights" aesthetic in recent African American poetry, focusing on four broad trends: a poetics of introspection that turns away from politics; a critical reexamination of African American history and heritage; a personalization of collectivist protest in the tradition of the Black Arts Movement; and black literary collective action. Michael Leong (Chapter 2) follows a parallel path in describing the "counter-modes" that twenty-first-century Asian American poets have developed in response to both racialized constraints and established poetic practices; these surrealist, documentary, and phenomenological modes, pioneered by writers of the 1980s and 1990s, have been developed into mature traditions since 2000. David A. Colón (Chapter 3) argues that the locations that have traditionally grounded Latinx writing are increasingly destabilized in the twenty-first-century; his account of the field focuses on the legacies and effects of colonialism, transnationalism, and migration. And Mishuana Goeman (Chapter 4) emphasizes a twenty-first-century "trans-indigenous" poetics that crosses the boundaries of settler colonial states.

Taken together, such approaches form the foundation of a twenty-first-century scholarship that rejects any notion of a neutral, universalizing poetics in favor of a poetics that is deeply implicated in the social and historical structures and conflicts that have characterized the early twenty-first-century. Even late-twentieth-century claims on behalf of the "politics of poetic form"[3] have increasingly been confronted with the need to account for the social locations that shape the politics and form of poetry. If, in the US context, race and indigeneity have arguably been at the center of such an implicated poetics, the politics of twenty-first-century poetic form has equally been conditioned by shifting discourses of gender and sexuality; by geopolitical upheavals, from the 9/11 attacks to ongoing US wars in the Middle East; by a renewal of protest and political resistance, from Occupy Wall Street to Black Lives Matter; by a rising sense of environmental crisis and catastrophe, centered on climate change and the notion of the Anthropocene; and by a rapidly evolving media landscape, with the dawn of the Internet and the rise of the social media age.

Accounts of twenty-first-century American literature have often taken the terrorist attacks of September 11, 2001, as violently inaugurating a new historical era. The notion of a "post-9/11" literature corresponds to the widespread public sense of a sharp rupture that altered Americans' sense of themselves and the world. Yet as the US response to the attacks rapidly shifted from shock to war, many poets found themselves in familiar postures of protest and resistance – even if in a new context. As Stephen Voyce's chapter in this volume (Chapter 13) reminds us, the post-9/11 US wars in Afghanistan and Iraq give rise to our current era of "unending" and "everywhere" war, as well as to what Voyce calls a post-9/11 "poetry of war resistance." The 2003 collection *Poets Against the War* began when the poet Sam Hamill was invited to the White House by First Lady Laura Bush; the event was postponed after Hamill made it known he would use the event to protest against the war in Iraq. Hamill solicited poems protesting the war through a website – a fact that seems trivial today but that served as one marker of the way poetry was quickly adapting to the new media of the internet age; the site ultimately received submissions from more than 13,000 poets.

Did American poetry change after 9/11? Some critics have argued that it did. Ann Keniston and Jeffrey Gray's 2012 anthology *The New American Poetry of Engagement* claims that, after 9/11, American poets "turn[ed] toward a more engaged poetry" (6), writing under a new pressure to "incorporate, chronicle, or allude to public events" (3) – a claim echoed in Voyce's observation of a resurgence in documentary poetry. Keniston and Gray suggest, in short, that post-9/11 poetry is a newly public poetry, a turn away from modernist hermeticism and post-confessional solipsism. As I have argued elsewhere, however, such sweeping statements about what American poetry as a whole is doing in the twenty-first-century are increasingly likely to miss large swaths of the poetic landscape, in part because they are tied to outdated assumptions of which poets and themes are "central" to US poetry.[4] Keniston and Gray's anthology is focused almost entirely on the work of white poets whose relationship to global violence and trauma is that of observers. Yet, as Voyce correctly observes, some of the most powerful American poetry written in response to the post-9/11 era has been produced by Arab or Muslim American poets, who emerge from communities that have been targets of discrimination, profiling, and violence since 2001. The question of American poetry's political engagement in the twenty-first-century looks very different – and, indeed, more continuous with the work of the twentieth century – when white poets are decentered from the discussion.

The desire to claim new political relevance for American poetry in the twenty-first-century is also, of course, a response to perennial discussions of poetry's decline into irrelevance. The 1980s and 1990s saw a number of such laments, from Joseph Epstein's "Who Killed Poetry?" (1988) to Dana Gioia's "Can Poetry Matter?" (1991) to Vernon Shetley's *After the Death of Poetry* (1993). While such commentators identified various culprits in poetry's decline, the general symptoms seemed clear: new books of poetry seldom sold more than a few thousand (or a few hundred) copies; general-interest magazines and book reviews (themselves in sharp decline) discussed poetry with decreasing frequency; and trade publishers were increasingly retreating from publishing any poetry at all. If poetry appeared to be in ongoing retreat in its traditional venues, however, the early 2000s also offered new contexts and new spaces for poetry's ongoing relevance. In particular, the expansion of poetry beyond the traditional printed page and into new media – from television to the Internet – created both new audiences and new opportunities for cultural critique.

In 2002, *Def Poetry Jam* premiered on the HBO cable network. Presented by hip-hop producer Russell Simmons, *Def Poetry Jam* featured poets including Nikki Giovanni, Amiri Baraka, Beau Sia, Willie Perdomo, and Staceyann Chin. As Javon Johnson and Anthony Blacksher discuss in more depth in Chapter 11 in this collection, *Def Poetry Jam* brought the genre of spoken word – whose contemporary history encompasses the Nuyorican Poets Café of the 1970s and the emergence of the poetry slam in the 1980s – to a broad national audience. In addition to popularizing (and, as Johnson and Blacksher suggest, possibly ossifying) the distinctive style of spoken word, *Def Poetry Jam* primarily featured poets of color, thus offering a (perhaps too easy) dichotomy in American poetry at the dawn of the twenty-first-century. If "poetry" was dying in America at the end of the twentieth century, the rise of spoken word seemed to indicate that it might be a certain traditional mode of poetry, focused on the printed page and dominated by white writers, that was in decline; but that a new mode of poetry, grounded in oral performance, aimed at younger audiences, and led by poets of color, might be supplanting it. Although academic scholarship on spoken word poetry is still limited, future histories of American poetry will certainly see the mainstreaming of spoken word as a significant feature of the early twenty-first-century – a mainstreaming that would only accelerate in the internet era.

In fact, by the early 2000s, TV itself seemed in danger of becoming a "legacy" technology, as increasing access to the Internet and the growing popularity of the Web threatened to erode TV's place as the dominant medium of mass communication. The discourse of this era frequently tied the precipitous decline of print culture – of books, magazines, and news-papers – to the rise of the Internet. It was perhaps fitting, then, that one of the first poetic movements of the twenty-first-century to be graced with a recognizable label was defined by its relationship to online culture. The term "flarf" emerged in 2001 – appropriately enough, on an email list – among a small group of writers to describe what poet K. Silem Mohammad called "liberal borrowing from internet chat-room drivel and spam scripts, often with the intention of achieving a studied blend of the offensive, the sentimental, and the infantile" (qtd. in Magee). Its signature technique was what its practitioners came to call "Google-sculpting," in which the results of often nonsensical or absurd Google search-engine queries were appropri-ated, arranged, and collaged.[5]

In retrospect, a number of elements stand out about flarf. As an (often ironic) avant-garde or literary movement, it extended the tradition of the twentieth-century poetic avant-garde – a position that had been occupied for much of the 1980s and 1990s by language writing – into the twenty-first-century. Yet while many of its techniques were familiar, its source material was the new forms of digital media. Moreover, in retrospect, flarf may be most striking for being tethered to a very particular era of the Internet: the relatively static, text-based world of chat rooms, listservs, and the early Web, before the era of social media and streaming video. As a response to the cultural shift toward online media, flarf might be seen as a claim on the Internet as an extension of print culture, into which traditional text-based poetry can still make a powerful intervention.

The rise of flarf is part of an era in which a range of poets flocked to new media venues and forms, responding to the utopian potential that still clung to the Web's early days. An active group of poets embraced the emerging form of blogging, particularly on the Blogger platform, beginning in 2002 and 2003. As with flarf, poetry blogging displayed important continuities with the poetry communities of the 1990s, particularly through the prominence of the blog of Ron Silliman, one of the central figures of language writing. Yet the format also attracted younger poets from around the country, especially from the San Francisco Bay area, and including somewhat more women and poets of color than actively participated in 1990s online communities such as the Buffalo POETICS email list.[6]

If the Internet seemed in this period a new potential space for creating poetic community, a longer-lasting impact was arguably made by some of the more formal organizations of poets that emerged during the 2000s, particularly among poets of color. This new development was spearheaded in the mid-1990s by Cave Canem, founded by the poets Toi Derricotte and Cornelius Eady to address what the organization's mission statement calls "the under-representation and isolation of African American poets in the literary landscape." The 2000s saw the appearance of two additional organizations inspired by and modeled on Cave Canem: Kundiman, serving Asian American writers, in 2004; and Canto Mundo, serving Latinx writers, in 2009. All three organizations sponsor an annual retreat for writers from their respective communities, while also supporting a range of other programming. All three groups can be seen as squarely within the lineage of earlier literary movements that argued for distinct traditions and spaces for writers of color, particularly from the 1960s forward: the Black Arts Movement as well as the Asian American and Chicano literary movements. At the same time, these poetic formations of the 1990s and 2000s were quite different from their 1960s and 1970s predecessors, focusing more on formal institution-building and shifting from an oppositional, outsider stance to one arguably more oriented toward gaining access for poets of color to "mainstream," historically white-dominated literary institutions (publishing, prizes, and academic employment). The remarkable literary success of poets from all three groups, which includes Pulitzer Prizes, MacArthur "genius" grants, and hundreds of book publications, speaks to their effectiveness as formations that have used the idea of distinct literary spaces for writers of color to reshape the wider literary landscape.

Of course, Cave Canem, Kundiman, Canto Mundo, and other comparable groups have emerged in a landscape of literary institutions that has shifted dramatically from the late twentieth century to the early twenty-first-century. The poetry culture whose "death" was decried in the 1980s and 1990s was one tied to a mid-twentieth-century US intellectual landscape, centered on New York City, in which prestigious literary journals, book reviews, and general-interest magazines, aimed at the abstract ideal of an educated general reader, shaped national tastes in poetry. Robert Lowell, who died in 1977, is often cited as the last of the "great," undisputed central figures whose poetry mattered to this imagined general public, before its splintering into obscure subcultures or its retreat into the academy. Of course, so-called academic poetry had been the target of critique by other poets for decades; Donald Allen's *The New American Poetry* made "academic verse" the adversary of its poetic avant-gardes. By the 1990s, however, the "academic verse" against which some critics railed was more likely to be of a different kind: that produced by graduates of university creative writing programs. Vernon Shetley, who dubbed such writing the "MFA mainstream," was not alone in regarding academic creative writing as a dulling and conformist influence in contemporary poetry, a view shared, as Kimberly Quiogue Andrews notes in Chapter 14 of this collection, by partisans of the avant-garde such as Marjorie Perloff and Charles Bernstein.

From the perspective of a couple of decades into the twenty-first-century, such debates around the impact of academic creative writing now seem almost quaint: for many American poets today, the world of poetry and that of the creative writing program have become essentially coextensive, with the university now serving, as Andrews puts it, as "the foremost patron of the poetic arts." While discussion of the influence of the MFA in the 1990s focused primarily on the effects of the "workshop style," a twenty-first-century examination of poetry and the academy must be far more attuned to the institutional and economic conditions for poetry set by the university creative writing program. Aspiring young poets are increasingly likely to see pursuit of the MFA (or even the PhD) in creative writing as *the* path to becoming a "professional" poet and to adopt the professional goal of academic employment alongside those of journal and book publication.

New contexts for the production and reception of poetry in the twenty-first-century United States have inevitably given rise to new preoccupations, and new stylistic expressions, among contemporary poets. The chapters in this collection highlight a number of these evolving concerns. Christopher Nealon (Chapter 12) and Jonathan Skinner (Chapter 10) examine poets who respond to the twenty-first-century's increasing sense of global crisis, from the financial crash of 2008 to the rapidly progressing threat of climate change. Nealon traces the ongoing development of an anti-capitalist poetry that can be seen as part of a renewal of political poetry in the current century, seeing in poets such as Daniel Borzutzky, Allison Cobb, and Wendy Trevino a politically radical poetics that "explores links among kinds of violence – racial, sexual, economic – and kinds of depredation – colonial, environmental – that liberal political language has tended to grasp in parallel, rather than as part of a totality." Environmental crisis has become an especially urgent topic for contemporary poets; Skinner examines how poets such as Juliana Spahr, Danez Smith, Stephen Collis, and Layli Long Soldier write "under the sign of the Anthropocene," grappling both with this term's potential for creating global solidarities and with the inequalities that it may efface.

New contexts and content have given rise to new formal developments in twenty-first-century poetry. Ann Vickery (Chapter 5) examines the impact of third- and fourth-wave feminisms in a wide variety of recent poetry by women, including the coining by Arielle Greenberg of the "gurlesque," one of the first new poetic tendencies of the new century to gain a recognizable label; Greenberg and other practitioners see the gurlesque as embodying a more "playful" and "brash" relationship to signifiers of femininity than is characteristic in the poetry of second-wave feminism. Vickery also traces new feminist trajectories for styles that bridge the transition from the late twentieth century to the early twenty-first, including performance poetry, post-language writing, and digital poetics. In Chapter 6, Stephanie Burt's articulation of a "nearly baroque" style in poets such as Angie Estes, Robyn Schiff, and Lucie Brock-Broido similarly identifies this mode as a "femme aesthetic" that "defend[s] traditionally feminine ideas of beauty and extravagance" as a way of mapping "the aspiration, and the limits, in the contemporary lyric poem."

The intersection of poetics and disability has been another arena in which a developing and maturing political movement has given rise to an increasingly complex formal landscape. Declan Gould's chapter in this collection on disability and poetry (Chapter 7) maps an emerging distinction in twenty-first-century poetry between a "disability poetry" that is aligned with the disability rights movement and draws on a wide range of aesthetic influences and a "crip poetry" that is aimed primarily at disabled audiences and that places itself within a tradition of disabled culture and activism.

Finally, the status of the lyric in contemporary poetry has been an ongoing concern in twenty-first-century poetics. If the late twentieth century saw a heightening of skepticism over the project of lyric poetry, with challenges to the "lyric I" of confessional and post-confessional poetry issuing from the ranks of experimental writing, the early twenty-first-century has seen, if not precisely a "return" to lyric, then a renewed interest in exploring the potential of the category of lyric to be turned to new, and often more politically engaged, ends. The work of Claudia Rankine again has been a touchstone of this effort, with both her 2004 collection *Don't Let Me Be Lonely* and her 2014 *Citizen* bearing the subtitle *An American Lyric*. Sarah Dowling's chapter in this collection (Chapter 8) offers an argument for the way queer indigenous and queer of color poets in particular are reimagining the twenty-first-century lyric, showing how the relationality characteristic of lyric poetry is exploded and expanded into a "queer bioethics" in work such as Tommy Pico's *Nature Poem* (2017).

If the theme of much of this account of twenty-first-century American poetics has been contemporary poetry's shifting centers of gravity, it is also true that those shifts have not been without resistance. Many of the controversies that have occupied poets and scholars of poetry – and even attracted national and international media attention – in the first decades of the century can be seen as symptoms of these seismic shifts in the poetic landscape, particularly around issues of race. The year 2011 saw two such events. The first was a debate between poets Claudia Rankine and Tony Hoagland that began with a panel discussion at the Association of Writers and Writing Programs (AWP) conference, which has taken on increasing importance as the major professional conference for academic creative writers. Rankine offered a critique of Hoagland's poem "The Change," in which Rankine wondered whether Hoagland's depiction of a thinly veiled version of Venus Williams – a "big black girl from Alabama" with "some outrageous name like Vondella Aphrodite" – defeating a white opponent was "a performance of the n-road." Rankine also shared a response from Hoagland, who called Rankine's reading "naïve"; the poem was not "racist" but "racially complex," expressing the fact that Americans "drank racism with our mother's milk." Hoagland's declaration that "it seems foolish and costly to think that the topic of race belongs only to brown-skinned Americans and not white-skinned Americans" reveals his debate with Rankine as a struggle over *ownership* of particular kinds of poetic content – and, in particular, over the conversations about race that continue to dominate American public discourse.

If the Rankine/Hoagland debate was mostly an "insider" conversation – one that happened between poets, staged at a conference for creative writers – a far more public incident occurred later in the year, one that brought competing narratives of contemporary poetry into open conflict. Helen Vendler, one of the most eminent critics of contemporary poetry, published a sharply critical review in *The New York Review of Books* of the new *The Penguin Anthology of Twentieth-Century American Poetry* (2011), edited by Rita Dove. Vendler charged Dove, a Pulitzer Prize–winning poet who was the first African American writer to hold the title of US Poet Laureate, with privileging "multicultural inclusiveness" over aesthetic value, to which Dove replied that Vendler was displaying "the wild sorrow of someone who feels betrayed by the world she thought she knew" (n. pag.). If the sharp distinction Vendler makes between "inclusion" and "quality" seems increasingly dubious in the multipolar world of twenty-first-century poetry – a point Dorothy Wang takes up in her coda to this collection (Chapter 15) – it is an opposition that has not entirely been abandoned either, as Dove also asserts that "literary merit" was her only criterion.

Perhaps the larger point to be taken away here is that late-twentieth-century narratives of American poetry have been irreversibly disrupted in the early twenty-first-century – largely, if not solely, by issues around race. An avant-garde lineage that might have been traced from language writing through flarf to conceptual poetry[7] has been challenged by critiques of conceptual poetry's racial politics and of the broader "whiteness" of the avant-garde. Several of the highest-profile poetry controversies of the mid-2010s, from the backlash against a poem by Calvin Trillin about Chinese food[8] to a white male poet's use of the name "Yi-Fen Chou" in *The Best American Poetry 2015*,[9] were sparked by the growing influence of younger writers of color, whose social media responses led to wider mainstream coverage. All of these cases revealed that old assumptions about who is reading and writing poetry must be discarded: readers and writers of color, in particular, are in the room and cannot be erased in favor of a concept of the (presumptively white) general reader of poetry.

If the discourse of the "death" of poetry that dominated the 1990s has not completely disappeared,[10] it has seemingly given way to a new optimism about the state of poetry in America. A survey released in 2018 by the National Endowment for the Arts reported a surge of poetry readership from 2012 to 2017, with *Washington Post* book critic Ron Charles reporting that "The share of adults reading poetry grew by an astounding 76 percent" and that "The percentage of poetry readers age 18–24 *doubled* during that period" (n. pag.). Many observers have attributed this surge in poetry readership to social media, and in particular to Instagram, which has become a platform for some poets to reach thousands, even millions, of readers. Rupi Kaur, a Canadian poet who has become the most famous poet of Instagram, has parlayed her nearly 4 million Instagram followers into eye-popping book sales, with more than a million copies of her book *Milk and Honey* (2014) sold.

The success of Kaur and other Instagram poets provides a striking bookend to the tentative, critical, and at times utopian relationship with digital technology that characterized the first years of the twenty-first-century. If flarf and the poetry blogosphere can be seen in retrospect as attempts by existing poetry communities to establish new networks and incorporate the emerging world of online discourse into traditional poetics, Instagram poets appear to have created an entirely new poetry world, one whose connection with traditional poetries is limited, but also one whose frank approach toward marketing and monetization has created a new poetic economy distinct from the nonprofit economy of the university and small-press publishing. While many poets and critics have bemoaned what they see as the poor quality of Instagram poetry, it might be more accurate to say that Kaur and other Instagram poets have further revealed the multiplicity of poetry worlds, economies, and audiences that characterize twenty-first-century poetry.[11]

This collection can best be understood, then, as an effort to define new paradigms that might help us grasp the unfolding projects of twenty-first-century American poetics. Understanding that the narratives and binaries of twentieth-century poetry have come under increasing scrutiny and challenge, these chapters map both continuity and change, while acknowledging how deeply poetry is implicated in contemporary social and political upheavals. What emerges is a nexus of subjects for contemporary poetry – race, gender, sexuality, disability, war, neoliberalism, the environment – that shape, and are being shaped by, a new array of poetic forms and aesthetics.

Notes

1. See Armantrout. Armantrout's essay responds to a question posed by Charles Bernstein.
2. The incident was widely reported in the media; for more, see Brown.
3. For example, see Bernstein.
4. See Yu, "Engagement, Race, and Public Poetry."
5. Andrew Epstein's "Funks of Ambivalence: On Flarf," which reviews the 2017 *Flarf: An Anthology of Flarf*, provides a useful overview of the movement and its reception; see also Bernes and Damon.
6. For an account of this period from an active participant, see Corey.
7. The close links between flarf and conceptual poetry were evident from the staged "rivalry" between the two movements around 2009–2010, including essays and readings by Goldsmith, Vanessa Place, and Drew Gardner.
8. Trillin's poem in the *New Yorker,* "Have They Run Out of Provinces Yet?", was widely criticized, particularly by Asian American writers, for its representation of Chinese culture. See Yu, "White Poets Want Chinese Culture Without Chinese People."
9. The author, poet Michael Derrick Hudson, revealed in a contributor's note that he used the name "Yi-Fen Chou" as a means of increasing his chances of publication. The incident received coverage from the *Guardian* (UK), NBC News, and *Slate*. Roundups of the discussion can be found at the Poetry Foundation, "Yi-Fen Chou Is a Real Person," and the Asian American Writers' Workshop, "After Yi-Fen Chou."
10. An interesting example of the new context for such sentiments is Bob Hicok's essay "The Promise of American Poetry," in which Hicok laments that he is "dying" and increasingly neglected as a poet, but links this to his status as a straight white male writer at a time when the "hottest" writers are poets of color or queer writers. For a response to Hicok, see Yu, "The Case of the 'Disappearing' Poet."

11. For further discussion of Instagram poetry and what it reveals about the economies of contemporary poetry, see Yu, "Instagram Poetry and Our Poetry
Worlds."

Works Cited

"After Yi-Fen Chou: A Forum." *The Margins*, Asian American Writers' Workshop,
September 15, 2015, aaww.org/after-yi-fen-chou

Armantrout, Rae. "Why Don't Women Do Language-Oriented Writing?" *Collected
Prose*. Singing Horse Press, 2007, pp. 13–15.

Bernes, Jasper. "Art, Work, Endlessness: Flarf and Conceptual Poetry among the
Trolls," *Critical Inquiry* vol. 42, no. 4, 2016, pp. 760–782.

Bernstein, Charles, editor. *The Politics of Poetic Form*. Roof, 1996.

Brown, Kara. "A Conversation with Johari Osayi Idusuyi, the Hero Who Read through
a Trump Rally." *Jezebel*, November 12, 2015, https://theslot.jezebel.com/a-con
versation-with-johari-osayi-idusuyi-the-hero-who-1742082010

Charles, Ron. "Poetry Reading by Young People Has Doubled since 2012."
Washington Post, September 12, 2018, www.washingtonpost.com/entertain
ment/books/poetry-reading-by-young-people-has-doubled-since-2012/2018/09/
12/a5724954-b6bd-11e8-94eb-3bd52dfe917b_story.html

Corey, Joshua Corey. "The Golden Age of Poetry Blogging," *Plume* 71, June 2017,
https://plumepoetry.com/the-golden-age-of-poetry-blogging/

Damon, Maria. "Between Friendship Network and Literary Movement: Flarf As
a Poetics of Sociability." *Among Friends: Engendering the Social Site of
Poetry*, edited by Anne Dewey and Libbie Rifkin. University of Iowa Press,
2013, pp. 130–150.

Dove, Rita. "Defending an Anthology." *New York Review of Books*, December 22,
2011, www.nybooks.com/articles/2011/12/22/defending-anthology

Epstein, Andrew. "Funks of Ambivalence: On Flarf." *Los Angeles Review of Books*,
July 22, 2018, https://lareviewofbooks.org/article/funks-of-ambivalence-on-flarf/

Gardner, Drew. "Flarf Is Life: The Poetry of Affect." *Boston Review*, February 11,
2014, bostonreview.net/poetry/drew-gardner-flarf-life-poetry-affect

Goldsmith, Kenneth. "Flarf Is Dionysus. Conceptual Writing Is Apollo." *Poetry*
July 1, 2009, www.poetryfoundation.org/poetrymagazine/articles/69328/flarf-
is-dionysus-conceptual-writing-is-apollo

Hicok, Bob. "The Promise of American Poetry." *Utne Reader*, Summer 2019,
www.utne.com/arts/new-american-poetry-zm0z19uzhoe

Hoagland, Tony. "Dear Claudia: A Letter in Response." *Poets.org*, Academy of
American Poets, March 14, 2011, poets.org/text/dear-claudia-letter-response

Keniston, Ann and Jeffrey Gray, editors. *The New American Poetry of Engagement:
A Twenty-First-Century Anthology*. McFarland, 2012.

Magee, Michael. "The Flarf Files." http://writing.upenn.edu/epc/authors/bernstein/
syllabi/readings/flarf.html

Mullen, Harryette. "Poetry and Identity." *Telling It Slant: Avant-Garde Poetics of
the 1990s*, edited by Mark Wallace and Steven Marks. University of Alabama
Press, 2002, pp. 27–31.

Rankine, Claudia. "Open Letter: A Dialogue on Race and Poetry." *Poets.org*, Academy of American Poets, February 14, 2011, poets.org/text/open-letter-dialogue-race-and-poetry

Vendler, Helen. "Are These the Poems to Remember?" Rev. of *The Penguin Anthology of Twentieth-Century American Poetry*, edited by Rita Dove. *New York Review of Books*, November 24, 2011, www.nybooks.com/articles/2011/11/24/are-these-poems-remember

"Yi-Fen Chou Is a Real Person, & Everything Else Circling 'The Bees.'" *Harriet*, Poetry Foundation, September 10, 2015, www.poetryfoundation.org/harriet/2015/09/yi-fen-chou-is-a-real-person-everything-else-circling-the-bees

Yu, Timothy. "The Case of the 'Disappearing' Poet." *New Republic*, August 7, 2019, newrepublic.com/article/154694/case-disappearing-poet

"Instagram Poetry and Our Poetry Worlds." *Harriet*, Poetry Foundation, April 24, 2019, www.poetryfoundation.org/harriet/2019/04/instagram-poetry-and-our-poetry-worlds

"White Poets Want Chinese Culture Without Chinese People." *New Republic*, April 8, 2016, newrepublic.com/article/132537/white-poets-want-chinese-culture-without-chinese-people

"Engagement, Race, and Public Poetry." *Jacket2*, March 20, 2015, https://jacket2.org/article/engagement-race-and-public-poetry-america

I

KEITH D. LEONARD

New Black Aesthetics: Post–Civil Rights African American Poetry

The renowned editor Charles Rowell was right to declare that African American poets have achieved a new kind of freedom in the twenty-first-century, but he did not name that freedom rightly. In "Writing Self, Writing Community," his introduction to *Angles of Ascent: A Norton Anthology of Contemporary African American Poetry* (2013), Rowell asserts, "After incalculable sacrifices, the long struggles, and the sociopolitical challenges of their ancestors as artists and advocates for freedom and respect under the Declaration of Independence, the U. S. Constitution, and post-mid-nineteenth-century progressive laws, contemporary African American poets have declared a space, however incomplete, to create as they please" (xxxix). Crediting the artists of the 1960s Black Arts Movement, the self-proclaimed "spiritual sister" of the Black Power movement, with persuasively asserting their commitments to community, collective action, and social revolution through their art, Rowell declares that, "instead of engaging their poems as instruments in the sociopolitical struggles of African Americans, contemporary black American poets are now writing self against the backdrop of community" (xxxix). Rowell understands this new priority on "the interior landscape of the poet" to be the commonly held fulfillment of the principles of freedom promulgated in the 1960s. This priority is also for Rowell the pinnacle of an aesthetic "angle of ascent" that was facilitated in part by access to predominantly white institutions of higher education, including MFA programs that offer rigorous training in craft. For Rowell, this training has helped contemporary poets to exceed the aesthetic limits of the Black Arts Movement's call for a revolutionary black art actively defiant of any mainstream norms of aesthetic meaning and value; and, for a certain swath of contemporary poets, these assessments are quite apt, but Rowell's emphasis on the personal captures only a narrow field of contemporary practice. Indeed, contemporary poets have pursued multiple angles of ascent through their modes of introspection, their artistry proliferating into a remarkable variegation of freedoms.

The personal introspection Rowell prizes is thus but one aspect of a broader inward-turning whose central principle is continuous with the defining priorities of the Black Arts Movement, a principle that might be more aptly named self-determination, the asserting of the terms by which to define one's own existence. Not just concerned with reflecting on the personal against the communal, in other words, most contemporary African American poets have embraced black culture as a historical and cultural landscape to be mapped into new frontiers in order to *make* the individual black self (not only to reflect on it) and then to develop terms for the liberation of that self, individual and collective, from social and cultural limitations of all kinds, including those within black culture. They reject the binary oppositions between self and community, internal landscape and protest, literary and political, that Rowell implicitly endorses and whose logic has been used to exclude African American poets from access to publication and prizes and, at times, from access to their own minds. These poets expand the personal so that, as the poet and scholar Evie Shockley observes, what distinguishes black aesthetics is not any particular politics or literary form or sensibility but rather "the subjectivity of the African American writer – that is the subjectivity produced by the experience of identifying or being interpolated as 'black' in the U.S. – actively working out a poetics in the context of a racist society" (9). Even when writing the personal, in other words, contemporary poets engage directly with how being interpellated into dominant ideologies of race creates all manner of tensions between that social constitution of identity and their self-perception. Part of contemporary poetic freedom has come from directly confronting the effects of these social forces outside of both self and community by seeking to constitute in their own terms that complex and inchoate entity called blackness that is as much a product as the subject of that "active" mind. The scholar Bertram Ashe put it well: "These artists 'trouble' blackness," he writes, "they worry blackness; they stir it up, touch it, feel it out, and hold it up for examination in ways that depart significantly from previous – and necessary – preoccupations with struggling for political freedom, or with an attempt to establish and to sustain a coherent black identity" (614). Crucially, this troubling comes not from a rejection of blackness and its politics in favor of a discrete, apolitical individuality but, as the poet, critic, and curator Kevin Young concludes, from how these poets "see and saw blackness as a given, both as subject matter and as subjectivity," allowing them "to stand at the crossroads of culture at which the black artist bargains, trades, borrows, makes, steals, and stories in a world of his or her own making" (289). Here is a personal, collective, historical, and aesthetic self-examination – this empowering inward-turning – that has made contemporary African American aesthetic freedom possible.

Moreover, this freedom remains engaged in remaking the larger culture in varying modes of social resistance, with these poets' aesthetic innovations and social spaces constituting what they have made of the revolutionary blackness to which the Black Arts Movement aspired. Whatever one's judgments about greater achievements, then, it is crucial to recognize important continuities. Radical 1960s artists as disparate as Larry Neal, Nikki Giovanni, Don L. Lee, Hoyt Fuller, Carolyn Rodgers, and Sonia Sanchez pursued what they called *the* "Black Aesthetic," an ostensibly singular and "radical reordering of the western cultural aesthetic" (Neal 29) keyed to calling a black audience to nationalist revolution through a turn to black vernacular cultural traditions, improvisational performative practices inspired by jazz, and innovative revisions of Standard English syntax, in the interest of remaking the black mind. Although they never agreed on any singular political program, they were united in declaring that cultural self-determination was central to any liberation. Their legacy was thus to grant contemporary poets license to see their own ways to and through this aesthetic self-determination. Shockley rightly urges readers to see how this inheritance produced "'black aesthetics,' plural: a multifarious, contingent, non-delimited complex of strategies that African American writers may use to negotiate gaps or conflicts between their artistic goals and the operation of race in the production, dissemination, and reception of their writing" (9). By the twenty-first-century, these pursuits of self-examination and self-determination comprised at least four broad and overlapping realms of practice: the apolitical introspection Rowell prizes; a rethinking of African American history and heritage beyond the terms of simple affirmation; a personalized mode of collectivist protest in line with Black Arts Movement practices; and a black literary collective action enacted by the numerous African American writers collectives and workshops that have arisen since the 1960s. Poets operating in all four of these realms adapt traditional and innovative techniques and turn to American, African, European, Middle Eastern, and Asian sources for the means to refute the very cultural logic that opposed self and community, art and politics, in the first place. The result has been not only individual aesthetic freedom and achievement but also a powerful and empowering transformation of US poetry – in its social and aesthetic forms – in their own images.

Understanding what contemporary African American poets have in common with each other and with the Black Arts Movement thus requires comprehending this self-determining "active mind" as it seeks to dismantle the oppressive logic of Western poetics in which aesthetic achievement is opposed to race politics and African American identity. In a 1963 review of the poetry of Gwendolyn Brooks, the poet and critic Louis Simpson exemplified this dehumanizing logic from which black writers have long sought to be free. "I am not sure it is possible for a Negro to write well without making us aware he is a Negro," Simpson averred. "On the other hand, if being a Negro is the only subject, the writing is not important" (Simpson 23). Harvey Curtis Webster was more explicit, declaring that Brooks "refuses to let Negro-ness limit her humanity" (21). For these critics, the particulars of black life limit access to the common feelings and experiences – called "humanity" – recognizable as such only in certain forms, rhetoric, images, or subject matter, none of which derive from black life. Such critics thus fail to recognize the cultural and emotional resonances – the humanity – of being "Negro." This failure constitutes what Addison Gayle aptly called "cultural strangulation" in his 1972 essay of that title. Gayle traces the historical emergence in Western iconography of the color "white" as a symbol of good and beauty and right (and even of the human) and "black" as a symbol of evil and ugliness and wrong, identifying this emergence as the defining feature of the so-called "white aesthetic." He concludes, "the extent of the cultural strangulation of Black literature by white critics has been the extent to which they have been allowed to define the terms in which the Black artist will deal with his own experience" (Gayle, "Cultural Strangulation" 212). The long life of this logic can be seen, for example, in Helen Vendler's suggestion in her 2011 review of Rita Dove's editing of *The Penguin Anthology of Twentieth Century American Poetry* that most of those writers of color that Dove included, concerned as they are with race politics, are not worth remembering.

Gayle spoke for the whole movement when he foresaw rightly that dismantling this logic requires an embrace of the multiplicity of black culture and experience as self-evidently valid sources of human selfhood and beauty. He put it this way: "the acceptance of the phrase 'Black is Beautiful' is the first step in the destruction of the old table of the laws and the construction of new ones, for the phrase flies in the face of the whole ethos of the white aesthetic" (Gayle 212). Thus, when leading Black Arts Movement theorist and poet LeRoi Jones/Amiri Baraka asserted that it was the role of the black artist to destroy America as he knows it, he had in mind this reorientation toward self-defined terms for dealing with African American experience and the creation of intellectual and cultural spaces in which this black self-examination could take place freely. Ron Karenga asserted aptly that "the fact that we are black is our ultimate reality" (10), locating knowledge and ethics in blackness itself. The statement thus affirms the Black Aesthetic principle that, to quote Nikki Giovanni's 1968 poem "Of Liberation," "Blackness is its own qualifier / Blackness is its own standard" (9). Jones/ Baraka's poem "Black Art" is one of the most anthologized poems of the movement because it makes plain the aim of this self-determination: "Let Black people understand / that they are the lovers and the sons / of lovers and warriors and sons / of warriors Are poems & poets & / all the loveliness here in the world" (n. pag.).

Even the twenty-first-century poets committed to the personal introspection that Rowell privileges garner the fullest access to their interior landscapes by following aspects of this Black Arts Movement roadmap. Pulitzer Prize–winner Dove captures well this complex connection between her interior landscape and this revolutionary discourse of black self-determination. Recalling that she would "get an occasional slap of the wrist because my poetry was, for some people, 'not black enough,'" she observed that "The Program," as she called the movement's revolutionary aesthetic disciplines, had, "after some political victories that served the purpose, stumbled into dead ends, artistically speaking" (Rowell xlv). Resisting the fidelity to "the blighted urban world inhabited by the poems of the Black Arts Movement" that "was not mine," Dove developed artistic means more commensurate with "the gamut of middle class experience, in a comfy house with picket fences and rose bushes on a tree-lined street in West Akron" that she had in her childhood (Rowell xlv). Yet even given this significant class and geography difference, for Dove the departure from any Black Arts Movement orthodoxy was not entirely a principled rejection since that rejection was itself a similar kind of self-determination: "The time was ripe; all one had to do was walk up to the door they had been battering at and squeeze through the breech [sic]" (Rowell xlv). Fellow Pulitzer Prize–winner Yusef Komunyakaa made a similar point: "In many ways, the Civil Rights Movement had intellectually prepared us for this necessary juncture in African American creativity ... An internal dialogue is possible through metaphorical inquiry that is highly political and enduring, an inquiry that continuously reinvents itself. We wanted a poetry that would speak to and for the whole person" (Rowell xliv). Komunyakaa's winning volume *Neon Vernacular* (1993) resists what he saw as "the Program's" narrowing of black personhood by substantiating the centrality of jazz, that defining African American musical form, to his artistic introspection. Komunyakaa enacts what one scholar described as "the individual artist's improvisational expression of a fundamental human loneliness lingering beneath black skin," an "expressive necessity" that "is necessarily manifest in distinctive cultural forms" (Leonard 825). Nonetheless, Komunyakaa knew well that jazz and the blues functioned as a communal expressivity for African Americans, making its introspection representative of that collective. What Komunyakaa has done is effectively elaborated on the sense that blackness is central to the "whole person" implicit even in the most strident Black Arts Movement proscriptions.

The difference that the Black Arts Movement made for personalized lyric introspection is thus not only that such personae have community as a backdrop. It is also that they should be more rigorously imbedded in their entire social and ideological worlds. Pulitzer Prize–winner Gregory Pardlo captures this expansive and rigorous self-awareness well: "The poem I write is not only a reflection of how I view the world; it is a reflection of how I *choose* to view the world" ("Logic of Ekphrasis" 348). He goes on: "Whether I externalize the authority that is rightfully mine, and choose instead to represent reality inhabited by some widely held value or belief, or I claim for myself the authority to re-present reality in a way that suggests choice, liberty, and agency . . . I am always engaged in some form of representation" ("Logic of Ekphrasis" 348). In the process, Pardlo confronts "an obligation to the idea of justice or balance" that requires "shoulder[ing] the weight of cultural, racial, and literary expectations" ("Logic of Ekphrasis" 348). For example, the first poem in his prizewinning volume *Digest* (2014), entitled "Written By Himself," plays with tropes of birth and self-narration from slave narratives and blues songs as each cultural form uses those tropes to claim the existence and the authority of an erased or burdened self: "I was born in minutes in a roadside kitchen a skillet / whispering my name. I was born to rainwater and lye; / I was born across the river where I / was borrowed with clothespins" (3). The "I" is clearly not Pardlo. He declares, "I wanted to interrogate the historical narrative of black suffering by foregrounding the essence of that narrative as text, by foregrounding its materiality, and separating that materiality from the historical *facts* of black suffering. Materializing the conceptual elements in the poem allows me the wiggle room I need to decouple notions of ontology and ideology" ("Logic of Ekphrasis" 351). Being versus ideology: this pursuit is a species of the 1960s radical self-determination because, as contemporary poets recognize, assertions of black being can thoroughly transform Western racial logic, which is predicated on the absence of that being, as in Simpson's and Webster's reviews. The freedom contemporary African American poets pursue and achieve derives from the various ways in which they explore how to extricate this emotional being from the material effects of dehumanizing ideology.

This shared aesthetic project is exemplified even more fully in the work of those poets who eschew personal introspection in favor of elaborating on African American history, heritage, and memory. For example, Natasha Trethewey seems to articulate quite a traditional sense of the personal in history:

I want to create a public record of people who are often excluded from the public record. I want to inscribe their stories into the larger American story.

> I want readers who might be unfamiliar with these people, their lives, and their particular circumstances to begin to know something about them, to see in the people that I write about some measure of them, and to, I think, enlarge the community of humanity. (1025)

Yet in order to unearth the "ontology" of the emotion of forgotten people, Trethewey shifts the burden of the personal from the traditional lyric "I" typical of many introspective poems to an intersection of multiple voices incorporated from a variety of preexisting, nonpoetic texts. She develops her book *Bellocq's Ophelia* (2002) by interpreting photographs of mixed-race prostitutes in New Orleans, and she won the Pulitzer Prize for *Native Guard* (2006), which juxtaposes elegies for her murdered mother with poems translating into verse archival material about enslaved Africans throughout the South and about the African American Civil War soldiers in Mississippi who were known as the Native Guard. In many instances in each volume, Trethewey uses ekphrasis – the writing of a poem to describe another art form – to move from the alleged objectivity of historical materials, usually photographs, into the realm of the imagination, creating a line of access to the interior landscapes of figures other than herself through the documents through which they have been (mis)represented. She disciplines these multiple voices into rigorously crafted sonnets, villanelles, and pantoums, and into patterned verse forms of Trethewey's own making, in order to untether those forms from the strangulating assumptions about the whitewashed conception of beauty and humanity associated with them. Poetic form becomes historical inscription, not just "white" standards of artistic virtuosity, challenging the authority of traditional historical knowledge by making self-critical poetic interpretation at least as legitimate. Instead of offering only a celebration of African American history or representative poetic mastery, then, Trethewey remakes the concepts of history and of aesthetic mastery in relationship to one another in order to remake the black historical self.

In his Pulitzer Prize–winning *Olio* (2016), Tyehimba Jess takes an even more expansive approach, making historical texts themselves into poems. Seeking the emotional resonances of African American blackface minstrels in particular, the book defines its method, "olio," as "a miscellaneous mixture of heterogeneous elements; hodgepodge," as "a miscellaneous collection (as of literary or musical selections)" and "also: the second part of a minstrel show which featured a variety of performance acts and later evolved into vaudeville" (n. pag.). Jess told assembled students at Interlochen Arts Academy in Michigan that "Characters have depth. They have multiple dimensions, right? A caricature, you only show one side of a person.

They're oafish. Or they're silly. Or they're dumb, etcetera. A character, you see multiple sides of their humanity" (n. pag.). Jess tells aspects of these characters' hodgepodge stories with and through the caricatures they were sometimes forced to inhabit as he juxtaposes photos of them or diaries from them against historical documents of vaudeville or the events of the day. Even more than Trethewey's work, *Olio* predicates its critique of racism on the premise that its mixed methodology is necessary as it juxtaposes fact and fiction, ideology and emotion in order for each to reveal the truth each gives to the other.

This emphasis on emotional resonances in places other than the lyric voice has also led to stirring revisions to the techniques of radical protest for which the Black Arts Movement is often disparaged. Instead of creating characters who are symbols or metonyms of black struggle or black heroism, or making urban blight metonymic of all black struggle, as their predecessors sometimes did, poets like Patricia Smith and Nikky Finney evoke African American political interests by locating aspects of history within the personal rather than the symbolic, allowing for a more robust sense of how the individual interior affirms itself in part by relating to and expressing communal social situations and collective history. Smith successfully translates the protest ethos of her award-winning slam-poetry practice, where rhymed oral storytelling often revolves around personal experience of and commentary on social injustices much like Black Arts Movement protest, onto the page of formal poetics. Her volume *Incendiary Art*, a finalist for the 2018 Pulitzer Prize, meditates on the lynching of Emmett Till and on ongoing state violence against African Americans by moving inside and outside of fully realized personae to enhance the poet's protest. One of Smith's many title poems, "Incendiary Art," characterizes the social conditions that should remind us that black men are "meant as meat" and yet that "Our sons don't burn their cities as a rule, / born, as they are, up to their neck in fuel" (10). The poem "Incendiary Art: The Body" adds in its concluding lines that "there are unstruck matches / everywhere" (Smith 129). These lines indicate that the rule of burning cities is not assigned by the black denizens but by the society that provides the fuel of exclusion and poverty. The lines also affirm that these "sons" are remarkable for not burning up cities more often as a matter of course, their restraint a rule more impressive than the rule of burning that might be more appropriate to their condition. Smith renders history and oppression as emotional forces, not just social ones, then, and reveals – even enacts – in her carefully crafted poems how political expression is and, to be effective, *must* be an incendiary *art*. Beauty inheres in the emotional and imaginative life necessary to survive and to resist, such that communal acts of anti-racist violence, when they do happen, affirm the "being" of these "sons" as much as it protests against policy, and as meaningfully as any other art form could. Similarly, Finney has affirmed the internal lives of numerous African American women, historical and fictional, by critiquing the violence to which they are subject, including from instances of misogyny in Black Arts Movement thought. In her poem "Clitoris," for example, Finney personifies this sexual pleasure node to evoke the oppressive ideologies by which women are likewise "meant as meat" (56). At the same time, the personified clitoris reclaims its pleasure, allowing the objectified part to replenish the whole person. Smith and Finney have thus found modes of artistry that extend the "dogmatism" believed to be an aesthetic limit to Black Arts Movement verse into a fully realized emotional experience capable of conveying the intricate beauty inhering in being constituted by racism and nonetheless finding the means to resist. One becomes free to see the beauty in incinerating injustice both outside of and within the community.

These challenges to the binaries of self versus community and art versus politics enacted by self-determination thus call for a thorough revision of traditional ways of reading of the relationship among blackness, form, and political meaning in all contemporary verse. As mentioned, Shockley shifts attention away from the predominant approach of seeking to define distinctively black poetic forms – inherited from the Black Arts Movement – and toward the black mind's active creation of beautiful solutions to the aesthetic problems caused by race politics. Writing about black experimental writers in ways applicable to more traditional ones, Anthony Reed characterizes such black formalism as "racialized reading" that misinterprets poems as straightforward, prosaic commentaries on the poet's biography and/or race politics and relies on a "romance of resistance" in which dissidence depends on a (falsely) coherent black identity. Instead, Reed "locate[s] a new conception of literary politics rooted in literature's raising new questions, proposing new modes of being together, and offering new conceptions and theories adequate to the complexity of our common pasts and presents" (1). These "literary politics" – not unlike Shockley's aesthetic problem-solving – derive from the techniques, like Trethewey's multiple voices or Pardlo's emphasis on materiality, by which literature makes "legible the outlines of its time, its framing of legible speech and illegible noise, and its injunction to think beyond the present strictures of 'allowable thought'" (6). Reed thus encourages readers to recognize not only explicit commentary but also how poems can reach beyond the immediate conditions as each "announces a challenge – and an opportunity – to disarticulate race as a pseudo-ontological category from the ethico-political obligations thought to derive from race as 'lived experience'" (6). Recognizing race as ideology rather than ontology, Reed suggests, will direct readers to attend to the implications of a poem directed away from current terms of racial conflict and affirmation and toward possible, and possibly more liberating, alternatives. He calls it imagining a future. Even in poems like Smith's or Finney's, then, where a current situation is often specified, the way to read their poems most fully, following Reed's apt declarations, is to trace how formal innovation and emotional complexity locate empowerment not only in critique and affirmation but also in reframed thinking. One must read for the attempt to change what can be thought.

The experimental poets for whom Reed develops his approach are even more likely to be misread than Smith and Finney in a binary opposition of self and community, since these poets are inclined to do away altogether with traditional notions of self and any associated categories, including those being asserted in this chapter. In their introduction to *Every Goodbye Ain't Gone: An Anthology of Innovative Poetry by African Americans* (2006), Lauri Ramey and Aldon Nielsen urge readers to resist "the plain pure surface of identitarian free verse ... [that has come] to be all of that long black song that America could hear singing" (xix), verse exemplified by, say, Dove's poems in the persona of her grandmother. Even "Clitoris" might qualify. Nielsen and Ramey call attention to poets who pursue nonrepresentational, nonnarrative, anti-lyric practices, artists whose "troubling" of blackness is meant to trouble *all* of the languages by which *any* meaning is asserted in order to remake race and its logics from the unsteady ground up. For example, Nathaniel Mackey has written numerous "songs" for the Andoumboulou, who are the first – meaning original – people, imperfect in their primacy, in the cosmology of the Dogon. Shifting the emphasis in jazz poetics from languages of individual loneliness, Mackey understands sound and semantics to be aspects of one another, with sound sometimes operating as a primary meaning-making principle over traditional syntax. Mackey develops an improvisational sense of poetic composition in which, much like a jazz solo, unexpected conjunctions of sound and syntax enact the idea of imperfection as the source of human beauty and possibility. Grant Jenkins argues that Mackey returns the idea of myth to its Greek root "mu," for "mouth," in his serial long poem of that title. Consequently, "Mackey's version of myth foregrounds often overlooked aspects of humanity ... such as asymmetry, regress, residue, insurmountability, and 'whatsaying,'" a term Mackey often uses to "draw on myth not as the foundation for an identity but as 'troubling' or 'worrying' tradition" (Jenkins 36). Musical ritual and African cosmologies do not for Mackey affirm an empowered version of the "Negro" as "pseudo-ontological," as Reed might put it. Instead, again quoting Jenkins, Mackey's song, "rooted in what is absent, regards source; that is, speaks about its own sources and the lacunae that haunt them" and focuses "on the correspondence with an interlocutor, not on the futile search for identity in origins" (36). The idea that black music and African ritual authenticate blackness shifts from source to collaboration, a shift that invites collective creativity in responding to the existential burden of meaning-making in the absence of any absolute authority. Mackey thus endorses a meaning-making ethic that liberates affirmation from the strictures of the self-contained liberal humanist perfectible self of Enlightenment thought that managed to its detriment to justify democracy and slavery at the same time and that, in its unquestioned dominance in the West, seems to constitute self-sufficient perfection as the limit of allowable affirmative thought. That Mackey won the National Book Award for combining aspects of "Mu" and "Song of the Andoumboulou" into the volume *Splay Anthem* (2006) suggests that other thoughts might be allowable after all.

It may seem odd to suggest that the mainstream success of many of the practitioners of these multiple black aesthetics testifies to the fulfillment of radical mandates of the Black Arts Movement, but it is clear that the institutional authority these poets have gained allowed them to make poetic culture in their own images, thereby fulfilling some of the radical ideals of the movement. In addition to such individual accolades as Pulitzer Prizes and major fellowships, Trethewey, Dove, Young, Finney and others have also published anthologies and collected works of other poets, curated archives, guided Library of Congress programming, cultivated students in MFA programs, and participated in one or more of many African American writers' collectives, that twenty-first-century enactment of the 1960s radicals' call for independent black literary institutions. The most substantial of these has been Cave Canem, founded by Cornelius Eady and Toi Derricotte in 1996 and responsible for supporting many if not most of the major writers of the contemporary moment.[1] The organization annually provides thirty-six poets – who are accepted after an application process – with a week-long retreat with workshop leaders selected from among the most lauded of contemporary poets, functioning much like the MFA programs that Rowell endorses. It launched poets like Trethewey, whose first manuscript was selected by Dove for the first ever Cave Canem prize.

Cave Canem is impressive, but perhaps the more significant organizations have been the informal collectives that have had no endowments or application processes and that have nonetheless provided space for African American poets to write with one another with support but without the burden of fundraising. The now-disbanded Dark Room Collective, founded by Sharan Strange, Janice Lowe, and Thomas Sayers Ellis, created an informal African American reading series and writers' workshop in a Cambridge Victorian in the late 1980s to affirm linkages between generations of African

American writers and to cultivate a community. The reading series got so well-known it moved to Boston University. Strange worried that the group "capitulated to the university and the museum in the end" but, as she recognized, not without "changing those places in important ways" (n. pag.). Indeed, close to as many prominent contemporary poets had contact with the Dark Room as have gone through Cave Canem, and most have made major marks on mainstream poetry. Affirming the "change" Strange hoped for, the Affrilachian Poets, a loose collective in and around the University of Kentucky who claim for African Americans the heritage of Appalachia usually figured as white, exemplifies the powerful dissidence these informal institutions can enact.[2] Offered the 2016 Governor's Award in the Arts, which is meant "to recognize individuals and organizations that have made extraordinary and significant contributions to the arts in Kentucky," the group refused it in protest of what they perceived to be the unjust policies of Governor Matt Bevin's administration towards the poor and the LGBTQ community. Similarly, formed within Cave Canem, the Black Took Collective, three queer African American poets, sought to change blackness from within by exorcising "an apparition, a familiar – the reiterative and irascible black poem, cloaked in 'authenticity,' encircling black cultural experience with a stifling string of sites/cites/sights: the South, rivers, 'Mother Africa'" among other conventions. Urging black self-determination to be more inclusive and thus more dissident, Black Took offers in their multimedia, nonnarrative performances, staged across the country, a postmodern, queer-theory critique of civil rights–era affirmation. Such collectives, workshops, and communities – too numerous to name here – enact the collective self-assertion for which the civil rights era had called.

This is the freedom that leads to the power of contemporary African American poetics, and part of that power is its capacity to unite across boundaries, including between elite and popular. One cannot comprehend the contemporary scene without seeing how spoken word and slam poetries have sent poets from stages large and small throughout the country to the pages of books published by presses large and small. Patricia Smith is not alone, then, given how Jessica Care Moore in her performances, press and foundation has sustained the aesthetics of spoken word and supported the work of spoken-word poets who have not made a mark on the mainstream but who have made their marks nonetheless. When Michael Brown was shot in Ferguson, Missouri, the aftermath of that travesty motivated #BlackPoetsSpeakOut, an online community of poets, many of whom will not get MFAs, posting videos in response to and in protest of state violence and mass incarceration. It might be fair to say that it would be of this underground that Amiri Baraka and Nikki Giovanni would have been most proud. After all, the existence of these nontraditional sites of practice and proliferation parallel to the Pulitzer Prizes and Cave Canem alumni only proves the point: contemporary African American poets have indeed come to create as they please. Looking inward and outward at the same time, these African American poets from all walks of life and institutional trajectories have changed the face of US poetry for good.

Notes

1. See Derricotte; Jones.
2. See Burris.

Works Cited

Ashe, Bertram, editor. "Post-Soul Aesthetic." Special issue of *African American Review* vol. 41, no. 4, Winter 2007, pp. 598–835.

Baraka, Amiri. "Black Art." *Genius*, https://genius.com/Amiri-baraka-black-art-annotated

Burris, Therissa. "Claiming a Literary Space: The Afrilachian Poets." *An American Vein: Critical Readings in Appalachian Literature*, edited by Danny L. Miller, Sharon Hatfiled, and Norman Gurney. Ohio University Press, 2005, pp. 315–336.

Derricotte, Toi. "Cave Canem: An Introduction." *Callaloo: A Journal of African American Arts and Letters* vol. 22, no. 4, 1999, pp. 974–1027.

Dove, Rita. *The Penguin Anthology of Twentieth Century American Poetry*. Penguin, 2011.

Du Bois, W. E. B. *The Souls of Black Folk*. 1903. Penguin, 1996.

Finney, Nikky. *Head Off & Split*. Northwestern University Press, 2011.

Gayle, Addison, editor. *The Black Aesthetic*. Doubleday, 1972.

"Cultural Strangulation: Black Literature and the White Aesthetic." *Within the Circle: An Anthology of African American Literary Criticism from Harlem Renaissance to the Present*, edited by Angelyn Mitchell. Duke University Press, 1994, pp. 207–212.

Giovanni, Nikki. *Black Feeling, Black Talk, Black Judgement*. William Morrow, 1970.

Jenkins, Grant. "'re: Source': African Contexts of Nathaniel Mackey's Ethics." *African American Review* vol. 49, no. 1, Spring 2016, pp. 35–52.

Jones, Meta DuEwa. *The Muse Is Music: Jazz Poetry from the Harlem Renaissance to Spoken Word*. University of Illinois Press, 2011.

Karenga, Ron. *The Quotable Karenga*, edited by Clyde Halisi and James Mtume. Saidi Publications, 1967.

Leonard, Keith D. "Yusef Komunyakaa's Blues: The Postmodern Music of Neon Vernacular." *Callaloo* vol. 28, no. 3, Summer 2005, pp. 825–849.

Mackey, Nathaniel. *Discrepant Engagement: Dissonance, Cross-Culturality, and Experimental Writing*. Cambridge University Press, 2009.

Neal, Larry. "The Black Arts Movement." *The Drama Review: TDR* vol. 12, no. 4, Summer 1968, pp. 28–39.

Nielsen, Aldon. *Black Chant: Languages of African American Postmodernism.* Cambridge University Press, 1997.

Nielsen, Aldon and Lauri Ramey, editors. *Every Goodbye Ain't Gone: An Anthology of Innovative Poetry by African Americans.* University of Alabama Press, 2006. *What I Say: Innovative Poetry by Black Writers in America.* University of Alabama Press, 2015.

Pardlo, Gregory. "The Logic of Ekphrasis: An Interview with Gregory Pardlo Part I." Interview by Charles Rowell. *Callaloo* vol. 39, no. 2, Spring 2016, pp. 345–354. *Digest.* Four Way Books, 2014.

Reed, Anthony. *Freedom Time: The Poetics and Politics of Black Experimental Writing.* Johns Hopkins University Press, 2014.

Rowell, Charles, editor. *Angles of Ascent: A Norton Anthology of Contemporary African American Poetry.* Norton, 2013.

Shockley, Evie. *Renegade Poetics: Black Aesthetics and Formal Innovation in African American Poetry.* University of Iowa Press, 2011.

Simpson, Louis. "Taking the Poem by the Horns." *On Gwendolyn Brooks: Reliant Contemplation*, edited by Stephen Caldwell Wright. University of Michigan Press, 1996, p. 23.

Smith, Patricia. *Incendiary Art: Poems.* Northwestern University Press, 2017.

Strange, Sharan. "Total Life Is What We Want: A Brief Dark Room History." *Mosaic Literary Magazine* vol. 16, 2006.

Trethewey, Natasha. "Inscriptive Restorations: An Interview with Natasha Trethewey." Interview by Charles Rowell. *Callaloo* vol. 27, no. 4, Autumn 2004, pp. 1022–1034.

Tyhimba, Jess. Interview by Dan Wanschura, "The Unconventional Poetry of Jess Tyhimba." *NPR*, July 15, 2017, www.npr.org/2017/07/15/537381252/the-unconventional-poetry-of-tyehimba-jess

Vendler, Helen. "Are These the Poems to Remember?" *The New York Review of Books*, November 24, 2011.

Webster, Harvey Curtis. "Pity the Giants." *On Gwendolyn Brooks: Reliant Contemplation*, edited by Stephen Caldwell Wright. University of Michigan Press, 1996, p. 21.

Young, Kevin. *The Grey Album: On the Blackness of Blackness.* Graywolf Press, 2012.

2

MICHAEL LEONG

Traditions of Innovation in Asian American Poetry

In the search box of the online MLA International Bibliography, I type the phrase "asian american poetry." A drop-down list appears, suggesting an alternate phrase: "asian american poverty." I insist on my intended search and receive forty-five results, but just to be sure – perhaps I mistyped – the electronic database asks: "Did you mean: asian american poverty."

For all the forces – human, machinic, or otherwise – that wish to ignore it, Asian American poetry in the twenty-first-century is enjoying an increasing amount of community building. It resists impoverishment. There are new publication venues, such as the *Asian American Literary Review* and *Lantern Review*, both established in 2010. The arts organizations Kundiman (founded in 2004) and the Asian American Writers' Workshop (founded in 1991) continue to extend their programming: the former established an annual book publication prize in 2009 and the latter launched the online magazines *The Margins* and *Open City* in 2012. The new century has also witnessed the first academic monographs on Asian American poetry by Xiaojing Zhou, Yunte Huang, Josephine Nock-Hee Park, Timothy Yu, Steven G. Yao, Joseph Jonghyun Jeon, and Dorothy J. Wang; such groundbreaking scholarship has done much to historicize and interpret a rich body of work. Needless to say, there is still more work to be done.

I'd like to foreground the impact the innovative legacies of the 1980s and 1990s have had on the early twenty-first-century as a way of appreciating this synchronic moment of transgenerational affiliation. Senior poets – largely born in the 1950s and who had developed a formidable poetics by the 1990s – continue to publish significant work alongside younger writers born in the 1970s and 1980s. These new generations are "push[ing] the boundaries set by their predecessors" (Yu 818) just as writers from older generations, now important presences within various communities, remain aesthetically surprising. The 1980s and 1990s witnessed within Asian American letters the success of a mainstream lyricism, generously represented in Garrett Hongo's anthology *The Open Boat* (1993). Yet this era was also a crucial incubation period for a counter-tradition less concerned with the well-crafted image, narrative continuity, and epiphanic closure in favor of juxtaposition, abstraction, appropriation, collage, syntactic experimentation, associational logic, absurdism, fabulism, assemblage, parody, recombination, non sequitur, and other nonnormative techniques of sensemaking.

According to Josephine Park, "Asian American poetry is shot through with discontent" as it "expresses difficult and even shattering situations marked by raced constraints" (101). I want to extend this sensible observation to argue that a contemporary counter-tradition is also shot through with a formal discontent, that is, an impatience with mainstream modes of poetic expression. Discontent is doubled: contemporary Asian American writers are reflecting the consequences of "raced constraints" while they resist prescribed modes of poiesis. I examine three prominent counter-modes – surely they are not the only ones – identifying representative writers from both older and younger generations. In emphasizing points of aesthetic connection across generations, I don't wish to posit simple examples of monocausal influence (though, in some cases, there is strong evidence, if not direct acknowledgment, of indebtedness), nor do I wish to deny the importance of affiliation with non-Asian Americans. Rather, I'd like to acknowledge the pioneering poets who came into prominence in the 1980s and 1990s for laying the discursive groundwork for future innovations while also honoring their ongoing evolution into the twenty-first-century. The younger writers – mostly born in the 1970s and 1980s – that I mention are not included in Victoria Chang's anthology *Asian American Poetry: The Next Generation* (2004), which demonstrates that contemporary Asian American poetry is a rapidly growing body of work that has yet to be fully charted and analyzed.

What I am calling counter-modes offer powerful alternatives to the confessional and culinary lyricism exemplified by Li-Young Lee's "Eating Alone" and David Mura's "Gardens We Have Left." I mean "culinary" in a double sense: first, to designate the poets' imagistic descriptions of Asian food, such as "the aroma of *sukiyaki*" (Mura 221) and "[s]hrimp braised in sesame / oil and garlic" (Lee 33).[1] Second, I intend "culinary" to capture the Brechtian sense of art that is palatable for bourgeois consumption. In contrast to the easily digestible poetry that dominated the end of the twentieth century, three major counter-modes have come to characterize some of the finest achievements of contemporary Asian American innovative poetics: (1) *a surrealist mode*, pioneered by John Yau (b. 1950) and practiced by younger poets such as Paolo Javier (b. 1974); (2) *a documental mode* of postmodern montage, evident in the work of Theresa Hak Kyung Cha (1951–1982), Walter K. Lew (b. 1955), Myung Mi Kim (b. 1957), and Divya

Victor (b. 1983); and (3) *a phenomenological mode* practiced by Mei-mei Berssenbrugge (b. 1947) and Sueyeun Juliette Lee (b. 1977).[2] These rubrics are not mutually exclusive: the surreal, documental, and phenomenological can intersect. Moreover, the aesthetic identities of these poets certainly exceed my heuristic categories. Ultimately, I am less interested in upholding the coherence of a typology than in specifying what we might mean by terms such as "experimental" or "alternative" – and in demonstrating that a pan-Asian American poetry has been at the forefront of innovative poetics in myriad ways.

The Surreal Mode

John Yau begins his essay "Between the Forest and Its Trees" by capitalizing on the double sense of "sentence," showing it to be both a grammatical unit and a means of disciplinary control: "I (or another faceless one with my name) was sentenced to sentences before I spoke [. . .] I learned the differences between acceptable and unacceptable sounds" (37). Later, Yau shows how he has been sentenced to various social, aesthetic, and racial identities: "I am the Other – the chink, the lazy son, the surrealist, the uptight East Coast Banana" ("Between" 40). "Surrealist," in this context, is a pejorative term, but Yau's invocation of Rimbaud suggests that surrealism, with its emphasis on otherness and the perpetual transformations of identity, is a potent mode for subverting stigmatizing identitarian categories. Yau's insubordinate surrealism of "unacceptable sounds" often draws on the fact that he was sentenced to language in the first place. Writing a sentence entails, as it does for any writer, an abstraction from his racial embodiment: it produces a discursive being, "John," a "faceless one." Indeed, Marjorie Perloff could write of Yau's late 1970s phase: "there was no indication, at this stage of Yau's career, that the poet is in fact Chinese-American" (n. pag.). Writing, of course, has no face even though we imagine it issues from one. Perloff's comment suggests that without the appropriate ethnic signifiers ("[s]hrimp braised in sesame oil," for example), it is assumed that Asian American poets – by default – write with white faces. Knowing that his writing always emerges from the imagined face of a discursive and racially ambiguous doppelgänger, Yau has become a master of the uncanny dramatic monologue, often appropriating the voices of white actors that have played yellow-face roles or creating bizarre parodic personae, such as Genghis Chan.[3]

Yau's strategy in confronting "raced constraints" inheres in his use of prosopopoeia as racialized impersonation, as a surrealist act of face transplantation. As his writerly "I" is faceless, Yau freely engages in a complex prosopopoetics, a making of performative faces. His "Peter Lorre Records

His Favorite Walt Whitman Poem for Posterity" conjures the image of the Austro-Hungarian American actor that played, among other roles, Mr. Moto, a Japanese detective that is a master of disguises.[4] Lorre called himself a "face maker," a moniker that aptly applies to Yau's poetry practice.[5] By bringing together Lorre, who was frequently typecast in roles of "'otherness,' 'deviance' and 'inauthenticity,'" and Whitman, the quintessential poet of American democracy, Yau takes on nothing less than American social relations and its discontents (Thomas 6). Recoding the liberating fluidity of Whitmanian identity in a grotesque register, Yau has Lorre record a string of ethnic and abject epithets: "Call me Zanzibar Sam, Bulging Pharaoh, Narcoleptic Swill" (*Borrowed* 60). These appellations – less a "Song of Myself" than a "Song of My Stereotypes" – are a poetic continuation of "chink, lazy son, surrealist, uptight East Coast Banana." The poem ends with a kitschy deformation of what Whitman calls "the Me myself" and "the other I am" (30): "Inside me dwells a nude drummer toy, all pomade and fancy, / while the outer me, the bun you tufted, was heavy-lipped // reflection of uncanny twittering amidst gnawed leaves" (Yau *Borrowed* 60). Yau turns *Leaves of Grass* into "gnawed leaves," a punning maneuver of poetic composting. "Heavy-lipped" is another phrase he strategically recycles from "Song of Myself" in which Whitman's open-hearted persona extends an invitation that, nevertheless, trades in the language of racial stereotype: "the heavy-lipped slave is invited" (44). Yau uncompromisingly questions the potentially restrictive and stigmatizing terms of any gesture of social inclusion.

In *Bijoux in the Dark* (2018), Yau extends his impersonation of Hollywood actors with "O Pinyin Sonnet (9)," which is in the voice of Mark Wahlberg, who assaulted Thanh Lam and Johnny Trinh on April 8, 1988. Yau's poem caustically parodies Wahlberg's 2014 application to have this racially charged crime stricken from his record: "I disagree with the concept / of an 'eye for an eye,' when it means / that that old gook would get mine, / and all I would get back is his broken bean" (*Bijoux* 41). The poem's deliberately plodding rhymes poke fun at Wahlberg's brief hip-hop career in the early 1990s. Moreover, Yau has Wahlberg absurdly misunderstand Matthew 5:38 (as well as its Old Testament precedent), drawing attention to the fact that, while in police custody, Wahlberg referred to "slant-eyed gooks" (Djansezian n. pag.). With this paronomastic "O Pinyin Sonnet," Yau follows not lex talionis but a poetic justice as he prosopopoetically swaps an "I" for an "I."

Charles Borkhuis has described how John Yau's poetry of the late 1980s developed into "a linguistic parasurrealism," creating productive tensions between "surrealist affinities" and a self-reflexive textual practice associated with Language writing (250). The recent "Genghis Chan: Private Eye XXXVII (Fifth Ideogram)," for example, conjures ominous signs and a menacing, uncanny soundscape, showing how Yau's linguistic parasurrealism has evolved (Borkhuis 250):

FUR REIGN   HACK SENSE

Ewe Ear

Damn

Every Wear (Yau, *Further Adventures* 70)

Yau's post-Poundian ideogram invokes fragmented animal imagery (a ewe ear, which suggests the violence of earmarking livestock, and fur, which calls to mind the fur-covered teacup of Meret Oppenheim's *Object*) while also exploiting homophonic double meanings to wryly comment on twenty-first-century xenophobia. By "hack[ing] sense," Yau hacks apart sense-making; so too does he hack into – like a computer hacker – dominant linguistic codes of English that police the boundaries of cultural belonging.

To update Borkhuis's insight about the "new avant-garde hybrids" (237) that have amalgamated within contemporary poetry, we should consider the deliriously disjunctive poetry of Paolo Javier.[6] Works such as *60 lv bo(e)mbs* (2005) and *Megton Gasgan Krakooom* (2010) have established Javier as one of the premier Asian American practitioners of linguist para-surrealism. His *Court of the Dragon* (2015) is "a book of (il) lyric, mediumistic poems" fueled by "occult praxes and hypnagogic processes." Containing references to Robert Desnos, Frank Lima, Mina Loy, Salvador Dalí, Paul Éluard, Federico García Lorca, among others, *Court of the Dragon* wears Javier's "love of the [surrealist] movement/s on its sleeve"[7] (Javier, "statement," n. pag.). The volume's serial poems are dense, incantatory thickets of linguistic amalgams: "o language hyena record coral reef couch reverie disappearance / hurricane crescendo or catfish city sublimate English / think of sew logic onto calendar away from canopy egret / name English yours divinity instance relief distend" (Javier *Court* 38). Javier is a "language hyena," a trickster that scavenges polyglot terrain, sampling words and phrases from Tagalog, Latin, Japanese, and Spanish while calling forth a crescendo of non-intentional and unsublimated English. Forgoing conventional syntactic articulations, Javier continually advances a Dionysian poetics of extremity: "why sing Apollonian guile / or stab waste resurgent ventricle quantity / inquire song engender sign replace wreath destiny acquiescence extremity" (*Court* 50).

In the book's title, Javier invokes the "Cour du Dragon" section of Max Ernst's *Une semaine de bonté* (1934) and Robert W. Chambers's "In the Court of the Dragon" (1895). There is certainly something of Ernst's collagic surrealism and Chambers's uncanny Gothicism in Javier's poetry, but the phrase "court of the dragon" goes beyond reference to the ancient passage-way from Paris's 6th arrondissement. "Court" in *Court of the Dragon* signifies an architectural space enclosed by walls as well as a place of adjudication. Late in the book, after references to Miguel López de Legazpi, the conquistador who established Spanish colonialism in the Philippines in 1565, and "U.S. encounters" (*Court* 104), a litotes for the Filipino-American War and its legacy, Javier invokes this usage of "court": "in the court of the dragon we lay out our case" (*Court* 120). The early-sixteenth-century Hunt–Lenox Globe has inscribed on its depiction of Southeast Asia the notorious phrase *HC SVNT DRACONES* ("Here there be Dragons") ("The Hunt–Lenox Globe"). *Court of the Dragon* is a court of divine decolonial justice, and just as Javier names English as his own, he resignifies the dragon as a surrealist force that refuses to be caged, carto-graphed, or colonized.

According to Phan Nhien Hao, "Nowadays you can find traces of surreal-ism in nearly all modern and postmodern works" (71). Various strains of surrealism are, indeed, ubiquitous in contemporary Asian American writing. In the epigraphs to her first book *Xing* (2011), Debora Kuan cites both John Yau and André Breton, and the influence of those writers is observable in her "Minority Assignment #2": "We sultry the lampshade & suture the lamb-chop. / We but widows wasp & swap" (19). Vi Khi Nao's *Umbilical Hospital* (2017) follows the profane excess of Georges Bataille: "Scintillating asshole shimmering brightly like the / North Star & what about the hybrid between a / grassbunny & a frog?" (20). There is what I've called, following James Clifford, an "ethnographic surrealism" in Linh Dinh's *Some Kind of Cheese Orgy* (2009); there is a recombinant surrealism in Eileen Tabios's *Murder Death Resurrection* (2018); and there is a surrealist formalism in Lo Kwa Mei-en's *Yearling* (2015) and *The Bees Make Money in the Lion* (2016). [8] It is curious, then, that "Asian American Surrealism" has not become a usable critical category. An internet search for that phrase yields only one result from a spam site: "asian-american surrealism formication calcareous glazed physiology" (juhhabazaa – donderdag).

The Documental Mode

The employment of found text, images, and other appropriated docu-ments has become increasingly prevalent in twenty-first-century

American poetry. Though such practices are mostly legible under the rubric "documentary poetics," for the sake of clarity, I employ the term "documental" rather than "documentary" to refer to poems that incorporate prior records. Terminological confusion can stem from the fact that "documentary," as an adjective, has included competing meanings that may or may not intersect: first, "of the nature of or consisting in documents" and, since the early twentieth century, "factual, realistic; applied esp. to a film or literary work, etc., based on real events or circumstances" ("documentary, adj. and n."). Though there is ample theorization around this second category, particularly in film studies, the first category has received scant attention in relation to contemporary poetry. Documents are both material instantiations of information and discursive objects that underwrite modern sociality. [9] The cultural labor of the documental poet is to resocialize documents by bringing items from private archives into public view and/or rhetorically transforming publicly available information.

The 1982 publication of Theresa Hak Kyung Cha's groundbreaking *Dictee* represented – because of her untimely death that same year and the text's belated critical reception – a deferred beginning to a new wave of late-twentieth-century and early-twenty-first-century documental impulses among Asian American and non-Asian American poets alike. Cha's book mixes myth, memory, and history by interpolating letters, photographs, maps, and film stills into her poetic prose and fragmented verses. To chart Cha's legacy is to appreciate how Asian American poets have been at the cutting edge of contemporary documental practices.

Walter K. Lew's *Excerpts from: ΔIKTH 딕테/딕티 DIKTE, for DICTEE (1982)* (1992) is an epic montage that functions as a Nekyia, a calling on the dead by way of docu-mancy. Reading *Excerpts from:* is akin to participating in a syncretic ritual, as one encounters, among found photographs of necropoli, textual fragments from sources such as Cha's *Dictee*, Dante's *Inferno*, Marguerite Yourcenar's *La Nouvelle Eurydice*, and Lew's own journals. Lew juxtaposes the *Homeric Hymn to Demeter* with the Korean shaman song about Princess Pari and includes a series of detourned drawings from a didactic 1968 children's book about Yu Kwan-sun and a meta-documentary reproduction of a photo from the "Les Deux Orphelines" section of Chris Marker's *Coréennes*, all of which Lew captions with snippets from a French essay about the Eleusinian Mysteries. The gestures are critical – indeed, the title page dubs the work a "critical collage" – in exploring the ideological juncture between Koreanness and femininity; so too does Lew initiate new mythic meanings and typological echoes to extend Cha's afterlife.

Fittingly, Lew excerpts material from *Excerpts from:* in *Treadwinds: Poems and Intermedia Texts* (2002), which reflects traces of Cha's documentalism as well as the post-Poundian, post-Zukofskian poetics of Ho Hon Leung, whom Lew champions in his visionary anthology *Premonitions* (1995). Lew's title *Treadwinds* suggests the need for new global constructs in contrast to the trade winds that historically structured the pathways of European imperialism. In *Treadwinds*, he combines personal, historical, descriptive, and ekphrastic verse, found documents, and multilingual collage in the spirit of what he has called "matrices." In 1983, Lew presciently – premonitionally – conceptualized the Asian American matrix poem, which includes "a wide range of rapidly juxtaposed languages, media, historical frameworks, motifs, and rhetorical moods. It is almost demanded by the normally multicultural situation of Asian Americans and the accelerated information flow and collisions of contemporary society in general" (qtd. in Stefans 587).[10] Exceeding conventional metrical verse, "matrical" poems demand a conceptual prosody and a materialist orientation towards the page. As the time-space compression of globalization has intensified, creating more multicultural collisions, the documental matrix recommends itself as a crucial form within Asian American postmodern practice.

Myung Mi Kim, another heir of Cha, has developed a distinctively astringent *mise-en-page*, including within her matrices "polyglot, porous, [and] transcultural presence[s]" as well as a generous amount of negative space, a move that focalizes attention on the stark juxtapositions produced by a traumatizing modernity (*Commons* 110). For example, the "Siege Document" section of *Commons* (2002) features five polyalphabetic tercets that consist of lines in Hangul flanked, above and below, by normative and nonnormative Romanizations. The final line of the page translates the fifth tercet into English, demonstrating a range of translational, transliterative, and pronounciational gaps. The name "Siege Document" suggests Kim's adherence to Walter Benjamin's dictum that "[t]here is no document of culture which is not at the same time a document of barbarism" (392). Indeed, she treats the document as a signature technology of the Enlightenment, a codification of inscriptions that perpetuates various acts of violence – physical, discursive, epistemological – in the name of progress.

To counter the domination made possible by the mobilization of documents (from the school primer to the coercive treaty), Kim's idiolectic poetics relies on strategies of dissident transcription that brush found documents against the grain. Kim's long poem *Penury* (2009) continues her documental practices of austere redaction:

> The said release   annexed   surrendered
>
> Majority of members
>
> In consideration of lawful money
>
> The said water frontage and the above described lands
>
> Rolling country   small poplar bluffs
>
> One Arrow transcript (69)

It is all too easy to project on to Kim's writing what isn't there. Reading *Penury*, Judith Halden-Sullivan says, "Sometimes I heard an immigrant struggling to learn a new language" (138). This dangerous assumption – that poets born in Asia always bluntly literalize their immigrant condition through a poetics of voice – causes her to misread the passage above: "Should the term be 'One Arrow,' or does it just *sound* like it to an immigrant's ear? Could it be 'one-hour' transcript – the duration of a language test? Or one-hour transit – a bus schedule?" (Halden-Sullivan 140).

When confronting documental poetry, it is, of course, helpful to find the source document, which, in this case, is the Canadian governmental record *Indian Treaties and Surrenders from No. 281 to No. 483, Vol. III*. For example, section no. 359 is a 1894 document attesting that "One Arrow's Band of Indians [...] Do hereby release, remise, surrender, quit claim and yield up to Our Sovereign Lady the Queen" a "certain parcel or tract of land [...] in the Indian Reserve No. 95" (144–145). Therefore, to read Kim's passage, knowledge of "Asian rhetorics" (139), to use Halden-Sullivan's phrase, is less useful than knowledge of settler colonialism in North America. The Cree chief One Arrow (Ka-Payak-Waskunam), who had a peripheral but tragic role in the North-West Rebellion of 1885, haunts Kim's text. Captured and compelled to participate in a trial he could barely understand, One Arrow was imprisoned in Manitoba Penitentiary. After his release in 1886, he died in exile, too ill to travel home. One Arrow's remains were exhumed and returned to Saskatchewan in 2007. Given the fact that the terminal phrases "rolling country" and "small poplar bluffs" come from a surveying document of the One Arrow Indian Reserve, we might consider Kim's dissident transcription as a documental exhumation, a way to textually reconnect Chief One Arrow with the rolling country of his homeland.

"Myung has taught me," says Divya Victor, "how to ask the harder question of a text [...] how to phrase an ethical problem as a material one" (qtd. in

Fitzgerald n. pag.). Victor studied with Kim in The Poetics Program at the University at Buffalo, but she is also referring to the ways Kim's books, more generally, contribute to a matrical/materialist tradition. Victor's *Kith* (2017) represents one of the most exciting documental works produced by an Asian American poet born in the 1980s. It is, as she says, "a documentary poetics for those of us without documents" (n. pag.). At just over 200-pages, *Kith* is, so to speak, a collection of many "kindred" mini-books under the sign of transgenerational, transcultural, transhistorical, and translingual "knownness" (kith, coming from the Old English *cȳððu*). It combines oral legend, prose poems, list poems, visual poems, creatively annotated photographs sourced from family albums, quotations, and ritualistic verses and diagrams. It juxtaposes memoir, lyric art-historical essay, and image-text collage in a postcolonial key.

Victor's matrices cleverly blend the documentary, documental, and meta- or mock-documental and accumulate a range of conceptual rhymes and resonances. One page from her series "Salt" records that "a cyclone off the coast of Gujarat / killed thousands of salt workers /who earned 350 rupees (£5) a week"; this statement is followed by "In 1998, £5 could buy," then a series of twenty numbered blank spaces (144).[11] The first three lines of this page, informed by a 1999 article from *The Guardian*, are documentary in a conventional sense: the journalistic language is based on a real disaster, both natural and social. In shifting to the meta-documental, Victor reinforces our sense of global inequality by creating a mock school assignment, a move that reroutes our affective thinking in complex and uncomfortable ways. We grasp the radical incommensurability between the thousands of salt workers, who were not warned of the cyclone's advance, and the twenty notional commodities worth £5 apiece as well as the steep hurdles separating salt farmers from literacy; interviewed by *The Guardian*, a salt trader says, "we don't ask if they can read or write. We just give them a job and, literate or illiterate, we pay them the same. So they can't be bothered to read or write" (Goldenberg n. pag.). Moreover, by presenting us with a preprinted instructional form to be filled in, Victor mimics a text that assumes an educational subject in formation; this page importantly resonates with a found text later in *Kith* from the 1848 *Phrase Book: Or, Idiomatic Exercises in English and Tamil: Designed to Assist Tamil Youth in the Study of the English Language*, a pedagogical document in service of the civilizing and Christianizing missions of the British empire. Later in the "Salt" series, Victor recodes the ruled space of the instructional workbook in a movement away from ideological enculturation towards commemoration: "in memory of _____, _____," and so on (*KITH* 154). In this way, Victor's ethics of memory emerges from the matrix of the material page.

Considering other works such as Sun Yung Shin's *Skirt Full of Black* (2007) and *Unbearable Splendor* (2016); Tan Lin's *HEATH* (2007–2012) and *BIB., REV. ED.* (2011); Craig Santos Perez's ongoing long poem *from Unincorporated Territory*, which consists of *[hacha]* (2008), *[saina]* (2010), *[guma']* (2014), and *[lukao]* (2017); Barbara Jane Reyes's *To Love as Aswang* (2015); Don Mee Choi's *Hardly War* (2016); Cheena Marie Lo's *A Series of Un/Natural/Disasters* (2016); and Janice Lobo Sapigao's *like a solid to a shadow* (2017) is only to begin to acknowledge the full range of documental modes that are thriving within Asian Pacific American poetry.

The Phenomenological Mode

For decades, Mei-mei Berssenbrugge has practiced a poetics of radical attention, observation, and description, drawing on an abstract, self-reflexive discourse to meditate on the intricate ways an embodied subject meaningfully interacts within time and space with other subjects and objects. *Sphericity* (1993), for example, ends: "A sensitive empiricism identifies with the object, and energy becomes / a theory of value, moving swatch of sunlight, continuum of spatial units or integers of lit grasses, commas, / a breath feather in space. Phenomenology of the space depends on the concrete value of its boundary, / not where she stops, but an opacity from which to extend her presence" (42). These long lines, which have come to characterize her mature writing style, offer an abundance of analogies: read aloud, a comma – a crucial mark of punctuation for Berssenbrugge – is unpronounced, "a breath feather in space," while it is also a graphic "boundary" on the page from which a sentence can extend new meanings. Berssenbrugge's twenty-first-century work has evolved to embrace the sentence as a basic unit of semantic as well as structural measure. As she says in *Sphericity*, "The sentence is her concrete measure of time" (40).

More explicitly anchored in "narrative and persona," Berssenbrugge's recent poems have become more accessible, trading less in "technical terminology." Nevertheless, they still carry forward her long-standing interests in Husserlian phenomenology, ecology, and Asian religiosity and retain certain conceptual and lexical complexities. In "Green," one of the strongest pieces in *Hello, the Roses* (2013), she writes, "I'm interested in the resonance of disjunction, of one thing next to another, blue mountain at sunset and yellow air. // The glow is an inner informational process connecting, moment-to-moment, in a kind of spontaneous karmic outline, crow in wind, elms" (45). Berssenbrugge continues to use the comma – in acts of grammatico-phenomenological appositionality – to connect one thing to another, to delineate a rich, sensory field of interobjectivities. One can say that her entire poetics is animated by a "resonance of disjunction," which importantly stems from her mixed-race, multicultural identity. During a 2006 interview, she said, "I try to expand a field by dissolving polarities or dissolving the borders between one thing and another. Sometimes I think it's because I'm from one culture – I was born in Beijing – and grew up in another" ("Mei-mei Berssenbrugge").

In the title poem of *Nest* (2003), dedicated to Gayatri Chakravorty Spivak, Berssenbrugge reflects on the disjunction between her mother tongue, Chinese, and her daughter's, English, allowing her to build a range of resonances: "Change of mother tongue between us activates an immunity, margin where dwelling and travel are not distinct // [...] // I observe a lighted field seem to hang in space in front of me. // Speaking, not filling in, surface intent, is a cabinet of artifacts, comparisons, incongruity" (46). In the penultimate line of this section, Berssenbrugge dissolves the comma one would expect between the words "field" and "seem"; such a mark of punctuation would graphically articulate the instance of *diazeugma* (disjoining), the rhetorical employment of a subject with multiple verbs. Fittingly, this sentence expresses a sudden disjoining between the speaker and herself, between the split sense of herself as both subject and object within a phenomenological field. In the next sentence, Berssenbrugge surprisingly creates two nonparallel series separated by a copula. In the first series, Berssenbrugge cites, as she often does, the concept of Husserlian intentionality as she puts speaking in apposition with "surface intent." The series in the predicate is also a kind of congruous incongruity; though a congeries of plural ("artifacts, comparisons") and singular items ("incongruity"), it is a subtle rhetorico-prosodic amplification that moves from a trisyllabic to a tetrasyllabic and, finally, to a pentasyllabic word. Ultimately, Berssenbrugge "dwells" – in a Heideggerian sense – in a language that is a complex nested construction of many margins even as she risks rhetorical disjointedness. According to Lawrence-Minh Bùi Davis, "'Asian American' has always been an inelegant conglomeration, of peoples from all across the world, from nations and cultures too disparate to gather coherently, and equitably, together" (n. pag.). On an individual level, any particular Asian American may also be "an inelegant conglomeration," a cabinet of potentially polarizing comparisons. Berssenbrugge's poetry powerfully responds to this conundrum of Asian American identity by transforming apparent disjunctions, disjoinings, and incoherencies into new forms of elegance.

In the essay "The Seamless World: Mei-mei Berssenbrugge's Poetry," Sueyeun Juliette Lee has observed that Berssenbrugge "draws the reader's attention to the very limits of perception" (69); moreover, Lee suggests that "her poems' phenomenal aspects also speak to socio-political orientations" (59). Lee takes such a poetry of perceptual focus into a speculative direction, asking readers to imagine how it feels to inhabit and conceptualize a sensuous world on the brink of catastrophe. In *Solar Maximum* (2015), one of her speakers says, "A gradual violence takes shape, here in the space we renamed twilight. Its halo hangs over the single ocean, radius a triumphant index of all the walls we've left to climb" (7). Like Berssenbrugge, Lee often creates a "resonance of disjunction" between scientific and affective discourses.

The title poem of Lee's *No Comet, That Serpent in the Sky Means Noise* (2017) powerfully links an eco-phenomenological attention to the northern hemispheric sky with an elegiac attunement to historical trauma as it makes reference to No Gun Ri, the site of a 1950 massacre of hundreds of South Korean refugees by US forces: "A white shadow stands at No Gun Ri [...] What is stood on bends, resounds. The hollow ear tinctured with lacking a grave" (80). The section entitled "현무," which alludes to the set of constellations called *hyeonmu*, begins with another image of a human ear, as if the aural hollow of attentive listening could provide memorial shelter for the dead: "Silence meant that there were disconnections in the atmosphere, the inner hairs of my ears curling themselves without a quiver or lightest touch of alarm. Plenary attitudes detach, disengage themselves from the white washed walls striking poses in the afternoon" (Lee *No Comet* 85). In "현무," Lee counterpoints the "slow violence" of environmental disaster with the whitewashing and slow forgetting of historical atrocity: "For even the ozone layer this is something of a tragedy" (85).[12]

Though I have emphasized, here, the reflective/speculative nature of Lee's phenomenological mode, she flexibly draws on what I've been calling the surrealist and documental modes as well, with all three modes sometimes appearing within a single volume. In an essay on Myung Mi Kim, Lee says, "I personally cannot imagine what sort of writer or individual I would be without having encountered her. I wish the same transformative experience to her future readers" (n. pag.). What I have been suggesting here is that aspiring Asian American poets can access multiple traditions of innovative practices that now-established writers consolidated in the 1980s and 1990s. Furthermore, if we can read Lee reading Kim and Berssenbrugge as notable instances of intergenerational connection so too can we read John Yau reading fellow Asian American poets as an affirmation of an innovative tradition's twenty-first-century continuance. As a prolific contributor and editor to the online arts magazine *Hyperallergic Weekend* since 2012, Yau has written reviews and review-essays on his contemporary Marilyn Chin as well as younger poets Cathy Park Hong, Sawako Nakayasu, Brandon Som, Monica Youn, and Muriel Leung. The introductory framing to his piece on Nakayasu advocates for an Asian American poetics grounded in "an engagement with the materiality of language" and an "openness to experimentation" in contrast to "the lyric poetry of the generation that emerged in the 1970s and '80s" (Yau "Language" n. pag.).

Ultimately, inhabiting surrealist, documental, and phenomenological modes have been important ways for Asian American poets to resist what Rey Chow calls "coercive mimeticism," mainstream cultural pressures that compel ethnic subjects "to objectify themselves in accordance with the already seen" (107). There is much more to say about Asian American poetic innovation, but I have run out of space: I mention this, risking rhetorical ineloquence, to suggest that contemporary Asian American poetry needs more space, discursive and otherwise. We need more critical language to place it, to show how it refuses to stay in its place.

Notes

1. For an exploration of what Frank Chin notoriously called "food pornography," see Wong 55–71.
2. For a previous typology of contemporary innovative Asian American poetry, see Stefans. See also Yao 15–16, who groups together John Yau, Myung Mi Kim, and Mei-mei Berssenbrugge under the broad banner "ethnic abstraction."
3. See Leong "Neo-Surrealism's Forked Tongue."
4. Yau's "Peter Lorre" series in *Borrowed Love Poems* – particularly "Peter Lorre Speaks to the Spirit of Edgar Allan Poe during a Séance" – bears comparison to Frank Chin's "Railroad Standard Time," in which the narrator describes "reading Edgar Allan Poe" to his father "in the voice of Peter Lorre by candlelight" (5).
5. See Thomas.
6. In December 2018, Javier, as Program Director of New York City's Poets House, organized a tribute to Yau, suggesting an intergenerational aesthetic affiliation.
7. Paolo Javier. "Statement." Received by Michael Leong, December 8, 2018.
8. See Leong "Forms of Asian Americanness" 138–139.
9. See Ferraris and Buckland. For a more detailed discussion of documental poetics, see Leong *Contested Records*.
10. Lew has more recently turned to the hybrid essay that "matrically" combines mock academic prose, diagrammatic images, and visual poetry. See Lew, "Shapely Vulgates: Respirational Form in Korean Orthography, Sexual Positions, and Vernacular Architecture." See also a compressed version of "Shapely Vulgates" with an alternative layout in *The Body in Language: An Anthology*, edited by Edwin Torres.
11. This page is comparable to the opening of the "Hummingbird" section in Myung Mi Kim's *Dura* (1998).
12. See Nixon.

Works Cited

Benjamin, Walter. *Walter Benjamin: Selected Writings 4: 1938–1940*, edited by Howard Eiland and Michael W. Jennings. Harvard University Press, 2006.

Berssenbrugge, Mei-mei. "Blurring the Borders between Formal and Social Aesthetics: An Interview with Mei-mei Berssenbrugge." Interview by Zhou Xiaojing. *MELUS* vol. 27, no. 1, 2002, pp. 199–212.

Hello, the Roses. New Directions, 2013.

"Mei-mei Berssenbrugge by Michèle Gerber Klein." Interview by Michèle Gerber Klein. *BOMB* 96, July 1, 2006, https://bombmagazine.org/articles/mei-mei-berssenbrugge

Nest. Kelsey St., 2003.

Sphericity. Kelsey St., 1993.

Borkhuis, Charles. "Writing from Inside Language: Late Surrealism and Textual Poetry in France and the United States." *Telling It Slant: Avant-Garde Poetics of the 1990s*, edited by Mark Wallace and Steven Marks. University of Alabama Press, 2002, pp. 237–254.

Buckland, Michael. *Information and Society*. MIT Press, 2017.

Chin, Frank. *The Chinaman Pacific & Frisco R.R. Co.* Coffee House, 1988.

Chow, Rey. *The Protestant Ethnic and the Spirit of Capitalism*. Columbia University Press, 2002.

Davis, Lawrence-Minh Bùi. "Introduction." *The Asian American Poets Issue*, special issue of *Poetry* July/August 2017, www.poetryfoundation.org/poetrymagazine/articles/142893/introduction-

Djansezian, Kevork. "Should Mark Wahlberg Be Pardoned for 1988 Assault." *NBC News*, December 9, 2014, www.nbcnews.com/news/asian-america/should-mark-wahlberg-be-pardoned-1988-assault-n263831

"documentary, adj. and n." *OED Online*, Oxford University Press, June 2019, www.oed.com/view/Entry/56332.

Ferraris, Maurizio. *Documentality: Why It Is Necessary to Leave Traces*, translated by Richard Davies. Fordham University Press, 2013.

Fitzgerald, Adam. "#Actual Asian Poets: A Celebration of Asian and Asian American Poetry." *Lithub*, October 8, 2015, https://lithub.com/actual-asian-poets/

Goldenberg, Suzanne. "Storm Haunts the Forgotten Labourers of the Salt-Pans." *The Guardian*, February 11, 1999, www.theguardian.com/world/1999/feb/11/7

Halden-Sullivan, Judith. "The Game of Self-Forgetting: Reading Innovative Poetry Reading Gadamer." *Reading the Difficulties: Dialogues with Contemporary American Innovative Poetry*, edited by Thomas Fink and Judith Halden-Sullivan. University of Alabama Press, 2014, pp. 127–145.

Indian Treaties and Surrenders From No. 281 to No. 483, Vol. III. C.H. Parmelee, 1912.

Javier, Paolo. *Court of the Dragon*. Nightboat Books, 2015.

"juhhabazaa – donderdag 07 april 2016 15:18," *Wehlse Tennisvereniging*, http://wehlsetennisvereniging.nl/index.php/component/vitabook/?new=tr&start=157650

Kim, Myung Mi. *Commons*. University of California Press, 2002.

Dura. Nightboat Books, 2008.

Penury. Omnidawn Publishing, 2009.

Kuan, Debora. *Xing*. Saturnalia, 2001.

Lee, Li-Young. *Rose*. BOA, 1986.

Lee, Sueyeun Juliette. *No Comet, That Serpent in the Sky Means Noise*. Kore, 2017.

"'shaped like relation suggested like progress': Celebrating Myung Mi Kim's *Dura*." *Building Is a Process / Light Is an Element: Essays and Excursions for Myung Mi Kim*, edited by Michael Cross and Andrew Rippeon. *Electronic Poetry Center*, http://writing.upenn.edu/epc/authors/kim/building/index.html

Solar Maximum. Futurepoem, 2015.

"The Seamless World: Mei-mei Berssenbrugge's Poetry." *Nests and Strangers: On Asian American Women Poets*, edited by Timothy Yu and Mg Roberts, Kelsey St., 2015, pp. 52–77.

Leong, Michael. *Contested Records: The Turn to Documents in Contemporary North American Poetry.* University of Iowa Press, 2020.

"Forms of Asian Americanness in Contemporary Poetry." *Contemporary Literature* vol. 57, no. 1, 2016, pp. 135–140.

"Neo-Surrealism's Forked Tongue: Reflections on the Dramatic Monologue, Politics, and Community in the Recent Poetry of Will Alexander and John Yau." *Contemporary Literature* vol. 55, no. 3, 2014, pp. 501–533.

Lew, Walter K. *Excerpts from: ΔIKTH 딕테/딕티 DIKTE, for DICTEE (1982).* Yeuleum Sa, 1991.

"Shapely Vulgates: Respirational Form in Korean Orthography, Sexual Positions, and Vernacular Architecture." *West Coast Line* vol. 50, 2007, pp. 16–28.

"Shapely Vulgates: Respirational Form in Korean Orthography, Sexual Positions, and Vernacular Architecture." *The Body in Language: An Anthology*, edited by Edwin Torres. Counterpath, 2019, pp. 310–316.

Treadwinds: Poems and Intermedia Texts. Wesleyan University Press, 2002.

Mura, David. "Gardens We Have Left." *The Open Boat: Poems from Asian America*, edited by Garrett Hongo. Doubleday, 1993, p. 221.

Nixon, Rob. *Slow Violence and the Environmentalism of the Poor.* Harvard University Press, 2011.

Park, Josephine. "Asian American Poetry." *The Cambridge Companion to Asian American Literature*, edited by Crystal Parikh and Daniel Y. Kim. Cambridge University Press, 2015, pp. 101–113.

Perloff, Marjorie. "Review of *Forbidden Entries*." *Boston Review*, Summer 1997, http://bostonreview.net/archives/BR22.3/Poetry3.html

Phan, Nhien Hao. *Night, Fish and Charlie Parker*, translated by Linh Dinh, Tupelo, 2006.

Stefans, Brian Kim. "'Remote Parsee': An Alternative Grammar of Asian North American Poetry." *Telling It Slant: Avant-Garde Poetics of the 1990s*, edited by Mark Wallace and Steven Marks. University of Alabama Press, 2002, pp. 576–608.

"The Hunt–Lenox Globe." *Treasures of the New York Public Library*, http://exhibitions.nypl.org/treasures/items/show/163

Thomas, Sarah. *Peter Lorre: Face Maker: Constructing Stardom and Performance in Hollywood and Europe.* Berghahn, 2012.

Vi, Khi Nao. *Umbilical Hospital.* 1913 Press, 2017.

Victor, Divya. "On How and Kith: An Interview with Divya Victor." Interview with Mg Roberts. *Entropy*, October 22, 2018, https://entropymag.org/on-how-and-kith-an-interview-with-divya-victor

KITH. Fence/BookThug, 2017.

Whitman, Walt. *Poetry and Prose.* Library of America, 1996.

Wong, Sau-ling Cynthia. *Reading Asian American Literature: From Necessity to Extravagance*. Princeton University Press, 1993.

Yao, Steven G. *Foreign Accents: Chinese American Verse from Exclusion to Postethnicity*. Oxford University Press, 2010.

Yau, John. "Between the Forest and Its Trees." *Amerasia Journal* vol. 20, no. 3, 1994, pp. 37–43.

Bijoux in the Dark. Letter Machine Editions, 2018.

Borrowed Love Poems. Penguin, 2002.

Further Adventures in Monochrome. Copper Canyon, 2012.

"Language Is Not Colorless: The Amazing Writing of Sawako Nakayasu." *Hyperallergic Weekend*, April 26, 2016, https://hyperallergic.com/201934/lanu gage-is-not-the-amazing-writing-of-sawako-nakayasu/

Yu, Timothy. "Asian American Poetry in the First Decade of the 2000s." *Contemporary Literature* vol. 52, no. 4, 2011, pp. 818–851.

3

DAVID A. COLÓN

Locations of Contemporary Latina/o Poetry

In his book *Notes on the Return to the Island* (2017), Bonafide Rojas glosses the frames that define being Puerto Rican, and he does so with persistent attention to place. The collection begins with the poem "At the Top of El Morro," El Morro being a site in Puerto Rico with immense historical significance. A Spanish citadel erected in Old San Juan during the sixteenth century, it functioned for a dozen generations as a near impenetrable fortress, even after the United States stole it. El Morro is the most iconic monument in Puerto Rico, a public symbol of Puerto Rico's history of colonization and military occupation, and for this very reason it is the island's major tourist destination – a UNESCO World Heritage Site that hosts two million visitors a year. Its garrison stone walls are more than twenty feet thick and its vast green esplanade is a lovely place for children to fly kites: a structure at once terrible, glorious, decrepit, and awesome, housing gift shops stocked with magnets and postcards flaunting its own likeness in tropical auras. El Morro is an understandable place for Rojas to start, and the opening lines of "At the Top of El Morro" are just as apt: "today we celebrate / the death of the past / that has haunted us / since the very beginning // we mourn the living / & wash our hands / of all the names / that tried to destroy us" (15).

A resident of the Bronx, Rojas is Nuyorican, and the premise of *Notes on the Return to the Island* is that Rojas is a diasporic subject returning to his ancestral homeland and "trying to find questions / that these dark roads, street lights & / bridges might be able to answer" (24). *Notes on the Return to the Island* has many poems about Puerto Rican places, among them: "First Night in Santurce," "Waiting for the Bus in San Juan," "Easter Sunday in Mayagüez," and "Lessons on a Park Bench in Rio Piedras." Yet, for Rojas, Puerto Rican places are not solely on the island. "Lessons on a Park Bench in Loisaida"[1] and "Open Letter to New York" are also among these *Notes*, as is his version of the register of culturally sanctioned Puerto Rican municipalities in "Townships": "adjuntas. aguada. aguadilla. aguas buenas. aibonito. allentown. / añasco. arecibo. arroyo. barceloneta.

barranquitas. bayamón. / bridgeport. the bronx. brooklyn. boston. buffalo. cabo rojo" (120). Rojas intersperses the alphabetized list of Puerto
Rican towns and cities with select US mainland destinations turned
viable communities.[2] "Townships" is a manifest not of the island but
of the *people* – a reckoning of the Puerto Rican diaspora, *el pueblo
boricua*, reinforced by the poem's central inclusion of "el barrio" and
its universality. Once the United States annexed Puerto Rico after the
Spanish-American War, the Foraker Act (1900) established Puerto Rican
"citizenship." During World War I that changed with the Jones–Shafroth
Act (1917), precipitated by the National Defense Act (1916). Largely
intended to fulfill the need for more conscripted American soldiers, the
Jones–Shafroth Act made Puerto Ricans US citizens of a second class,
denied numerous political rights[3] but free to move to the mainland
without legal obstacle. In the century since, Puerto Ricans have populated a revolving-door migration that continues to this day, a condition
that situates Puerto Rican diasporic identity at the junction of inter-
lingualism, interculturalism, and transnationalism.

Notes on the Return to the Island is haunted by this uniquely reconstituted
transnationalism. The first entry of "Thirty Ways of Looking at a Nuyorican"
declares, "i do not wake up / to roosters, i wake up / to construction sights / &
exhaling buses" (26); the thirtieth reads, "patria. sangre. libertad." (29). The
development of reflections, anecdotes, and ideas over the course of the poem is
akin to its "library of dead heroes / that i have stolen" (27), oscillating through
affective phases of self-doubt, indifference, pride, and indignation. The entire
collection expresses a confluence of validation and anxiety, as if this were
a natural condition of being Puerto Rican in the shadow of our inherited
socioeconomic and political precariousness. Yet to describe *Notes on the
Return to the Island* as simply a transnational book would miss Rojas's
intervention. The concept *transnational* implicitly retains nationality as
a quantifiable category that can be combined and recombined, hybridized
even – the movement indicated in *trans-* is between states. The concept of
transnationality denotes travel or movement or transgression between such
discrete political entities, or at the very least denotes simultaneous membership
in two or more polities, however one may define membership. The Puerto
Rican diaspora's condition is different, more reminiscent of a metaphysical
Anzaldúan borderland of cultural autonomy, not beholden to its constitutive
elements but rather having passed into a phase of being wholly new, its own
thing. It is more *post-transnational* than transnational in that to identify as
a diasporic Puerto Rican (much like identifying as Chicano/a) is to assert
contact zones, not nationality, as sovereign. In this way, Rojas's poetry speaks
to broader themes and cultural dynamics in contemporary Latina/o poetry.

Like the various forms of citizenship (global, cultural, legal, dual) that are a consequence of emergent Latina/o communities, transnationalism has already splintered throughout Latina/o experience and cultural production. If *transnational* indicates the interplay between polities, and *post-transnational* suggests a borders-are-the-sovereign framework, then there are other mutations to be seen in Latina/o poetries. In their site-specific expressions of affect, many contemporary Latina/o poets envision futures, a kind of *pre-post-transnational* mindset that foresees the specter of sovereign contact zones yet to come. Others eschew either the terms or the compulsion to engage transnationalism in what one might refer to as a form of avoidance or *circumnationalism*. Still others, and perhaps like Rojas at times, issue *indignationalism*, especially when addressing the psychic strain of "belonging to the United States, but not a part of the United States."[4]

Clearly the locations of contemporary Latina/o poetry are neither politicized nor aestheticized all in the same manner. The formal range of expression that Latina/o poets in the twenty-first-century produce is as diverse as our range of heritage nationalities and local geographies. An intriguing instance of the convergence of radical experimentation in both realms (of aesthetics and geopolitics) lies in Hugo García Manríquez's conceptualist book, *Anti-Humboldt: A Reading of the North American Free Trade Agreement* (2014). Published as a collaboration between Editorial Aldus (Mexico City) and Litmus Press (Brooklyn), *Anti-Humboldt* is a collection of erasure poems[5] crafted from the text of NAFTA (1994) documents. The book is presented in a reversible bilingual format but, as translation, the two texts are not faithful. In his epilogue, García Manríquez explains that "the passages in English and Spanish do not always mirror each other – they come from different sections of the documents" and thus the experiences differ by language. Yet he believes "that the very incommensurability between passages and languages articulates such a 'reading in unison' with the very task of translation: to aspire not to synthesis but to circulation between interstices. Dissonances that allow us to imagine critical resistance" (Garcia Manríquez 72–73).

In *Anti-Humboldt*, resistance reigns. With the title, García Manríquez invokes the explorer-naturalist Alexander von Humboldt (1769–1859) and the problematic legacy of his scientific expeditions in the Americas. Authorized by Spain's Bourbon monarchy and financed by his own inheritance from his mother's late husband, Humboldt travelled throughout Spanish America from 1799 to 1804 to audit and account the natural resources of the empire's holdings in the New World. While Humboldt's findings and hypotheses "produced a significant body of work for various fields, such as geology, natural history, and sociology,"

García Manríquez asserts that this Enlightenment project was fraught with large-scale ethical complexities: that while his credited advancements in botany, geography, and meteorology were key to scientific advancement and often remembered as utilitarian, Humboldt's "work must be read in the light of intense spatial reconfigurations of capital during that period" (74). The extent of the Spanish Empire was at its greatest at the turn of the nineteenth century, but just a few years after Humboldt's mission, Napoleon invaded Iberia, spurring the mass liberation movement that saw most Spanish territories gain independence between 1808 and 1826. As the *Anti-Humboldt*, García Manríquez's offering of *A Reading of the North American Free Trade Agreement* layers a counter characterization of this history as its backdrop:

> Asymmetries inherent to neoliberalism have impacted communities on both sides of the border. In this sense, the bilingual space of *Anti-Humboldt* would represent an invitation for a reading in unison from multiple social spaces, particularly United States and Mexico, which frequently seem incommunicado. The interruption of the neoliberal language can turn the document into a possible space of encounter. [...] In the open arc from Humboldt, in the early 19th century, to NAFTA in the late 20th century, a spectre emerges: the reinscription of the living as mere "standing reserve," or *Bestand*, in Heidegger, that is, the modern instrumental orientation which has turned nature and the world into entirely disposable and meaningless supplies and things. (72–75)

The text of NAFTA itself supports this view. It is thoroughly bureaucratic, in other words, ideological in its preamble and clerical in its enumerations. Through *Anti-Humboldt*'s paratactic framing of NAFTA as a document to be regarded for its potential as literature, flits of allegory, irony, and rhythm emerge from the erasure of restrictions and lists, including lists of commodities ranging from textiles to livestock to machinery: "8430.50.99 Other (**self**propelled machinery **and apparatus**). / 8430.61.01 Graders (pushers). / 8430.61.02 Tamping or compacting rollers. / 8430.62.01 **Scarification** machine (ripping machine)" (García Manríquez 33). Because the physical act of passing one's eyes over the grayed-out textual gaps is needed in order to register each darkened set of letters, the raised text inherently reads at a slower pace than the whole. Moreover, conventional reading usually makes the eyes focus on a few points per line, with the forms of most letters noticed essentially by peripheral vision. Here, however, the raised text, in such short selections, makes the eyes zero in directly on each grapheme, and this somatic experience adds a layer of emphasis onto the meaning of each bit of darkened text. This is García Manríquez *reading* NAFTA, manipulating the aesthetic through a clandestine but no less compulsory programming of how your eyes take it in as you read it. At the same time, the text highlights words principally for either their subject rhyme or their potential to aggregate into impressions, not for phrases that syntactically hold together or construct syllogism. Coupled with the substance of word choice, the mood of the raised text feels almost ghostly in the way its dark selections tend to be very short, scattered about the page, glimpses of thought rising from an underworld; and in the erasure process, by stripping words and phrases out of their original context, so, too, are they stripped of their mundanity. Particularly by having to ignore so much of the host text in order to read the poetry, there is a home key of loss.

Anti-Humboldt's cadence is somber, its mood abstract, and its syntax improvisational, all of which makes it feel as if a voice trying to communicate from the other side. The experience of reading it strangely feels like a séance for a sentenced civilization. Considered thusly as a voice, the raised text of *Anti-Humboldt*, in its ghostly feel, conjures comparison to a sort of enciphered oracle. Since García Manríquez's book was published on NAFTA's twenty-year anniversary, and combined with its American site-specificity, it evokes a futurist sentiment: that within its transnational context and its overstocked ledger, *Anti-Humboldt* envisions a rebirth of neo-capitalism. This pre-post-transnational *mindset that foresees the specter of sovereign contact zones yet to come* anticipates new tragic consequences of late capitalism. In moving product, so, too, are bodies moved. People become commodified and in that process they become dehumanized. Global capitalism is indifferent to human experience and this indifference is inherently a violence, just as labor is an end only possible through exploitation.

Such tragic consequences surge at the intersections of Latin American migration. The dehumanization of bodies swept up in the trawlers of global capitalism is prosperity's sin, and by design these casualties are meant to be hidden from public view in the same ways that industrial sites are most often strategically located out of the purview of neighborhood communities. Yet a poet turning their eyes to this can reveal and recover the legacy of lives silenced by state-sanctioned corporate predation, as does Valerie Martínez in her collection, *Each and Her* (2010). *Each and Her* is rooted in the borderlands where "Ciudad Juárez sits at the front lines of globalization" (Martínez 14). The concern of this volume is intently focused on lamenting the migrant girls and women recently lost to an epidemic of violence in this region, a poetic account that can be thought of, in a way, as a literary precedent for the #SayHerName movement.[6] The book opens with a sudden, two-part preface. An epigraph of a couplet by Adrienne Rich, "Nothing less than the most radical imagination / will carry us beyond this place," is followed, on the next page, by the statement:

> Since 1993, over 450 girls and women have been murdered in or near the cities of Juárez and Chihuahua, Mexico, along the U.S.-Mexico border. Some were students; many were workers in the maquiladoras. The murders are linked by evidence to torture, sexual violence, and mutilation. Many young women migrate from others areas of Mexico to border cities both for education and for work. Despite local and federal investigations, intermittent arrests, and an international awareness of the murders, they continue in what appears to be a higher rate than in previous years. According to press reports, 28 women and girls were murdered in Ciudad Juárez and the surrounding areas in 2004. The number was 58 in 2006 and 86 in 2008. (n. pag.)

In her service to the victims – past, present, and future – of this humanitarian crisis, Martínez engages in the work of a poet-cartographer. For the ways they chronicle passage over territories by citing the names of towns, cities, and counties, many of the poems in *Each and Her* are reminiscent in substance of early Spanish colonial *crónicas* but composed in a minimalist-impressionist (perhaps pointillist) manner akin to García Manríquez's erasure poems: "they pack what they have / travel north / from Durango / Sinaloa / Nuevo León / Coahuila // rivers of dots / on a migratory map // *papa* / *hay muchos* / *empleos allí*" (Martínez 3). These workers on the move wind up "between / the Mexican interior / and U.S. border // three thousand maquiladoras / more than a million workers / at fifty cents an hour," only to exclaim, "*imagine!* / *bastante para todos nosotros*" (Martínez 6). As the book unfolds, the nameless subjects of mass migration come into focus. Martínez's focus, as promised from the outset, becomes female migrants and their vulnerability at the hands of shadowy perpetrators and an authoritarian state. Poem 39 in its entirety reads: "the missive / from the attorney general / of the state of Chihuahua // *You, Parents,* / *for raising up daughters* / *whose conduct does not conform* / *to the moral order*" (39). Poem 49 is comprised of a single newspaper quote attributed to an "unidentified man" (Martínez 77) that is cited in Teresa Rodríguez's book, *The Daughters of Juárez: A True Story of Serial Murder South of the Border* (2007): "'Sometimes, when you cross a shipment of drugs to the United / States, adrenaline is so high that you want to celebrate by killing / women!'" (49). The portrait of this chilling discourse suspended between dangerous rogues and government officials represents a crossfire of depraved, misogynistic sociopathy within which migrant Latinas are caught, tortured, and die. Martínez uses each page to try a new approach to capturing the horrors: to give us, the audience, a multitude of perspectives for consideration. Lists of names, prose poems, quotes from source texts, and suggestive invocations fill out the spectrum of Martínez's referents. As unsettling and infuriating as the narrative fragments of these victims' traumas are, the insinuation of how this cycle will continue to be perpetuated is no less unnerving: "in the desert of Lote Bravo // two teenage boys / and their dogs // follow a trail // in scraps / of women's clothes" (Martínez 43).

Migrations are not the only forms of travel that deliver capital (financial, cultural, political, or human) across borders. So does tourism. A promising aspect of contemporary Latina/o poets' engagement with the theme of tourism is how, for this generation, facing a distanced facet of one's heritage can be accompanied by a concomitant feeling of shame. The broader poetic antecedent of this idea comes from the nineteenth century, and particularly Nathaniel Hawthorne (1804–1864). Hawthorne wrote his novel *The Marble Faun* (1860) during an extended stay in Rome, and from that experience – being an Anglo-American privileged enough to afford passage and lodging and to seek no income from employment – he conceived of the idea of "touristic shame": the affect of reflecting on how shallow and inequitable the experience of tourism is. *Touristic shame* is a species of colonization, different in aims and diluted in its depth of violence but no less structured by the same social dynamics and systems of capital. Hawthorne's idea was that not only is the economic disparity that affords aristocratic classes the luxury of recreational travel perverse but also the experience of touring a foreign land cannot permeate beneath a surface consideration of one's new environment, never picking up any substantive learning of a place's history or traditions or character.

Many contemporary Latina/o poets express this very sentiment, but with a twist: they tour the places of their direct ancestors. As such, I consider these poetic moments as instances of *touristic vergüenza*: the touristic shame of a Latina/o visiting an ancestral place and either not feeling connected or else realizing a poignant connection only for the first time. These Latina/o experiences are captured in a wide variety of poems with settings all over the world. An extended stay in Spain is the premise of Francisco Aragón's poem "To Madrid" from his collection, *Glow of Our Sweat* (2010). The epigraph of the poem reads, "July 20, 2005, Madrid." The date and location are significant because, that day, the Spanish newspaper *El País* ran a feature about the first same-sex marriage performed in Madrid, just a couple of weeks after gay marriage was legalized. That same issue also contained a story about the memorial services held for the 52 killed and 700 injured from a suicide bombing on July 7 in London (Aragón 70). As a foreign visitor, a gay man, a heritage Spanish speaker, and a Latino, Aragón reflects on how, that day, these identities were intersected through the pages of *El País*, "giving news of the living, // the dead: a first marriage (you're / suddenly the freest state // on earth): London burying her own" (37). The poem also reflects on the events of "a year ago": the March 11, 2004, bombings of commuter trains approaching the Atocha station in Madrid that killed 191 people and injured 1,800. These terrorist attacks were initially blamed on Basque extremists in spite of evidence to the contrary, and this spin, along with the ruling Popular Party's endorsement of the US war in Iraq, led to the Socialist Party returning to power after winning elections held just three days later (Aragón 70). The way Aragón ends this poem with an epiphany that suggests having been unaware of how myriad forms of protest politics in pursuit of sovereignty and equality are with him now as much as they have shaped the long history and emergence of his peoples (Latina/o and queer) is a unique instance of *touristic vergüenza* in contemporary Latina/o poetry: "I see // that you are not, really, / part of my past" (37).

Aracelis Girmay's debut collection *Teeth* (2007) situates further aspects of the complexity of touristic experience into a range of locales. Girmay, a native Californian educated on the East Coast, "is of Eritrean, Puerto Rican, and African American descent" (Girmay n. pag.). Her poems in *Teeth* speak to a number of places she has visited, some with ancestral ties and some without. Her poem "Ride" stages a scene in Puerto Rico where a woman takes the bus across town from Old San Juan to Barrio Obrero. In Barrio Obrero, the feminine speaker notes all the "doo-rags, cornrows, / brown skin, white skin," then suddenly: "A little boy says '*Parmiso, Mrs., pero tu tiene' la hora?*" (Girmay 20). He has asked her for the time of day but she does not give it to him. Instead, she says, "I think I hear him say *Let's take over the bus. /* I think I hear him say *Let's ride it into Banco Popular.*" Her train of thought veers immediately into considerations of protest, inequality, and opportunity, hoping to "fill our bags, & build proper houses / with radios & speakers in all the rooms" and ultimately get "refrigerators full of refrigerated foods" and "a printing press, / libraries, gardens, schools / for all the people" (Girmay 20). Girmay is deft at portraying a recognizable mind-set, a benevolent-savior mindset of a person referred to as "*Mrs.*" instead of *Señora*. The little boy also uses the familiar *tu* instead of the formal *usted* – common in Puerto Rico among strangers, even between generations, so reading this choice is inconclusive. These circumstances combine to leave the impression that if the woman in the poem is not a *gringa*, at least she probably appears to a from-the-mouths-of-babes local as potentially *Americana*; and if the speaker of the poem is in fact ethnically Puerto Rican but not a permanent resident of the island, then the touristic vergüenza that Girmay displays is not instilled in a conscious epiphany. It is more likely in the Anglophone woman's indifference to the sense of entitlement she wields as she ignores the boy's immediate concern while confidently deciding the good – and expensive – ways to fix Barrio Obrero.

Girmay's poem "Limay, Nicaragua" includes inspired understatement of surface perceptions in which the simple mention of "bones" implies a subtle but perceptible awareness of cultural history: "Mountains / jangled with bones, / fields, roads, / rivers jangled, / volcanoes jangled / with bones / on their backs, / into the earth / nevermind merengue / nevermind the cooking / nevermind the quiquiriquí / of roosters / singing *Rise*" (61). Hawthorne's idea of touristic shame (as well as "touristic aggression") relies on the premise that a tourist only sees surfaces at the expense of internalizing histories, but here Girmay manages to blend ekphrasis with a nuanced sense of knowing. In spite of the suggestion to "nevermind" culture, the "roosters / singing *Rise*" feel as if they are announcing the dawn at the same time as calling up the bones from the mountains and volcanoes: reveille for both the living and the dead. Thus, Girmay's travel poems achieve a suitable balance of surface and insight as they develop imagery. The opening lines of "The Rain at Dzorwulu" (set in Ghana) read, "Remember the road from Dzorwulu, / & how it took you down / into the deep, high grasses to cross a field / that rattled with the tails of lizards / cutting through the dried, sharp blades / & how this made you remember where / it is you came from, & the sea" (Girmay 101). Girmay's keen eye for detail, her ear for nature's music, and the poem's address of "you" invest her touristic ethos with credibility; and guilt is not an affect that *Teeth* pursues when pondering corners of the world.

More than ever, Latina/o poets are producing works that look ahead with the same drive as those that turn to the past. The implication of futurism in a conceptual framework such as pre-post-transnationalism is that speculating on what it *will* mean to be Latina/o is the vanguard of our sense of self in the present. *Latinxfuturist* poems abound in contemporary collections of verse as well as come to the fore in poetry readings and performances. On October 28, 2015, the Eck Visitors Center at the University of Notre Dame hosted a poetry event headlined by Roberto Tejada, Carmen Giménez Smith, Rodrigo Toscano, and Rosa Alcalá. The program was called "Angels of the Americlypse: Readings and Colloquia – New Latin@ Poetries and Literary Translation." The title of the event was borrowed from a section of Toscano's book, *Collapsible Poetics Theater* (2008) called "Pig-Angels of the Americlypse: An Anti-Masque for Four Players." An absurdist, Fluxus-inspired performance piece riffing through stubs of jumbled topics never seen to their logical ends, "Pig-Angels of the Americlypse" lent itself not only to the title of the event at Notre Dame but also to the title of Giménez Smith and John Chávez's anthology by Counterpath Press, *Angels of the Americlypse:*

New Latin@ Writing (2014). Clearly the portmanteau "Americlypse" derives from *America* and *apocalypse*, but its implications for new Latina/o poetics are less obvious. In its connotation of looking forward to an end of days and a final reckoning, the banner of the Americlypse has many Latina/o poets contemplating what latinxfuturist poetics should be. At the Notre Dame reading, Alcalá performed her prose poem "Voice Activation" from her most recent collection, *MyOTHER TONGUE* (2017) and she read the poem with an arresting impersonation of a digitally automated voice: emotionless, off-cadence, falling when ordinarily it would rise. Her flaccid, halting, bot-like tone infused irony into the opening lines: "This poem, on the other hand, is activated by the sound of my voice, / and, luckily, I am a native speaker. Luckily, I have no accent and you / can understand perfectly what I am saying to you via this poem" (Alcalá 21). The irony that Alcalá achieves in her latinafuturist praxis, while provocative for its novelty, has at bottom a sentiment that aligns with a long-standing intuition: that even an artificial copy of a person made in the Anglo image might very well be implicitly measured by the American public as more human than a genuinely human Latina/o.

Toscano's most recent book, *Explosion Rocks Springfield* (2016), takes latinxfuturism in numerous directions. In lieu of having true titles of their own,[7] all of the poems in the collection begin with a heading of the same line: "The Friday Evening Gas Explosion in Springfield Leveled a Strip Club Next to a Daycare." The line refers to the true events of November 23, 2012, in Springfield, Massachusetts and Toscano's wording is practically verbatim from the Associated Press's coverage of the incident. Toscano employs this premise, site-specific and crammed with irony, as a leitmotif for direct entry into an array of absurdist possibilities. Many of them can only be characterized as futurist, either for their oddly cavalier use of technical jargon or in their obscure speculative fantasies. One of them begins, "The Jupiterian midday lead effusion on Ganymede liquefied a zinc bed next to a crater rim. / The Uranian morning argon ionization on Oberon dispersed a helium cloud next to an ammonium pool" (Toscano 40). Several poems riff on the X-Bot server moderation app: "X-bot – rolled up to the spot. / X-bot – performed what was taught. / X-bot – applied what it's got. / X-bot – content with its lot" (Toscano 83). "'The Opportunity Button calibration was up to date'" ends with the lines: "Oh, one more thing, the Cosmic Transport Wormholes have since closed up, but one is / sure to open up soon, especially if you commit to this Invisible Pink Leopard Print Full / Body Suit in a pitch dark closet, the sun directly overhead" (Toscano 71). In these particular poems, the manner in which Toscano fuses absurdism to futurism within the realm of colloquial expression is native to the improvisational temperament of his well-defined aesthetic. In many respects, it evokes the thesis of Edwin Torres's manifesto-poem "The Theorist Has No Samba!": "I propose a New Instantism. Take spontaneous out / of the ether and smack it into the throes of the wild / screaming bastard maggot that IS poetry! I propose a / New NEWness, where we refuse to comply by the aged / fumblings of mere MEANING" (Torres 42).

Torres's collection *The PoPedology of an Ambient Light* (2007) not only provides a workable theoretical defense for Toscano's poetics but it is also one of the more latinxfuturist collections to emerge in recent memory. Composed in a variety of forms – from verse to prose poems to concrete poetry – *The PoPedology of an Ambient Light* revels in speculative experimentation. Like Toscano, Torres routinely integrates high-tech verbiage into his work, making the field of scientific discourse the source of poems' vocabulary. Nevertheless, both poets just as often engage with the *idea* of scientific discourse, that is, a language field developed purely for the purpose of empirical inquiry and experiment. As such, many of the poems that result read as if they had been rendered into products of mathematical or chaotic *methods*. Others read as if they were verse tainted by some sort of experiment gone awry: a confessional poem poisoned with radiation, say, or a text file corrupted by a virus. "Transla-lation-tion" opens with the lines, "what im doing in twilt sleep / drivel what key to bud him / nananoid of left ruff him / sick jijick of fluffin day vagabond glugg" before abandoning any pretense of resembling an attempt at meaning and completely devolving into sheer artifice: "jdsfdskghslhfclrdt;od?" (Torres 149–150). Latinxfuturist potential is outlined in the work of both of these poets in ways that pair the posthuman with the Latina/o. The nature of this combination is evident in Torres's reminder that "oh yeah, se habla / password" just before he apologizes for being so obscure: "yo, take it suavé pana mia, / estoy reaching . . . " (107). As an emergent method of poetry that regularly leads to artifice and absurdity, latinxfuturism might very well be the latest iteration of our preoccupation with cultural survival. In the unfathomable, yet-to-come poetic worlds and that Torres and Toscano create, there remain incontrovertible traces of intelligent Latina/o life.

The present state of the locations of contemporary Latina/o poetry is destabilizing, a process that is gaining momentum and increasingly becoming difficult to reverse. Our Latina/o literary legacy, tracing the lines from our heritage nationalities to our anti-US imperialist ancestors to our civil rights–era forebears and into the twenty-first-century, has always been rooted in *place*. No ethnic community in the United States finds more things to know in posing the question *Where are you from?* than Latinas/os. But art imitates life, indeed, and the Latina/o life in the United States, on the cusp of the third decade of this century, is one that accepts the fact that where we are from is more and more an internalized state of being. As the largest ethnic minority population in the United States and increasing at its second-fastest pace, the political forces we are being subjected to in this life are running an out-of-hand deficit well into the trillions of fears. To seek political asylum in the United States as a Latin American is akin to committing fraud in the public imagination. To be smashed by a category-5 hurricane in the Caribbean is a ruse to steal hard-earned money in the eyes of the heartland. More and more, we are growing accustomed to the understanding that where we Latina/o diasporic subjects are from is the province of our own allegiance, discretion, and imagination. Our places are becoming processes and our poets are writing them down. In the words of Aracelis Girmay, a poet from so, so many places: "Here are your eyes. Here are your eyes like tanks / filling with water. Here is your way home" (25).

Notes

1. *Loisaida* is Nuyorican slang for the Lower East Side of Manhattan.
2. *Notes on the Return to the Island* was published before the Hurricane María catastrophe of 2017, therefore "Townships" precedes release of Lin-Manuel Miranda's disaster relief single "Almost Like Praying," which sets all the names of Puerto Rico's townships to music.
3. Puerto Ricans on the island are not permitted to vote in any US federal elections. Puerto Rico is represented in US Congress by a Resident Commissioner in the House of Representatives. Until 2019, the Resident Commissioner could not cast a vote; beginning with the 116th Congress, new House Rules now allow the Resident Commissioner to cast a symbolic vote, that is, only if that vote is not a tiebreaker and thereby not decisive of a legislative outcome. The PROMESA Act (2016) that established an oversight board to manage Puerto Rico's debt crisis explicitly states that eligibility to serve on the commission requires that the considered "individual is not an officer, elected official, or employee of the territorial government, a candidate for elected office of the territorial government, or a former elected official of the territorial government," denying the opportunity for Puerto Rico's democratically elected representatives to participate in developing the economic recovery strategy of their own commonwealth.
4. Puerto Rico's political status as articulated in Downes v. Bidwell, 182 U.S. 244 (1901).
5. An *erasure poem* is one that utilizes a found text or source text and highlights, boldfaces, lightens, or otherwise visually signals certain words within the source to produce a text within the text.
6. Martínez states in her notes that the "most current and comprehensive list of names and dates of the murdered and disappeared women of Juárez can be found at http://womenofjuarez.egenerica.com/content/view/36/2 (accessed November 2, 2009)" (75).

7. The table of contents of *Explosion Rocks Springfield* lists the poems by their respective first lines.

Works Cited

Alcalá, Rosa. *MyOTHER TONGUE*. Futurepoem Books, 2017.

Aragón, Francisco. *Glow of Our Sweat*. Scapegoat Press, 2010.

García Manríquez, Hugo. *Anti-Humboldt: A Reading of the North American Free Trade Agreement*. Editorial Aldus/Litmus Press, 2014.

Girmay, Aracelis. *Teeth*. Foreword by Martín Espada. Curbstone Press, 2007.

Martínez, Valerie. *Each and Her*. University of Arizona Press, 2010.

Rodríguez, Teresa. *The Daughters of Juárez: A True Story of Serial Murder South of the Border*. Atria Books, 2007.

Rojas, Bonafide. *Notes on the Return to the Island*. Grand Concourse Press, 2017.

Torres, Edwin. *The PoPedology of an Ambient Light*. Atelos, 2007.

Toscano, Rodrigo. *Explosion Rocks Springfield*. Fence Books, 2016.

   Collapsible Poetics Theater. Fence Books, 2008.

4

MISHUANA GOEMAN

Sovereign Poetics and Possibilities in Indigenous Poetry

Contemporary Native American and Indigenous poetry is disrupting, crossing, and transgressing boundaries set up by settler states who enact policies and promote an erasure, elimination, and eradication of Native culture, political authority, and, as many poets suggest, our very nonconforming subjecthood. Poetic possibilities reflect the movement and motions toward seriously engaging trans-Indigenous possibilities: coming to the table already knowing that we have had ways of speaking to and with each other since time immemorial, while also remaining attuned to the cultural specificity reflected in past craftmanship of earlier published poets. Chadwick Allen, in his book *Trans-Indigenous Methodologies* (2012), reminds us that thinking through and with each other as Indigenous subjects is not about authenticity or defining or even making "real" the Indian in public imagination as it may have in times past, "but rather how to recognize, acknowledge, confront, and critically engage the effects of differential experiences and performances of Indigenous identities" (xxxii).

The erosion of these asymmetries of power began with formative poets who thought beyond binaries, such as the late Paula Gunn Allen, Janice Gould, and Beth Brant, as well as the 2019 US Poet Laureate, Joy Harjo. Yet there were still few spaces and places in which Native American, Pacific Islander, and Indigenous folks could speak to their experience in the world. Harjo recognizes the trans-Indigeneity that is now occurring in an interview with poets.org by thinking of the diverse roots it takes to come to a poem for contemporary poets today, stating "I always tell my students about poetry ancestors. Every poem has so many poetry ancestors. How can we construct a poetry ancestor map of America that would include and start off with poetry of indigenous nations?" ("An Interview" n. pag.). From oral stories passed down through elders, which made up much American Indian poetry in its earlier decades, to contemporary poetry that incorporates the international while remaining immersed in place, to the visual that opens new terrains, to the digital that provides a space for organizing across borders, or the contemporary landscapes in which Native people are present, contemporary poets are rising. In the words of Harjo's new poem, "We are still America. We/ know the rumors of our demise. We spit them out. They die/ soon" ("An American Sunrise" n. pag.).

As poets talk with and among each other in international gatherings or converse in digital projects across the Web, poets bring into the conversation a further breaking down of ethnographic containers and bring forth new collaborations. In these places and gatherings, which tend to ethically acknowledge whose lands we are standing on and the histories that led to occupation and domination, poets are not homogenizing identities as they break free from the containers that hold us in patterns of erasure and elimination, but learning about specificities. This attention to the place-based and to the connections we have with each other – and this includes the nonhuman – are key to understanding main tenets of Indigenous poetry. Allen relates the stakes in employing trans-Indigenous methods as such:

> The point is to invite specific studies into different kinds of conversations, and to acknowledge the mobility and multiple interactions of Indigenous peoples, cultures, histories, and texts. Similar to words like translation, transnational, and transform, trans-Indigenous may be able to bear the complex, contingent asymmetry and the potential risks of unequal encounters borne by the preposition across. It may be able to indicate the specific agency and momentum carried by the preposition through. ... At this moment in the development of global Indigenous literary studies (primarily) in English, trans- seems the best choice. (xiv–xv)

The scalar possibilities in Indigenous poetry enable the methods Allen advocates for in the quote above. While readers can find similarities between Indigenous poets from vastly different geographic areas and histories, specificity is key to rethinking race, gender, sexuality as a means of categorical difference. Rather poetic relationality is the generative practice that has sustained communities across decades of settler violence.

Sovereign poetics are a means of enacting and expressing a self-determined justice. The cultural difference ascribed to Indigenous poetry in its nineteenth- to twentieth-century explorations left much poetry unexplored beyond an ethnographic reading. This left out the rich ways that it resists, undermines, and theorizes state power. Deep meanings of Indigenous poetry may be lost, if we continue to package Indigenous poetry as one of mere cultural difference, rather than political, theoretical, and visionary concepts attempting a balancing of asymmetrical power relations that began with European writings labeling Indigenous cultures inferior as they attempted to grapple with a world they could not recognize. Audra Simpson makes clear that the politics of difference "is a form of politics that is more than representational, as this was a governmental and disciplinary possession of bodies and territories, and in this were included existent forms of philosophy, history and social life that Empire sought to speak of and speak for." In this chapter, I encourage a thinking beyond representational differentiation and point toward a deeper thinking that trans-Indigenous poetic methods evoke at different scalar points.

Sovereignty in the North American context, for instance, becomes a large component of North American Indigenous poetry. Sovereign poetics is a framework used by many outside the United States as well, as people fight for territorial control in the Pacific. Chamoru poet Craig Santos Perez reminds readers, "If we are what we imagine, then we must be able to imagine sovereignty" (n. pag.). Sovereign poetics, however, is not about sovereignty for sovereignty's sake, which repeats settler structures or those "recognized" or "given" by the settler state. Instead, poets open a critical sovereign space in which they can, following the words of Joanne Barker, "confront the imperial-colonial work of those modes of Indigeneity that operationalize genocide and dispossession by ideologically and discursively vacating the Indigenous from the Indigenous" (6).

Janet Rogers's poems in *Peace in Duress* (2014) do just this. She confronts the vacating of the Indigenous in her poem "Is it Easier to move from an Indian to Acculturated Eurocentric Assimilated Brown Skin? Or the Other Way Around," reframing the "liberal work . . . that seek[s] to translate Indigenous peoples into normative gendered and sexed bodies as citizens of the state" (Barker 6). The push and pull of connection and specificity, erasure and presence, race and political citizenship – all the uneasy terrain of Indigenous peoples who struggle for justice in settler colonial states – emerge as she "Confront[s] the violence by resisting the violence." She muses on the terrain of the sovereign self: "We live on the other side/ Of privacy after Practical/ Matters are exhausted" (Rogers 114), referring to the impact of racial and gender policies that have particularly and uniquely affected Haudenosaunee people, who live under the onslaught of Canadian settler erasure policies in the *Indian Act*. "Our real selves are tested" (114), Rogers asserts, thinking through the implication of Bill C31, which returned state Indian status to Indian women disenfranchised through marriage policies. Through complicated procedures tied up with colonial blood laws and patriarchal inheritance practices, many found themselves returning to status, yet with new pressures.

For "Indians," whether one has the status of Indian or is erased through legislation as one of the "Acculturated Eurocentric Assimilated Brown Skins" named in the title, the very word and being of Indians is political.

Citing a feminist reframe, Rogers cracks open the context of colonial status impositions: "There can be no separation / Between personal and political" (115). In particular, she looks at the Guswenta, or what is known in English as the Two Row Wampum, throughout her poetry as she wrestles between the settler and Haudenosaunee relationship. Rogers speaks to a specific context in her community of the pressure to marry and reproduce babies, who become, under these regimes, "brutes" and "assaults." "They are colonizing gender and measuring / Commitment to land with reproduction, reproduction, / reproduction ... " (116), Rogers writes, making a direct reference in the indefinite pronoun to the collaboration between appointed tribal councils and settler states' "corrections" of years of gender and racialized dispossession.

Such legal practices stand in contrast to the sovereign poetics Rogers evokes in a set of three connected pregnancy poems (or creation poems), whose ontological meanings rest in the creation story of Sky Woman. In this story, Sky Woman falls through the world, pregnant with all that we will need to live and thrive in the world below. In "Sky Woman Falling (a POV blog) part 1," Rogers undoes a conventional liberal American concept of "freedom," with its investment in whiteness,[1] and instead asserts, "This is freedom of flesh and emotion. / So this is where ancestors leave to / circle around to meet you again" (59). In laying out a genealogy to Sky Woman, Rogers asserts an inherent, rematriated sovereignty at the end of the second poem, after acknowledging the help of the nonhuman in the process of creation: "A home, where she would be placed and left alone to live / out her will" (61). This world, however, is not one of exclusion or small territories bounded by settler economic tyranny and terror. In her home, "The new world is expanding." Again, Rogers uses a repetitive American patriotic refrain to undo it. In the power of her creation, in the birth of her child, she asserts "We are the people. / My girl joins me on the soil. The earth is witness to her birth. / Land Memory has begun" (62). It is not the state that witnesses or assigns a number to her child or next generation; nor can the state deny it, as the earth's witnessing overpowers the foreignness of settler states. The woman in the present, acknowledging and recognizing the power of her creation that is linked to her ancestors, is "Home. I am Home. / I made it" (62). In this ambiguous moment of making home, or surviving despite the structures of settler patriarchy, she asserts the power of creation.

Rogers complicates sovereignty and its ties to a gendered patriarchy that privileges male right and might over the creative forces that the land remembers. Poets engaging in forms of sovereign embodiment insist that we assert an inherent sovereignty that predates "Laws of compliance and adherence" (Rogers 115). Within the framework of Rogers's poetry, adherence is a risky

64

choice, for "We are broken people breaking laws / designed to confine us to violation." In the use of a poetic legal language, she makes clear the choice of refusal and defiance in the face of the onslaught of continued colonial law, even that which seeks to repair its past wrongs such as Bill C31.

Refusal to adhere to these insistent colonial forms of membership is key to survivance, as Audra Simpson, also writing from Haudenosaunee political philosophies, makes clear in her book *Mohawk Interruptus: Political Life Across the Borders of Settler States* (2014). Simpson is clear that the everyday refusal of community members to adhere to colonial rule is a form of enacting a "nested" sovereignty and acknowledging settler sovereignty is historical and temporal. Settler sovereignty and how American Indians come to be nested sovereignties has an unremitting history; poetry has the ability to collapse the linear narrative, to expose the twisted meaning and roots of words that enable new perspectives on what is too often normalized as having no beginning or end. "Don't believe a story that does not begin / With person, place and time / This is a legacy in words archived for / The future it is a grand experiment" (115), Rogers warns the reader. These lines stand alone and play off each other, as do previous lines in the poetry; Rogers unravels the legal jargon and weaves it together again through women's activated words. In doing so, she addresses colonialism without closing off the ability to disrupt its path in a story of deficiency or declension.

The power of Rogers's collection lies in its specificity, even as she speaks to much larger scalar issues. Poetic interventions such as this provide new terrains to refuse settler states' definitions of citizenship, sovereignty, and our relationships to each other. In the ending words of *Peace in Duress*, "Of your education we will teach them / From here how to be human" (Rogers 117).

Understanding the history of Indigenous people as separate political entities, in order to avoid the pitfalls of homogenizing through constructed racial categories that have become settler commonsense, is key to the formulation of trans-Indigeneity. Poetry enables a reframing that resituates our histories temporally as living histories by unpacking the linearity and power associated with telling a history of the United States. Understanding that the past intrudes on the present as an asymmetry of power structures stitched together through language enables a forward movement for justice. In the words of Patrick Wolfe, settler colonialism is "not just an event but a structure." Nick Estes reminds us in the very title of his book *Our Histories Are Our Future* (2019) that we must "chart a historical road map for a collective future" (22). This map is never simple and filled with a cacophony of voices. Indigenous poets often wrestle with the settler-states that seek to homogenize their dealings with them as a place-based people, while using concepts of difference to discredit their very existence. Poets are at the forefront of developing new scalar models of relationships. As they do so, they (re)create with traditional and contemporary materials that remind all of us what it means to live in a settler world, and what it means to be in this together, Indigenous and settler.

Qwo-Li Driskill's poem "Map of the Americas" hauntingly starts in the form of a double helix and with the aspirational lines, "I wish when we touch / we could transcend history / in double helixes we build ourselves," reflecting on the embodiment of colonization in both its genealogical categorizations and its sexual ones. The double helix, that biological element that ties us all together, far transcends the fragile borders of American empire, race, and homonormative boundaries. Driskill contemplates their desire for their lover and a relationship – "Look: my body curled and asleep/ becomes a map of the Americas" – before proceeding to lay out a poetic history of trans-Indigeneity in the form of a familiar word map of the colonized Americas, starting with "My Hair / spread upon the pillow" and ending with "my feet / that reach / to touch / Antarctica" (10). The use of the space and placement of the words to create a map of the Americas in relation to their body parts affirms Indigenous embodiments that belie the cartesian map we have come to recognize. The embodiment of history and the everyday reminds the reader that Indigenous people "walk out of genocide to touch you" (10). Driskill uses words in relation to the body, the existing and surviving body, to provide new frameworks considering how the past interacts with the present. What does it mean to walk out of these histories? Indigenous poetry disrupts the settler vernacular of place and belonging. Indigenous bodies and embodied words haunt the present moment. Poets speak to the harm caused by the onslaught of everyday settler life *in the present*.

In toying with a settler vernacular of progress and of linear pasts tied into the racial making of the nation, the reader must rethink simple solutions to come to grips with a nation founded on genocide. In this settler vernacular, for instance, apologies become a means with which to move on, to progress in American liberal ideology. An acknowledgment of past occupancy or past wrongdoings in an apology is a settler apology that can never suffice. Or, in the words of poet Layli Long Soldier to a fourteen-year-old girl who writes a savior letter wanting to repair through apology, "Dear Girl, I honor your / response and action, I do. / Yet the root of reparation is repair. My tooth will not grow back. / The root gone" (84). Colonialism in forms of land dispossession, biopolitics, necropolitics, and disposability continues in Indigenous communities, yet there is a growing resurgence that refuses this as a thing of the past or as necessary to security in the Americas. Long Soldier's collection

Whereas (2017) toys with the 2009 Barack Obama apology to Indigenous people in order to respond to centuries of settler moves consolidated in language. The words of the "Whereas" series of poems, which echo and respond to the language of the US government apology, fight against the words of a state vernacular.

By weaving in and out of historic events, by playing with colonial defin-itions and diction throughout the text, and by using the archive and forms of governmental practices, Long Soldier rethinks the settler practice of telling history and then providing an insincere apology. In particular, she reframes what is too commonly referred to as the Indian wars, a title that belies the treaty-making promises and the violence put upon people who sacrificed much to have peace. To be more specific in language – as Long Soldier puts it in her poem 38, "I will comprise each sentence with care, by minding the rules of writing dictate" (49) – this historic period is more accurately labeled the Dakota Uprising. In part 1, "These being the Concerns," Long Soldier situates herself in the beginning poem, "He Sapa," by specifically placing herself in Lakota territory on the hills and in relation to her relatives human and nonhuman. The Black Hills are a land in conflict, as it is labeled property and subsumed under settler management with a constant threat of being mined; Long Soldier reminds and asserts that "Its rank is mountain and must live as mountain" (6). In the concrete poem "Three," Long Soldier beauti-fully lays out the ethnographic containers that cannot reflect the expansive relations in the earlier two poems. Horizontally at the top of the page, she states, "This is Where you see me in which to place me," after which she uses the words in various sequences to create a box for the reader. She plays with the space on the page, creating a mirror effect as the words twist to create a container, moving to the words, "This is how to place you in the space in which to see" (Long Soldier 8). In the repetition – a means to create a settler grammar of place – and the physical resemblance to a box, the reader's common-sense knowledge of Indians and the Indian wars begins to erode as the words and her play with them that continue throughout the text reframe colonial historic containers: "The Dakota people were starving. / The Dakota people starved. / In the preceding sentence, the word 'starved' does not need italics for emphasis. / One should read 'The Dakota people starved' as a straightforward and plainly stated fact. / As a result– and without other options but to continue to starve– Dakota people retaliated" (Long Soldier 51).

What current Native American and Indigenous poetry accomplishes is a disruption of ways of knowing that form through settler patterns of language. Whether reflecting on politics or on nature, poets respond to the ways of seeing that the settler state has laid out and normalized as permanent and the only way of the world. Poetry disrupts common-sense language and thus settler common-sense, or what Mark Rifkin calls the quotidian practices that manifest themselves through the law and through structures too often taken for granted.

When Heid Erdrich lays out the dictionary meaning of desecrate in the beginning of her poem with the same name, she incorporates the familiar structure of the dictionary. By using synonyms – "Shave," "Tear," "Render," "Melt," "Bulldoze", "Rubble-pile," "Rake," "Burn," "Salt," "Blow," "Wreck" – to elicit a reaction to a desecration of objects and places in our society commonly held to be sacred and respected, Erdrich is asking for empathy on the part of readers and for a rethinking of the destruction of Native cultures and places. Whether it is "Render Chocolate Jesus down to kisses" or "Melt, thaw and absolve into dew ... " (a line from Hamlet, a sacred English text so to speak), Erdrich is using common forms to compel an anti-colonial alternative to definitions of the sacred (13). Through the affective quality of poetic reasoning, the settler might come to understand desecration of sacred land sites – or land in general – as not limited to an unfortunate consequence of colonialism in the past or a possible development in our future circumstances.

Poetry has the force to undo a colonial unknowing, which Vimalassery, Pegues, and Goldstein define as "[p]roduced and practiced in concert with material violences and differential devaluations" and "striv[ing] to preclude relational modes of analysis and ways of knowing otherwise" (1042). Colonial unknowing "is always itself a response, an epistemological counter-formation, which takes shape in reaction to the lived relations and incommensurable knowledges it seeks to render impossible and inconceivable" (Vimalassery, Pegues, and Goldstein 1042). Erdrich "renders" this impossibility of settlers respecting Native sites as absurd. Rather, the lack of care is willful, and holding up such desecrations as settler rights makes them no more, as she writes in her definition, "vandals" using the "graffiti of words to do so" (13).

Leanne Betasamosake Simpson takes up seeing in form and quite literally in her poem "I am Graffiti" in the stunning collection *This Accident of Being Lost* (2017). She not only acknowledges "the "big pink eraser" of settler colonialism but lets the readers know that Indians are well aware of its function at all political spectrums: "erasing Indians is a good idea / of course / the bleeding -heart liberals / and communists / can stop feeling bad for stealing / &raping / &murdering / &we can all move on / we can be reconciled" (Simpson 25). She forms alliances beyond that of a settler state that blinds a general population into thinking of history as gone; the state acts as though the apology is enough, or as though reconciliation politics mired in settler desires to continue destruction of land, peoples, and nonhumans is the answer. Simpson's repetition of "except, mistakes were made" (Simpson 25), coupled with language of counting and accounting for them, reminds the reader that Indians are the beautiful "graffiti" denying settler permanence. Throughout *This Accident of Being Lost*, a book containing prose and poetry (or stories and songs, as she notes in the summary, a common historic crossover in Indigenous poetry), consistently undoes a natural political ordering in which liberals fetishize and erase Indians and conservatives want to kill and be Indians. Before describing in the next prose segment a gun class she takes to be able to assert tribal sovereignty, Simpson ends this poem on Indigenous futurities: "we are the singing remnants / left over after / the costumes have been made" (26). The graffiti and remnants of Indian foment in a liberal imagination unsettle political orders that could destroy us all.

Words matter, as poets so deftly show, as does their dismembering in settler common-sense. The representational frames in the present and the material violences are very real and too often felt materially on the ground. Sovereign poetics provide new ways of thinking the ongoing contexts and aftermath of colonialism. Billy-Ray Belcourt writes an ode to his home territory: "history lays itself bare / at the side of the road / but no one is looking" (42). His poetry, like many other contemporary young poets, brings attention to history, makes us look at the structures, the diction, and the consequences of colonialism, but does not do so to erase, look past, or disembody the material reality of Indigenous people. At times, the wittiness and play at words in this sovereign poetics laughs at our condition, pointedly recognizing the precipices we have been on throughout history and are on as a planet with the destruction of land and climate demise. Or, in the words of Billy-Ray Belcourt, poetry creates a shared feeling that can move toward collectivity and understanding that can be generative: "It insists that the loneliness [caused by settler frameworks] is endemic to the affective after life of settler colonialism, but that there is something about this world that isn't quite right, that loneliness in fact evinces a new world on the horizon" (59).

Notes

1. See Harris 1707; Nichols.

Works Cited

Allen, Chadwick. *Trans-indigenous Methodologies for Global Native Literary Studies*. University of Minnesota Press, 2012.

Barker, Joanne. *Critically Sovereign: Indigenous Gender, Sexuality, and Feminist Studies*. Duke University Press, 2017.

Belcourt, Billy-Ray. *This Wound Is a World: Poems*. Frontenac House Poetry, 2017.

Driskill, Qwo-Li. *Walking with Ghosts: Poems*. Salt Publishing, 2005.

Estes, Nick. *Our History Is the Future: Standing Rock Versus the Dakota Access Pipeline, and the Long Tradition of Indigenous Resistance*. Verso, 2019.

Erdrich, Heid E. *National Monuments*. Michigan State University Press, 2008.

Harjo, Joy. "An American Sunrise." *Poetry*, February 2017, www.poetryfoundation.org /poetrymagazine/poems/92063/an-american-sunrise

"An Interview with Joy Harjo, U.S. Poet Laureate." *Poets.org*, March 31, 2019, https://poets.org/text/interview-joy-harjo-us-poet-laureate

Harris, Cheryl. "Whiteness As Property." *Harvard Law Review* vol. 106, no. 8, 1993, pp. 1707–1791.

Long Soldier, Layli. *Whereas*. Graywolf Press, 2017.

Nichols, Rob. *Theft Is Property!: Dispossession and Critical Theory*. Duke University Press, 2020.

Perez, Craig Santos. "The Indigenous Sovereign Imaginary." *Poetry Foundation*, April 26, 2012, www.poetryfoundation.org/harriet/2012/04/the-indigenous-sovereign-imaginary

Rifkin, Mark. "Settler Common Sense." *Settler Colonial Studies* vol. 3, no. 3–4, 2013, pp. 322–340.

Rogers, Janet. *Peace in Duress*. Talonbooks, 2014.

Simpson, Audra. *Mohawk Interruptus: Political Life across the Borders of Settler States*. Duke University Press, 2014.

Simpson, Leanne Betasamosake. *This Accident of Being Lost: Songs and Stories*. Astoria, 2017.

Vimalassery, Manu, Juliana Hu Pegues, and Alyosha Goldstein. "Colonial Unknowing and Relations of Study." *Theory & Event* vol. 2, no. 4, October 2017, pp. 1042–1054.

Wolfe, Patrick. "Settler Colonialism and the Elimination of the Native." *Journal of Genocide Research* vol. 8, no. 4, 2006, p. 388.

5

ANN VICKERY

Changing Topographies, New Feminisms, and Women Poets

Following second-wave feminism and the emergence of new communication technologies, American women's poetry diversified and proliferated during the 1990s. It included critical framings such as Rachel Blau DuPlessis's *The Pink Guitar: Writing As Feminist Practice* (1990); new magazines like *Chain* (with its first issue on gender and editing); new women-run presses like Kore Press, Tinfish, Perugia Press, a+bend Press, and Tender Buttons Press; and anthologies like *Moving Borders: Three Decades of Innovative Writing by Women* (1998), *Out of Everywhere: Linguistically Innovative Poetry by Women in North America and the UK* (1996), and *The New Fuck You: Adventures in Lesbian Reading* (1995). *Chain* and *Out of Everywhere* considered transnational constellations. There was a shift away from poetry movements and camps to more dispersed networks and affiliations, heralded by volumes like *Writing from the New Coast* (1993). A critique of the nation-state and colonialism would also intensify. The year 1999 would see the publication of *Through the Eye of the Deer: An Anthology of Native American Women Writers* and Haunani-Kay Trask's *Light in the Crevice Never Seen*, the first collection of poetry by an indigenous Hawai'ian to be published in the mainland. The latter appeared alongside Trask's critical volume on the Indigenous sovereignty movement, *From a Native Daughter: Colonialism and Sovereignty in Hawai'i* (1993). As Myung Mi Kim stated in "Anacrusis," the new millennium was set to begin with "A valence of first and further tongues. A fluctuating topography, a ringing of verve or nerve – transpiring" (n. pag.).

Gurlesque and Third-Wave Feminism

Prefigured by experimentally perverse works like Lee Ann Brown's *Polyverse* (1999) and Dodie Bellamy's *Cunt-Ups* (2001) and correlating with third-wave feminism, Arielle Greenberg would coin the term "gurlesque" to identify a new trajectory in women's poetry. Unlike the "earnestness, sensitivity, or self-seriousness that marked many . . . poems stemming from second wave feminism" (Greenberg, "Notes" 4), third-wave feminist writers "have the privilege to be more playful with and brash about their relationship to the markers of traditionally feminine identity, as well as sexuality" (Greenberg, "Feminist Poetics" 39). Sexual agency and pleasure are central elements of gurlesque poetics, with gender understood as social construction rather than essence. Citing Judith Butler, Greenberg notes that the girl as a subject position is particularly laden with "myth, fantasy, glamour, danger, fragility, mortality, immortality, sexuality and wholesomeness" that "comes to stand in for a wealth of 'gender trouble'"("Feminist Poetics" 39).

In its stress on artifice and performance, gurlesque poetry incorporates a sense of burlesque in a heightened, sometimes ironic, attention to the gendered body on display. It also considers the body through a grotesque lens as being "open, protruding, irregular, secreting, multiple and changing" (Russo 8). While gurlesque poetics has "fun with the feminine," it can sometimes "be almost shockingly straightforward about the dark areas of sexuality" (Greenberg, "On the Gurlesque"). This is evident in Chelsey Minnis's "Wench": "It is rough to be a seafoam wench. Like cocksucker. Like kissing someone and then spitting into their mouth" (120). In "celebrating the same cultural trappings it seeks to critique" (Greenberg, "On the Gurlesque"), gurlesque poetry questions or reverses gendered power relations. Danielle Pafunda, for instance, writes, "When he was mine, I'd milk him" (128). Politically, gurlesque can appear ambivalent. After writing a poem entitled "The Enormous Cock," Tina Brown Celona's speaker in "Sunday Morning Cunt Poem" "started up again about my cunt." Exploring the challenges in reappropriating traditionally derogatory terms, "Some said it was a vicious swipe at feminism. Others said it was a vicious feminist swipe" (277).

In invoking Butler's concept of gender as contingent and performative, Greenberg suggests a capacity of gurlesque poetics to break taboos. Yet a number of poets associated with gurlesque explore the continuing power of social narratives through fantasy. Cathy Park Hong's poetry often features women characters who struggle with subjugation and silencing. Invoking the casual freedom of white, teenage boys in the sitcom of the same title, "Happy Days" notes the desire to be "ensorcelling" (n. pag.). The poetic speaker, however, is "always a meter maid, never a mermaid" (n. pag.). Catherine Wagner reconceptualizes the sexualized female body as an alien-like reproductive space in "This is a fucking poem." Extending Kafka's metamorphosis, the girl-insect is potentially self-consuming as she is vulnerable to abuse by others.

While gurlesque reworked grrl-culture and girly kitsch, Morgan Myers was critical of nostalgia for a stylized object culture endangered by twenty-first-century technology. A key critique of gurlesque was its hetero-normativity. Although Lara Glenum promoted gurlesque as queering het-erosexuality (n. pag.), Amy King argued that its anthology *Gurlesque: The New Grrly, Grotesque, Burlesque Poetics* (2010) failed to acknowledge origins in lesbian burlesque and to extend its scope to queer writers. Others also critiqued its selection of predominantly white and middle-class con-tributors. Working on an expanded edition, Greenberg admitted that the collection was limited and that "part of the idea of third wave feminism is . . . a more complex notion of gender, one which intersects more thought-fully with queer, working-class, non-white and other identity politics" ("Some (of My) Problems with the Gurlesque").

Performing Resistance and Fourth-Wave Feminism

Much of gurlesque's emphasis on the cultural fashioning of gender can also be found in hip-hop and performance poetry. As Angela Aguirre states of Chingona Fire, a Chicana feminist poetry collective: "It is as much about the lipstick as it is about fighting the patriarchy" (n. pag.). While still largely elided critically, hip-hop and performance poetries are widely circulated and have immense democratic potential and immediacy in an era of social media, smartphones, and YouTube. Whereas gurlesque focuses on the *artifice* of gender performance, hip-hop and performance poetries focus on *authenticity* and forms of truth-telling. Susan Somers-Willett discerns that the poet's "speech, dress, gestures, voice, body, and so on all reflect in some ways on the poem at hand and these various aspects of embodiment convey nuances of cultural difference that the page cannot" (18). Maria Damon argues that such poetries require "close listening" for "some transmission/recognition of resonant difference . . . a gestalt that effects a 'felt change of consciousness' on the part of the listener" (330). Even though popular genres and modes "have often been positioned as counter to feminist politics and feminist subjects" (McBean 15), they are a primary vehicle of what has been termed fourth-wave feminism. According to Prudence Chamberlain, fourth-wave feminism emerged around the mid-2000s and is characterized by "online activism, rape culture, humour, and intersectionality and inclusion" (2).

Third- and fourth-wave feminism are not discrete and there are similarities in an attention to self-agency and the use of humor. Yet fourth-wave femin-ism is often more overtly political. In "What It's Like to Be a Mixed Girl (For Those of You Who Aren't)," Tara Betts writes: "it's brothers blurting / damn I thought you was white / then asking for your phone number / it's being painted with zebra stripes / with brushes that assume you're confused" (33). Writing of a girl found in a drainage ditch, she states, "Brown skin / turned ash and bone. / She could have been me" (Betts 47). With both foregrounding acts of violence on the female body of color, Betts and Patricia Smith would post mug shots of the alleged assailants of Megan Williams on the Harriet blog of Poetry Foundation with the statement: "This is where poetry comes from" (Reyes, "On Feminism" 341).

As with gurlesque poets, slam poets like Imani Cezanne rework aspects of feminine identity that second-wave feminism excoriated. Critiquing social pressures on women to make themselves small, she promotes high heels as a means to walk tall. Lily Myers also considers the "circular obsession" carried intergenerationally by women to make space for others in "Shrinking Women." Slam poets like Yesika Salgado and Rachel Wiley critique social alignments of desirability with slimness in "How Not to Make Love to a Fat Girl" and "10 Honest Thoughts on Being Loved by a Skinny Boy" respectively. Performance poet and artist Petra Kuppers also considers how gender and ableist attitudes intersect in *PearlStitch* (2016), advocating bodily mutability: "Change gender / Change genus / Change somatic structure / Change your mind / just keep in motion" (99). In "trail mix," hip-hop poet La Tasha N. Nevada Diggs ridicules right-wing movements to restrict bodily self-determination by giving zygotes the same rights as American citizens. Like other performance poets, Diggs shifts across colloquial registers, her work riffing off the sounds, rhythms, and rhymes of the inner urban diasporic neighborhood. Coming out of the #MeToo movement, Khadijah Queen's *I'm So Fine: A List of Famous Men & What I Had On* (2017) critiques the constant surveillance of the male gaze, celebrity culture, and toxic masculinity. In her penultimate poem, Queen marks turning forty as "the accumulation of bliss & survival" (68). She only divulges her name in the postscript poem, declaring "My mother said I should keep some things to myself" (Queen 69).

Reconceptualizing Belonging and the Public

While Jeffrey Gray and Ann Keniston suggest that the millennium has seen a resurgence of public poetry (1), what constitutes the "public" has been reconceptualized through feminist and queer theorizations of materiality and intimacy. As Heather Milne notes, twenty-first-century America is marked by continuing economic inequity, sexual violence, and conservative attempts "to remove the right to bodily self-determination" (2). Neoliberal regimes of power have reinforced ideologies of gender, heteronormativity, racism, and nationalism, with processes of imperialism, militarization, and globalization leading to those culturally marginalized even more vulnerable to the conditions of precarity.

Following Steve Evans's identification of survival as a major trope in the 1990s for American poetry, a sense of precarity would be heightened in the new millennium through man-made crises and natural disasters (90). The events of 9/11 signaled a new era of Terror and suspended agency. As Juliana Spahr writes in *This Connection of Everyone with Lungs* (2005), "While we want to believe that we all live in one bed / of the earth's atmosphere, our bed is just our bed and no one else's / and we can't figure out how to stop it from being that way" (30). In "First Writing Since," Palestinian-born poet Suheir Hammad declared amidst all the uncertainty:

> But i know for sure who will pay
> in the world, it will be women, mostly coloured and poor. Women will
> have to bury children, and support themselves through grief.   (n. pag.)

Nicole Cooley foregrounds breaches of trust and questions of responsibility in the wake of 9/11 but also Hurricane Katrina and the Gulf Coast Disaster in *Breach* (2010). In "Old Gulf Postcards," she remembers "driving to Gulfport with my mother, / beaches my daughter will never see . . . Between the gone and the not-recovered, no one / steps out of their house to wave" (Cooley 53). In this changed landscape, "Nothing could keep any girl safe from the levee's edge. / Nothing I write could make a clean river of light" (Cooley 71–72). Evelyn Reilly wonders whether "we are in a moment of amplification" regarding the ecological, such that in an "inverse of 'no poetry after Auschwitz,' we are in a moment of 'all poetry after Katrina' . . . or whatever it is that comes next" (n. pag.).

Resonating with the work of Cecilia Vicuña, poets like Jen Hofer have turned to site-specific poetry in critiquing the long-term cultural and environmental impact of colonial, military, and industrial activities. Using donated and foraged materials from Wendover, Utah to construct a paper quilt in "Uncovering," Hofer selected "The Road to California" quilt pattern as one developed during the Western Expansion of white people into indigenous and Mexican territories. Presenting a fragmented, multi-perspectival counter-history, the quilt became a way of "thinking about what a poem can be or do. About how persons relate to place, and about what we choose to remember" (n. pag.).

Kaia Sand's "She Had Her Own Reason for Participating" would be culled through the Portland Police surveillance files kept on activist groups, newspaper articles, and materials by the activists themselves. Focusing on sentences and phrases that began with "she," the resulting poem would be stamped on copper index plates as a means of reworking information and to bring to the surface what police investigators feared about women. In *Landscapes of Dissent: Guerilla Poetry and Public*

Space (2008), she and Jules Boykoff identify a wave of activist poets who generate locational conflict in reclaiming public spaces. Kristin Prevallet's *Shadow Evidence Intelligence* (2006) not only reproduces signs, posters, and business cards from public protests over the Iraq War but also questions the way authorities might read information during war. As she notes of an aerial surveillance photograph, "There are many ways to define proof" (Prevallet 23). Jena Osman's *Public Figures* (2012) juxtaposes homeland memorial statues with incoming texts about drone attacks in Iraq, raising questions about perspective and meaning-making. Joseph Harrington suggests that such work "is not about presenting documentation so much as it is about the process of documenting and the documenting of process" (77).

Legacies of Colonial and Racial Violence: Writing As Resilience

As Arif Dirlik suggests, the local becomes a "site of both promise and predicament" (22). Globalization of the English language and the imperial reach of American culture saw the local either elided or commodified (a latter example is the Coca-Cola ad that had "America the Beautiful" sung by bilingual Americans in seven different languages). This would be countered by a rise in decolonizing poetics, with particular attention given to the discursive and material subjection of the female body of color and modes of resilience. Having earlier published *Eros and Power: The Promise of Feminist Theory* (1984), Haunani-Kay Trask would denounce feminism as "just another haole intrusion into a besieged Hawaiian world" ("Feminism" 909). Not only "too white," feminism tended to be "aggressively American": "Any exclusive focus on women neglected the historical oppression of all Hawaiians and the large force field of imperialism" ("Feminism" 909). Demonstrating the linguistic structures of power, Hawai'ian Filipino poet Kathy Dee Kaleolkealoha Kaloloahilani Banggo codeswitches between standard English and Hawai'ian Creole to describe being raped in "Fly, Da Mo'o & Me": "Befo time, I wuz bright" but now "I stay stink. I stay ugly" (13). With the violation represented in Creole, Morris Young suggests that "[l]anguage becomes the means for creating knowledge and seeking social justice" (115).

Layli Long Soldier's *Whereas* (2017) engages with the Congressional Apology to Native Americans in 2009, an event that was largely unknown to Native Americans. While directing the poem to Barack Obama's delivery and the document's language, Long Soldier's repetition of the term "whereas" enacts the linguistic and lived effects of occupation. While another would say "*at least* there was an Apology," she draws attention to its inadequacy as an occupied body on occupied land: "Whereas I have spent my life in unholding" (n. pag). Long Soldier notes the challenges of being a dual citizen of the United States and the Oglala Sioux Tribe, framing the collection with the imperative: "I must work, I must eat, I must art, I must mother, I must friend, I must listen, I must observe, constantly I must live" ("The Freedom" n. pag.). Like Long Soldier, Cheryl Savageau mobilizes storytelling as a decolonizing mode. While presenting both women and land as under siege in *Mother/Land*, she de-privileges European point of contact narratives and celebrates a Native American understanding of the New England environment. In "America, I Sing You Back," Allison Adelle Hedge Coke takes a maternal stance. She vows to "sing you home into yourself, and back to reason." Her repetition of "My song" and a guiding "I" denote strong presence in a lullaby-like ritual of care after damage.

The focus on maternal legacies can also be found in the work of poets like Kimiko Hahn. In "Foreign Body," Hahn explores intergenerational support in writing "on my other's body, / I mean, my mother's body." It is, she declares, the "one body I write on" and "can lean against- / against not in resistance" (n. pag.). She, in turn, must make way as "my own daughter turns sovereign" (Hahn n. pag.). Recognizing this paradox between plenty and empty in *The Bounty* (1996), Myung Mi Kim navigates "the mental, emotive, and psychic space in which one's family of origin crossed with whatever families we make and build otherwise" (Keller, "Interview" 342). In *Commons* (2002), she asks: "What is English now, in the face of mass global migration, ecological degradation, shifts and upheavals in identification of gender and labor? ... What are the implications of writing at this moment, in precisely this 'America'?" (110). Whereas *Commons* turned to "ideas of translation, translatability, transliteration, transcription," her later work *Penury* (2009) questions the possibility of ever articulating authentic subjectivity. Fragmentation foregrounds forced loss and violence as transcription becomes increasingly problematic. Reduced, at certain points, to a series of slashes, the reader is left to "contemplate the generative power of the designation 'illegible' coming into speech" (*Commons* 110).

Tracie Morris notes that she "teases apart the meaning that is embedded with sound and separates that from literal meaning" ("Artist to Artist" n. pag.). Suffering is conveyed in her late 1990s sound poems like "The Mrs Gets Her Ass Kicked" and "A Little," the voice breaking from song to stutter, slur, screech, or splutter. Resisting colonial legacies, stereotypes, and rhythms in "Chain Gang" and "Slave Sho to Video aka Black But Beautiful," Morris slides from negating to questioning to affirming the black female body through phonemic repetition and improvisation. Invoking Jyoti Singh Pandey who was gang-raped and murdered on a Delhi bus in 2012, Bhanu

Kapil also explores the limits of representation in *Ban en Balieue* (2015). Writing of Ban, a young girl caught in a race riot, Kapil blurs Ban with Bhanu and raises questions around what is narratable and why certain bodies are abused. Dawn Lundy Martin considers how the black female body is repeatedly violated and reduced in both language and daily life in *Life in a Box Is a Pretty Life* (2014). She reflects on how racial and sexual boxes of identity overlap to frame and isolate: "almost everything we've ever desired is diminished when enclosed" (Martin 29). Demonstrating a limited agency, Martin's speaker nevertheless declares resistance: "I refuse to sing to you" (68). In *Citizen: An American Lyric* (2014), Claudia Rankine sees identity manifesting "as if skin and bone were public places" (144), yet argues that the black female body "can't hold / the content it is living" (143). While the media has focused on the loss of black male lives, she finds the continuing "invisibility of black women [. . .] astounding" (Cocozza n. pag.).

In "I Do," Filipina-American poet Eileen Tabios lists the limited range of identities available for migrant women in the United States and how they reinforce an underclass: "Because I do know English, I have been variously called Miss Slanted Vagina, The Mail Order Bride, The One With The Shoe Fetish, The Squat Brunette Who Wears a Plaid Blazer Over a Polka-Dot Blouse, The Maid" (n. pag.). Countering the dominance of English poetic forms, Tabios reworks the Japanese haiku and haibun in inventing the hay(na)ku, a six-word tercet, and "haybun," a hay(na)ku tercet of prose. Alternatively, Barbara Jane Reyes mixes English with Spanish and Tagalog in *Invocation to Daughters* (2017) to resist religious, capitalist, and patriarchal discourse. Noting how language has been used to consume, strip, and "control our bodies, redact consent from our tongues," she impels, "Daughters, let us create a language so that we know ourselves, so that we may sing, and tell, and pray" (8). As her final poem declares, "I am not the polite little colored girl you are looking for. You did not fashion me in your image … I am not your ethnic spectacle. I am not your cultural poverty … I do not ask for your permission to speak … I am not your object lesson. I don't need your absolution" (Reyes, *Invocation* 71).

Post-Language Poetics and a New Lyric

The new millennium is perhaps best characterized by writing that is linguistically innovative and embodied. Known variously as post-language poetics, a new lyricism, or hybrid poetry, it seeks, as Cole Swensen suggests, "to renew the forms and expand the boundaries of poetry – thereby increasing the expressive potential of language itself – while also remaining committed to the emotional spectra of lived experience" (xxi). Of this more inclusive poetics, she adds that, "While political issues may or may not be the ostensible subject of hybrid work, the political is always there" (xxi).

Introducing *American Women Poets in the 21st Century* (2002), Juliana Spahr discerns: "Lyric is not and never has been a simplistic genre, despite its seeming innocence." While lyric has had a "troubled history of relation with women," form was "no longer the clear marker of intention or meaning that it was thirty years ago" (10). Emerging out of the "Where Lyric Meets Language" conference, the volume gathered Language writers but also those with a history of critical exclusion from movements or groups. It also included those who worked between art and poetry like Barbara Guest and Mei-mei Berssenbrugge. Seeking to move "away from too easily separated and too easily declarative identities," it foregrounded "how the social and the cultural keep intruding" (Spahr, "Introduction" 2–3).

Elizabeth Willis notes that the new lyric "is not self-expressive except to the extent that ideas of self or voice are never entirely absent from the tonal shadings of language" (228). Linked to this is the difficulty of naming psychic states. Nick Selby points out that poets like Lisa Jarnot question the ethical reach of lyric while deconstructing assumptions of nation (203). For Jarnot, lyric cannot be transcendent or autonomous. Her poem "The Bridge" explores the continuum of the history of war (from Greek to American Independence to contemporary) and how we might think about the continuum between the poet of such history and the poet of everyday intimacies, in particular what does or does not survive. Jarnot often deploys repetition, such as in "Right View," which deconstructs a privileging of the human through the term's adjectival excess: "human city," "human cars," "human confusion" (86). The poem speculates on the capacity of human as animal and the challenges of imagining what might be beyond the limits of the poem or environment impacted by the human: "The view that I have is of / the human animal that I am / in the human room" (Jarnot 86).

In *From Dame Quickly* (2009), Jennifer Scappettone takes the forked tongue and bodily excess (as "neither fish nor flesh") of Shakespeare's character to subvert commerce and perhaps signal a new revolutionary class. Others explore lyric's capacity for contemporary intimacy. Harryette Mullen's "Any Lit" riffs off the division between "blackness" and "humanity" but also the "you" and "I": "You are a union beyond my meiosis / You are a unicycle beyond my migration" (6–7). Parodying Shakespeare's sonnet 130 and the dark lady muse, Mullen writes playfully in "Dim Lady": "If Liquid paper is white, her racks are institutional beige . . . And in some minty-fresh mouthwashes, there is more sweetness than in the garlic breeze my main squeeze wheezes" (20). Commodity fetishism is defused through colloquial improvisation, which draws attention to other processes of making meaning.

Coining her poem a "son-not" (Thaggert 46), Evie Shockley's "my last modernist poem #4 (or re-re-birth of a nation)" critiques calls of a post-race Obama-led America in *the new black* (2011). Karen Volkman also brings a rhythmic and linguistic playfulness to the sonnet in *Nomina* (2008). Exploring refusal and nameless freedoms, she concludes in "Sonnet (Nothing was ever what it claimed to be)," "sheen that bleeds blue beauty we are taught / drowns and booms and vowels. I will not" (n. pag.). Laynie Browne extends the sonnet's scope for intimacy to the everyday in *Daily Sonnets* (2007).

The reconceptualization of the lyric has gone hand in hand with a reconceptualization of elegy, or perhaps more accurately anti-elegy, as poets dismiss poetic consolation and attempt to articulate a present absence that may be only registered bodily. Each grieving over the loss of a son, Akilah Oliver crosses genres and the borderlands of memory in *A Toast in the House of Friends* (2009) while Mary Jo Bang explores forms of afterwardness in *Elegy* (2007). Maggie Nelson foregrounds the limits of representation in approaching both romantic loss and physical loss in *Bluets* (2009) while Lisa Samuels concludes with the word "live" (122) after navigating childhood discontinuity, absence, and lack of connection in *Anti-M* (2013).

Digital Platforms and Networking

While the twenty-first-century continued to see the proliferation of micro-publishing focused on noncommercial material objects for select audiences, digital technologies brought paradigmatic shifts to the ways in how poetry circulated and who could write it. The Internet enables immediately downloadable versions while social media platforms like Instagram and Twitter have created new poetic forms and audiences. With 440,000 followers, Instagram poet Cleo Wade, who has been dubbed the "millennial Oprah" (Goodman), quotes Coretta Scott King that "Freedom is never really won / that / We must earn it / And win it / In / Every generation" in "Who We Are Right Now "("Tribute"). Wade's *Heart Talk: Poetic Wisdom for a Better Life* (2018) promotes female solidarity, self-empowerment, kindness, and well-being mantras in broad-stroke terms: "Our hearts are warm when we are able to show with generosity, patience, and compassion for the ones we love, but we must remember that it is impossible to be truly there for others without taking care of ourselves first" (96).

Within hours of being posted on a general-interest website *The Awl*, Patricia Lockwood's "Rape Joke" attracted 10,000 Facebook likes and rapidly went viral. It would, according to *The Guardian*, "casually reawaken[...] a generation's interest in poetry" (Groskop n. pag.). Lockwood takes a tragi-comedic approach: "The rape joke is if you write a poem called Rape Joke, you're asking for it to become the only thing people remember about you" ("Rape Joke" 301). Her "sexts" on Twitter revel in the absurd and internet slang: "I am FWB with Scrooge McDuck. He asks me to pretend to rob him. 'IS IT A BEAGLE BOY,' he gasps, as I break into his money bin" ("Sexts" n. pag.).

A burgeoning number of listservs, online journals, and blogs would host new writing and generate new reading networks. Listservs like Poet-Moms provided a support space who might have lessened access to communities. Wom-Po was a broad base for informal conversation around women's poetry. As Lesley Wheeler notes, its egalitarian openness was imperfect but valuable (55). Pussipo, a listserv specifically for experimental women's poetry, also enabled women, according to Danielle Pafunda, to "find the numbers to make an impact on the larger scene, celebrate each other's successes, and cast off many of those patriarchal conventions which can promptly diffuse one's participation in mixed-gender forums" (qtd. in Wagner, "Post-Marginal" n. pag.). Both Mendi Obadike and Evie Shockley commented on the listservs' unspoken white references and frameworks (Wheeler 64; Wagner "Post-Marginal"). Wheeler accedes that while Wom-Po sought to be transnational, it tended to be American-centric. Alternatively, Annie Finch points out how online communities have helped raise awareness and solidarity around gender transnationally, citing the response to poet Nadia Anjuman's murder in 2005. The Internet also increasingly houses digital libraries and archives. An example of the latter is the timeline of *Mezzo Cammin*, an online journal on formal poetry by women.

Numbers Trouble

In 2007, Jennifer Ashton claimed that "on a numerical level the problem of underrepresentation [of women's poetry] has been corrected" (213). In response, Juliana Spahr and Stephanie Young analyzed rates of publishing, reviewing, and academic tenure and concluded that there still existed a marked gender imbalance. This would be reinforced by VIDA: Women in Literary Arts, a feminist organization that began in 2009 by tabulating reviews of books by men and women. Spahr and Young cautioned against numerical parity: "our fear is that when we lean too heavily on the numbers, we end up arguing for our share of the American privilege pie and doing little else" ("Numbers Trouble" 100–101). They argued that feminist activism is required to change contemporary writing communities that often parallel a "larger cultural dismissal of feminism" (Spahr and Young, "Numbers

Trouble" 89). This dismissal extended from expressions that "feminism is irrelevant and outdated or just plain over or boring or pathetic or whiny" (Spahr and Young, "Numbers Trouble" 90) to moments of aggression. They would also note a sense of exhaustion that Jennifer Scappettone diagnoses as a result of bearing the persistent weight of social inequities. She contends that younger experimentalists use different tactics "from those of the eighties or the nineties" ("Bachelorettes" 180). These are emblematized in Spahr and Young's own "Foulipo," which deploys the female body strategically through enacting simultaneously generative and restrictive processes. Eliding the "r" (are) foregrounds both absence and presence, while linguistically announcing "the messy body" in the context of patriarchal dominance: "one that still lets us deal with the I AM HEE . . . " (Spahr and Young, "Foulipo" 42).

Spahr and Young staged a call-out to poets around the world through the "Tell US Poets" project, collecting responses in *A Megaphone: Some Enactments, Some Numbers, and Some Essays about the Continued Usefulness of Crotchless-pants-and-a-machine-gun Feminism* (2011). They included Reyes's critique of their call-out as a command from a site of privilege and their assumption that 'other' communities deemphasize feminism due to an "inherent or essential misogyny" ("On Feminism" 336).

Beginning with the Women of Color Count in 2014 and extending their intersectional count the following year, VIDA would track disparities such as discovering that 73 percent of women who published in *Poetry* in 2014 were white. One strategy of countering gender imbalance in reception was feminist scholarship that included important volumes by Linda Kinnahan, Elisabeth Frost, Lynn Keller, Nicky Marsh, Deborah Mix, and Heather Milne. Rachel Blau DuPlessis extended a feminist focus to critiquing poetic navigations of masculinity in *Purple Passages: Pound, Eliot, Zukofsky, Olson, Creeley, and the Ends of Patriarchal Poetry* (2012). *Nests and Strangers: On Asian American Women Poets* (2015) celebrated the heterogeneity of Asian American women's poetry. *Women Poets on Mentorship: Efforts and Affections* (2008) collected responses from writers who had grown up with second-wave feminism and were able to benefit from the influence of a previous generation of women poets.

The new millennium would see continuing growth in feminist and women-run journals and presses. There has also been a proliferation of women's poetry anthologies, including sequels (*Eleven More American Women Poets in the Twenty-First-Century* [2012] and *Out of Everywhere 2: Linguistically Innovative Poetry by Women in North America and the United Kingdom* [2015]) and anthologies with a renewed sense of activism and urgency like

Women of Resistance: Poems for a New Feminism (2018) and *Letters to the Future: Black Women/Radical Writing* (2018).

Conceptual Writing

An anthology that is transnational in scope, *I'll Drown My Book: Conceptual Writing by Women* (2012), would be partly motivated, according to one of its editors Laynie Browne, by a potential underrepresentation of women ("Conceptual" 14). While another of its editors, Caroline Bergvall, notes the "initial propensity for exclusionary models" (20), she views conceptual writing as "a way out of a societal status quo that must silence or symptomatize the female, minoritarian or differential writer" (18). Bergvall adds that "conceptual methods paired with psychoanalytic and specifically feminine investigations have provided an ideal combination to seek out the somatic, cognitive and symbolic bases for language and gender development" (20).

In "Conceptualism is Feminism," Vanessa Place argues that "woman only exists contextually – one can only be woman relative to man" (8) yet "[c]onceptualism, like feminism, asks one equally to consider the '='" (9). Characterizing Place as a "contemporary Echo," Naomi Toth distinguishes Place from Echo in the "level of choice in what she hears." These choices are deliberately controversial in order to create "unease and discomfort among audiences" (n. pag.). An example is Place's recital of rape jokes in "If I Wanted Your Opinion, I'd Remove the Duct Tape" (collected in "Rape Jokes"). The use of her female body and voice mediates distance from the bodies they channel as the vast majority of sexual crimes are committed by men. Place's redirection deploys what Bergvall identifies as an Irigarayan tactic of female mimicry, creating friction rather than equation (18). Jeff Dolven argues that Place's performance stages "the urgency of a consent that is public and inclusive" (276) while Place herself calls it "a response to an unbearable call" ("Rape Jokes" 260).[1]

Conclusion

As evident in this chapter, much poetry of the twenty-first-century is marked by a poetics of refusal and resistance. Anne Boyer notes that, "Refusal which is only sometimes a kind of poetry, does not have to be limited to poetry, and turning the world upside down, which is often a kind of poetry, doesn't have to be limited to words" (n. pag.). In *Hardly War* (2016), Don Mee Choi matches five repeated lines in Korean with conclusion of five repeated lines in English: "I refuse to translate." While speaking of "disobeying history, severing its ties to power," she also attempts to "string together the faintly remembered, faintly imagined, faintly discarded" (Choi 4). Michael Davidson notes that, "Critical negativity is not a simple reverse of humanist categories of self and identity into their opposites but an attempt to make new art out of rupture and refusal" (604). It is worth dwelling on his emphasis on remaking and movement. In *Memory Cards: Simone Weil Series* (2017), Susan M. Schultz cautions against a no that "stays still-in-movement like snapchat" (90). She suggests that "Kindness, like trauma, repeats itself. But it needs first to pierce the skin" (Schultz 90). This register of a poetics of care and resilience requires what Myung Mi Kim termed "verve and nerve," force and embodied impact. Against the backdrop of feminist waves, new technologies, and increasing precarity, twenty-first-century poetry by women demonstrates a multiplicity of perspectives, connection and loss, and continuing revolutions across the borders of gender and genre.

Notes

1. For a discussion of the controversy surrounding another work of Place's, in which she tweeted selections from *Gone with the Wind*, see Chapter 9 by Sueyeun Juliette Lee in this collection.

Works Cited

Aguirre, Angela. "How I Define My Chingona Fire." *HuffPost*, January 24, 2017, www.huffpost.com/entry/how-i-define-my-chingona-fire_b_5887de69e4b 0a53ed60c6a35

Ashton, Jennifer. "Our Bodies, Our Poems." *American Literary History* vol. 19, no. 1, 2007, pp. 211–231.

Bang, Mary Jo. *Elegy*. Graywolf Press, 2019.

Banggo, Kathy Dee Kaleolkealoha Kaloloahilani. "Fly, Da Mo'o & Me." *Whetu Moana: Contemporary Polynesian Poetry in English*, edited by Albert Wendt, Reina Whaitiri, and Robert Sullivan. University of Hawai'i Press, 2003, p. 13.

Barnhart, Danielle and Iris Mahan, editors. *Women of Resistance: Poems for a New Feminism*. OR Books, 2018.

Bellamy, Dodie. *Cunt-Ups*. Tender Buttons Press, 2001.

Bergvall, Caroline. "The Conceptual Twist: A Foreword." *I'll Drown My Book: Conceptual Writing by Women*, edited by Caroline Bergvall, Laynie Browne, Teresa Carmody, and Vanessa Place. Les Figues Press, 2012, pp. 18–22.

Bergvall, Caroline, Layne Browne, Teresa Carmody, and Vanessa Place, editors. *I'll Drown My Book: Conceptual Writing by Women*. Les Figues Press, 2012.

Betts, Tara. *Arc & Hue*. Aquarius Press/Willow Books, 2009.

Boyer, Anne. "No." *Poetry Foundation*, April 13, 2017, www.poetryfoundation.org /harriet/2017/04/no

Boykoff, Jules and Kaia Sand, editors. *Landscapes of Dissent: Guerilla Poetry and Public Space*. Palm Press, 2008.

Brown, Lee Ann. *Polyverse*. Sun & Moon Press, 1999.

Browne, Laynie. *Daily Sonnets*. Counterpath Press, 2007.

"A Conceptual Assemblage: An Introduction." *I'll Drown My Book: Conceptual Writing by Women*, edited by Caroline Bergvall, Laynie Browne, Teresa Carmody, and Vanessa Place. Les Figues Press, 2012, pp. 14–17.

Celona, Tina Brown. "Sunday Morning Cunt Poem." *Gurlesque: The New Grrly, Grotesque, Burlesque Poetics*, edited by Lara Glenum and Arielle Greenberg. Saturnalia Books, 2010, p. 277.

Cezanne, Imani. "Heels." Uploaded by *Button Poetry*, December 29, 2014, https://buttonpoetry.tumblr.com/post/106570099862/imani-cezanne-heels-they-said-women-like

Chamberlain, Prudence. *The Feminist Fourth Wave: Affective Temporality*. Palgrave Macmillan, 2017.

Choi, Don Mee. *Hardly War*. Wave Books, 2016.

Cocozza, Paula. "Poet Claudia Rankine: 'The invisibility of black women is astounding." *The Guardian*, June 30, 2015, www.theguardian.com/lifeandstyle/2015/jun/29/poet-claudia-rankine-invisibility-black-women-everyday-racism-citizen?CMP=share_btn_fb

Coke, Allison Adelle Hedge. "America, I Sing You Back." *Poetry Foundation*, www.poetryfoundation.org/poems/89062/america-i-sing-you-back

Cooley, Nicola. *Breach: Poems*. Louisiana State University Press, 2010.

Critchley, Emily, editor. *Out of Everywhere 2: Linguistically Innovative Poetry by Women in North America and the UK*. Reality Street, 2015.

Damon, Maria. "'Was that "Different," "Dissident," or "Dissonant"': Poetry (n) the Public Spear – Slams, Open Readings, and Dissident Traditions." *Close Listening and the Performed Word*, edited by Charles Bernstein. Oxford University Press, 1998, pp. 324–342.

Davidson, Michael. "Introduction: American Poetry, 2000–2009." *Contemporary Literature* vol. 52, no. 4, 2011, pp. 597–629.

Diggs, La Tasha N. Nevada. "trail mix." *Poets.org*, www.poets.org/poetsorg/poem trail-mix-audio-only

Dirlik, Arif. "The Global in the Local." *Global/Local: Cultural Production and the Transnational Imaginary*, edited by Rob Wilson and Wimal Dissanayake. Duke University Press, 1996, pp. 21–45.

Dolven, Jeff. "Rape, Jokes, Consent." *Studies in Gender and Sexuality* vol. 18, no.4, 2017, pp. 274–276.

Dunn, Carolyn and Carol Comfort, editors. *Through the Eye of the Deer: An Anthology of Native American Women Writers*. Aunt Lute Books, 1999.

DuPlessis, Rachel Blau. *The Pink Guitar: Writing as Feminist Practice*. Routledge, 1990.

Purple Passages: Pound, Eliot, Zukofsky, Olson, Creeley, and the Ends of Patriarchal Poetry. University of Iowa Press, 2012.

Evans, Steve. "The American Avant-Garde After 1989: Notes Towards a History." *Assembling Alternatives: Reading Postmodern Poetries Transnationally*, edited by Romana Huk. Wesleyan University Press, 2003.

Finch, Annie. "2000–2009: The Decade in Poetry." *Poetry Foundation*, December 21, 2009, www.poetryfoundation.org/articles/69457/2000–2009-the-decade-in-poetry

Gizzi, Peter and Juliana Spahr, editors. *Writing from the New Coast*. Garlic Press, 1993.

Glenum, Lara. "Notes on the Gurlesque: Queering Heterosexuality," *Exoskeleton*, March 26, 2010, http://exoskeleton-johannes.blogspot.com/2010/03/note-on-gurlesque-queering.html

Glenum, Lara and Arielle Greenberg, ed. *Gurlesque: The New Grrly, Grotesque, Burlesque Poetics*. Saturnalia Books, 2010.

Goodman, Lizzie. "Is Cleo Wade the Millennial Oprah?" *The Cut*, December 12, 2016, www.thecut.com/2016/12/cleo-wade-instagram-poet.html

Gray, Jeffrey and Ann Keniston. "Introduction: Contemporary Poetry and the Public Sphere." *The News from Poems: Essays on the 21st-century American Poetry of Engagement*, edited by Jeffrey Gray and Ann Keniston. University of Michigan Press, 2016, pp. 1–10.

Greenberg, Arielle. "Some (of My) Problems with the Gurlesque." *Evening Will Come: A Monthly Journal of Poetics*, no. 38, February 2014, www.thevolta.org/ewc 38-agreenberg-p1.html

"Feminist Poetics, in Waves: Part 2." *American Poetry Review*, September/ October 2013, pp. 39–41.

"Notes on the Origin of the (Term) Gurlesque." *Gurlesque: Gurlesque: The New Grrly, Grotesque, Burlesque Poetics*, edited by Lara Glenum and Arielle Greenberg. Saturnalia Books, 2010, pp. 1–8.

"On the Gurlesque." *Small Press Traffic*, April 2003, www.smallpresstraffic.org /article/on-the-gurlesque

Greenberg, Arielle and Rachel Zucker, editors. *Women Poets on Mentorship: Efforts and Affections*. University of Iowa Press, 2008.

Groskop, Viv. "Rape Joke: What Is Patricia Lockwood's Poem Really Saying?" *The Guardian*, July 26, 2013, www.theguardian.com/society/shortcuts/2013/jul/26/ patricia-lockwood-poem-rape-joke

Hahn, Kimiko. "Foreign Body." *Poetry Foundation*, July/August 2017, www.poetry foundation.org/poetrymagazine/poems/142874/foreign-body

Hammad, Suheir. "First Writing Since." *HOW2* vol. 1, no. 8, 2002, www.asu.edu /pipercwcenter/how2journal/archive/online_archive/v1_8_2002/current/forum/ hammad.htm

Harrington, Joseph. "The Politics of Docupoetry." *The News from Poems: Essays on the 21st Century American Poetry of Engagement*, edited by Jeffrey Gray and Ann Keniston. University of Michigan Press, 2016, pp. 67–83.

Hofer, Jen. "Materiality: Mortality: Notes on the Making and Context of 'Uncovering: A Quilted Poem Made From Donated and Foraged From Wendover, Utah.'" *Alligatorzine* vol. 127, 2012, www.alligatorzine.be/pages/ 101/zine127_01.html

Hong, Cathy Park. "Happy Days." *The Paris Review*, no. 211, Winter 2014, www.theparisreview.org/poetry/6684/happy-days-cathy-park-hong

Hunt, Erica and Dawn Lundy Martin, editors. *Letters to the Future: Black Women/ Radical Writing*. Kore Press, 2018.

Jarnot, Lisa. *Ring of Fire*. Salt, 2003.

Kapil, Bhanu. *Ban en Bailieue*. Nightboat Books, 2015.

Keller, Lynn. "An Interview with Myung Mi Kim." *Contemporary Literature* vol. 49, no. 3, 2008, pp. 335–356.

Kim, Myung Mi. "Anacrusis." *HOW2* vol. 1, no.2, 1999, www.asu.edu/pipercwcen
    ter/how2journal/archive/online_archivev1_2_1999/current/readings/kim
    .html
    Commons. University of California Press, 2002.
    Penury. Omnidawn, 2009.
King, Amy. "The Gurlesque." *Amyking.org*, May 29, 2010, https://amyking.org
    /2010/03/29/the-gurlesque/
Kotz, Liz and Eileen Myles, editors. *The New Fuck You: Adventures in Lesbian
    Reading.* MIT Press, 1995.
Kuppers, Petra. *PearlStitch.* Spuyten Duyvil, 2016.
Lockwood, Patricia. "Rape Joke." *Studies in Gender and Sexuality* vol. 18, no. 4,
    2017, pp. 299–301.
    "Sexts from Patricia Lockwood." *Rhizome*, January 24, 2012, https://rhizome.org
    /editorial/2012/jan/24/patricia-lockwood/
Long Soldier, Layli. "From *Whereas*," *Poetry Foundation*, January 2017, www.poetry
    foundation.org/poetrymagazine/poems/91697/from-whereas
    "Layli Long Soldier: The Freedom of Real Apologies." *On Being with Krista
    Tippett*, March 30, 2017, https://onbeing.org/programs/layli-long-soldier-the-
    freedom-of-real-apologies-oct2018/
Martin, Dawn Lundy. *Life in a Box Is a Pretty Life.* Nightboat Books, 2015.
McBean, Sam. *Feminism's Queer Temporalities.* Routledge, 2015.
Milne, Heather. *Poetry Matters: Neoliberalism, Affect, and the Posthuman in
    Twenty-First-Century North American Feminist Poetics.* University of Iowa
    Press, 2018.
Minnis, Chelsey. "Wench." *Gurlesque: The New Grrly, Grotesque, Burlesque
    Poetics*, edited by Lara Glenum and Arielle Greenberg. Saturnalia Books,
    2010, pp. 120–121.
Morris, Tracie. "A Little." *Penn Sound*, http://writing.upenn.edu/pennsound/x/
    Morris.php
    "Chain Gang," http://writing.upenn.edu/pennsound/x/Morris.php
    "The Mrs. Gets Her Ass Kicked." *Penn Sound*, http://writing.upenn.edu/penn
    sound/x/Morris.php
    "Artist to Artist: Queen Godl Interviews Tracie Morris about Poetry, Performance
    and East New York." *Creative Capital*, February 18, 2014, https://creative-
    capital.org/2014/02/18/artist-to-artist-queen-godis-tracie-morris/
Mullen, Harryette. *Sleeping with the Dictionary.* University of California Press, 2002.
Myers, Lily. "Shrinking Women." Uploaded by Button Poetry, www.youtube.com
    /watch?v=zQucWXWXp3k
Myers, Morgan. Review of *Gurlesque: The New Grrly, Grotesque, Burlesque
    Poetics.* Rain Taxi, Summer 2010, www.raintaxi.com/gurlesque-the-new-grrly-
    grotesque-burlesque-poetics/
Nelson, Maggie. *Bluets.* Wave Books, 2009.
Oliver, Akilah. *A Toast in the House of Friends.* Coffee House Press, 2009.
O'Sullivan, Maggie, editor. *Out of Everywhere: Linguistically Innovative Poetry by
    Women in North America and the UK.* Reality Street, 1996.
Osman, Jena. *Public Figures.* Wesleyan University Press, 2012.
Pafunda, Danielle. "Fable." *Gurlesque: The New Grrly, Grotesque, Burlesque Poetics*,
    edited by Lara Glenum and Arielle Greenberg. Saturnalia Books, 2010, p. 128.

Place, Vanessa. "Rape Jokes." *Studies in Gender and Sexuality* vol. 18, no. 4, 2017, pp. 260–268.

"Conceptualism is Feminism," www.academia.edu/2778773/Conceptualism_is_feminism

Prevallet, Kristin. *Shadow Evidence Investigation.* Factory School, 2006.

Queen, Khadijah. *I'm So Fine: A List of Famous Men & What I Had On.* Yes Yes Books, 2017.

Rankine, Claudia. *Citizen: An American Lyric.* Graywolf Press, 2014.

Rankine, Claudia and Lisa Sewell, editors. *Eleven More American Women Poets in the 21st Century.* Wesleyan University Press, 2012.

Rankine, Claudia and Juliana Spahr, editors. *American Women Poets in the 21st Century: Where Lyric Meets Language.* Wesleyan University Press, 2002.

Reilly, Evelyn. "Environmental Dreamscapes and Ecopoetic Grief." *Omniverse,* http://omniverse.us/evelyn-reilly-environmental-dreamscapes-and-ecopoetic-grief/

Reyes, Barbara Jane. "On Feminism, Women of Color, Poetics, and Reticence: Some Considerations." *A Megaphone: Some Enactments, Some Numbers, and Some Essays about the Continued Usefulness of Crotchless-pants-and-a-machine-gun Feminism,* edited by Juliana Spahr and Stephanie Young. Chainlinks, 2011, pp. 335–342.

Invocation to Daughters. City Lights Books, 2017.

Russo, Mary. *The Female Grotesque: Risk, Excess, Modernity.* Routledge 1994.

Salgado, Yesika. "How Not to Make Love to a Fat Girl." Uploaded by Button Poetry, www.youtube.com/watch?v=fHH0KC-xZXc

Samuels, Lisa. *Anti M.* Chax Press, 2013.

Sand, Kaia. "She Had Her Own Reason for Participating." *KaiaSand.net,* http://kaiasand.net/she-had-her-own-reasons/

Savageau, Cheryl. *Mother/Land.* Salt Publishing, 2006.

Scappettone, Jennifer. *From Dame Quickly.* Litmus Press, 2009.

"Bachelorettes, Even: Strategic Embodiment in Contemporary Experimentalism by Women," *Modern Philology* vol. 105, no. 1, 2007, pp. 178–184.

Schultz, Susan M. *Memory Cards: Simone Weil Series.* Equipage, 2017.

Selby, Nick. "Mythologies of 'Ecstatic Immersion': America, the Poem, and the Ethics of Lyric in Jorie Graham and Lisa Jarnot." *American Mythologies: New Essays on Contemporary Literature,* edited by William Blazek and Michael K. Glenday. Liverpool University Press, 2005, pp. 202–225.

Shockley, Evie. *the new black.* Wesleyan University Press, 2011.

Sloan, Mary Margaret, ed. *Moving Borders: Three Decades of Innovative Writing by Women.* Talisman House, 1998.

Somers-Willett, Susan. *The Cultural Politics of Slam Poetry: Race, Identity and the Performance of Popular Verse in America.* University of Michigan Press, 2009.

Spahr, Juliana. *This Connection of Everyone with Lungs.* University of California Press, 2005.

"Introduction." *American Women Poets of the 21st Century: Where Lyric Meets Language,* edited by Claudia Rankine and Juliana Spahr. Wesleyan University Press, 2002, pp. 1–17.

Spahr, Juliana and Stephanie Young. "Foulipo." *A Megaphone: Some Enactments, Some Numbers, and Some Essays about the Continued Usefulness of Crotchless-*

plants-and-a-machine-gun Feminism, edited by Juliana Spahr and Stephanie Young. Chainlinks, 2011, pp. 31–42.

"Numbers Trouble." *Chicago Review* vol. 53, no. 2–3, 2007, pp. 88–111.

Swensen, Cole. "Introduction." *American Hybrid: A North Anthology of New Poetry*, edited by Cole Swensen and David St. John. W. W. Norton, 2009, pp. xvii–xxvi.

Tabios, Eileen. "I Do." *Poetry Foundation*, www.poetryfoundation.org/poems/53813/i-do

Thaggert, Miriam. "Black Modernist Feminism and This Contemporary Moment: Evie Shockley's the New Black." *Feminist Modernist Studies* vol. 1, no. 1–2, 2017, pp. 44–50.

Toth, Naomi. "Echo's Echoes, or What to Do with Vanessa Place." *Jacket2*, May 1, 2018, https://jacket2.org/article/echos-echoes-or-what-do-vanessa-place

Trask, Haunani-Kay. "Feminism and Indigenous Hawaiian Nationalism." *Signs* vol. 21, no. 4, 1996, pp. 906–916.

Light in the Crevice Never Seen. Calyx Books, 1999.

From a Native Daughter: Colonialism and Sovereignty in Hawai'i. University of Hawai'i Press, 1993.

Volkman, Karen. "Sonnet (Nothing was ever what it claimed to be)." *Poets.org*, www.poets.org/poetsorg/poem/sonnet-nothing-was-ever-what-it-claimed-be

Wade, Cleo. "Poet Cleo Wade's Powerful Tribute to Gloria Steinem, Coretta Scott King, and More on International Women's Day." *W Magazine*, March 8, 2017, www.wmagazine.com/story/cleo-wade-poem-international-womens-day

Heart Talk: Poetic Wisdom for a Better Life. Atria/37 INK, 2018.

Wagner, Catherine. "This Is a Fucking Poem." *My New Job*. Fence, 2009.

"Post-Marginal Positions: Women and the UK Experimental/Avant-Garde Poetry Community: A Cross-Atlantic Forum." *Jacket* no. 34, 2007, http://jacketmagazine.com/34/wagner-forum.shtml

Wheeler, Lesley. "A Salon with a Revolving Door: Virtual Community and the Space of Wom-Po." *Contemporary Women's Writing* vol. 7 no. 1, 2013, pp. 54–72.

Wiley, Rachel. "10 Honest Thoughts on Being Loved by a Skinny Boy." Uploaded by Button Poetry, www.youtube.com/watch?v=tRFOTqTicvY

Willis, Elizabeth. "The Arena in the Garden: Some Thoughts on the Late Lyric." *Telling It Slant: Avant-Garde Poetics of the 1990s*, edited by Mark Wallace and Steven Marks. University of Alabama Press, 2002, pp. 225–235.

Young, Morris. "Beyond Rainbows: What Hawai'i's 'Local' Poetry Has Taught Me About Pedagogy." *Poetry and Pedagogy: The Challenge of the Contemporary*, edited by Joan Retallack and Juliana Spahr. Palgrave Macmillan, 2006, pp. 105–128.

Yu, Timothy, editor. *Nests and Strangers: On Asian American Women Poets*. Kelsey Street Press, 2015.

6

STEPHANIE BURT

The Nearly Baroque in Contemporary Poetry

Read a great deal of academic critics' takes on contemporary poetry and you will surely find debates as to whether some poets are subversive; whether they are political, or radical; whether they are authentic, or believable, or (if the critics are young enough) "relatable"; whether they continue, or alter, or repudiate, a Romantic, or else a modernist, tradition; whether their work owes much to one or another institution; whether and how it is truly new. You are less likely to find, among the earlier schools and movements critics invoke, the rococo, or the Baroque; and you are unlikely to find, among academic analysis, self-conscious interest in beauty.

Yet some contemporary poets embrace the idea of beauty, and its concomitants: the pretty, the stylish, the attractive, and the femme. Some of the same poets look back to the styles, and the periods in art history, called rococo and Baroque. These poets – worth calling, together, the nearly Baroque – represent a kind of aesthetic success, and a formal inquiry, unique to our day. When this inquiry began, its representative poets were almost all white cisgender women. Now, however, its scope has changed: we can find the nearly Baroque as well – or at least elements of its success – in some poets of color, and in some trans poets, whose work also rewards rereading now.

"It's the opposite of Baroque so I want / none of it," Angie Estes declared in a poem called "Sans Serif," from *Chez Nous* (2004). That brisk and irregularly rhymed poem announced Estes's opposition to any programmatic version of modernism, and to any attempt to make poems resemble spontaneous, unornamented speech. It now looks like a manifesto for a tendency. Call it the nearly Baroque, or the almost rococo. It is by no means simple in its practice; it seeks the opposite of simplicity, preferring the elaborate, the contrived, taking toward soundplay and simile the attitude of King Lear: "O reason not the need!"

Yet it can seem just simple enough in its goals. The twenty-first-century poets and poems of the nearly Baroque want art that puts excess, invention, and ornament first, art that cannot be reduced to its own explanation, art that shows off at once its material textures, its artificiality, and its descent from prior art, its location in history; they want an art that can always give, or show, more. Some poets have pursued a nearly Baroque aesthetic for almost the whole of their careers; Angie Estes and Robyn Schiff seem to me the clearest examples, and – along with the late Lucie Brock-Broido – the most important. My sense of the nearly Baroque comes first from what they create, why they matter, and what they can do.

Other poets – among them Nada Gordon, Ange Mlinko, Kiki Petrosino, Geoffrey Nutter, and Brenda Shaughnessy – have come to a similar aesthetic more recently. Enough such poets exist that the trend deserves attention not just in the context of one or another career but in the larger picture of present-day poetry. At the same time, that present is a moving target: after describing the nearly Baroque, and offering what I hope comes across as a credible appreciation, I'll reach its potential weaknesses, some less evident in 2014 (when the present chapter began its life) than in 2019 and beyond.

Nearly Baroque contemporary poems exhibit elaborate syntax, and self-consciously elaborate sonic patterning, without adopting pre-modernist forms: if they derive overall form from one earlier poet, it is always Marianne Moore. The poems have subjects – things and characters in a preexisting, historical world – and often include proper nouns. They rarely focus on one subject, however; instead, they weave together several topics or scenes in sinuous, multiply subordinated sentences. They may compare their own intricacies to other intricately made things: textiles, jewelry, household machines, braids, spiral staircases, DNA.

The nearly Baroque is a femme aesthetic, and all its practitioners know it; almost all are women. They defend traditionally feminine ideas of beauty and extravagance against the macho (or butch) insistence on practicality, on political utility, on conceptual novelty, or on efficiency that has characterized trends and schools from modernism to conceptualism (and beyond). At the same time these poets tend to note – they may sound guilty about – the serious effort and energy devoted to making such complicated, luxurious, or apparently useless things as contemporary literary poems. That's one reason their work can help us think about why we want, or need, art at all.

"Baroque" in its usual sense denotes art, literature, and music from approximately the last two-thirds of the seventeenth century, from Bach to Bernini to Góngora, distinguished by complexity, virtuosic technique, asymmetry, grandeur, theatricality, and violence. "Baroque artists do not stage the natural or the realistic," writes the art historian Roy Eriksen, but instead "produce marvel and even shock" (8). Rococo style, the eighteenth-century successor to the Baroque in at least some of the arts in at least some of western Europe, substituted decoration for grandeur, flirtation for violence, the pastoral for the sublime, prerevolutionary Paris for Rome, but remained elaborately theatrical, showing, to quote the critic William Park, "masterfully rendered natural objects that insist upon their artifice" (25). Art historians disagree as to whether the rococo is the late Baroque, or the antithesis of the Baroque, or somehow both.

Estes describes and demonstrates the nearly Baroque in simile after simile. Take the first lines in the first poem in *Enchantée* (2014), "Per Your Request" (the title runs into the poem): "gilded bronze rosettes once pressed / through the Pantheon's dome like stars ... and history posed especially / for you, its spree became / repose" (3). We live in history, like it or not (these Roman sights say); we were never here first. The poem concludes with riffs on the sounds in *crow* before it returns to *rose, pose, request*: "a crowbar that pries open // the day: a posse of roses coming / to possess you" (Estes, *Enchantée* 4).

Crows seek carrion; posses arrive to arrest and confine, as the grave confines its dead. Estes's roses are omens: *Enchantée* sounds a lot like *Chez Nous*, and like Estes's *Tryst* (2009), but it differs from them in its concentration of elegies. In "I Want to Talk About You," "Fifteen flocks of fifteen to twenty starlings ... suddenly rise" in "a reveling that molts sorrows to roost // rows, roost rows to sorrows as they soar" (Estes, *Enchantée* 5). These starlings mourn, too, shifting in flight as anagrams shift: "*grass lint, snarl gist, gnarls / sit*. Art slings them this way, *last grins*" (Estes, *Enchantée* 6). Again Estes summons the Baroque by name: "I once dreamed a word entirely / Baroque: a serpentine line of letters leaning / with the flourish of each touching the shoulder / of another ... " (Estes, *Enchantée* 56).

This word could stand for any of Estes's poems. In them, as in much Baroque and rococo art, motion is life, and nothing will stand on its own. ("The S-curve, the serpentine line," writes Park, is "universally acknowledged as one of the defining features of the rococo ... Such curves are commonly thought to be feminine" [19].) Estes's imagined motions, the serpentine curves of her irregular lines, take her not only from art work to art work but also from place to place, stitching together in her imagination, within a single poem, "the chasm of the Siq, the city of Petra / carved on its side" in present-day Jordan, "the unclaimed / cremated remains of those known as / the incurably insane at Oregon State Hospital," "the lapis lazuli of Hokusai seen / from outer space" (Estes, *Enchantée* 53). Her poem "History" starts with Mallarmé and Loie Fuller; brings in William James and Joseph Conrad; and explains how

> Leonardo's double-helix
> staircase at Chateau Chambord wraps
> its arms around its own quiet

> center, makes sure that the person going
> up and the one coming down
> never meet.   (Estes, *Enchantée* 13)

Estes's spiraling lines make such staircase-shapes too, except that she does want the people in her poems, as well as their topics, to meet. She writes "on behalf of life, its befogged aioli / logic, its belief-a-go-go" (Estes, *Enchantée* 25) and, for her, complexity, asymmetry, sensory delight, ornament *are* life: they are signs and reasons for it. Simplicity, on the other hand, reductiveness, single answers, and plainness are death; they are what we get when we stop asking for more.

Gilles Deleuze defined the Baroque not as a period but as "an operative function," a way of thinking, acting, or being, that "endlessly produces folds" (3). In Deleuze's Baroque "unfolding is thus not the contrary of folding, but follows the fold up to the following fold" (6). In this definition – derived from Deleuze's interpretations of G. W. Leibniz – everything is connected to everything, nothing moves in a straight line, and anything that looks like a whole is a part: "what is folded ... only exists in an envelope, in something that envelops it" (22). These folds within folds represent the inseparability, but also the distinction, of body and soul (Deleuze 35).

We can find these *ideas* – the inevitability of metaphor, the enfolding of matter and spirit, the strange isolation of souls – all over contemporary poetry. Yet the nearly Baroque poem pursues them as a matter of style: to read such a poem is to follow involutions, unfolding and re-foldings, re-linkings whose analogies do not end but double back into what one of Mlinko's titles calls "A Not Unruffled Surface," marked by *trouvailles* if not by *trompe l'oeil*. Its poets seem uncommonly fond not only of long, complex sentences but of simile, in part because similes can form braids, or chains: *A is like B is like C which resembles D.*

The first American book to feel and sound nearly Baroque might be Robyn Schiff's first book, *Worth* (2002). Most of its poems took their titles either from species of finches or from houses of fashion. Some of them read as if Schiff had immersed herself in Deleuze: "House of Dior," for example, begins: "Now we are on the chapter of pleats. / The impatience to fold, the joys of having folded, / the pleasures of folding them again" (16). One of Schiff's figures for poetry itself, from *Revolver* (2008), is "de la Rue's Envelope Machine," "with output of twenty-seven hundred / envelopes an hour" (*Worth* 5). The mass production of envelopes is – Schiff's syllabic stanzas say – a "paper-folding mystery" involving "the instantaneous / transformation of / matter," almost like the placement of souls within bodies, or the making of words into poems" (Schiff, *Worth* 5). All these processes might harbor a dangerous secret: "Friend, don't / unbend, to see what's written, even one wing of / the paper crane the king's master / folder made of the document you're // transporting" (Schiff, *Worth* 6). The sentences fold and unfold, concealing internal rhyme (friend, unbend), and they suggest that poems encode sentiments that, put into plaintext, could kill the bearer.

Schiff gets her ideas from all over but her reticulated style from Marianne Moore; Adam Edelman's "The Poetics of Robyn Schiff" quotes Schiff as saying that reading Moore "gave me permission ... to become the writer that I wanted to become." Yet the traits that Moore reserves for villains – showiness, boastfulness, conscious striving for effect – are everywhere in Schiff. Everything marvelous has to be both good and bad, both ingenious and dangerous (much of *Revolver* concerns the fabrication of weapons). Elaborate language, rococo detail-work, can also suggest that we live in an *ancien régime*, where "the future is a Louis XVI teacup / saving itself for you" (Schiff, *Revolver* 44). Elaboration can, however, also become a morally upright protest against any demand that our work must turn a profit or show a heteronomous use. Perhaps poetry needs no use at all; or perhaps it should do many things, all of them mysterious and beautiful and inefficient, like an "Eighty-Blade Sportsman's Knife, by Joseph Rodgers and Sons": "my heart flipped / the various blades open / in silence inside the closed box" (*Revolver* 20–21).

Schiff's newest work emphasizes the dangers, the bad faith, within the artifice, the illimitable associations and likenesses, which poetic language (or perhaps any language, any human action) contains. Much of it also addresses motherhood. In "Nursery Furniture," Schiff helps install a new rocking chair for her new baby, and its imperfect complications – themselves pursued in spiraling syllabics– remind her of the tangled-up lines in nature, connecting everything dangerous to everything else: "I held the ideal steel coil to the / light and saw the spiral / staircase out of the machine the clematis in my yard / unwinds up along its own concertina / wire, wheeling soft turbines up the / porch screen" (*A Woman of Property* 8). These architectural means of protection or concealment speak to the means of concealing the body – the clothing, the couture – in Schiff's earlier work: Angela Ndalianis names, in her own list of what counts as neo-Baroque, "Coco Chanel, Helena Rubenstein and Elsa Schiaparelli" (10), about whom both Schiff and Estes have written poems.

Lucie Brock-Broido's theatrically overextended sentences – like those in Estes and Schiff – use their attention to beauty, their attempt to make something overtly artificial, as a way to counteract entropy, practicality, time, and death. If Schiff's nearly Baroque spirals into itself, Brock-Broido's expands, into a theatricality that knowingly approaches melodrama. Much of her final book, *Stay, Illusion* (2013), comprises elegies for her father: "If my own voice falters, tell them hubris was my way of adoring you, / The hollow of the hulk of you." The same poem continues: "Will you be buried where: nowhere. // Your mouth a globe of gauze and glossolalia. / And opening, most delft of blue" (6). To hear such oversaturated poems is like looking at the Baroque ceilings that just barely resolve into scenes of gods and goddesses, or saints and miracles – were they more crowded they would make no sense at all.

Brock-Broido's style owes little to Moore: when she credits a precursor it is Emily Dickinson (as in her Dickinsonian title and Dickinson-inspired project of 1992, *The Master Letters*). Yet reading *Stay, Illusion* alongside *Enchantée*, or alongside *Revolver*, it can seem as if Brock-Broido had been waiting for other poets, readers of Moore, admirers of Bernini, to catch up. Her style now looks like what I am tempted to call – following the architectural historian Stephen Calloway – the Baroque Baroque, a mode of excess doubled and tripled, of decadence brought up to date without apology. One of the late Brock-Broido's key words is "extravagance": "extravagance of gesture" (90); "a basin of water, light, shuddering with its own / Extravagance, gone dull from keeping constant company with relentlessness" (79). That is Baroque indeed, as is the overextension (beyond what modern prose permits) of sentence and syntax. So is the frequent reference to art history; and so is the self-consciousness about frames, and framing devices, in poems that take their titles from the elements of a poetry book – "Selected Poem," "Collected Poem," "Contributor's Note."

All the poets of the nearly Baroque show off a complicated and unconventional technique (you might call them all show-offs). None seriously propose that their poems have spiritual or supernatural force. Even Brock-Broido, so drawn to religious imagery, frequently disclaims religious commitment (see her poem "Physicism," from *Trouble in Mind* [2014]). The death penalty is so emblematically wrong because this life is the only one: that is the sense behind Brock-Broido's elegies for people put to death by the American criminal justice system. Commemorating the author and reformed gang leader Tookie Williams, Brock-Broido imagines "A thousand inmates' spoons for music / While the paper kite flies like a boy-weed caught // In wind from San Quentin to nestle in the next / Prison and the next" (18).

That sense of material life as the only life brings all these poets closer to rococo. The art critic Glenn Adamson explains, "The rococo dispensed with some features of the baroque (such as its pervasive religiosity) and exaggerated others (its 'extravagant' use of ornament)," so that "this seemingly most artificial of styles gave a special place to . . . 'the real'" (143, 145): it treated its materials as indispensable and irreplaceable occasions for the flourish of the maker's hand. These poets treat their materials – words – that way too.

Nutter's poem "Purple Martin" aligns itself decisively, and a bit sadly, with the term, as with other manifestations of decadence: "the foyer painted black with golden leaves / of rococo design ... Yes, Herr Rektor, Man is not a hammer / and the mind is no machine, and the scalloped / shapes of basins under fountains have no function" (91–92). "Purple Martin" amounts to a verse essay in defense of the artifice that it describes: it might say, instead, *reason not the need*, or (with Estes) "glamour is its own / allure" (*Chez Nous* 1).

I have called these poets nearly Baroque, not neo-Baroque, in part because they can get closer to rococo and in part because "neo-Baroque" has a stack of liens on it: Latin American poets and fiction writers (especially Severo Sarduy and José Lezama Lima) have claimed "neo-barrocco" or neo-Baroque for themselves. The Latin American neo-Baroque is at once more violent, and more implicated in public history, than any of my Anglophone examples. That makes the Latin American version less femme and more compatible with a radical – indeed a revolutionary – politics. Both Paul Nelson and Roberto Tejada recommend the Latin American neo-Baroque as a model for North American avant-gardes.

The American Anglophone nearly Baroque can respond to radical politics too. So apprehensive about the powers in its elaborately crafted things (knives; viral DNA; hunters' calls; bourgeois humanism), Schiff's poetry can seem conscious of neo-avant-garde attacks on beauty, craft, and workmanship – on what Marcel Duchamp called "retinal art" – even as it exemplifies the versions of craft it attacks. These attacks in turn harmonize with – sometimes they simply are – the attacks on voice, and on notions of lyric selfhood, that Gillian White identified in her influential study *Lyric Shame* (2014). Brock-Broido's brand of self-consciousness turns attention from voice to page, from the sense of a live voice to the sensuous feel of handwritten letters and perfect-bound books; her politics (as finally expressed in *Stay, Illusion*) are certainly on the left. Yet neither Schiff, nor Brock-Broido, nor the later poets Brock-Broido, for many years a teacher at Columbia University, influenced most directly have had much truck with the post-language-writing, Marxist or Marxist-influenced avant-garde.

Can a poet who did emerge from that background become, or share goals with, the nearly Baroque? The answer, heavily qualified, seems to be yes: one such poet is Nada Gordon, who emerged from the sarcastic bad-is-good, publicity-is-better early 2000s school called Flarf. Gordon's *Vile Lilt* (2013) defends ornament through advice that verges on parody: "Wear your costumes with conviction – by which / we mean decide which picture you will make of yourself, / make it and then enjoy it!" (13). Gordon's hot words sound like older defenses of (inter alia) drag queens, whose lives are as authentic as anyone else's, though their wigs and scarves are longer; she goes on to align herself with such aesthetes as Oscar Wilde, declaring "Flowers are nature's readymades. The words of 'others' / are warm salt blossoms" (15). Gordon's copious poem (she calls it a "torrid cornucopia") goes on to recommend "Proper regard / for the 'intimate little feminine things' – that is the secret / of charming individuality. Gathered rosebuds, re-strewn" (14–15).

Between the density of her description and the clichés that she incorporates, Gordon sounds partly, but only partly, sarcastic. We should be *able to* define ourselves through charm, through miniature detail, especially if we are women (these poems imply), but we should never be *required* to do so. "Can one possibly escape / our theme – Woman as Decoration?" Gordon asks. "No, for she is carved in wood and stone ... She gleams in the jeweled windows of the monitor" (17). This iconic, historically durable Woman is the muse of Gordon's poetry now, and also the muse of the decorative arts, including dress ("One sets out gaily to study costume" [Gordon 17]). Nutter also wonders whether his poetry comes close, or too close, or just close enough, to the arts of decoration: to fireworks, for examples, with their "lavender // globes of opalescence" (56), or to a "sweet and useless ball of sugar icing" (119). Estes's *Chez Nous*, too, likens poetry to dessert, to "*l'opera* cake," "icing," an eclair, an *amuse-bouche* (4–5, 28).

Ange Mlinko, like Gordon, began as another kind of poet, one whose effects of improvised fragmentation came partly from indie rock, partly from the New York School, but she too has now incorporated the devices, the concerns, of the nearly Baroque. Mlinko's new work keeps asking whether art in general and her art in particular is overelaborate, useless, decadent, like the "eggshell balcony railings" in seaside suburbs, "green-grape sunlight spilling on the metallurgical sound of the waves – more like staves – collapsing, / and so collapsing every riff into one note" (10). Perhaps poems are like the doomed textiles of Arachne, or the unraveled thread of Ariadne ("I mix up Arachne with Ariadne: / similar name, similar gesture" [Mlinko 13]). Yet perhaps the thread of Mlinko's own art maintains its claims on us after all: perhaps it can rescue us from feeling insignificant, or overwhelmed. Mlinko's "Cantata for Lynnette Roberts" (named for a form whose origins are Baroque) takes up arts marked as feminine (sewing, home gardening) in Mlinko's suburban existence, and it asks how Mlinko, like the Welsh modernist poet Roberts, could make an art at once modern, individual, complicated, and connected to women's experience neither warlike nor "hard": "'I was rendering a "whipping" stitch,' Lynette wrote, on a silk-and georgette petticoat, the utility of which would be tested in Dover, where Keidrych had been called up to man the antiaircraft guns ... " (62–63). This work, too, with its overflowing, unpredictable lines, shows what the media critic Angela Ndalianis calls a "central characteristic of the baroque," a "lack of respect for the limits of the frame" (25).

Marsha Pomerantz seems, compared to Schiff or Estes, like an outsider; she lived in Israel for much of the past thirty years and made a career outside the poetry world, as an art curator; and she too writes poems that prefer elaboration and indirection to full frontal anything: in "Slut," from *The Illustrated Edge* (2012), "it is the *almost* and the *after* I // am after," "the angled glance / off the edge of an eyeful" (67). Pomerantz has just retired as a curator at the Harvard Art Museums and her art-historical interest shows in "Turner II" (the second of two poems about the same painting). The poem appears as double-spaced lines, shot through with repeated phrases, in what might be read as prose: "For *The Burning of the Houses of Parliament* Turner reversed // the direction of the wind so that flames went toward the Thames, // maximizing reflection. In life I like to maximize reflection don't you ... " (72). Art must let itself reverse direction, must permit folds, must permit interruptions, even falsifications, must juxtapose the pretty, or the girly, with the unruly, and with the bloody, in order to represent anything like sense in an otherwise "uncombable" life.

Baroque-era poetry in Spanish and Portuguese, as Ndalianis notes, sometimes used visual elements to create "the form of the multicursal labyrinth" (84) with lines that could be read in several directions, "played" like mazes, or game boards. One Spanish poem was "constructed like a chessboard, with text included in alternate squares" (84). Pomerantz has published a poem, called "Potsy with Patty in the Driveway," arranged in sets of hopscotch squares. I could add examples from other early career books, but the point – the outline of the style and the reasons behind its power – should already be clear.

It is no coincidence that almost all the poets named in this chapter are women. The nearly Baroque aesthetic – like the rococo – lends itself easily to a defense of the feminine, or the femme, against sexist claims that poets must seek importance, contemporaneity, utility, "masculine persuasive force." The same elaborate styles can also become a defense of something instead of nothing, a way out of nihilism. The British critic and poet Angela Leighton has argued that aestheticism is always close to nihilism, belief in form or beauty for its own sake close to belief in "nothing" (266). The nearly Baroque argues otherwise, making us, as Marc McKee puts it, "celebrant in the throes of nothing," emphasizing delight in our alterable material world (n. pag.). Yet the poems are not all sublime celebration; they can sound sad about their inability to make their poems more useful, or more durable, than they are.

The nearly Baroque can even amount to a dare. Since contemporary poetry (at least, the kind that comes in printed books) feels like an ornament anyway, feels unnecessary, or self-indulgent, or obsolete, in a way that was not true in the days of Frost or Moore, why not ramp up the ornamental content? Why not – if you are already being treated as mere decoration – become as decorative as you can? "If rococo ornament was a triumph of craft," Adamson explains, "a moment when workmanship took on the ambitions of complete control over materiality, its innovations were confined within the logic of the detail. They were only possible because they seemed to be trivial" (149). He might be describing the aspirations, and the limits, in the contemporary lyric poem.

I have been trying to recommend these poets: I admire them very much. Yet I have also been laying out a way to read them skeptically, as symptoms of a literary culture that has lasted too long, stayed too late. *Engagée* readers might say that the nearly Baroque celebrates, and invites us to critique, a kind of last-gasp, absurdist humanism. We value what has no immediate use, in order to avoid becoming machine parts, or illustrations for radical arguments, or pawns for something larger, whether it is existing institutions or a notional revolution: and we must keep moving, keep making discoveries, as the scenes and lines and similes of the nearly Baroque poem keep moving, because if we stop we will see how bad – how intellectually untenable, how selfish, or how pointless – our position really is. The same readers might say that these nearly Baroque poems bring to the surface questions about all elite or uncommercial art: Is it a waste? What does it waste? Can it ever get away from the violence required, if not to produce it, then to produce the society whose members can enjoy it? The rococo is the art of an *ancien régime*: it may be that the nearly Baroque poetry of our own day calls our regime *ancien* as well. It does not pretend to predict what could replace it.

*

Since the first version of this chapter appeared (in 2014) the white parts of the American poetry world have become more alert to race and to racism (which is not to say that we are aware enough). Poets of color have come to seem more clearly central to American poetry generally (as viewed by prizes, awards, and editorial positions, as well as by uncountable conversation). The de facto segregation of "minority" poets to "minority" syllabi, and of "racial" criteria from aesthetic ones (as described, for example, by Dorothy Wang), has become as obviously indefensible as it was always ethically wrong; and out trans poets, thin on the ground five years ago, are no longer hard to find.

All these developments resonate with the aesthetic of the nearly Baroque. Both Schiff and Brock-Broido, in some of their latest work – including work quoted in this chapter – try to work as white allies in anti-racist projects; they address Jim Crow, residential segregation, and the carceral state. Poets who work in the nearly Baroque idiom now (more than when this tendency began) take account of the actual bodies and bodily histories that do not fit well with conventional standards of prettiness, ornament, femininity, or beauty. Poets of color who foreground race have sometimes chosen not so much exactly the strategies described in this chapter but related ones, ones that benefit from the comparison. Poets whose interest in femininity and its opposites comes from lived transfeminine or nonbinary identity have put the techniques of the nearly Baroque to use. Jos Charles's much-noted *feeld* (2018) depends obviously on medieval English, and on the kinds of puns and nonstandard spellings she found in the sixteenth century (especially Edmund Spenser), but it is hard not to see its verbally rich, unfolding explorations of ambiguity and trans identity as, also, nearly Baroque: "gendre like all / sirfase is a female depositrie room" (2).

Other new poets come close not so much to the nearly Baroque, to the rococo, but to the violence of the first Baroque, as recommended by McSweeney, Tejada, or Nelson. Juliana Huxtable, for example – who is also a DJ, a model, and a visual artist – won a Lambda award in 2018 for a book of prose poems whose elaborately explicit, sometimes even run-on, sentences pursued the evolving and often self-contradictory standards of beauty in modern trans life, and in night-life: "UNIVERSAL CROP TOPS FOR ALL THE SELF-CANONIZED SAINTS OF BECOMING. PRIMAL SELF RECOGNITION DISASSEMBLES AS IT FORMS, TRANSFERRING CORPORAL MATTER INTO THE VIRTUAL AS IT DOUBLES BACK AS A FANTASY OF OURSELVES . . . OR PERHAPS A NIGHTMARE" (16).

A later prose block attacks the gender binary that (Huxtable suggests) underlies our "SYSTEMS FOR MAPPING DESIRE," our internal standards of beauty: "THEY ALL SEEMED SATISFIED TO LIVE IN A WORLD OF TOPS/BOTTOMS, MASCS/FEMS DIVIDED INTO VARIOUS . . . . AFFILIATIONS" (37). Huxtable will defeat these binaries through an endless proliferation of sometimes violent (to use Deleuze's favorite term) Baroque folds. Elsewhere she practically quotes the art historians who contrast Baroque color to classical line: in Huxtable's prose poem "LINES EXTEND. THE WEIGHT OF PASSAGE PLAYS OUT IN THICKNESS AND NUMBERS EMERGE AT THEIR BREAK POINTS. COLORS SHIFT AND STATIC POSES IN PROFILE RESEMBLE INSTALLATIONS . . . . THE PAST 500 YEARS DISAPPEAR INTO MICRO-METERS THAT ECLIPSE SIGHT" (127).

This aesthetic – best pursued in ongoing prose poems, not in self-limiting lines – is not the nearly Baroque, but it might be the Baroque Baroque. It also approaches the melodramatic, unbalanced excess of the Latin American neo-Baroque, the space in which, to quote the contemporary American poet Joyelle McSweeney, a writer can "let Art's occult and obscene powers over take you and push you to territory beyond your grasp as a poet" (n. pag.). McSweeney's piece, published in 2014, responds to an earlier version of the present chapter, objecting to my own omission of the Latin American move-ment, and of US, Asian or European writers it might have inspired, among them Johannes Göransson, Chelsey Minnis, Lucas de Lima, Seyhan Erözçelik, Tim Jones-Yelvington, Achille Mbembe, Jasbir Puar.

The writers in this second group cross national as well as linguistic bor-ders, and many of them (like Huxtable) work across or between genres rather than confining themselves principally to page-based verse. Many of them aspire to an aesthetic of violence, of revolution, as well as of folds, elabor-ation, involution. Some of these Baroque Baroque, or neo-Baroque and violent, writers draw directly on the Latin American past: Roberto Tejada, for example, opens his most recent book of prose by reprinting a prose poem that combines images of the sea, of life undersea, with words from the island of Cuba, by the Cuban leader or dictator Fidel Castro: "A record of survivors unsettled by the semidarkness of the undersea night, the velodrome cradle undertow, and marveled by these monuments in place of the invertebrate culture unique to saltwater, rewarded as we were with a glimpse into a landscape few of us will ever know … " (16). The sentence continues all the way down the page. A similar blend of elaboration with aggression, disorientation with intertwined images, governs some of the poems in Ginger Ko's first volume, *Mother Lover* (2015). "Flora" records a refusal to remarry: "There is no room in my heart for important men who surround themselves with flowers. Take the garland of wives and daughters from around your neck. That you feel safe they would not choke you makes me sick … " (40). We are far, here, from the grace of Estes's Rome; and yet there are those S-curves, those vivid colors, that concentration on detail over structure, and that assertion of gendered will against the direction of a male plot.

A poet like Estes defends her idea of beauty, ornament, *otium* against the ancient accusation that these things are feminine, frivolous, of no conse-quence. The poets I have been describing here – poets of Baroque Baroque extremes, poets who (to quote McSweeney) "go all the way" – trade subtlety for overflow and transform an excess of ornament into something like a weapon, as if they had to defend themselves right away; they are not accused, or overlooked, so much as they seem to respond to physical threat, or else they appear as already damaged by it. That damage also informed the scary and still underrated poems in Brenda Shaughnessy's *So Much Synth*

(2016), which toggled between a memoiristic plain style and a self-conscious defense of always-already-wounded, disqualified, half-repaired beauty, as in the poem called "Dress Form": "Myself I'm like a dress my mother made / me, a fabric self split open with a sigh / as I grew" (21).

Attention to Shaughnessy has accreted around her experience as the mother of a son with profound disabilities, especially as described in her volume *Our Andromeda* (2012). That attention has obscured the power in poems like "Dress Form," whose spiraling sentences stop short, or rip themselves open, in order to consider the aspirations to beauty of an anomalous body, an Okinawan American body, a queer body, a body that feels otherwise displaced. If she is like a dress form (that is, the model that dressmakers use to see if a dress fits) then the counterpart to a dressmaker's needle must be something that penetrates the poet's skin, both beauty and "wound": "tattoo needles don't use thread but ink / to mark a place in this ever-moving skin / and that wound is ornament" (21).

Whiteness, like heterosexuality, like slender cisgender adulthood, is the default, goes unremarked, or unmarked; by contrast, Shaughnessy asks about her perhaps imaginary tattoo, "who / needs a mark to know what's marked? / I would pray to the dark in the dark" (21). The long poem that anchors *So Much Synth*, called (after a song by Duran Duran) "Is There Something I Should Know?," envisions the teenage poet's encounter with beauty not as a way to adorn or complete the self but as an escape from it, embodied in the lyrics to "A Little Respect," the 1988 hit song by the dance-pop duo Erasure (60–61). Shaughnessy, the poem explains, once envisioned herself in a ballet, "the slightly chunky ballerina // ever-cast as the ginger-bread lady or Rat King, / Never Sugar Plum" (57). At least she was in the ballet. Her body shape, her queer identity, and her identity as Asian American, "half-Japanese," with no visible pop culture role models, all enter this long poem in which the poet remembers trying and failing to see herself in conventional models of beauty (65). She will have to fashion her own models instead – as, in so much of *So Much Synth*, she does.

Shaughnessy and Huxtable, Tejada and Ko, are not white, and are not quite rococo, and are taking the Baroque aesthetic in other directions, directions that may (or may not) grow out of a bad fit between their experience and European-derived feminine beauty norms. Shaughnessy's version of beauty is awkward, always in progress, sometimes embarrassing, never complete (perhaps like a teenaged self). It feels like an act of resistance to many parts of culture at once, not only the part that tells girls to shrink, to occupy no space, not to grow up, but also the part that excludes people who look or think or feel as Shaughnessy has. The violence in her poetry – the violence against which beauty and elaboration count as partial defenses – is intimate, social, small-scale. In Ross Gay's rightly celebrated *Catalog of Unabashed Gratitude* (2016), on the other hand, beauty looks like a defense, and far more than a defense, against a violence that is also systemic: "There is, in my yard, a huge and beautiful peach tree. / I planted the thing as a three-foot whip ... Now the tree reaches almost / into the grumpy neighbor out back's yard, the one who once / snarled at me and my house *why would anyone paint a house that color?*" (68). Here are defenses of beauty that are not defenses of the Baroque, nor of the femme, nor of elaboration at all: they show, no less than Tejada or Huxtable do, that some elements of the nearly Baroque style can thrive, and attract admirers, and succeed aesthetically, in a contemporary environment, far from that style itself.

Gay's deliberately, insistently affirmative poem, like the rest of the book in which it occurs, identifies beauty and pleasure not with artifice but with nature; not with complexity (though his sentences often become grammatically complex) but with the sincerity of unpremeditated speech; and that version of natural beauty, "abundant and floral" (35), where "once a small seed / took hold" (72), sets itself not against a mommy track, not against accusations of triviality, not against sexism, not against an austerely political modernism, but against a society that permits the economic neglect, the isolation from nature, and often the murder of black men. The central poem in Gay's book mourns one murdered black man, the Indiana writer Don Belton, and – as elegists have done all the way back to "Lycidas," and farther back than that – the poet complains that his artifice, his "artifacts," his constructed beauty, cannot become nature or cancel out death: "I can't even make a metaphor / of my reflection upside down and barely visible / in the spoon. I wish one single thing made sense" (40).

It makes no sense to call Gay nearly Baroque, or Baroque at all, though it would make a great deal of sense to call him Romantic. Yet Gay, no less than Estes, builds into his volume a contemporary defense of the aesthetic, not as a pure or disinterested or elevated category of experience but as a quality whose "specificity" – and whose worth – "is not contingent on its purity," as John Guillory put it (336); and Guillory continues: "the experience of any cultural work is an experience of an always composite pleasure"; as against a canon restricted to certain works or certain ways of reading, his influential argument of 1993 urged readers to recognize "the ubiquity of aesthetic" (that is, of potentially aesthetic) "experience" (336).

Beauty is there for us if we want, or need, it, as long as we do not try to simplify it, to separate it from something else, to restrict it to "classics" or rank it on a linear scale: and classic, of course, is one opposite for Baroque, as linear scales are one opposite for the serpentine line. A poem like Gay's lament for Belton – or like Estes's own series of elegies, like Schiff's elaborations, like Shaughnessy's memory-poems – cannot make everything make sense: it cannot overturn the prose of the world, nor can it reverse all social injustice. It can, however – whether it stresses its artifice, or its proximity to nature; its femme identity, or (with Gay) its masculine friendship – say to a world of bare facts: there is more than you see here, more than the bare necessities we are told to want; there may even be "a posse of roses," "a serpentine line," a fig tree blooming, somewhere waiting for you.

Works Cited

Adamson, Glenn. "The Real in the Rococo." *Rethinking the Baroque*, edited by Helen Hill. Ashgate, 2011, pp. 143–160.

Brock-Broido, Lucie. *Stay, Illusion*. Knopf, 2013.

Charles, Jos. *feeld*. Milkweed Editions, 2018.

Deleuze, Gilles. *The Fold: Leibniz and the Baroque*, translated by Tom Conley. University of Minnesota Press, 1993.

Edelman, Adam. "The Poetics of Robyn Schiff: History, Fragmentation, and Ekphrasis." The Writing University, University of Iowa, www.writinguniversity.org/writers/robyn-schiff

Eriksen, Roy, editor. *Contexts of Baroque*. Novus, 1997.

Estes, Angie. *Enchantée*. Oberlin College Press, 2013.

  Tryst. Oberlin College Press, 2009.

  Chez Nous. Oberlin College Press, 2004.

Gay, Ross. *Catalog of Unabashed Gratitude*. University of Pittsburgh Press, 2015.

Gordon, Nada. *Vile Lilt*. Roof, 2013.

Guillory, John. *Cultural Capital: The Problem of Literary Canon Formation*. University of Chicago Press, 1993.

Huxtable, Juliana. *Mucus in My Pineal Gland*. Capricious and Wonder, 2017.

Ko, Ginger. *Mother Lover*. Bloof, 2015.

Leighton, Angela. *On Form*. Oxford University Press, 2010.

McKee, Mark. "At the Edge of a Deep, Dark Wood, Re-Purposed Dolphin Speaks." *Diagram* 4, https://thediagram.com/7_4/mckee.html

McSweeney, Joyelle. "I Want to Go All the Way." *Poetry Foundation*, April 16, 2014, www.poetryfoundation.org/harriet/2014/04/i-want-to-go-all-the-way

Meek, Sandra. *Road Scatter*. Louisiana State University Press, 2012.

Mlinko, Ange. "A Not Unruffled Surface." *Poetry*, June 2008, www.poetryfoundation.org/poetrymagazine/poems/51178/a-not-unruffled-surface

  Marvelous Things Overheard. Farrar, Straus and Giroux, 2013.

Ndalianis, Angela. *Neo-Baroque Aesthetics and Contemporary Entertainment*. MIT Press, 2004.

Nelson, Paul. "The Neo-Baroque: A Missing Group in the New American Poetry." *paulnelson.com*, December 6, 2012, http://paulenelson.com/2012/12/06/neo-barroco/

Nutter, Geoff. *The Rose of January*. Wave, 2013.

Park, William. *The Idea of Rococo*. University of Delaware Press, 1992.

Pomerantz, Marsha. "Potsy with Patty in the Driveway." *Raritan* vol. 33, no.2, 2013, https://raritanquarterly.rutgers.edu/issue-index/all-volumes-issues/volume-33/volume-33-number-2

  The Illustrated Edge. Biblioasis, 2012.
Schiff, Robyn. *A Woman of Property*. Penguin, 2016.
  Revolver. University of Iowa Press, 2008.
  Worth. University of Iowa Press, 2002.
Shaughnessy, Brenda. *So Much Synth*. Farrar, Straus and Giroux, 2016.
  Our Andromeda. Copper Canyon Press, 2012.
Tejada, Roberto. *Still Nowhere in an Empty Vastness*. Noemi, 2019.
  "Avant-Garde in Crisis." *Lana Turner*, www.lanaturnerjournal.com/contents-current/roberto-tejada-avant-garde-crisis

7

DECLAN GOULD

Disability Aesthetics and Poetic Practice

Led by Ed Roberts and the Center for Independent Living in Berkeley, California, the Disability Rights Movement began in the 1970s, advocating for legal reform, organizing protests, smashing curbs, and building ramps in the dead of night in order to make sidewalks accessible to people who use wheelchairs.[1] Disability rights advocates' focus on increasing accessibility on a systemic level is informed by the social model of disability, which views physical, social, and political structures as the cause of the exclusion and stigma that people with disabilities face. This politicized way of seeing disability resists the medical model, which sees disability as an individual, biological problem to be fixed, and perpetuates the perception that people with disabilities are broken, wrong, and therefore not deserving of full citizenship or equal rights.[2] Owing in no small part to the oppression created by the medical model, up until the late 1970s, American poets with disabilities, such as Larry Eigner, Josephine Miles, Hannah Weiner, and Vassar Miller, tended to leave disability out of their poetry or to refer to it only indirectly (one exception to this tendency was the poet Adrienne Rich, who lived with severe rheumatoid arthritis and openly wrote about the pain caused by this disability as early as 1973).[3] Despite their unwillingness to speak directly about disability in their poetry, mid-twentieth-century disabled poets have had a strong influence on many contemporary poets with disabilities, such as Jennifer Bartlett and Jillian Weise, who have found a lineage in earlier poets like Eigner and Miles.

The Rehabilitation Act of 1973 and the Americans with Disabilities Act of 1990 made it illegal to discriminate against people on the basis of disability, just as the Civil Rights Act made discrimination based on race illegal in 1964. In the wake of this legal reform, and supported by the first literary magazines

I would like to thank Michael Davidson for his generous feedback. I am also greatly in debt to Brian Teare for his invaluable insight during our talks about this chapter. In addition, I would like to thank Petra Kuppers for the vote of confidence and Jordan Burgis for his support throughout this project. Finally, I would like to thank Timothy Yu for including my chapter in this collection.

and anthologies devoted to the perspective of people with disabilities (including *Kaleidoscope*, founded in 1979, and *Toward Solomon's Mountain*, published in 1986), American poets increasingly began to bring disability into their poetry in a more direct way in the 1980s and 1990s. Along with their embodied experiences living with disability, the work of many of these poets, such as Laura Hershey, Jim Ferris, Kenny Fries and Stephen Kuusisto, represents their involvement in the Disability Rights Movement and disability culture and puts disability at the center of the poetry by writing primarily for disabled (rather than nondisabled) readers. Following Ferris's terminology in "The Enjambed Body: A Step Toward a Cripple Poetics," I call the twenty-first-century poets who continue this tradition of disability culture poetry "crip poetry."[4] In contrast, I call the twenty-first-century poets who develop disability poetics that are not written primarily for disabled audiences, and that are often based in other aesthetic movements and/or identities, "disability poetry." Such poetry is more closely affiliated with disability studies – the interdisciplinary field of disability scholarship that has been steadily growing since the founding of the Society for Disability Studies in 1986 – in the sense that, while it is concerned with investigating disability's many valences and with creating new ways of understanding disability, it does not necessarily share crip poetry's allegiance to disability activism or disability culture. The first category that I describe, Deaf poetry, consists largely of American Sign Language (ASL) poems that are performed rather than written and that develop out of and speak primarily to Deaf culture, which has its own rich history apart from the Disability Rights Movement.

The Deaf community has a well-established culture, which includes its own language, art, institutions, and social mores. In the 1980s, Deaf poets began to move beyond phonocentric translations of English poetry into ASL, developing visually centered poetic devices like movements that use cinematic effects, handshape constraints, and visual rhyme (Bauman, Nelson, and Rose 9). A defining moment in Deaf poetry occurred in 1984, when Beat poet Allen Ginsberg met with Deaf poets at the National Technical Institute for the Deaf in Rochester, NY. According to H-Dirksen L. Bauman et. al., "Ginsberg asked for volunteers to translate the image of 'hydrogen jukebox' from his famous long poem 'Howl.'" They continue:

> [Deaf poet Patrick] Graybill performed the image of a man putting a coin in the jukebox, the record moving into place, the needle touching down, and the record spinning faster and faster to the beating music until finally whipped into the fury of a hydrogen explosion of music (clip 1.6). As Graybill finished his image, Ginsberg exclaimed,
> "That's it! That's what I meant!" (6)

Building on the foundation established by early Deaf poets like Graybill, Clayton Valli, Ella Mae Lentz, Debbie Rennie, and Peter Cook (who collaborated with hearing poet Kenny Lerner), twenty-first-century Deaf poets like Douglas Ridloff, Sean Forbes, Dack Virnig, and Angel Theory use Deaf poetry to preserve ASL and to enrich Deaf culture. As Ridloff, who runs the monthly New York City ASL Slam, states, "When ASL is translated into English for poetry, 95% of the time it's lost in translation. That's why I ask the [live ASL] interpreters not to translate the poems" (n. pag.). While it may not be possible to translate Deaf poetry into English in a way that would capture all of the nuances of this art form, there is evidence that the performative aspects of Deaf poetry align with the growing interest among twenty-first-century poets more broadly in finding ways – as Michael Davidson puts it – to return "aesthetics to its original meanings in eighteenth-century philosophy: *aesthesis* or corporeal perception" and to explore the more embodied, visual elements of poetry and poetic practice (Bauman, Nelson, and Rose 5).

In her Keynote Address at the 2018 New Disability Poetics Symposium, "Dis Poetics / Crip Poetics," Meg Day drew a clear line between disability poetics and crip poetics, stating that "Disability poetics isn't for us," in the sense that, because its primary audience is not disabled people, it does not go far enough toward resisting the "co-opting" of disability by nondisabled poets (through, for example, objectifying disability metaphors and tragic or reductively inspirational representations of disability that are not written by disabled people). As a result, Day has come to identify with crip rather than disability poetry because, for her, only crip poets, such as Gaia Thomas, Raymond Luczak, Daniel Simpson, Ona Gritz, Leroy Moore, Eli Clare, Stephanie Heit, John Lee Clark, and Travis Lau, truly put disabled people at the center of its poetic practice. This commitment to centering people with disabilities is apparent in "what is in the hand carries what is in the head," from her chapbook *We Can't Read This*. In this poem, Day (whose influences include Deaf poet Clayton Valli, queer poet Eileen Myles, and Language writing-adjacent poet Juliana Spahr) uses a series of colloquial turns of phrase to demonstrate the power of ASL and the people who speak it: "the whole world is in our hands / handfuls of it / we are a handful / hand to mouth" (*We Can't Read This* 14). From the outset of this reiterative poem, her use of the first person plural, "our," foregrounds the perspectives not only of disability but of disabled people as a group who have common experiences with both the joys of speaking ASL and with resistance to the dominant ableist culture, which perhaps at times causes them to be perceived by nondisabled people as "a handful." In addition, by referring to familiar sayings like "hand to mouth" and "talk to the hand" in the context of crip poetry, she defies the negative connotations of these phrases, thereby expressing the vitality and value of ASL.[5]

In Day's poetry, these moments of pride and resistance are interwoven with complex questions about Deaf, hearing, disability, nondisabled, queer, and heteronormative cultures' relationships with one another, and about her own relationship to these cultures as a queer woman who is profoundly deaf and who has a "deep investment and involvement in Deaf culture" but who is not culturally Deaf (Day, "Queerness" n. pag.). These questions collide in "the first time," where Day recalls a memory of a youthful romantic encounter: "the first time you bilabial epiglotal tuning forked against my ear, there were voiced gutturals all around. they said if I transparencied a bird & you classifier inflected a fish, then where would we retroflex gloss a nest?" (*We Can't Read This* 12). This highly musical, imagery-rich prose poem connects the specialized terminology of speech therapy to homophobia and ableism by using it to describe the dominant (i.e., heteronormative, nondisabled) culture's disapproving response to Day's sexuality. By using the discourse of speech therapy to mimic this condemnation of her queer, crip sexuality, Day suggests that the medical, educational, and religious institutions that enforce what Robert McRuer calls "compulsory able-bodiedness" also enforce what Rich calls "compulsory heterosexuality" (89). In addition, the cryptic word choice of this poem means that its crip, queer valences will largely be lost on people who are not part of the disability or Deaf communities, and who are therefore likely to be less attuned to the negative connotations that the discourse of speech therapy carries in the Deaf community, or to the irony of Day's instrumentalization of this normalizing language in the service of queer, crip sexual innuendo.

Leah Lakshmi Piepzna-Samarasinha writes poems for disabled readers – more specifically, for "the glitterfemme canes. the wheelchair pushers [...] for my lovers. for my friends. the beautiful ones in the ugly city. the ugly-beautiful ones in the beautifulugly city. for us" (n. pag.). While Day's poetics of inquiry and implication invite readers to reflect on how the very structures of our language perpetuate ableism and audism (and how this system can be turned against itself), Piepzna-Samarasinha, who uses a cane and lives with both fibromyalgia and psychiatric disability, takes a more instructive, narrative approach, encouraging readers to "figure out a way to love yourself" and to "find the people you can sketch the secret inside of the world with" (41). She celebrates working-class, disabled, queer, femme, and trans people of color's hardscrabble resilience and ability to find strength in vulnerability, describing the complex, loving relationships that are cultivated in these communities as well as the struggles with oppression and abuse that they face as a group and as individuals. Her fourth book of poetry, *Bodymap*

(2015), shows readers what it looks like to celebrate the beauty of people with disabilities – even those with painful chronic illnesses like fibromyalgia – in a world that sees them as broken and inferior: "fibro hips like butterfly wings, that tremor tremor tremor. so fast nobody could see it. little earthquakes on the left wing, on the right wing. fibro hips like butterfly wings tremoring [...] fibro hips that shake and shake and that I do not curse and fear anymore" (28). For Piepzna-Samarasinha, the work of liberating herself and others from "internalized ableism" (44) is an ongoing, collective healing process that involves activism and performance art (she is a member of Sins Invalid, a widely lauded disability justice performance project) as well as poetry.

While *Bodymap* uses triumphant analogies like the one quoted above to redefine beauty in the image of disability, the analogies in Amber DiPietra and Denise Leto's collaboratively written chapbook, *Waveform* (2011), invite disabled readers to see their differences as natural, functional ways of being. For example, they propose that "the idea of a manatee" might help DiPietra – who lives with chronic arthritis and whose writing is influenced by lyric, confessional, and Language poetry – better understand her slow-moving body, observing that "A manatee gets to shift vertically while always remaining at a / glide, horizontal" and that "Manatees are better at detecting broadband, rather than tonal, / sound" (*Waveform* n. pag.). Throughout the emails that DiPietra and Leto exchanged and then cut up and intertwined to create "Waveform," this analogy of the slow but nonetheless graceful, otherworldly manatee repeatedly reinscribes and undoes itself, in the sense that the authors acknowledge its limitations and imagine alternative analogies even as they return to this image of the manatee's "Shrunken forelimbs and slow" (*Waveform* n. pag.). These unstable analogies draw attention to an important aspect of DiPietra and Leto's crip conception of disability: For them, the lens of disability illuminates the always-already unstable state of all bodies and makes visible the instability of the language with which we attempt to categorize our bodies. As they write, "When continuous = / > discontinuous we have to invent new ways of being a writer" (*Waveform* n. pag.).

This drive toward unstable analogy is both therapeutic and a continuation of the constraint of collaboration that was used to create this text, through which they create an alternate world – albeit a fragile, contingent, and complex one – within and among themselves. DiPietra sees *Waveform* both as a "textual performance" of her and Leto "getting to know each other" and as a performance text (i.e., scores for and enactments of performances that investigate the interrelatedness of text, writing process, and body). She and Leto – who lives with laryngeal dystonia (a neurological condition that causes involuntary movements of the muscle that controls the voice box) and whose influences include Barbara Guest, Norma Cole, and Oulipian constraint-based writing – have done many "adaptive" readings, in which DiPietra helps Leto "to voice parts of the text [...] sometimes it is like an echoing, and sometimes it is like me towing her into the sound."[6] These performances begin with DiPietra reading the beginning of a line aloud, and then Leto riding the momentum of DiPietra's voice and joining in when she is able. As DiPietra explains, this process of "chunking and towing" is "like towing into a wave [...] like when you have to get on the jet ski to be towed into them when you're surfing." In the video of their reading at San Francisco State, sometimes, Leto drops back out, unable to gain the momentum and rhythm necessary to continue ("Amber DiPietra and Denise Leto Reading & Discussing Their Poetry" n. pag.). Other times, DiPietra's voice cedes to Leto's as she rides the wave of DiPietra's voice to the end of the stanza. In the moments when they are reading simultaneously, their voices intertwine to create a new, third voice that is both steady and wavering, recognizable as language as well as audible trace of Leto's dystonia and DiPietra's difficulty tracking the line visually, a voice of unpredictable modulations and fragmented syllables that is amplified through supportive collaboration.

This investment in collaboration and interdependence is also evident in Petra Kuppers's collaboration with Neil Marcus, *Cripple Poetics: A Love Story* (2008), which combines lineated epistle, instant message, photos of the authors' intertwined bodies, and lyric poetry, which together tell a story of two disabled people falling in love, cultivating their dance and poetry practices, attending pain support groups, symposia, and concerts, and debating the pros and cons of reclaiming the word "crip" (an abbreviation of the historically derogatory term "cripple") for purposes of disability liberation (111). This collaboratively written poetry builds on the disability justice movement's investment in moving beyond what Lennard Davis calls the "humanistic model" (30). Davis explains, "In a dismodernist mode," the aim is "to create a new category based on the partial, incomplete subject whose realization is not autonomy and independence but dependency and interdependence" (30). This prosody of disability – or dismodernism – rests upon an ethics of and orientation toward the care of self and others and toward interrelation rather than individualism.

An early practitioner of performance-informed crip poetry, Kuppers, who has used a wheelchair her whole life, has been artistic director of a collective performance project for people with disabilities called The Olimpias since 1998 (Anger n. pag.). Like Day, Kuppers drops allusions to disability and queerness throughout *PearlStitch* (2016), which is based in part on her work with The Olimpias (Kuppers, "Pearl Stitch/Spherical" n. pag.). For example, readers familiar with disability culture will likely read Kuppers's lines about the Greek god Hermes's slyness and Mother Ann Lee's (the founder of the Christian sect known as the Shakers) interpretation of shaking as prayer as allusions to disability culture, where slyness signifies resourcefulness and shaking is associated with a variety of physical disabilities (Kuppers, *PearlStitch* 1). Likewise, as Marissa Perel points out, readers familiar with queer cultures will likely read lines about the dangers of public transportation as a reference to the homophobic harassment that often takes place in these kinds of public spaces (25). This specificity means that much of the cultural knowledge present here may be lost on readers who are not familiar with crip or queer coteries (Gould n. pag.). A love song for those deemed nonproductive, illegible, or otherwise invalid, *PearlStitch* offers not a universalizing anthem for the misfits and monsters but rather caring via observation and listening. Kuppers expresses this love through complex and unwavering description and engagement, approaching queerness and disability in a sensual, seductive way, writing, "I need to feel your footsteps / your wheels' path your snaking ways" (*PearlStitch* 23). Questions about the meaning and mutability of a body's form, how bodies in relation come to constitute one another, and the kinds of alchemical social processes that can change the makeup of this material are central to *PearlStitch*: "Change gender / Change genus / Change somatic structure / Change your mind / just keep in motion" (Kuppers, *PearlStitch* 99). This vision of metamorphosis is complicated by Kuppers's insistence on weaving the violence, anger, and pain of living in an ableist, homophobic society into the fabric of her poems, such as when she writes, "taste do not even scream, frozen / startle reflex like a fucking possum his meat on my teeth groping deeper why don't I bite down" (*PearlStitch* 43). Like *Bodymap*, in *PearlStitch* this embrace of the different and changing shapes a body may take must also include the mark left by violence and invalidation.

Constance Merritt also refuses to look away from the invalidation and violence experienced by many people with disabilities, but rather than offering the healing incantations of *PearlStitch*, the narrative, free verse poems in *Blind Girl Grunt* (2017) serve as witness and testament to this ongoing injustice. For example, in "Invisible Woman, Dancing," Merritt gives a firsthand account of attending a Halloween party at a private women's college in the South in the early aughts. Merritt – whose influences include James Agee, Pablo Neruda, and blues music – compares the erasure that she experiences at the hands of the other (white, nondisabled) partygoers to having come "as a ghost to the party," because although she is not actually wearing a Halloween costume, her blackness and blindness – her "brilliant skin" and "ruinous eyes" – render her "presence so insubstantial / eyes pass through it, hands / reached through air" (1). However, this erasure is coupled with a kind of hypervisibility, as some of the partygoers, protected by the "purity and privilege" of "the flag of whiteness," respond to Merritt's presence by staring at rather than ignoring her: "Staring into that void they glimpsed themselves, / turned back, shuddering, to the masquerade" (1). Acutely aware that these gazes are yet another form of erasure, Merritt understands that the people who stare at her see a projection of their own fears and prejudices.

As Jillian Weise observes in her blurb for *Blind Girl Grunt*, the end of "Invisible Woman, Dancing" is "explosive" – in the last stanza, Merritt casts a malediction upon all racists and ableists, willing "These words" – the poem itself – to become "kerosene, dry wood, locked doors, a match" (3). Like Merritt, Weise, in "Elegy for Zahra Baker" from *The Book of Goodbyes* (2013), responds to the nondisabled people whose objectifying stares are their own kind of invalidation. In contrast with Merritt's lyrical imagery, Weise sharply retorts, "How much would you pay me to say the name of the condition I have? Would I just need to say the name or would you require an examination? How much for the box of legs in the attic?" (62). Weise, who uses a prosthetic leg and whose influences include Josephine Miles, Ishmael Reed, and Alejandra Pizarnik, explores the spectacle of disability further in "The Ugly Law," where she is by turns disturbed, indignant, and finally bewildered by the nineteenth-century municipal ordinances known as "the ugly laws," which made being in public while disabled an offense punishable by fine or even institutionalization and which are described by Susan Schweik in her book *The Ugly Laws* (2009): "*Any person who is diseased, maimed, mutilated or* / Can I continue reading this? Will it affect my psyche // so that the next time Big Logos comes over / I will not be there in the room?" (12). By juxtaposing her growing doubts about her nondisabled lover (referred to throughout the book as "Big Logos") with direct quotes from the ugly laws (in italics), Weise captures the jarring rupture that they represent, putting both her society and her relationship in a new and disturbing light.

In *Virginia State Colony for Epileptics and Feebleminded* (2017), Molly McCully Brown reflects on how, as a person living with cerebral palsy, a "window less than half a century wide" kept her from being incarcerated in the institution that her book is named for, which is located just miles from where she grew up in Amherst, Virginia (4). While Weise's use of disability history provides an informative but disruptive interjection into the present, Brown – whose influences include Eavan Boland and Louise Glück – intersperses "invented sterilization forms" (which are based on documents from The Image Archive on the American Eugenics Movement) with poems in the voices of fictional colony inmates, nurses, and doctors (73). Brown memorializes the inhumane living conditions (which according to Brown included solitary confinement, unpaid labor, sexual abuse, and involuntary sterilization) that were perpetrated within the walls of early and mid-twentieth-century institutions like the Virginia State Colony, which was "formally enmeshed in the eugenics movement" and which sterilized more than 70,000 people in Virginia alone. These rhythmic, musical poems are also a way for Brown to see herself as part of a longer lineage of people with disabilities who were grossly misunderstood, as seen in "Numb," which presents the internal monologue of an inmate who has been labeled "idiotic" (and who very well may be diagnosed with cerebral palsy today) immediately following her involuntary sterilization (64). By (re)constructing the eloquent, complex inner lives that the Virginia Colony inmates had despite their horrifying living conditions, Brown implies that their experiences gave them unique insights into the fear and ignorance that have driven many aspects of American society, both past and present.

The writers that I have categorized as disability poets disclose their embodied differences in their poetry and actively engage with the somatic and socially constructed aspects of disability but do not write primarily for disabled audiences, nor do they see themselves as primarily in conversation with the disability community. Some of these poets, such as Eleni Stecopoulos, Tito Mukhopadhyay, Jennifer Bartlett, and Adam Mitts, raise questions about the very idea of identity, deconstructing this concept and emphasizing the fluidity and fragmentation of lived experience, while others have strong ties to other identity groups and/or schools of poetry beyond disability, such as Michael Davidson, Norma Cole, Pattie McCarthy, C. S. Giscombe, Susan Schultz, Rachel McKibbens, Khadijah Queen, Canadian poet Jordan Scott, and British poet and performance poet Aaron Williamson. For example, in *Patient* (2014), Bettina Judd connects her undiagnosed ovarian torsion (which doctors mistook for cramps) and the subsequent death and removal of her left ovary to the long history of racism in the field of medicine, writing "*Gynecology was built on the backs of Black women, anyway*" (90, italics original). Like Brown, Judd connects her lived experience with historical figures, whose voices she writes in (a gesture that is part of a long tradition of feminist, queer, and African American poets making their erased histories visible by going to the archives and recovering previously lost or ignored historical figures). Yet while Brown adopts a lineage of people with disabilities, the primary lineage that Judd identifies with is three of the enslaved black women – Anarcha Westcott, Betsey Harris, and Lucy Zimmerman – who J. Marion Sims (known as the father of modern gynecology) performed experimental surgery on, without anesthesia, and likely without their consent. Judd suggests that she is connected to Wescott, Harris, and Zimmerman – along with Joice Heith, a black woman whose teeth were pulled out by P. T. Barnum in order to falsely display her as George Washington's nanny – due to their shared experience with violent, racist medical treatment: "Hospital curtain, showman's speculum, surgeon's auditorium. There is an opening here, a thrusting, a climax, a little death. Who will rise from that, and how? You, in bed with me, Anarcha. You, brushing my head Joice. Why do you mourn me and sing, as if I am the one who has died?" (9). By demonstrating how disability is created and exacerbated by racism, Judd's capacious poems connect these seemingly separate experiences to broader historical and sociopolitical contexts, opening up the possibility for solidarity and resistance across time and between individuals. By writing in the voices of nineteenth-century black women who experienced "ordeal[s] with medicine," she also amplifies and humanizes their marginalized perspectives (Judd 1).

While Judd adopts a lineage based on race, gender, and shared experiences with medicine, Airea Matthews's process of making meaning of her intersecting experiences with psychiatric disability, race, and gender develops through her "many literary ancestors, including Margaret Walker, Anne Sexton, and Gertrude Stein" (Mishler and Matthews n. pag.). In *Simulacra* (2017), Matthews compares witnessing her father's heroin addiction to watching him fall daily "[...]six / feet into a vat of tar. Burned / his neck, ankles, veins" (80). Matthews then reflects on her own addiction and stint in a rehab facility, where one of her nurses was named Anne Sexton (16, 20). In "Sexton Texts as Dead Addict's Daughter During Polar Vortex," this nurse's double, the mid-twentieth-century confessional poet Anne Sexton (who also had a psychiatric disability), becomes the narrator's confidant (Matthews 20). By channeling Anne Sexton, who "writes" the messages in the right-hand column, the narrator finds an interlocutor who empathizes with her experiences with a psychiatric disability that causes her to feel hollow and hopeless, without reducing this experience to a pathological label or disclosing a particular diagnosis. Through this call and response of mutual understanding, Matthews constructs a flexible, cross-racial identity that enables her negotiation of the contemporary sociopolitical climate (Shockley n. pag.).

In *Hospitalogy* (2013), David Wolach also seeks understanding in intertextuality, in the form of the many dedications and quotes by other writers that pepper this series of poems about the hospital stays occasioned by their mitochondrial disease (which can cause a wide range of symptoms, including muscle pain and weakness, gastrointestinal and mobility problems, and migraines).[7] These references are Wolach's way of achieving a mediated form of solidarity and "abstracted commons" from inside the hospital-industrial complex ("Body Maps" 335; *Hospitalogy* 89). This practice of citation allows Wolach to politicize and mobilize disability because it enables them to engage with and choose a community despite and beyond their position inside the hospital, an institutional structure that they find dehumanizing because it treats them and their fellow patients as *"things"* rather than as complex individuals (*Hospitalogy* 121). For Wolach, however, this kind of intertextual community-building does not revolutionize the "hospital-industrial complex," because world remaking is not yet reachable or even conceivable in any structural or specific sense and because it is intrinsically unpredictable (*Hospitalogy* 123). Instead, they show that, while disability can be aesthetically, politically, and socially generative, it can also create constraints that make the act of writing more difficult, in Wolach's case by forcing them to literally write their poems from within "hospitals and medical clinics," just at confessional poets Robert Lowell, Sylvia Plath, and Anne Sexton and New York School poet James Schuyler wrote some of their most well-known poems while undergoing treatment at mental institutions like Mclean Hospital ("Body Maps" 334). Wolach mentions exploratory surgery, heartburn, and headaches in passing, but rather than giving sustained descriptions of these painful experiences, they turn this disembodiment into a political, aesthetic strategy by representing their body as an abstraction (*Hospitalogy* 4, 22, 24). For example, they write: "And if love is an act of sub / Mission, bedsores are your deductible" (*Hospitalogy* 8). Here, painful ulcers are imagined as partial payment for medical care, which in turn gets ironically framed as love. By diagramming their experience, Wolach reveals the structure of their pain and the ways that it is caused not only by their mitochondrial disease but also by their subjection to the hospital-industrial complex.

Like Wolach, Brian Teare shows how disability can be the impetus for generative writing constraints. Since the constraints caused by his disability (which is never named in the poems) include – at various points – nausea, pain, headaches, mental fogginess, and severe digestion problems, *The Empty Form Goes All the Way to Heaven* (2015) shows that disability can lead to formal innovation but can also make writing more difficult. Specifically, the grid-like poetic forms that he creates literally allow Teare to produce writing while in pain, in the sense that the regular, linear appearance of the grid helps him to write through the "cognitive fog of illness" by providing a kind of anchor to which he can tether his language ("to fashion" 107). As Teare puts it, prior to acquiring a disability, his "previous poems had all been built through nearly continuous work whose integrity depended on an almost uninterrupted process of composition," but when his symptoms were flaring up, "The grid [...] accommodated long gaps of inactivity, I could hang a few lines or stanzas on the page and come back to them days or weeks later" ("to fashion" 107). In addition to accommodating the embodied aspects of Teare's disability, the grid form "could [also] accommodate uncertainty, silence, and contingency more fully" than his previous writing practice ("to fashion" 108). These concepts became increasingly pertinent to Teare during the five years that he underwent doctors' tests without receiving a diagnosis, which rendered him illegible in the eyes of Western medicine and which contributed to his understanding of disability experience as process rather than monolithic identity (*Empty Form* 58). As he writes in *The Empty Form*, "[...] being ill makes me │ │ / │ │ an object full of process [...] " He continues: "[...] if my voice also takes place as a shape │ │ / │ │ arranged to stop the pain when I pin the grid │ │ / │ │ with acupuncture needles the page clicks shut │ │ " (25). By referring to the vertical lines that frame this poem as "acupuncture needles" that "pin the grid," Teare reinforces the reading of this poem as itself a kind of grid. For Teare, these grid-poems have the potential to alleviate his symptoms. By giving him "[...] a shape │ │ / │ │ arranged to stop the pain [...]," this poetic form enacts his experience with disability and renders it legible not by being cured but by redefining the very terms of legibility and diagnosis themselves.

Most of the writers cited in this chapter are connected not only through overlaps in the poetic forms, themes, and questions that they explore but also through an ever-expanding web of disability-oriented literary magazines, anthologies, arts collectives, and symposia, including The Olimpias, the Nonsite Collective (a loosely affiliated, interdisciplinary Bay Area collaborative), *Wordgathering* (an online journal of disability poetry), *Beauty Is a Verb: The New Poetry of Disability* (an anthology of twentieth- and twenty-first-century writing by poets with physical disabilities), Zoeglossia (a summer retreat for writers with disabilities), the yearly meeting of the Disability Caucus at the American Writers and Poets Conference, and *The Deaf Poets Society* (an online journal of deaf and disability poetry).[8] As the ranks grow, relative newcomers like Matthews, Judd, Ulanday Barrett, Camisha Jones, and torrin a. greathouse are shifting disability aesthetics and poetic practice, and the mid-twenty-first-century promises to be a period where a field that has historically been dominated by straight white men with physical disabilities shifts to one that is increasingly populated by women, people of color, queer and trans people, people with psychiatric disabilities, and people who are neurodiverse.

Notes

1. See Williamson.
2. See Clare.
3. See Northern.

4. According to Sami Schalk, "Crip is shorthand for the word 'cripple' which has been (and is) used as an insult toward people with disabilities, but which has been re-appropriated as an intra-group term of empowerment and solidarity" (n. pag.).

5. The slang phrase "Talk to the hand" was popularized in the mid-1990s. A dismissive way of expressing one's lack of interest in hearing what another person is saying, this phrase was usually accompanied by a "stop" gesture (arm extended, palm facing the other person).

6. DiPietra, Amber. "Re: Proprioception." Received by Declan Gould, January 7, 2016.

7. Wolach uses the pronoun "d" or, alternatively, "they."

8. For example, Marcus, Leto, and DiPietra have participated in Kuppers's Olimpias collective, and all three were also involved in the Nonsite Collective, which also included Wolach. Further, Day, Weise, and Merritt all participated in the "'Against Death What Other Stay Than Love': Disabled Poets Read" session of the 2018 Split This Rock Poetry Festival, while Teare and Day both participated in the 2018 New Disability Poetics Symposium. In addition, Piepzna-Samarasinha contributed an essay to a collection of essays about twentieth-century disabled poet Laura Hershey edited by Day, and Brown is on the American Writers and Poets Disability Caucus Executive Board, working alongside Advisory Board members Weise and Day, while Judd and Matthews are both Cave Canem fellows.

Works Cited

Anger, Christina. "'U' Professor Dances with Her Disability." *The Michigan Daily*, February 15, 2010, www.michigandaily.com/content/petra-kuppers

Bauman, H-Dirksen L., Jennifer L. Nelson, and Heidi M. Rose, editors. *Signing the Body Poetic: Essays on American Sign Language Literature*. University of California Press, 2006.

Brown, Molly McCully. *The Virginia State Colony for Epileptics and Feebleminded: Poems*. Persea Books, 2017.

Clare, Eli. "Stolen Bodies, Reclaimed Bodies." *Public Culture* vol. 13, no. 3, 2001, pp. 359–365.

Davis, Lennard. *Bending Over Backwards: Disability, Dismodernism, and Other Difficult Positions*. New York University Press, 2002.

Day, Meg. "Queerness, Violence, and Poetry: A Conversation with Meg Day." Interview by Michael Stewart. *The Triangle*, May 3, 2017, www.thetriangle pa.org/2017/05/03/queerness-violence-and-poetry-a-conversation-with-meg-day/
We Can't Read This. Gazing Grain Press, 2013.

DiPietra, Amber and Denise Leto. *Waveform*. Kenning Editions, 2011.
"Amber DiPietra and Denise Leto Reading & Discussing Their Poetry." September 27, 2012, The Poetry Center, San Francisco State University, San Francisco, CA. MP4 file.

Gould, Declan. "'Spastic messiah / erotic daughter': On Petra Kuppers's *PearlStitch*." *Jacket2*, July 6, 2017, https://jacket2.org/reviews/spastic-messiah-erotic-daughter

Judd, Bettina. *Patient: Poems*. Black Lawrence Press, 2014.

Kuppers, Petra. "Pearl Stitch/Spherical," www-personal.umich.edu/~petra/under.html
Pearlstitch. Spuyten Duyvil, 2016.

Kuppers, Petra and Neil Marcus. *Cripple Poetics: A Love Story*. Homofactus Press, 2008.

Matthews, Airea. *Simulacra*. Yale University Press, 2017.

Mcruer, Robert. "Compulsory Able-Bodiedness and Queer/Disabled Existence." *Disability Studies: Enabling the Humanities*, edited by Rosemarie Garland-Thomson, Brenda Jo Brueggemann, and Sharon L. Snyder. MLA Publications, 2002, pp. 88–99.

Merritt, Constance. *Blind Girl Grunt: The Selected Blues Lyrics and Other Poems*. Headmistress Press, 2017.

Mishler, Peter and Airea Matthews. "Texting with Anne Sexton." *Literary Hub*, March 22, 2017, https://lithub.com/airea-d-matthews-texting-with-anne-sexton/

Northern, Michael. "A Short History of American Disability Poetry." *Beauty Is a Verb*, edited by Jennifer Bartlett, Sheila Black, and Michael Northern. Cinco Puntos Press, 2011, pp. 18–26.

Perel, Marissa. "*PearlStitch*: Petra Kuppers." *The Poetry Project* vol. 250, 2017, p. 25.

Piepzna-Samarasinha, Leah Lakshmi. *Bodymap: Poems*. Mawenzi House, 2015.

Ridloff, Douglas. "Spoken Without Words: Poetry with ASL Slam." Uploaded by Great Big Story, https://youtu.be/dmsqXwnqIw4

Schalk, Sami. "Coming to Claim Crip: Disidentification with/in Disability Studies." *DSQ* vol. 33, no. 2, 2013, http://dsq-sds.org/article/view/3705/3240

Shockley, Evie. "The 'She' That Means 'I.'" Panel on "New Approaches to Writing and Identity." Modern Language Association Conference, January 2, 2019.

Teare, Brian. "'to fashion a form that pains': Interview with Brian Teare." Interview by Declan Gould. *Denver Quarterly* vol. 52, no. 3, 2018, pp. 107–108.

The Empty Form Goes All the Way to Heaven. Ahsahta Press, 2015.

Weise, Jillian. *The Book of Goodbyes*. BOA Editions, 2013.

Williamson, Bess. *Accessible America: A History of Disability and Design*. New York University Press, 2019.

Wolach, David. *Hospitalogy*. Tarpaulin Sky Press, 2013.

"Body Maps and Distraction Zones." *Beauty Is a Verb*, edited by Jennifer Bartlett, Sheila Black, and Michael Northern. Cinco Puntos Press, 2011, pp. 334–339.

8

SARAH DOWLING

Queer Poetry and Bioethics

The American lyric poem deals with relation. In lyric poems, as we know, an "I" calls out to another, a "you." Whether explicitly or implicitly, lyric poems work the distance and the tension between these two figures; as readers, we are witnesses to the event of the speaker's movement outward, toward another. I want to say that this relation has always been queer. For one thing, the triumvirate of speaker, addressee, and audience stretches and bends dominant, dyadic models of love. For another, even the "straightest" lyric poems partake of a queer aesthetic, tending to enshrine impossibility and excess alike. While relation and the blatant apostrophes that mark it are not the only important things about lyric poems, they are among the most pervasive and underdiscussed features of the tradition (Culler 190). If the lyric's prolific and boundless calling-into-relation has failed to preoccupy critics, twenty-first-century poets – particularly queer Indigenous and queer of color poets – have taken particular interest in its voicy, vatic excesses, and in the transformative potential that they hold. What I'll argue here is that queer Indigenous and queer of color poets are remaking the American lyric, precisely through a recasting of the relations that are foundational to it. Queer Indigenous and queer of color poets are building on the lyric's historic breadth of address in order to refuse the bounded individualism that shapes the positions of and divisions between speaker and addressee. Their poems practice and theorize other forms of relation – which go well beyond what "queer" has hitherto meant – in order to speak to, from, and through intimate and intricate connections with land, with air, with water, and with innumerable and interdependent forms of life. What twenty-first-century queer Indigenous and queer of color poetries make clear is that the relationships that make and sustain life are not merely those between human selves. The works that I will consider in this chapter instead explore the possibilities of *sympoiesis* – they begin from the fact that no being is ever alone, calling out for an absent other. Rather, our lives are sustained in and through the existence of whole networks of other beings.[1] The poems I'll discuss retain the physicality associated with the lyric voice but reject its fantasy of a self-organizing, independent consciousness. They explore what might happen when the speaker's crystalline singularity is shattered – first, by a more accurate conception of the interdependence of living beings; and second, by historical and contemporary conditions of mass death. What I attend to in this chapter is the growing prominence, the growing relevance, and the growing urgency of lyric poems that – not only in theme but also in structure – rethink the fundamental relations that make life possible, and that make it livable.

I hope it is clear, then, that I am using the terms "queer" and "bioethics" as a kind of shorthand for describing concepts that are difficult to articulate within the epistemological frameworks that normally house discussions of American poetry. When I use the word "queer," I am not referring only or specifically to 2SLGBTQ+ identities, relationships, or experiences. Instead, I am using "queer" in the expanded and more overtly politicized sense wherein it denotes an opposition to normative conceptions of identity, and an imperative to denaturalize the natural. In this chapter, "queer" serves as an imperfect tool with which to gesture beyond the fundamental conceptions of human exceptionalism and bounded individualism that subtend the lyric tradition.[2] Similarly, when I use the word "bioethics," I am not referring to the study of ethical issues as they relate to medicine and healthcare. Rather, I am using the term in attempt to refer to the broader relations-with-life that are described and theorized in twenty-first-century queer poetries. When I use the term "queer bioethics," then, I am doing so in order to twist the expectations of fundamental personhood that readers bring to lyric poems, and to describe the expanded and expansive ways that twenty-first-century queer poetries theorize how beings relate to one another, materially and in time, through dense networks that include the human but extend far, far beyond it.[3]

I'll root my discussion in *Nature Poem* (2017), a book-length work by queer Kumeyaay poet Tommy Pico. Pico's gritty vocatives ("ugh"), the conversational quality of his writing, and his socio-geographic location in Brooklyn, NY, situate him firmly within whatever generation of the New York School is considered current at the turn of the third decade of the twenty-first-century. In addition to this social and stylistic positioning, Pico's first three books are emphatically lyric: Although book-length projects, they are composed in brief, sonically dense segments, and they share a distinctive "I," a persona named Teebs. This self-described "weirdo NDN faggot" (2) invites autobiographical readings while also offering a degree of artifice that distances the events and opinions described in the poems from Pico's "real life," to quote the title of his first book.[4] Together, Pico's use of this persona and his relationship to the New York School establish the "lyric-reading conventions" through which readers approach and understand his work. That is, readers are explicitly invited to imagine and project a particular speaker, Teebs, on to the poems – in constructing this organizing consciousness, and imagining the book to represent his thoughts, we produce a strategy for reading and making sense of the work.[5] Pico makes astute use of the conventions of lyric poetry and its associated reading practices in order to invoke, if not inaugurate something different – poetry that disidentifies with the form of the person, and that radically expands the tripartite relation of speaker, addressee, and audience that structures the American lyric tradition.[6] What I'll argue in this chapter is that Pico's *Nature Poem* exemplifies a broader trend in queer Indigenous and queer of color poetics in the twenty-first-century: It draws upon lyric conventions in order to demonstrate the profoundly sympoietic ways in which our lives are interlinked with and dependent upon those of other beings. In fitting his speaker, his addressees, and even his audience into complex assemblages of human and nonhuman beings, Pico argues against the bounded, autopoietic concepts of personhood that undergird the lyric. Responding to the racialization of personhood itself, Pico calls for a lyric poem whose significance inheres in another unit of meaning – not the person, but something else.

In their 1938 volume *Understanding Poetry*, Cleanth Brooks and Robert Penn Warren argue that, in understanding and appreciating a poem, readers attain a sense of "conquest over the disorder and meaninglessness of experience" (493). "Perhaps," they opine, "this sense may be the very basis for his exhilaration in the poem – just as it may be the basis for the pleasure one takes in watching the clean drive of the expert golfer or the swoop of a bird in the air, as contrasted with the accidental tumbling of a stone down a hillside" (493). Although Brooks and Warren do not use the word "lyric" in this passage, a number of critics have argued that their description of "successful" poems was instrumental to the making of an "American lyric subject," generally imagined as present in all poetry (Newman 209).[7] This lyric subject organizes and gives meaning to experiences that are otherwise disordered and meaningless; "his" conveyance of order, "his" sense-making, is imagined as an exhilarating "conquest" over the disorder of nature itself (as represented by the stone's accidental tumble down a hill). However, the "exhilaration" provoked by successful poems does not belong only to this lyric subject. Brooks and Warren are not discussing how one takes pleasure in *executing* a clean drive or a swoop through the air. Rather, they suggest that exhilaration is the reader's: It arrives through the act of observing the sense and order constructed in the poem. In other words, Brooks and Warren describe a two-part movement: The speaker separates himself from experience and from nature in order to exert control over the mess and meaninglessness of life. The reader in turn is exhilarated by the speaker's ability to perform this separation, and by the order and control displayed in the poem that is its result.

There is much to be said about the American lyric subject described (or birthed, or calcified) in *Understanding Poetry*. For the present, I will restrict myself to the claim that this figure's separateness from his surroundings and specifically from nature is a racialized and gendered division. As numerous theorists have shown, accounts of the subject as self-making, self-sufficient, and bounded produce this subject via comparison to other, more dependent figures.[8] That is, the autopoietic subject's abstraction from the bodily and the merely natural defines him over and against others who are incapable of autopoiesis. These too-fleshly figures are unable separate themselves from their environment, or to achieve the distance necessary for the production of meaning and aesthetic judgment. While the autopoietic subject achieves spatial and temporal separation from nature, those who are incapable of similar abstraction remain, in Denise Ferreira da Silva's words, "affectable" (xv). They are unable to conquer experience via abstraction, and instead remain mired in disorder and meaninglessness, tainted by their association with the bodily and the natural.

As I have argued elsewhere, there is precious little scholarship in poetics that considers how the racialization of subjectivity and of personhood shapes the American lyric subject.[9] However, it would be impossible not to observe that this question is at the heart of the most significant poetry published in the twenty-first-century.[10] Pico's work is one prominent example of this broader corpus. Without referring directly to Brooks and Warren's volume, *Nature Poem* challenges the foundational conception of the American lyric that it represents, though Pico focalizes his critique through the looser genre term "nature poem." Although numerous schools of American poetry embrace disorder and meaninglessness and reject the artistic project of conquering either, *Nature Poem* is somewhat different in emphasis. In this book, Pico makes clear that he is specifically rejecting discourses of conquest as forms of sense-making, and that he is interrogating the forms of personhood achieved through the separation from an entity called nature. Like many Indigenous poets and poets of color, then, he explicitly questions and critiques the settler colonial scripts encoded in white mainstream aesthetics. His book offers a complex meditation on the concept of a "nature poem": It critiques the ideas that humans are separate from nature, and that we can sit outside of it in order to contemplate it and confer order upon it. Equally, Pico rejects the popular notion that Indigenous peoples are "at one with nature" (Tosone n. pag.). As he points out, such stereotypical depictions reduce Indigenous peoples to "features of the landscape, not human beings, [but] things to be cleared and removed" (Tosone n. pag.). Implicitly, he defines nature itself as a discourse of conquest, often capitalizing it and turning it into a figure with which his persona, Teebs, interacts. Much of the time, Teebs and Nature are one another's antagonists, and Teebs often displays a flippant antipathy toward N/nature and elements thereof, stating at one point "I wd slap a tree across the face" (2) and at another "I can't write a nature poem / bc I only fuck with the city" (Pico 4).

While this apparent hostility goes a long way toward establishing Teebs's distinctive humor, it quickly becomes clear that Pico's critique is not directed toward N/nature, and that the book does not express a desire to achieve greater separation from it. Rather, Pico's critique is directed toward the "settler common sense" within which the entity called the individual or the person is imagined as a distinct and bounded entity, separate from its surrounding environment.[11] Pico's densely patterned repetition makes clear that a nature poem is impossible for anyone: It's a fallacy to imagine that we can separate ourselves from nature when our bodily selves exist only in relationship to other beings. Moreover, Pico reveals that it is particularly impossible for him, as an Indigenous person, to write a nature poem: "a nature poem," he explains, is "fodder for the noble savage / narrative" (2). That is, the nature poem – wherein a lyric subject separates himself from nature in order to mine meaning from it – is part and parcel of the broader discourse that reduces Indigenous peoples to and equates Indigenous peoples with mere nature.

Nature Poem begins with images of ecological collapse that demonstrate the impossibility of achieving any meaningful separation from nature, and the profound limitations of the bounded individualism and human exceptionalism that undergird the American lyric. Pico's densely textured and unpredictable use of repetition links his own body to the bodies of other creatures. These other animals are not symbols of a more important human experience that forms the meaning of the poem. Rather, Pico makes clear that all of the organisms he describes are intimately connected to one another, especially insofar they are all undergoing similar experiences by living in times of mass death: "The stars are dying / like always, and far away, like what you see looking up is a death knell from light, right? Light / years. But also close, like the sea stars on the Pacific coast. Their little arms lesion and knot and pull away / the insides spill into the ocean. Massive deaths" (1). At first, Pico's references to star death and to the epidemic of sea star–associated densovirus first observed along the west coast of North America in 2013 appear as images, examples, or metaphors.[12] That is, the poem initially seems testimonial: It describes pervasive conditions of "Massive" death that are at once "far away" and "also close." The pervasiveness of these deaths seems to prompt the speaker to reconsider his oath to "never write a nature poem." However, it is not simply that these conditions trouble the speaker's "sleep" and induce him to testify to the ecological crisis that he observes. The use of repetition – "arms," "fine," "insides," "spill," "pull," and "*pulled*" – makes links between the speaker's body and other nonhuman bodies, as well as with the broader cosmos. Just like the sea stars or the beach sand, his body is irradiated, attacked, pulled apart, and spilled. With all this spontaneous overflow, it becomes clear that the human experience does not stand out as different from or as superior to the experiences of other creatures; instead, Pico makes campy links between radically dissimilar forms of life. The images of deliquescing, stretching, and spilling bodies explicitly challenge the dominant conception of the human individual as a bounded entity, while the parallels between radically different organisms challenge conventional assumptions of human exceptionalism. For all the technological savvy indicated by our ability to watch workout videos on YouTube (which the poem elsewhere describes), Pico suggests that we are more like invertebrates than we are unlike them – we are related to and can't separate ourselves from these other creatures.

This refusal to separate from nature in order to impose sense and meaning upon it in the form of a poem becomes a refrain throughout the book, echoing in the declaration "I can't write a nature poem" (2, 4, 15, 50, 56), in the hedging descriptions of the "kind of nature I would write a poem about" (2, 7, 27), and in the vow that opens and closes the book, "I would never write a nature poem" (1, 67).[13] This refusal does not arise from mere exhaustion with the genre; that is, it is not based on Pico's sense that nature poems are no longer contemporary, or that they are irrelevant to urban (or urbane) queers. Instead, *Nature Poem* exposes the fallacies undergirding the very idea of nature, and uses the lyric's capacity for inaugurating relationships across radical difference in order to invoke (if not quite realize) another possibility. As Teebs encounters disorder and meaninglessness, as he is pulled apart and unbound, as he fucks and is fucked, we readers are provoked to a different exhilaration. This exhilaration does not arrive from our observations of the orderliness of conquest but from an assertion of connectedness that undoes our normative, and in some cases hard-won human distinctness. This is an exhilaration that disidentifies with personhood in order to transform and reinvigorate the lyric's relation-making power.

As *Nature Poem* moves toward its conclusion, Pico returns to the references to stars and sea stars that open the book, signaling a kind of closure. However, at this late stage he significantly complicates the ways in which he has described the relationship between Teebs and n/Nature, letting the antagonism between them dissipate. He writes: "You can't be an NDN person in today's world / and write a nature poem. I swore to myself

I would never write a nature / poem. Let's be clear, I hate nature – hate its *guts* / I say to my audience" (67). Pico's first line break suggests the ways in which being an "NDN person" is popularly construed as being at odds with the modernity of "today's world." To "write a nature poem," he suggests, is to fall backwards into anti-modernity and to confirm one's interlocutors' most demeaning misconceptions. That is, for him to write a nature poem would reconfirm readers' desires to consume a representation of an Indigenous person's special intimacy with – or fundamental inseparability from – nature. Seeking to counteract stereotype, Teebs declares "I hate nature – hate its *guts*." Yet this is reported speech; it's what he says to "my audience" and, presumably, for their benefit. What comes next is something that he says "to myself," but also something that, in characteristically lyric fashion, is read or heard or overheard by readers of *Nature Poem* – another audience, with a different kind of access to Teebs's interiority. The simple statement "*I don't hate nature at all*" inaugurates a shift in the poem's language, a swerve away from its normative, speech-based syntax. Entities – "places," "hills," "the river," "the bluffs," and "the jellybean moon" – are described as thinking, loving, gobbling, purring, laughing, and even "sugar[ing]." Rather than producing meaning through the separation of a single, thinking entity from nature, the conclusion of *Nature Poem* places its speaker within an environment replete with entities that act, emote, and interact with him. This emplacement, this situation among responsive entities who vocalize along with the poet, purring and laughing and allowing him to breathe, offers a transformative vision of sympoiesis. This multiplicity of active entities – proliferating through a disjunction between selves and audiences – points to the possibility of a lyric poem or a lyric subject not founded in crystalline singularity or in abstraction from experience. Pico's account of emplacement and the syntactic convolution that is its result ask the audience of his poem to find another kind of exhilaration, to find meaning in the speaker's profound connectedness rather than in his distinct and unique separation from a surrounding disorder.

Nature Poem twists and turns away from the normative expectations of personhood structuring the American lyric: It refuses any notion that the distinct and unique personhood of its speaker forms the source of the poem's meaning. In addition to Pico's descriptions of his speaker as situated among multiple speaking and acting entities – that is, his fundamental refusal to separate from nature – Pico also enacts sympoiesis through the saturation of his text with other texts, structuring the book through a mixtape's worth of pop songs. References to Guns N' Roses's "Welcome to the Jungle" (12), Amy Winehouse's "Love Is a Losing Game" (14), Cher's "Half Breed" (50), and Tracy Chapman's "Fast Car" (69) serve to place this book within a long lineage of queer poetry that takes pop music as its raw material. Pico's work differs from this largely urbane queer corpus, however, insofar as his use of and references to highly recognizable pop songs serve to amplify his queer bioethical critiques of bounded individualism and of human exceptionalism.

Pico's reference to Guns N' Roses is not only explicit; it's over the top: *"knees, knees* (in a Guns N' Roses way)" (12). The phrase *"knees, knees"* not only features repetition; the fact that it is italicized suggests that it is a quotation, while the parenthetical statement that follows it clarifies its source (perhaps encouraging readers to imagine it uttered in Axl Rose's nasal, uptalky whine). However, this parenthetical attribution, along with the use of repetition, enacts a swerve: *"knees, knees"* follows the lines "waterways / kiss the bees," such that the expression "the bees' knees" collides with Axl's faux-sexy warning. We are kissing the bees' *"knees, knees ... // goodbye."* The unaffected swagger evinced in the band's lyrics is referenced in the lines, "The world is a bumble bee // in the sense that *who cares?"* That is, bees have become a prominent symbol of the ecological devastation that a small minority of powerful humans have wrought. Pico's speaker's sense that no one *"cares"* is communicated not as direct, heartfelt realization but through a multilayered, quotational collage, performed with a nod to Guns N' Roses's hip-swiveling disdain for the feminine and the powerless. Italicized words reveal layers of attribution; they take the place of the speaker's intimate thoughts. Like "systemic pesticides," phrases and fragments are absorbed and accumulate; external elements appear in the speaker's "every cell," in his "soil" and "waterways." The lyric subject, like the bumblebee who succumbs to a buildup of toxins, is overwhelmed by the external elements from which he cannot be separated.

Much like Pico's opening references to marine life forms, the construction of his book as a mixtape refuses the models of speakerly singularity and (of course) of poetic originality that continue to dominate. Especially when considered in relationship to the conceit of critiquing the nature poem, Pico's writing-through of pop songs offers a striking example of what the late queer of color critic José Esteban Muñoz termed "disidentification." That is, Pico's text recycles and rethinks existing cultural texts: Saturated with material that is external to the speaker, the book exposes the universalizing and exclusionary force of dominant cultural scripts. Although the incorporation of these texts reveals the ways in which Teebs and others like him are prevented from transcending their social environments and attaining the universalizing abstraction of personhood, Pico's message is not one of straightforward rejection. Rather, in working on and through individual pop songs, and in working on and through the idea of the nature poem, he makes space for the "weirdo NDN faggot[s]" whom the dominant culture has made unthinkable. Beginning from the experiences of those who are forbidden from or opposed to attaining the significance that comes from conquering disorder, Pico composes a poem about another kind of nature, and theorizes a different relationship to it. He rejects the normative separation between nature and culture, pointing to the planetary consequences resulting from it. More specifically, he critiques the consequences of this separation for queer Indigenous people living in what is currently the United States.

The fact that *Nature Poem* is so deeply rooted in the practices and aesthetics of disidentification leads to some of the thorniest questions that the project considers – questions that are at the heart of twenty-first-century American poetics. Namely, *Nature Poem* asks what it means to disidentify with personhood itself, and with the models of it that are encoded in lyric poetry. Pico is very clear that the dominant cultural scripts for personhood – of which the lyric poem is one prominent example – were never meant to accommodate those whose disordered and unabstractable experiences reduce them to mere nature. *Nature Poem* shows that the American lyric partakes of a settler colonial ethos: It constructs significance and meaning by severing the webs of relation that would tie its subject into a network of other beings, and that would compel that subject to behave responsibly toward the beings to whom it is connected. In making this claim, *Nature Poem* takes its place alongside the most challenging and provocative poetry of the twenty-first century. Like Claudia Rankine's *Citizen: An American Lyric* (2014), Danez Smith's *Don't Call Us Dead* (2017), Bhanu Kapil's *Ban en Banlieue* (2015), Layli Long Soldier's *Whereas* (2017), Divya Victor's *Kith* (2017), and countless other recent texts by US-based writers of color, *Nature Poem* examines the affective and psychic costs of disidentifying with personhood itself. Working on and working with the lyric, it reveals the ways in which this tradition participates in the racialization of personhood, and also offers potential ways to transform the tradition such that it would see aesthetic value in, and confer aesthetic value upon, something other than abstraction from the body, from experience, and from nature.

In other words, *Nature Poem* asks whether the American lyric can do the cultural work of making another kind of meaning. Rather than asserting the singularity of abstract, autopoietic, race-neutral entities called persons or speakers, whose unique perceptions are apprehended by the reader as the significance of the poem, Pico, like other poets of color, turns to this tradition in order to interrogate its uncritical embrace of notions of personhood that depend upon abstractability, upon a universality conferred in disembodiment. *Nature Poem* performs a queer bioethics in that it refuses to jettison the body; it refuses to transcend bodily specificity. Instead, Pico works on and through the other features of the lyric in order to call for a "nature poem" of a different kind – one that refuses myths of autopoiesis. The voicy, conversational, socially embedded, and profoundly physical qualities often noted in Pico's work are its most distinctly lyric features, and these are the sources of the potential transformation it identifies for the American lyric tradition. Pico takes the lyric's expansive potential for inaugurating relations across difference – long a resource for queer American poetry – and uses these features to counteract the tradition's emphasis on human singularity. He calls for – and offers an example of – a poetry whose significance lies in relatedness, not in distinction. In its subject and in its structure, *Nature Poem* shows that bounded individualism and human exceptionalism are limited and limiting ways to make meaning – that in pursuing a meaning in which we escape networks of relation, we will write ourselves out of existence. Pico's queer bioethics lies in his critique of the privileging of human lives over those of other creatures, and in his simultaneous critique of the ways in which many of us are prevented from becoming human. He shows that a sympoietic lyric can do the work of producing another and a better kind of relation, and what could be queerer than remaking relations not only among humans but between humans and the other forms of life among whom we live?

Notes

1. I draw the term sympoiesis from Donna Haraway. She writes: "*Sympoiesis* is a simple word; it means 'making-with.' Nothing makes itself; nothing is really autopoietic or self-organizing. In the words of the Inupiat computer 'world game,' earthlings are *never alone*. That is the radical implication of sympoiesis. *Sympoiesis* is a word proper to complex, dynamic, responsive, situated, historical systems. It is a word for worlding-with, in company. Sympoiesis enfolds autopoiesis and generatively unfurls and extends it" (Haraway 58).
2. There is a growing body of work in queer theory that moves beyond the human in order to consider the ways in which different forms of life are connected. For two radically different examples of this dynamic body of scholarship, see Tortorici and Chen.
3. I draw the term "queer bioethics" from Lance Wahlert and Autumn Feister, who have pushed for a more justice-oriented bioethics, which they call "queer bioethics." Wahlert and Feister describe queer bioethics as follows: "[It] places the 'less powerful' center-stage; it challenges the status quo and the presumptive legitimacy of the normative; it employs powerful intellectual resources from neighboring fields (queer theory, disability studies, medical humanities, and the history of medicine); and, it challenges our complacency in the face of injustice and discrimination" (ii). Wahlert and Feister also argue that "queer bioethics mandates a change in both the topical and methodological approaches to queer identity" – notably, they argue that queer bioethics challenges clinicians' and theorists' "expectations and affirmations of fundamental personhood" (iii).

4. *IRL*, the title of Pico's first book, is a term used online to distinguish what happens "in real life" from what happens online, or "url." "NDN" is a term used by Indigenous peoples to refer to themselves; it is pronounced the same way as the word "Indian," and is often used online, as a self-identificatory shorthand. It is worth noting that Pico has a significant online presence, with approximately 9,000 followers on Twitter at the time of writing. While someone else ought to write an essay on the relationship of contemporary poetry to Twitter, I will simply observe that Pico's Twitter handle, @heyteebs, further blurs the lines between the speaker of his first three books and his own "authentic" utterances: Does it identify Pico as Teebs, or does it serve as an apostrophe addressing his poetic persona?

5. I'm borrowing the phrase "lyric-reading conventions" from Gillian White's excellent *Lyric Shame: The "Lyric" Subject in Contemporary American Poetry* (162).

6. See Muñoz.

7. See also White.

8. See da Silva; Lloyd.

9. See Dowling.

10. See Javadizadeh.

11. See Rifkin.

12. See Crane.

13. There are small variations across the repetition of these lines. For example, the phrase "I can't write a nature poem" sometimes appears as "I can't write a fucking nature / poem" (Pico 15). Similarly, the vow "I would never write a nature poem" also appears as "I'll never write a nature poem" (Pico 62).

Works Cited

Brooks, Cleanth, and Robert Penn Warren. *Understanding Poetry*. Henry Holt & Company, 1938.

Chen, Mel Y. *Animacies: Biopolitics, Racial Mattering and Queer Affect*. Duke University Press, 2012.

Crane, Brent. "Starfish Suffer Mysterious and Gruesome Demise Along West Coast." *The Guardian*, May 3, 2015, www.theguardian.com/environment/2015/may/03/starfish-sea-star-deaths-west-coast

Culler, Jonathan. *Theory of the Lyric*. Harvard University Press, 2015.

da Silva, Denise Ferreira. *Toward a Global Idea of Race*. University of Minnesota Press, 2007.

Dowling, Sarah. *Translingual Poetics: Writing Personhood under Settler Colonialism*. University of Iowa Press, 2018.

Haraway, Donna. *Staying with the Trouble: Making Kin in the Cthulucene*. Duke University Press, 2016.

Lloyd, David. *Under Representation: The Racial Regime of Aesthetics*. Fordham University Press, 2018.

Javadizadeh, Kamran. "The Atlantic Ocean Breaking on Our Heads: Claudia Rankine, Robert Lowell, and the Whiteness of the Lyric Subject." *PMLA* vol. 134, no. 3, 2019, pp. 475–490.

Muñoz, José Esteban. *Disidentification: Queers of Color and the Performance of Politics*. University of Minnesota Press, 1999.

Newman, Steve. *Ballad Collection, Lyric, and the Canon: The Call of the Popular, from the Restoration to the New Criticism*. University of Pennsylvania Press, 2007.

Pico, Tommy. *Nature Poem*. Tin House, 2017.

Rifkin, Mark. *Settler Common Sense: Queerness and Everyday Colonialism in the American Renaissance*. University of Minnesota Press, 2014.

Tortorici, Zeb. *Sins Against Nature: Sex and Archives in Colonial New Spain*. Duke University Press, 2018.

Tosone, Austen. "Tommy Pico's New Book Confronts American Indian Stereotypes." *Nylon*, May 9, 2017, https://nylon.com/articles/tommy-pico-nature-poem-interview

Walhert, Lance and Autumn Feister, "Queer Bioethics: Why Its Time Has Come." *Bioethics* vol. 26, no.1, 2012, pp. ii–iv.

White, Gillian. *Lyric Shame: The "Lyric" Subject in Contemporary American Poetry*. Harvard University Press, 2014.

9

SUEYEUN JULIETTE LEE

Trauma and the Avant-Garde

At its core, avant-garde work strives to rankle, stress, challenge, and even insult or outrage its audiences. By disrupting aesthetic conventions, or our sense of "taste," avant-garde work claims to invite its audiences to interrogate the institutional, cultural, and social norms that shape our perceptions of the world. When successful, avant-garde work functions as a true *vanguard*, (violently) ushering in new aesthetic possibilities for the field and expanding our worldviews. When it fails, it disappears from relevance and view.

The avant-garde is also a battle for resources. Avant-gardists are fighting for audiences, opportunities, prestige, and money. Their efforts to upend aesthetic conventions also serve to bring their work into (often) valuable legibility. At their most successful, avant-gardes became institutionally ascendant and their practitioners financially profited. We can look to T. S. Eliot as just one example of this phenomenon. Writing into the wound of what he perceived as history's collapse, his work radically departed from lyric norms, helped usher modernism into view, and later won the Nobel Prize. It isn't by chance that artists and now scholars use a military term to describe these disruptive aesthetic movements – the financial and social stakes are very real.

In twentieth-century US poetry, we can recognize avant-garde work for its disavowal of historic forms and genres, inclusion of nonliterary texts and materials, and centering proceduralism over craft. As we move into the twenty-first century, we can see how these institutionally ascendant practices have helped bring to light artists from marginalized communities who use these strategies to address the historic traumas and ongoing harms their people experience. How can we ever adequately represent the impacts of colonization, slavery, state-sanctioned ethnic cleansing, or war? In revoking traditional poetic forms and striking into new – in some cases unrecognizable – terrain, these writers produce liberatory work that demonstrates their resistance, resilience, and alterity in form and content. As these writers' work garners recognition and praise, more institutional resources and opportunities rightfully move their way.

As writers from historically oppressed communities working in an avant-garde framework have come into view, however, their work has illuminated deep tensions within contemporary writing communities regarding how avant-garde practices and practitioners are received. Who can write into the wounds of history? Can experimentation that is unaccountable to or disconnected from harmed communities have meaningful relevance? As history has repeatedly demonstrated, art practices – including avant-garde ones – are not immune from broader problematic cultural tendencies such as white supremacy culture. These considerations have massive implications for North American poetry since the market relies on established educational and cultural institutions for financial backing and visibility. Successful avant-gardists shape the next cultural wave.

I begin with a brief study of a series of events that broke out between 2013 and 2015 around Kenneth Goldsmith's work, in which the tensions between avant-garde practices, cultural trauma, and appropriate authorship spilled into public view. Next, I examine Douglas Kearney and Dawn Lundy Martin's work in the context of black pain and the excess of black signification. I close with a discussion of how South Asian diaspora writers Bhanu Kapil and Divya Victor inventively appropriate and redefine whiteness through a process I call "compos[t]itional witness."

The Traumatic Stuplime/Stupid Witness

The 2000s were going remarkably well for conceptual writer Kenneth Goldsmith. A provocateur and advocate of "uncreative writing," in which an author recomposes and reframes existing texts rather than writing original ones, Goldsmith slowly transformed his literary notoriety into real institutional power and visibility. In 2004, he started teaching at the University of Pennsylvania; by 2011, he was a featured reader at President Obama's celebration of American poetry at the White House. In 2013, he was appointed the Museum of Modern Art's first ever poet laureate and appeared on *The Colbert Report* – a satirical news and late night talk show with more than 1 million viewers per night – to promote his latest book *Seven American Deaths and Disasters*.

On August 9, 2014, black teenager Michael Brown was shot six times by officer Darren Wilson after Michael allegedly tried to grab the police officer's gun. His death ignited massive protests in Ferguson, Missouri and fueled a national grassroots movement to fight anti-black racist violence now known as Black Lives Matter. Five months after the shooting, when the national conversation about police violence in black communities was roiling, Goldsmith created a national literary scandal when he read a slightly altered version of Michael Brown's autopsy report as a poem titled "The Body of Michael Brown" onstage at an academic literary conference, Intercept 3.

Given the political and social climate at the time, the response to his performance was vehement and swift, warranting coverage by *The Guardian*, *The New Yorker*, *Hyperallergic*, The Poetry Foundation, *Los Angeles Review of Books*, and several other outlets. Writing for *Art In America*, Brian Droitcour reflected on his experience as a participant at the Intercept 3 conference and witness to the reading.

> While Goldsmith's lilting inflections brought out the repetitions, they seemed somewhat out of place. At times they seemed to disguise his discomfort with the text and his mispronunciations of medical terms. The last lines Goldsmith read were a description of Michael Brown's genitals; later fact-checking confirmed suspicions raised by the audience that the report had been altered to make it end there. It was a dramaturgical gesture to make for a "satisfying" ending, but the audience didn't want that tawdry satisfaction. It wasn't worth the violence done to the text and to the memory of Michael Brown. It was a grave misstep. (n. pag.)

Outrage centered on how Goldsmith's alterations reanimated traumatic anti-black racist histories, such as the medical subjugation of poor black communities, and accused him of trying to advance his notoriety at the expense of black pain. The outrage was particularly animated by Goldsmith's prominence as an avant-garde author who had gained immense institutional power.

A people of color–led coalition of writers anonymously banded together as The Mongrel Coalition Against GringPo to use social media to publicly address this incident and other racist offenses in the experimental writing community. They utilized sarcasm, meme culture, and call-outs to highlight the latent white supremacy in conceptual poetry's emerging canonization. Another of their targets was conceptual writer Vanessa Place, who since 2009 had been tweeting the text of *Gone with the Wind* from a Twitter account featuring a photo of Hattie McDaniel, who played the role of Mammy. Though Goldsmith ultimately offered an apology, the Mongrel Coalition's efforts did not impact his reputation, ongoing arts opportunities, or exposure. In 2015, he was interviewed by *The Guardian* about his latest work, *Capital*. The Coalition, however, was successful in ousting Place from the American Writing Program's subcommittee for the 2016 LA conference.

As two of the more visible practitioners of an institutionally ascendant mode of conceptual writing, Goldsmith and Place have been accused of perpetuating racist ideologies, exhibiting thoughtless white privilege, garnering notoriety and opportunities off the pain of historically oppressed communities, and have been held up as examples of white supremacy in the avant-garde. The accusations against these authors is directly tied to their aesthetic practice – primarily their use of appropriation and plagiarism, for how their work ambiguously de- or recontextualizes culturally traumatic texts.

In my essay "Shock and Blah: Offensive Conceptual Poetry and the Traumatic Stuplime," I identified the general dis-ease with this mode of conceptual writing in how such writing invokes a *traumatic stuplime*. The *traumatic stuplime* draws from traumatic materials in a procedural, repetitious manner that simultaneously inflames and exhausts emotional responses to the work, thereby invoking an anxious ambiguity over the author's intentions. The conceptual simplicity of such works creates an entangled psychological response from audiences and readers – the implication being that those who feel outrage are not sophisticated enough to appreciate the clever critique in the work.

Place has a much longer history of appropriating culturally traumatic materials in her work. For Goldsmith, however, the turn to trauma was relatively new. His major previous works, such as *Day* (2003), *Weather* (2005), *Traffic* (2007), and *Sports* (2008) were all centered in exploring relatively banal materials such as weather or traffic reports. *Seven American Deaths and Disasters* (2013) was his first foray into cultural trauma. He transcribed archival radio and news reports on nationally riveting events: the John F. Kennedy, Robert F. Kennedy, and John Lennon assassinations, the space shuttle *Challenger* disaster, the Columbine shootings, 9/11, and the death of Michael Jackson. Stephen Colbert offered a surprisingly resonant response to this book when he hosted Goldsmith on his talk show in 2013:

> All these things, these seven different events – we know what's happening when we read this. These people – who are just living their lives, thinking it's an ordinary day – don't know it's coming. When I read this, I feel like I'm some sort of time traveling aesthete who is coming in to sample other people's shock and tragedy. I'm tasting their disbelief and the way it's changing them forever. I am tasting them while I read it. And it feels vampiric. Are you giving us a feast of other people's blood? (n. pag.)

In her rebuke of Kenneth Goldsmith in *The New Republic*, poet Cathy Park Hong wrote:

> In fact, even before the performance, Goldsmith's "brand" was in trouble. His PoMo for Dummies "no history because of the internet" declarations became absurdly irrelevant when black men were dying at the hands of cops.

> Goldsmith, who previously exhibited zero interest in race, saw that racism was a trending topic and decided to exploit it to foist himself back in the center and people roared back in response. (n. pag.)

Should we see Goldsmith's interest in trauma as a cynical way to stay relevant? Or was he responding to the social current? The answer is perhaps both.

After further reflection, I now feel that another way we can understand the traumatic stuplime in Goldsmith's Michael Brown piece is one of *stupid witness*. Stupid witness implies that the readers/receivers of the work lack sophistication or intelligence, or that the work exhausts them from considering it clearly: *they just don't get it*. Stupid witness, more importantly, points us to the work's creator – *what were they thinking?*

The physiological and cultural relationship between trauma and stupidity is no joke. Common sense frequently flies out the window because crisis logic is often not logical at all. In a traumatic situation, many survivors describe being unable to react – even *witnesses* can be struck dumb for a period of time. I therefore find it no surprise that as a society we have yet to devise reasonable, humane, or thoughtful measures for addressing trauma; by nature, trauma wounds us so greatly that it overwhelms and stupefies.

I think stupid witness is a useful way to describe the ways white authors have problematically sought to address our cultural anti-black racism and violence. The trauma and outrage for black communities in the wake of Michael Brown's shooting are immeasurable. The stupidity of many white responses should also be expected as a cultural trauma response. White supremacy culture, which continues to dominate our institutions including art institutions, is incapable of adequately or meaningfully addressing black pain.

Black Pain/Signifying Surplus

I am no expert in black experiences or black pain. I am, however, someone who has paid careful attention to the historical and social dynamics of oppression, and how that has been expressed, explored, and disrupted through various aesthetic strategies. For me, any productive understanding of cultural trauma in a North American context must account for our collective anti-blackness. The intense variety and depth of anti-black oppression has fueled – and continues to fuel – many of the core social and economic structures that shape our reality.

The collective and accumulated legacy of anti-blackness that is instantly mapped onto black bodies and lives results in a massive excess of signification that black artists contend with. In *In the Break*, scholar Fred Moten articulates how "black performance has always been the ongoing improvisation of a kind of lyricism of the surplus – invagination, rupture, collision, augmentation. [...] It's an erotics of the cut, submerged in the broken, breaking space-time of an improvisation. Blurred, dying life; liberatory, improvisatory, damaged love; freedom drive" (7). Douglas Kearney and Dawn Lundy Martin, two very different black writers, contend with this "surplus" of signification in their work using divergent strategies.

Much of Kearney's work offers virtuosic performances of improvisation, collision, rupture, and augmentation through an often deliberate performance of excess in his typographic works, particularly evident in his series "That Loud-Assed Colored Silence" from his 2016 poetry collection *Buck Studies*. Presented as collaged torn and layered text with various white-outs, font sizes, and overwrites, these works are visually "loud" in a way that conjures layers of posters lining public walkways in metropolitan downtowns. There's an electric energy to how they confront the reader, asking them to abandon a conventional understanding of how a poem "should" appear on the page. These works invoke graphic design and literature.

In "That Loud-Assed Colored Silence: Protest," Kearney directly references and protests the surplus of signification that is blackness. If we imagine this work in visual layers, the base or farthest background layer references the famous civil rights protest song, "We shall overcome someday." However, the lyrics have been transformed – some of the parts that are legible read, "We are overcome. We are all afraid." The next layer appears in the largest font of the piece; "AIN'T I AN AM?" "I AIN'T WHAT!" and "I CAN'T AIN'T!" are further emphasized by their placement in rectangular boxes (Kearney 31).

The next layer up is composed of permutations of the now nationally recognized campaign and hashtag #BLACKLIVESMATTER, but transposed as #BLACKLIVESSTUTTER, #BLACKLIVESSTAMMER, #BLACKLIVESYAMMER, and #BLACKLIVESMUTTER. Significantly, all these permutations connect the movement for black liberation to a physical inability to speak clearly. The layers of different typographies reference different periods of time and competing rhetorics. This work refuses to let us ignore the violent erasure and consumption of black bodies across history through the visual layering of language. There is so much to say about his work as an act of survival – of taking debris, reframing the bits into a performative excess.

We can see his use of satire in "Well Hung," which simultaneously references racist generalizations around black men's genitalia as evidence of their hypersexuality – a racist trope that was frequently brought up as justification for the lynching of black men. His use of black humor, a biting satire demonstrated in his word play, is yet another strategy for how he contends with the signifying surplus that is blackness. Numerous types of text overlap and overwrite each other – repeating passages are often just clusters of sounds (aka phrases that read like noise such as "fap" or "ng," which also reference the sounds of sexual activity). In vertical text down the left side of the page, we read "Whacked blacks often got stiffs whacked off" (Kearney 24). Visually, he's created a pun – this text serves as a visual reminder of a length of taut rope while also referencing an erection. The "stiffs" simultaneously evokes corpses (stiffened in death) and the way white lynch mobs frequently castrated their black victims.

Kearney ably reworks the excess of meanings that coagulate around black (male) bodies into a visually rich, multilayered text that insists upon identifying *and* dismantling the various violences and histories that shape black experiences. Dawn Lundy Martin's work tends toward a minimalist gravity for addressing trauma and the signifying surplus of blackness. Her 2014 poetry collection *Life in a Box Is a Pretty Life* illustrates and destabilizes some of the ways that black female subjectivity continues to be framed by mis/conceptions and mis/representations of the black female body. *And what do we really know about the black female body?* Though never explicitly posited in her book, this question floats as a central premise around her pieces and requires us to consider the ways that representational violence, colonial history, and ongoing gender and racial prejudice continue to shape psychic realities.

A book-length work in hybrid prose and minimalist lyric sections, *Life in a Box Is a Pretty Life* is not always "pretty." With section titles like "WITHOUT KNOWING THE SLIGHTEST THING ABOUT WAR, I FIND MYSELF AN INSTRUMENT OF LABOR, INVESTIGATION, AND EXPERIMENT" (Martin 69) and "IT WILL BE HEARBY OBSERVED THAT NIGGAS GET SHOT IN THE FACE FOR THAT MENACING, THREATENING LOOK!" (Martin 42) the book can run rough over the reader in parts. Martin's poetry questions the basis by which we expect particular modes of pleasure from art. We can see how she elects this stance by opening her collection with an epigraph from black artist Kara Walker: "What strikes me is how easy it is to commit atrocities" (Martin i). The "easy" Walker alludes to reflects the "common sense" attitudes that ideologies masquerade under when uninterrogated. Walker's own art practice challenges the aestheticization of racial violence by forcing her viewers to confront these qualities in an art context, removing the "ease" in "pleasure" when we view her work. Walker's black-and-white cutouts charm with their beautifully delineated silhouettes. They also horrify viewers through their graphic depictions of violence, such as a child being choked or hanged. Her works regularly implicate the viewer by exploring the racialized dynamic between their gaze and the black body, which was perhaps best expressed in a recent interview she gave on the way the public responded to her gigantic sugar sphinx, "A Subtlety, Or the Marvelous Sugar Baby."

The box that Martin's title alludes to could be many things, but its shadowy power is persistently made evident. Whether the sexual box of the female body or the conceptual boxes we create in order to tick off categories, the box frames and focuses our attention while also isolating our view. Martin's work insists that these various "boxes" are vitally, complexly inhabited. Life persists within (and perhaps in spite of) the frame. The first section of the book, "MO[DERN] [FRAME] OR A PHILOSOPHICAL TREATISE ON WHAT REMAINS BETWEEN HISTORY AND THE LIVING BREATHING BLACK HUMAN FEMALE" invokes Carrie Mae Weems's "Framed by Modernism" photo series. A trio of portraits, the images capture Weems with painter Robert Colescott, who had asked her to take his picture. Taken in Colescott's studio, the photos present Colescott fully dressed and in the center of the frame, while, upstage and to the right, Weems leans in the corner, nude. Her nakedness and pose imply that she serves as the painter's model, but his back is turned to her in order to face the camera. In two of the shots, he covers his face in apparent shame while she slouches against the wall. Her interior life is not available to us, unlike Colescott's evident anguish. She remains a cipher, relegated to the corner. The question emerges: Can we truly see the artist (Weems) in the context of this framing? Can we know the black female subject by gazing at her body?

Like Weems, Martin also places herself within the frame and in view – but what are we capable of seeing? What can we see? How are we participating in what we have already seen? The incredible challenge of her work is that she trusts us to recognize the cipher of black female constructions, permitting us to roam with her as she inhabits and navigates through them. Martin demonstrates how frankly challenging it is to live in this described space – to arrive *in medias res* with a prehistory. She describes this experience as a "presence" or "haunting": "You are yourself and no other physical being is there, yet a feeling or sensation emerges as if from nowhere. Like the Negress. The black female body not in repose, instead walking or clickity clack. It knocks at the doors, which is the surface of existence" (Martin 1). This ghosting is problematically productive. "What would we do with her? How would we know ourselves?" What might happen if this body were mobilized, activated, given free rein to roam and roam past the frame? As a racialized female subject, I can appreciate this query. There is no blank field of being – not for anyone – but the power and paradox of race/gender frames can be incredibly stifling. How often is Martin "read" before we really read her work?

Composting Whiteness/Composing Witness

Bhanu Kapil's *Schizophrene* (2011) writes through and re-presents the partially destroyed contents of a failed "*epic* on Partition and its *transgenerational* effects" (emphasis original, 1). On the night she realized her epic had failed, Kapil tossed her manuscript into a snowy field. She recovered the text in the spring, only to discover that the snow melt and thaw, among other natural ecological processes, had partially digested portions of her text into illegibility. Kapil opted to recover the remaining text, maintaining the effaced portions as white spaces in her published book.

Divya Victor's poem "Laundry List" meditates on the 1919 Jallianwala Bagh massacre, where British Indian Army troops fired upon thousands of unarmed Indians gathered in a park. Victor offers a "speculative laundry list of outfits Left Behind by Corpses if all Victims were Female and British, Instead of Indian Women, Men, Children, and Infants" (134). Victor substitutes the Indians' possessions with those of contemporaneous English women, offering a litany of these women's garments *not* rotted with blood.

Kapil and Victor make use of whiteness as a conceptual tool for addressing cultural trauma. By presenting whiteness as a series of effacements and substitutions, both authors' works digest and transform the impossible onus of witness while elegantly highlighting the complex racial and colonial structures motivating the violence. Their projects ultimately demonstrate an ecological approach, where their compositional practices "compost" the cultural trauma through whiteness, repurposing it as a site for generating fertile possibilities of response.

I use the term "conceptual" rather than experimental in order to highlight how a central procedure shapes both of these authors' projects. I argue that the procedural aspects of their writing utilizes what I term a *compos[t]itional practice*. By turning to an ecological/biological metaphor, I want to highlight how these poets' "conceptual" works maintain strong relationships to bodies, geography, and history.

Composed in eight prose sections with a prefatory "passive note," *Schizophrene* attempts to address the legacy of India's Partition as Britain ceded its colonial power. The Partition occurred at the stroke of midnight, August 17, 1947, carving Pakistan out into two discontinuous sections from the Union of India. Primarily motivated by a desire to territorially segregate Muslims from Hindus, the Partition was unpopular and hotly contested, even among the Muslim polity whose interests the Partition ostensibly sought to protect. In Punjab, as noted by cultural historian Ian Talbot, "the important Sikh minority population had no desire to be included in a future state of Pakistan" (404).

The Partition caused incredible confusion and anxiety among the native populace, who were already rocked by intense sectarian, ethnic, and anti-colonial violence. It didn't help that no one knew precisely *where* the new state lines would finally be drawn. The public response was intense: "rather than ending the violence and distrust which had stalked India, [Partition] sparked off massive disturbances, especially in the Punjab region, the historic centre of recruitment for the Indian Army and an area which was awash with weapons" (Talbot 405). A historically diverse region, Punjab was also bisected by western Pakistan's new border. There "the killings approached a genocidal intensity [...] with ethnic cleansing practiced to clear entire districts of minority populations" (Talbot 406).

As a member of the "generation after," Kapil doesn't seek to represent or bear witness to these traumas by narrating them directly. In fact, *Schizophrene* is *not* documentary, neither referencing news accounts nor borrowing from other "official" accounts of the Partition. Instead, Kapil writes from her own thoughts and experiences, weaving in recounted memories and research notes, in a lyrically disjunctive, self-reflective format. Kapil's eschewal of the documentary impulse is rather remarkable. Other experimental or radically composed texts that have sought to address cultural trauma, such as Charles Reznikoff's *Testimony* (1978) or M. NourbeSe Philip's *Zong!* (2008), frequently rely on the transposition of documentary evidence as part of their general aesthetic of witness. Such practices tend to highlight the disjuncture between trauma and its historicization.

By seeking to address Partition by writing through her experiences and research through a lyrically diaristic and notational approach, Kapil, on the other hand, suggests that Partition *moves through her* while it also *evades* her as an object of study or totalizable understanding. Through these breaks and the shifting literary modalities of the text, *Schizophrene* captures a sense of the Partition's *psychic* legacy, which emerges auratically. The sense of threat that hangs over Kapil's being throughout the text is atmospheric in its proliferation across various geographies. It antedates her, haunting her numerous environments before she even steps foot there.

Born long after Partition, herself neither a witness nor a direct survivor, Kapil writes from the space of "postmemory." Coined and developed by cultural theorist Marianne Hirsch in her study of the Holocaust's cultural legacy, postmemory "describes the relationship that the 'generation after' bears to the personal, collective, and cultural trauma of those who came before – to experiences they 'remember' only by means of the stories, images, and behaviors among which they grew up" (5). As a diasporic member of the "generation after," Kapil is separated from the Partition by time and space. For Kapil, the Partition appears as a postmemory characterized by mental illness: Kapil places her project in relation to "the high incidence of *schizophrenia* in diasporic Indian and Pakistani *communities; the* parallel social history of *domestic violence*, relationship *disorders*, and so on" (emphasis original, i).

The aporiatic aspects of Kapil's "recounting" highlight postmemory's necessarily imaginative qualities. Removed across time, but nonetheless deeply affected by these cultural traumas, Hirsch describes how "[p]ostmemory's connection to the past is thus actually mediated not by recall but by imaginative investment, projection, and creation. It is to be shaped, however indirectly, by traumatic fragments of events that still defy narrative reconstruction and exceed comprehension" (5). Kapil writes from her own experiences in a lyrically disjunctive, self-reflective format, weaving in recounted memories and research notes: "I was visiting a person with a *head injury*. A bulky cloud of soot came out of her mouth when she spoke. 'Who's that?'" (16).

Kapil's poetic, fragmented approach points to how this cultural trauma exceeds her ability to address it. Recognizing this, Kapil "threw the book into the dark garden" (1), and the arc of this seed-like failed manuscript's flight becomes an organizing aesthetic of the final text. Constantly writing *toward* the disturbed psychological legacy of the Partition, *Schizophrene* persistently takes flight into numerous interrupted asides. In section "2: India Notebooks," Kapil interlaces two accounts: a scheduled interview with a researcher from the Institute of Community Health Sciences in London and a trip to Vimhans Hospital in New Delhi. Never offering a "full" account of these experiences, Kapil offers fragments of these events, punctuated with vibrant visual descriptions of the minor physical details in these spaces that captured her attention: "the freshly dyed black wool hanging from a line in the garden," and "[t]he garden with its triptych of fuchsia, green, and black. / Complicated zig-zag stems" (20). Importantly, both of these trips are abortive – she ends up *not* meeting with the doctor. She "documented the corridor then went home" (19). Likewise, in New Delhi, Kapil walks through the corridors and pharmacy of the hospital, but then finds herself in the art galleries beyond the waiting room, "where [she] wrote, simmering in a pink shirt, and hurt" (21).

These flights, evasions, and detours point to the Partition's abjection. Kapil's text suggests she can only address this cultural trauma by turning aside, by flinging it from her. This abjection emerges as a structural schizophrenia.

Cultural theorist Fredric Jameson argues that in a world dominated by the proliferation of simulacral images, our experience of events and places is set adrift in a flattened plenitude unmoored from any broader meaning-making narratives. Without a unified sense of history or our location in time, we experience a form of schizophrenia. As schizophrenics, we are reduced to experiencing "pure and unrelated presents" (Jameson 27), or "a new depth-lessness" (Jameson 6).

For Jameson, this schizophrenic condition has interesting psychological consequences. Isolated from other "activities and intentionality that might focus it and make it a subject of praxis," the present moment "suddenly engulfs the subject with undescribable vividness, a materiality of perception properly overwhelming, bearing a mysterious charge of affect" (27), what he also describes as "intensities." This fractured temporality opens the door to a new type of "hysterical" sublime, an overwhelming awe at "the great global multinational and decentered communicational network in which we find ourselves caught as individual subjects" (44).

Schizophrene demonstrates a similar fractal logic and intensity for the diasporic postcolonial subject. The work is almost exclusively in the present tense. While Jameson suggests that schizophrenic temporalities are unmoored from history, Kapil posits a different experience of the present – one rooted in trauma – which creates diasporic schizophrenia. In "7: Partition," Kapil posits an interwoven and *dense* temporality – one that *interjects* past cultural traumas into different geographies. From a traumatic standpoint, schizophrenic temporalities are neither flattened nor loosened from their meaning but proliferate – *thickened* with histories that press with dire intensity. Kapil deftly weaves together her mother's narration of the Partition with allusions to domestic abuse and race riots in London: "There are perhaps eleven faces pressed to the blood-specked window, banging on the glass with their foreheads. Being white, with the delicate skin that accompanies race, they bruise easily. They are looking at the unfolding scene with a boo and a hiss and a *You fucking Paki, what do you think you're doing?*" (49).

The "hysterical sublimity" she experiences is of a different tenor than Jameson proposes: By identifying trauma as the simulacral locus of prolifer-ating images and narrations populating the diasporic subject's landscape, *Schizophrene* points to the *density* of history, which accretes with dizzying psychic intensity, suggesting that schizophrenic temporalities have differen-tiated *geopolitical* valences. These accretions efface distances and spans of time, generating an alternative experience of a *thick present* for the diasporic postcolonial subject.

Her compos[t]itional practice both identifies this temporal/territorial dilemma and seeks to transform it. By flinging her book into the field, Kapil engages the landscape as a collaborating agent. Her use of the destroyed contents of her journal reflects the Partition's impossible cite-ability – it was a "dead" text: "The paper crumbled where I folded it in half. It was *brittle*. It was *damaged*. It was *dead*" (Kapil 61). Yet the visual lapses on the page suggest its persistence. Her collaboration results in an unsettling transformation: The ejected book takes on a strange new form. Digested by snow melt and thaw, "where it's rotted to the bone, the paper is covered with metallic fur, which is not paper" (Kapil 58).

Kapil cites/sights/sites this transformation in the white breaks of the book. Hardly empty, these are *compos[t]itional* spaces that digest and territorialize the Partition *differently*, recalibrating our attention to the bodies, places, and histories that the Partition consumed. The whiteness of these spaces imply the act of witnessing, troubling, plural agency. Rather than fixing this cultural trauma to the past and burying it, Kapil contends that it, like her thrown text, can remain animate *otherwise*. Through her compos[t]ition, Kapil seeks to wrest schizophrenia from its space of cultural overdetermination for the postcolonial diasporic subject, offering it instead as an arc of transformative, perhaps monstrous, possibility.

We can see a similar compos[t]itional strategy in Divya Victor's work to address colonialist violence in her latest collection, *KITH* (2017). The fourth section of a longer poem in series titled "Blood," "Laundry List" is a direct response to the Jallianwala Bagh massacre, in which, as Victor notes, "On April 13, 1919, British Indian Army soldiers under the command of Brigadier-General Reginald Dyer opened fire on an unarmed gathering of men, women and children picnicking in an enclosed urban garden called the Jallianwalla Bhag ... There were around 1000 fatalities" (133). In order to account for the dead, Victor offers up a "speculative laundry list" that offers a summation of the garments they left behind. As a speculative list, however, Victor replaces the Indians' possessions with articles belonging to British women.

The repetitiousness of Victor's replacements multiplies. On the one hand, it enacts an *abjected stuplimity*. The "stuplime," coined by aesthetic theorist Sianne Ngai, "is a response to encounters with vast but bounded artificial systems, permutation and combination, and taxonomic classification" (36). Where Kant's sublime invites us to experience a profound terror that preludes transcendence, stuplimity leads to "cosmic exhaustion rather than terror" (Ngai 36). It "reveals the limits of our ability to comprehend a vastly extended form as a totality, as does Kant's mathematical sublime, yet not through an encounter with the infinite but with finite bits and scraps of material in repetition" (Ngai 271). By being barraged with repetitious phrases and statements, as in Stein's, Beckett's, or Kenneth Goldsmith's numbingly detailed work, stuplimity is "simultaneously astonishing and deliberately fatiguing" (Ngai 261). Victor's "Laundry List" confronts us with an incredible volume of unassimilable data. The violence of this material elicits a fatiguing *horror*. Secondly, the replacements also abject the killed Indian bodies, literally ejecting them from the field of the poem and replacing them with whiteness's *literal* effects (read effects as articles of clothing).

Furthermore, the repetitiousness of Victor's poem enacts a form of aesthetic digestion, working over these various garments until they *mean differently* for us. The gleaming purity of these garments, persistently *not stained in blood*, become filled with the absented Indian dead. The garments finally "drop to pieces," becoming fertile ground for a different mode of witness.

Like Kapil's *Schizophrene*, Victor's work draws its power from writing otherwise, by taking flight, by turning away. Both authors' compos[t]itional practices bear strange fruit: They highlight the diasporic postcolonial subject's *impossibility*. "*You fucking Paki*" elides into a query of puzzlement, of illegibility: *What do think you're doing?* These projects invite us to perhaps embrace our monstrousness, our excess. "*You bleeding animal.*" How does one write as a bleeding animal? Perhaps the answer is through the guts, digestively.

Coda

By examining trauma and the avant-garde, I aim to account for the harm that white supremacy culture perpetuates in our communities and lift up the innovative ways writers of color have sought to dismantle and reckon with this legacy. What I hope to articulate is that the thick relationship between trauma and the avant-garde is not incidental but the (perhaps) inevitable result of an aesthetic strategy whose aim is to disrupt, upend, and interrogate social norms and inheritances. Cultural trauma's relationship to the avant-garde is hardly new – we can look to T. S. Eliot's work and rampant orientalism as an early manifestation of what we wrestle openly with now.

We currently persist in the midst of a collective and very public battle to reckon with our anti-black, misogynistic, homophobic, and xenophobic cultural histories. Social media and the twenty-four-hour news cycle has allowed for a stunning level of immediate visibility to the injustices and intense violences that oppressed communities face. Nationally, it seems we have fallen into a call-out culture as a mode of accountability, which has fostered a social climate of hypervigilance and triggered responses. Our collective capacity for nuanced discussions about aesthetics is understandably thin. The avant-garde will continue to challenge us around these dynamics; some will do so stupidly, others quite brilliantly. What ascends, however, requires our participation and support.

Works Cited

Colbert, Stephen. "Kenneth Goldsmith. *The Colbert Report*. Comedy Central, July 23, 2013.

Droitcour, Brian. "Reading and Rumor: The Problem with Kenneth Goldsmith." *Art in America*, March 18, 2015, www.artinamericamagazine.com/news-features /news/reading-and-rumor-the-problem-with-kenneth-goldsmith/

Hirsch, Marianne. *The Generation of Postmemory: Writing and Visual Culture after the Holocaust*. Columbia University Press, 2012.

Hong, Cathy Park. "There's a New Movement in American Poetry and It's Not Kenneth Goldsmith." *The New Republic*, October 1, 2015, https://newrepublic.com/article/ 122985/new-movement-american-poetry-not-kenneth-goldsmith

Jameson, Fredric. *Postmodernism, Or the Cultural Logic of Late Capitalism*. Duke University Press, 1991.

Lee, Sueyeun Juliette. "Shock and Blah: Offensive Conceptual Poetry and the Traumatic Stuplime." *Evening Will Come: A Monthly Journal of Poetics*, no. 41, May, 2014, www.thevolta.org/ewc41-sjlee-p1.html

Kapil, Bhanu. *Schizophrene*. Nightboat Books, 2011.

Kearney, Douglas. *Buck Studies*. Fence Books, 2016.

Martin, Dawn Lundy. *Life in a Box Is a Pretty Life*. Nightboat Books, 2014.

Moten, Fred. *In the Break: The Aesthetics of Black Radical Tradition*. University of Minnesota Press, 2003.

Ngai, Sianne. *Ugly Feelings*. Harvard University Press, 2005.

Talbot, Ian. "The Partition of India: The Human Dimension." *Cultural and Social History* vol. 5, no. 2, 2009, pp. 403–410.

Victor, Divya. *KITH*. Canada: Bookthug, 2017.

10

JONATHAN SKINNER

Blockade Chants and Cloud-Nets: Terminal Poetics of the Anthropocene

Poetry emerging under the sign of the Anthropocene must, like all cultural work, contend with the terminal horizon of anthropogenic climate change, one that variously shadows poetry's relevance. While this is not the first time that poetry has been asked to negotiate "intellectual formations that are somewhat in tension with each other," the possibilities for alignment – of human with planetary change – seem sharply curtailed (Chakrabarty 213). Such dissonance also is true for the dominant narratives of progress, of the ever less impeded flow of capital, and of "sustainable" global development, as catastrophes, ruptures, and eruptions of social resistance at terminal sites expose the precarity of the dominant petrocapitalist system. New levels of social and environmental complexity, in many regards effects of the same system, open up the possibility for, and the necessity of, uncommon forms of solidarity, in resistance movements run through with insurmountable difference. Poetry that resonates with the chants of protests and, provoked by the indeterminate cloud architecture of digital networks, attempts to weave what cannot be woven convokes these forms of solidarity while exposing the seams of difference. One important seam is a temporal difference between those for whom the Anthropocene harbors an imminent collective future and those for whom it names a long and already too present collective experience of oppression. While these collectives do not overlap, they find themselves forced together at the same barricades, subject to the same unpredictable clouds of atmospheric and digital weather. In many respects, place rather than identity, site rather than form or figure, determine the trajectories of this writing. Discussing poetry by Juliana Spahr, Danez Smith, Stephen Collis, and Layli Long Soldier, the following chapter sounds some of the key differences activating the uncommon solidarities of North American poetry in the emergent awareness of the Anthropocene.

Since even before its inception the twenty-first-century has felt terminal: Y2K, 9/11, War on Terror, Katrina, Great Recession, Deepwater Horizon, Brexit, and Trump, to name just a few of the events that seemed to harbor the end of an era. Other kinds of terminals have mediated these events: airplane terminals, oil pipeline and shipping terminals, gas pumps, banking and computer terminals. The neoliberal global economy had established these terminals as means of controlling and monitoring various critical flows, including those of data. At the same time, the new century has been punctuated by events that seemed to mark a new beginning: Obama, Arab Spring, Occupy, Standing Rock among them. The digital terminal, specifically social media, and the global spread of its algorithms via mobile computing, as a new and unpredictable factor in political movements and democracies, was integral to these hopeful events, while also harboring more dystopian possibilities. Through all this period extreme weather events such as Katrina, "superstorm" Sandy, tornado, heatwave, polar vortex, drought, fire and flood, or the variously named hurricanes battering the coasts with increasing frequency and intensity, kept climate change on the front pages and in the political discourse, while also emphasizing the resilience of the neoliberal economic system, even its ability to profit through "disaster capitalism" (Klein 8–9, 51). As of this publication (2020), nineteen of the twenty warmest years in the record of global average temperatures have occurred since the start of the century ("Global Climate Change: Evidence"). The Intergovernmental Panel on Climate Change (IPCC) 2018 *Special Report on the impacts of global warming of 1.5°C above pre-industrial levels (Summary for Policymakers)* confirms scientific consensus that the global mean warming of one degree Celsius above preindustrial levels reached in 2015 is anthropogenic, with more to come, due to carbon emissions from human activity since the Industrial Revolution (4). More than half of this warming occurred since scientist James Hansen first brought climate change to mainstream attention in his 1988 testimony to US Congress, with business as usual leading to a projected rise of at least four degrees Celsius in global temperatures by the end of the century (Wallace-Wells 4, 15).

In the 2016 Paris Agreement, 196 state members of the Conference of Parties to the United Nations Framework Convention on Climate Change (COP21) negotiated language agreeing to limit the increase in global average temperature to well below two degrees Celsius above preindustrial levels (Wallace-Wells 9). As current pledges to cut CO_2 emissions are still projected to push global warming to at least three degrees Celsius by the end of the century (without taking into account the Trump administration's declared intent to withdraw from the Paris Agreement), the IPCC reported in 2018 that stabilizing global warming at 1.5 degrees Celsius would require a 45 percent reduction of carbon emissions by 2030 (IPCC 12; Wallace-Wells 74). Upper-end projections based on "business as usual" see huge swaths of the Earth becoming uninhabitable by the end of the century

(Wallace-Wells 31). World Bank and UN projections estimate 140–200 million climate refugees by midcentury (8). In 2008, the Stratigraphy Commission of the Geological Society of London considered a proposal to designate a new formal unit of geological epoch divisions, the "Anthropocene," a term used from the early 1980s by ecologist Eugene F. Stoermer and popularized from 2000 by Nobel Prize–winning chemist Paul J. Crutzen, to indicate a geological epoch during which human activity has become the dominant influence on climate and the environment. While the term has yet to be ratified by the International Commission on Stratigraphy (ICS), the group has been directed to identify a marker allowing for a date to be inserted in the chronostratigraphy and is gravitating toward the "golden spike" of the US Army's Trinity test in 1945, the radioactive fallout from which offers a potentially distinct, globally synchronous marker for the current human presence on Earth (Davison n. pag.). (One skeptic, pointing out that the longest-lived radioisotope from radioactive fallout, iodine-129, has a half-life of less than 16 million years, has indicted a certain geological arrogance built into the Anthropocene concept [Brannen n. pag.].) This date also aligns the Anthropocene with the mid-twentieth-century "Great Acceleration" in human activity, population growth, and industrialization (Solnick 5). The twenty-first-century increasingly feels terminal for civilization as we know it, if not for the human species itself.[1]

Literary responses to the Anthropocene cover a spectrum, from focusing on "derangements of scale" and "scalar dissonance" to strange forms of intimacy, entanglement, and swerves of kin-making, to critiquing how the "Anthropocene" concept overrides less monumental distinctions (Clark 150–151; Keller 38; Farrier 9, 12). Historian Dipesh Chakrabarty may have been the first to point to the scale challenges of the Anthropocene as a crisis for his discipline, which is now required "to bring together intellectual formations that are somewhat in tension with each other: the planetary and the global; deep and recorded histories; species thinking and critique of capital" (213). While Jason W. Moore makes the critique of capital the focal point of climate change, Chakrabarty argues that "the whole crisis cannot be reduced to a story of capitalism" (221). This difference is crucial: While the Anthropocene forces species consciousness into the picture – the human species as the difference that makes a difference – for many, its generic emphasis, which I have characterized as monolithic, overrides critical distinctions in regards to class, race, gender, sexuality in one direction or in regards to multispecies assemblages in the other, distinctions constitutive of the Anthropocene itself (Clover and Spahr 157–160; Yusoff xii; Haraway 160). What all these critics and scholars can agree on is that work in the gravitational field of the Anthropocene both feels urgent and urgently forces scholars to redraw the boundaries of their disciplines.[2]

"Moaning Action at the Gas Pump"

After a lifetime of writing and thinking through a poetics adequate to the Great Acceleration, the poet Charles Olson condensed his method into five memorable lines: "the Blow is Creation / & the Twist the Nasturtium / is any one of Ourselves / And the Place of it All? / Mother Earth Alone" (Olson 634). Much has been written on Olson's poetics of type ("Blow"), trope ("Twist"), and topos ("Place").[3] For the purposes of this chapter, I would like to read Olson's "Mother Earth" and the topos it implies not nominatively, as theme, but verbally, as action – as if Olson were asking poets, where do they place their work? Even if Olson's efforts to bridge his political energy with his later poetic work met with limited success at best, his imagination of placement as integral to poetics addresses the incomplete political claims made on behalf of avant-garde writing. The Anthropocene places us all in a kind of terminal relation to the life of our species and to the ethics of our actions toward forms of life on the planet; in its shadow, an imagined political agency for "disruptive syntax," for instance, works well below the threshold of "scale derangement," nearing zero significance. A thematic and/or narrative read on "topos," for its part, expects poetry to do a kind of communication more effectively conducted in other media: Visual mass media, for instance, are much more effective at communicating stories. What if poets *placed* their work at the active terminals of the Anthropocene, in particular, at oil pipeline and shipping terminals, gas pumps, banking and computer terminals? Such work is not only performative, as suggested by Brenda Hillman's "Moaning Action at the Gas Pump,"[4] but written in imagined and often actual adjacency to direct, mostly nonviolent (though also in some cases violent) political action at terminal sites (Hillman 37).

"Has the earth lost its cool? / Did we lose a moist place within?" Cecilia Vicuña presciently asks in a "Letter to the Reader" in the catalog to her 1998 "Cloud-Net" installation, a gallery-sized woven net of raw wool (90). In this same letter (also presaging the "cloud"-based architecture of Web 2.0), Vicuña proposes "Clouds as the ethical model of what is to come" (92). She notes that, "To weave clouds at a moment like this is an attempt to change the pattern of destruction, as if this impossible gesture (you cannot 'weave' with unspun wool – it falls apart as you touch it) had the power to affect the climate and move people to thought" (19). The bright web invoked in Vicuña's "Cloud-Net," and her proposed collective weaving of a new "net worth" (a pun in the associated video), seems to be emerging from a loom of bodies both analogue and digital. The Occupy movement arguably was most directly inspired by the "Arab Spring" at the start of 2011, where cloud computing-based social media platforms such as Facebook and Twitter had been instrumental in the decentralized organization of and success of the popular uprising (Clarke and Koçak n. pag.). The Occupy poetry assemblies would model a poetry that reflects on its proximity to and engagement with sustained social insurrection, also transparent about the role of networked (if not net worth) social relations in these moments of change, always slightly beyond any group mastery, eluding the deliberate sort of "weaving" Vicuña proposes (Donovan 21–28, 56–58).

In the opening poem to her 2015 volume *That Winter the Wolf Came*, "Transitory, Momentary," Juliana Spahr weaves together sentences on migrating Brent geese, on lost singers of epiphanic songs, on police clearing occupied parks, on well fields "pumping out amber colored oils," on economics benchmarked against Brent Crude, on the loneliness of the many "pulled from intimacies by oil's circulations" (including labor in the shipping trade alienated from "the tongue in meaningful conversation"), and on a line of people barricading the entrance to the park, passing bricks onto a growing pile: "Some get out of the line and climb on the pile, hold both hands in the air because they know now is the transitory, momentary triumph and it should be felt" (13–14). Such a gesture binds the poem itself as a way of feeling to the transitory, momentary rewards of resistance, insurrections that go some way toward combating alienation but that fall short of the revolution necessary to overthrow the system. This prose poem sets the stage for poems (some in verse, some in prose) sounding ways of being together in a late capitalist extraction society in crisis. In the face of a gradually climbing Brent Crude Oil Spot price, which funds ever more risky extraction, ultra-deepwater drilling catastrophe, and species endangerment and extinction, feral alliances and on-and-off love affairs with "Non-Revolution" sound the call and response. An affect of radical ambivalence ("it's all good, it's all fucked") filters a mother's intense love for her son as for her comrades in the midst of insurrection and in her avowed attraction to its transitory epiphanies in the rush of engaged opposition: "All art either with the crowd or with the police. All art coming down to that simple divide" (Spahr 65, 69). Rather than shore up identity, however, engagement diffuses and blends differences: "I am unsure of my metaphors. Were we wolves? Were we even we? Were we lovers or were we just a brief hook up?" (Spahr 72).

With its Steinian repetitions, the collection seems more interested in registering the effect of this collective "sort of walking around the city" on its efforts to link global economic and ecological forces with personal relationship through parataxis than in affirming or negating particular identifications. In the next piece, "Brent Crude," the poetry searches for a rhythm – avowedly out of step as the speaker has started writing a poem about oil extraction in iambic pentameter – resonant with "the sounds of chants through the city" (Spahr 22). The following poem in the volume, "If You Were a Bluebird," chants the speaker's desire for relation, gathering, and togetherness through polyspecies assemblages of the Niger Delta and the Gulf of Mexico (ecosystems threatened and degraded by oil extraction), such as hingemouth, red snapper, reed cormorant, mudskipper, and bacteria, through habitats such as sandbanks and swamps, and through women gathering blood cockles, sabotaging oil extraction infrastructure, and attacking police stations (Spahr 29–35). The poetry's immediate social concerns are set in a global ecological context across uneven distributions of precarity. The poem about oil extraction in iambic pentameter, "Dynamic Positioning," is included in the volume: Here the meeting of poetic technique with the technique of ultra-deepwater drilling, around an operation gone wrong, entails the disassembly of the poem's prosody – as a run of eighteen lines in a row achieves the pentameter at the cost of semantic integrity, snapping all the end words in half (Spahr 48).

In an essay co-written with Joshua Clover, reflecting on the November 2, 2011, shutdown of the Oakland port and another West Coast follow-up action a few weeks later, Spahr locates the port "as an ecotonality where material intervention is possible" (164). Ports are the places where the underlying social relations of capital now present themselves, as capital increasingly seeks its profits in circulation. Clover and Spahr identify ecotones (a term from ecology denoting regions of transition between biological communities), which become productive within capital, and their analysis and literary reading pairs the ecotone of the port (where land meets sea and production meets circulation) with the ecotone of the Hawai'ian *Kumulipo* creation chant (as well as with the ecotone created by a differential gender politics): "These ecotones are one, *Kumulipo* and capital. Where the poem was, now we find the port" (163). In their analysis, capitalism exploits the differences of the ecotone to create differentials across which the production of surplus value can flow; ecology, economy, and even ecopoetics are intertwined in the apparatus of the port and the poem. Especially for middle-class North Americans, whose per capita CO_2 emissions ("carbon footprint") presently rate nearly four times the global average (and nearly fifty-five times that of the least developed countries), consciousness of something like the Anthropocene can be experienced as awareness of heightened responsibility paralyzed by diminished agency – whether in terms of the species life the Anthropocene proposes or in terms of the failure of democratic institutions, arguably the very institutions energized and circum-scribed by fossil fuels (Ritchie n. pag.).[5] (Ecocritics have referred this cognitive dissonance to the "scalar dissonance" of having to think human and planetary history together [Keller 38].) For such consciousness, the ecotonal apparatus of the port, like the pipeline, becomes a site vulnerable to collective action and resistance, local action with potentially global effects. Spahr's *That Winter the Wolf Came* attempts to bring poetry to this action and to this site. For related reasons, Clover and Spahr push back at Dipesh Chakrabarty's claim, in his much-discussed essay on the "Climate of History," that "the whole crisis cannot be reduced to a story of capitalism" (160). In their view, "[t]he drive to bring together the most cost-effective means of production with the lowest wages is intrinsic to capital's expansion and intensification, which is to say, it constitutes the Anthropocene" (157). Most certainly because it locates sites for effective action, they prefer the term popularized by Moore and others, Capitalocene. In another part of the essay, Clover and Spahr suggest that "the idea of gender abolition *is* the idea of annihilating the value-productive differential as applied to the specific category of gender" (155, emphasis in original). The speaker in Spahr's poetry is drawn to collective direct action that seems to promise abolition of such differentials – however transitory or momentary – all while bringing her differences as a white, cisgender, middle-class, poet mother with child in tow into the fray. In an essay for *Jacket2* coauthored with Jasper Bernes, Spahr and Clover have referred to poetry as the "riot dog" of Athens, "unable to do much to alter the balance of forces … Some barking. Some letting you know that the cops are at the door" (Bernes, Clover, and Spahr n. pag.).

The volume's final poem, "Turnt," interrogates what community means in the contingencies of digitally networked relations, as the speaker, who is "often a little late," moves "from isolation to the depths of friends," from an outer ring of emptied out blocks, with "night herons settled into trees," past riot police who ignore or even offer her directions, to a merging with others in the riot, where physical togetherness (a heart opening condition of being "turnt") is inseparable from the intimacies of digital communication, as text messages are sent back and forth, shops are looted, and cars get burnt: "The fire truck arrives. As I stand there watching it, it is as if everyone I have ever texted I love you to walks by. I love you we call out to each other." Sentiment is balanced by the irony of a digitally networked crowd looting the telecommunications ("t-mobile") shop, as a group of women stop to take selfies in front of the burning car. Even the speaker's "son is in my feed too" (Spahr 81–85). The affect can be understood as non-ironic inasmuch as the warmth of the crowd replaces the network's proxy connections. The poem ends with a confession: The names of all the beloveds texted throughout the poem are not true. Instead, an alphabetical list was generated from a list of the most popular baby names for various countries in 2015 and put into the poem one by one. While challenging the very intimacy, authenticity, and sincerity the affect of the poem has invoked, this gesture also addresses the poem to future readers, the yet to be literate, as if to say, we were here, we tried, we attempted this, together. The artifice locates the poem's truth in relation to an unidentifiable community, throwing into question the very togetherness (invoked in the book's first line as a wavering line of migrating Brent geese) that has motivated the poetry from the start, worrying its purpose and genre: "This poem is true. I have texted I love you and its variations over and over. / Sometimes I barely knew you. / But the names are not true. / This is not a coterie poem. / Is it a milieu poem? / Can it be a movement poem?" (Spahr 85). The profession of love to these future readers balances the loneliness of the speaker, bereft in her realization that to Non-Revolution she is just one in a string of lovers. While determined to be pragmatic in regards to the transitory, momentary romance of insurrection, and resolved not to get lost in epiphanic song, history strands the speaker with her now inadmissible feelings, voiced in a country song about abandonment playing in her app: "I'm through with all the crying the song states, even though the song gets all its power from being about the soft crying after being left standing on the street corner." As if to say: This poem is not sentimental about the events of the winter of 2011/12, while drawing so much of its meaning from the feelings those events uncovered. The speaker "begin[s] walking, determined, head down," enacting the gesture, seemingly impossible for poetry, to precede rather than follow the revolution (Spahr 76–77).

"Turnt" appropriates African American slang, current at the time, for "excited or energized," that is, turned up, and possibly under the influence of alcohol or drugs (OUP). The reasons for walking "determined, head down" are likely to be different for a black American male, who might have a divergent experience with the police on the peripheries of the riot and might be feeling less "turnt" about the riot itself. Occupy Oakland was notably more racially diverse than its East Coast counterpart, a fact the protesters seemed to highlight by renaming Frank H. Ogawa Plaza (itself an act of erasure with racial overtones) after Oscar Grant, a twenty-two-year-old unarmed African American man killed by Oakland police in 2009. Nevertheless, for black Americans, contact with police – often in the form of police killing young black men – tends to be the precipitating event rather than the aim of a riot. Danez Smith's poem "tonight, in Oakland" pursues eros under skies of drought, or drought as the weather for eros ("the sky has given us no water this year ... i've started seeking men to wet the harvest"), imagining a kind of sabbath from violence, or perhaps the courage to go outside, without which no sabbath is possible: "tonight i declare we must move / instead of pray ... tonight / guns don't exist. tonight, the police / have turned to their God for forgiveness" (79). (That said, the speaker does not walk but "ride[s their] bike to the boy" [Smith 79].) In this profane sabbath, Smith invokes togetherness that is not of the crowd but of two individuals, not through a chant but the refrain "tonight," queering religious feeling as gay desire under the open sky: "let everyone be their own lord. / let wherever two people stand be a reunion // of ancient lights. let's waste the moon's marble glow / shouting our names to the stars until we are // the stars" (79–80). The lights are cosmic: What might be unbearably *uneventful* for the white body, which actively seeks to be "turnt," is a moment of peace the black body wishes might last forever.

Yet the physical union, while private, is similarly anonymous, and in the poem's closing figure is wholly run through with the public plight of the black male body in America: "i will say *look / i made it a whole day, still, no rain / still, i am without exit wound //* & he will say *tonight, i want to take you / how the police do, unarmed & sudden*" (80). Smith, who identifies as nonbinary and who writes about the fact they are HIV positive, does not need climate change to feel close to extinction or the ways in which disease (whether in fact terminal or sustainable) brings biopolitics to the administration of otherness. Smith's poem underscores how the Anthropocene's violence against black bodies aligns, as Clover and Spahr argue, with the ecotonal differential of gender. The racial and sexual politics of disease in America foreshadow how climate change politics, with its discourse around reproduction, health, and futurity, might come to administer the category of the human over the coming decades. Who has a stake in that future? Who is to be included or excluded? It may be that such exclusions are too bound up with the very genealogy of the Anthropocene for the concept to serve a just and equitable future. It may be that Blackness (not to speak of Indigeneity) can in no way identify with this proposed common project so long as its emergence through colonial histories of scientific mastery, resource extraction, and chattel slavery – that, as Kathryn Yusoff argues, guided the "scientific" division between animate and inanimate matter at the birth of geology – remains unexcavated (5). In an earlier version of the poem published on the Poetry Foundation, a since redacted couplet brings the conclusion: "& tonight, when we dream, we dream of dancing / in a city slowly becoming ash." The poem's retrenchment or revision sharpens how, for the black American poet as for all who seek historical awareness, the "taking" and Blackening of bodies will always come prior, ontologically and epistemologically, to the cinders of environmental apocalypse.

"Smash the Petro State"

Stephen Collis opens his 2016 collection *Once in Blockadia*, a meditation on oil, gas, and shale extraction and on events surrounding the occupation of a bore hole testing site for a proposed pipeline through Burnaby Mountain, in Vancouver, BC with an epigraph from Naomi Klein: "Blockadia is not a specific location on a map but rather a roving transnational conflict zone that is creeping up with increasing frequency and intensity wherever extractive projects are attempting to dig and drill" (n. pag.). Among all the sites of extraction, production, distribution, consumption, and waste disposal identified by Clover and Spahr as ecotonalities where material, and perhaps poetic, intervention are possible, Blockadia focuses the attention on sites of extraction, in ways that continually force us to think beyond nation and state and across languages. Collis's *Once in Blockadia* brings together poetic and material intervention: The book's major occasions are actions sited at opposite ends of a pipeline being built to bring Canadian tar sands oil to shipping terminals in Burrard Inlet, near Vancouver.[6] The poet's home also is near Vancouver, and his place of employ (Simon Fraser University) sits directly above the proposed route of the pipeline through Burnaby Mountain. Collis became de facto spokesperson for a 2014 occupation (or blockade) of this site and was sued by the Kinder Morgan company responsible for building the pipeline, claiming 5.6 million dollars in damages (a case eventually dismissed). Poetry in the volume includes, among other materials, a court transcript of the submission for the plaintiff, an account of the blockade (incorporating material from "72 Theses Against Tar Sands Pipelines" the poet had attached to the gates of Kinder Morgan's marine terminal), a "blockade chant," a poem read at the police barricades, a "raw machine transcript" of a CBC Radio interview with the poet, a poem written during and after a Tar Sand Healing Walk ("Reading Wordsworth in the Tar Sands"), and "Home at Gasmere," a poem written between a visit to Grasmere in the UK and reflections on returning home to "Gasmere" (paired photographs of Grasmere and Burrard Inlet open the poem). Describing prose material from the poet's blog ("Beating the Bounds") as poetry, the lawyer in his argument for the plaintiff notes its connection to the direct action on Burnaby Mountain and concludes, "So underneath the poetry is a description of how the barricade was constructed" (Collis, *Once in Blockadia* 9).

Apart from "Blockade Chant"[7] and the poem read at the barricades, little of the work is recognizably protest poetry, but it takes its occasion from witness and direct action. The speaker of "Thirteen Trees" (titled after trees felled at the borehole site) picks up on the language used by the lawyer for the plaintiff: "Underneath the poetry / Not just description but the act / The biotariat at borehole 1 and 2 / Ravens and bears last Kinder last / Morgan or imagine pipes collapsing / Beneath re-Indigenized streets" (14). Such poetry departs markedly from modernist emphases on the autonomy of the work of art or unquestioned primacy of the poem. In the puns on proletariat, child and morning (in "last Kinder last / Morgan") these lines maintain an open choice between terminal and ongoing language, between poetry of (merely) description and poetry as act. As the speaker notes in a later section of the book titled "The Port Transcript": "Beneath the poetry / everything beyond the page / *what went unrecorded* / *mattered most* / and goes on resisting / as it can and as it must" (104, my emphasis). Collis has written of poetry's political function deriving from the contexts in which it is performed, heard, and read as an "embedded poetry." Poetry written from within social movements, addressed to those engaged in social movements, as a form of research and a mode of counter knowledge, might "generate a capacity for struggles to read themselves" ("On Embedded Poetry" n. pag.). According to Collis, the "biotariat" at borehole 1 and 2 names:

> that portion of existence that is *enclosed* as a "resource" by and for those who direct and benefit from the accumulation of wealth. So: labouring human beings generally; most animals and plants; forest, wetland and grassland eco-systems; water; land itself, as it provisions and enables biological life broadly; minerals that lie beneath the surface of the land; common "wastes" and "sinks" too, into which the waste products of resource production and use are spilled – primarily the atmosphere and the oceans, primarily in the form of carbon and petroleum products. The enclosed and exploited life of this planet.
>
> (Staples and King 25)

Enclosure entails boundaries, and *Once in Blockadia* includes a citation from Peter Linebaugh (*The Magna Carta Manifesto*) on "beating the bounds" (that is also the title of Collis's blog), "ceremonial walks about a territory for asserting and recording its boundaries" (Collis, *Once in Blockadia* 32). Collis and fellow activists detour this practice for walks tracing the proposed pipeline route (documented by a page-long, single sentence "layered with semantic history and compact with minute orientation" that mimics a 1671 "perambulation of the New Forest") and for a 2014 "Healing Walk" around a tar sands extraction site near Fort McMurray, sponsored by "Keepers of the Athabasca" (a river and watershed severely impacted by the tar sands operations): "Walking the route of the proposed new pipeline still an imaginary line in data bank accounts begin on river mud banks beneath bridge the pilings & log booms small midspan island treed & reedy temporary trail closed signs barbed-wire hypocrisy of man-made habitats ..." (33). Fellow Canadian poet Rita Wong, in her celebration of waters (*Undercurrent*), also has participated in and written for the Walks: "we walk for healing the scar sands, in a living pact with the bears, the eagles, / the muzzled scientists, the beavers who've built dams you can see from outer space," similarly emphasizing cross-disciplinary and cross-species solidarity (18).[8] The collaboration with Keepers of the Athabasca, whose leadership includes First Nations elders, also emphasizes cross-cultural solidarity, in particular solidarity across the troubled and often unspeakably painful lines of settler genocide, occupation, and theft of Indigenous commons, lines heightened by the fact that much First Nations territory across Canada is openly acknowledged as "unceded."

As Clover and Spahr have noted, in regards to the Anthropocene, "[t]he carbon footprint is just a beginning" (160). In their analysis, "*differentials are capital's ecology* ... the differentials that allow value to flow, to valorize and realize itself" (159). In other words, the ecology of the Anthropocene is capitalist:

> This is true whether the differentials are familiarly ecological (as in the case of resource extraction or forcing other regions to bear one's toxic burden) or whether they do not appear particularly ecological at all (as in the case of childcare) ... These differentials exist at every stratum, from the household to the geopolitical, from the brute materiality of the shipping container to the ethereal whirring of financial circuits, from the sex work down the street to the start-up known as the Dating Ring. (159–160)

This does not mean that every poem that confronts capital or that deals with globalization is ecological and thus self-consciously of the Anthropocene. Unaddressed here is the question of where capitalist differential shades off into ecological differential – a possible "derangement of scale" that Clover and Spahr's analysis doesn't fully address (Clark 150–151). Ecocritic Lynn Keller (following Derek Woods) has noted the primacy of "scale variance" for poets of the Anthropocene – that, when confronting what she calls "scalar dissonance" in thinking about the Anthropocene, some poets attempt to straddle the scalar rift between, for example, human and geological history while others register the disjunction of such rifts (38). In other words, Anthropocene ecopoetics might make such dissonance a part of its music – as with the kinds of prosodic, figurative, and affective dissonances explored in *That Winter the Wolf Came*. Collis's term "biotariat" signals alliance with the anti-capitalist emphasis put forward in Clover and Spahr's critique of the Anthropocene (Collis has indicated sympathy for their notion of poetry as "riot dog"), while more overtly expanding the emphasis to include the multiple, if not conflicting, perspectives of polyspecies assemblages as well as Indigenous points of view ("On Embedded Poetry" n. pag.). Collis embeds his poetry in collaboration with Indigenous activists and cites the Supreme Court of Canada's definition of Aboriginal title in *Tsilhqot'in Nation v. British Columbia*, supporting the biotariat's defense of unceded commons, as "collective title [that] cannot be encumbered in ways that would prevent future generations from using or enjoying it" (*Once in Blockadia* 35). Collis's inclusion of "transcripts" (of court proceedings, of media interviews, as well as, more loosely, of the port itself) invokes the collective context of his writing, without presuming to speak for all the perspectives involved. As Fred Moten puts it in his blurb for Layli Long Soldier's *Whereas* (discussed later in the chapter), "we have no right to *we* on and under the ground of this history." At the same time, the volume's return to Wordsworth inscribes Collis's project within the Romantic legacy for ecopoetics, including its alignment with "The method of our walking / From seeing to contemplating / To remembering ..." (62).

Once in Blockadia crosses back and forth between prose and verse. Prose sections blend a language of testimony, witness, and manifesto – sometimes didactic and descriptive, in series of sentences unsubordinated to an overt form of narrative or argument, and sometimes poetic in sound and syntax: "come wolves run wolves come leap becquerel leap along path no pipeline has" – while the verse tends toward allegorical statement: "I wandered lonely / as a sound cloud / until the one-way / street burst into / frantic act and a / king's carriage or / CEO's Escalade / fled into dark" (Collis 96). Occasionally a certain opacity reminds us that resistance is linguistic as well as bodily, reinforced by repeated nods to Louis Zukofsky's Objectivist integrals: "Upper limit elegy / Lower limit pastoral ... upper limit howl / Lower limit lament ... upper limit abolition / lower limit solidarity" (Collis, *Once in Blockadia* 64, 67, 92). Syntactic parallels across separate sections of the book – "Underneath the poetry ... beneath the glassy surfaces / of our smart phones" – embed the poetry in a cognitive mapping of social relations (including their digital mediations) across materialist surface readings (105). Practices of appropriation and erasure, as with a section derived from an erasure of Shell Oil's "Scenario Plans," inscribe the work in the umbra of investigative, documentary, and conceptual practices of the past two decades (Collis, *Once in Blockadia* 43–55). The "I" of "The Port Transcript" is relatively mobile, inhabitable, while the ruminative "I" of "Reading Wordsworth at the Tar Sands" and "Home at Gasmere" seems more occupied with the poet's Romantic inheritance under the sign of the Anthropocene. Here the turn to description, to sites that "swarm with sensation" (in Wordsworth's memorable phrase from "Home at Grasmere"), recollected in a not-so-tranquil untimely present, both invokes and challenges Romantic subjectivity (line

447). The access to memory and its affective structures through phenomena is flattened out by the uncanny temporality of the Anthropocene where, as David Farrier puts it, "distant pasts and futures flow through the present in all manner of sometimes surprising ways" (2). The "special now" of the lyric is lodged in the "crease of time" – "the appelation for the folding of radically different temporal scales: the deep time of geology and a rather shorter history of capital" – where it folds, pleats, splits, and ruptures (5, 7). As a speaker in "The Port Transcript" wonders, "I keep pondering this other tense – *I what we will have had to have done*" (Collis, *Once in Blockadia* 93). Similarly, in spatial terms the familiar negations of Romantic idealism are themselves negated by the flattening and negotiations of dialectic: "the aesthetics / Of the [Tar Sands] are pure negation … There is no viewpoint" (Collis, *Once in Blockadia* 66). Without going so far as to invoke the "flat ontology" of new materialism, Collis indicates clearly that anthropogenic material changes wrought at the scale of the planet will prevent us from ever being at home again with Wordsworth. As the word "home" indexes the *oikos* of ecology, this also is an admission that ecology at Grasmere/Gasmere is no longer an objective "natural order" independent of human choice and action.

"Together We Reach a Full Stop"

Poets of the Anthropocene find themselves forced into uncommon solidarities. Layli Long Soldier's *Whereas* (2017) ends with a stitching together of two texts, "Direct Action Principles," by two Indigenous activists engaged with the Dakota Access Pipeline (DAPL) protests, a 2016–2017 direct action involving thousands of activists opposed to the proposed DAPL connecting the Bakken oil fields in western North Dakota with southern Illinois, crossing beneath the Missouri and Mississippi rivers, as well as under part of Lake Oahe near the Standing Rock Sioux Reservation (and thus avoiding the predominantly white town of Bismarck, North Dakota). When read left to right across the seam, the montage fuses representation with action in ways that refuse a priori "identity": "you may ask / I acknowledge a plurality of ways / does that seem reasonable to you / to resist oppression / don't give any further info" (94). What matters is what occurs at the seam of Blockadia. The title poem of Long Soldier's book focuses on a 2009 "Congressional Resolution of Apology to Native Americans" signed by President Barack Obama. Written within the reductive legal structure of a "Whereas Statement," "[m]eaning whatever comes after the word 'Whereas' and before the semicolon in a Congressional document falls short of legal grounds," Long Soldier does the poet's work of exposing the language, structure, and syntax of the "resolution of apology" (70). As she puts it, "Whereas sets the table" (79). In a series of prose poems – though also sometimes written in long lines or through other treatments of language that use the full space of the page – Long Soldier details one Native American's responses to the violence settler language brings to the civic table, even or especially within the structure of an "apology."

As according to the speaker there is no word for "apologize" in many Native languages (though of course there are "definite actions for admitting and amending wrongdoing"), she wonders "how, without the word, this text translates as a gesture" (92). Her "response is directed to the Apology's delivery, as well as the language, crafting, and arrangement of the written document" (57). Some of the most painful yet also hopeful moments of the text entail family relations, where the bond of language and culture is broken: "what did I know about being Lakota? Signaled panic, blood rush my embarrassment. What did I know of our language but pieces?" (75). As with the negated negation of Collis's tar sands, the poems enact the difficulty of figuring out how to resist colonial oppression in the double negation of lacking what might offer resistance: "What is it to wish for the absence of nothing?" (65). What the speaker calls "American Indian emptiness" is a burden brought by the very term "American Indian": "for my work some burden of American Indian emptiness in my poems how American Indian emptiness surfaces not just on the page but often on drives, in conversations, or when I lie down to sleep" (62). Repair and shelter, as "the root of reparation is repair," come from awareness, from the lessons daughter teaches mother, as mother teaches (her) father – arrows shot backwards through time from the future: "my daughter understands wholeness for what it is, not for what it's not, all of it the pieces" (84, 76). In one episode, the speaker laughs at reading the phrase, "'the arrival of Europeans in North America / opened a new chapter in the history of Native Peoples.' Because in others, I hate the act // of laughing when hurt injured or in cases of danger. That bitter hiding." She then observes a similar self-protective laughter on her daughter's part, after a playground injury: "My daughter's quiver isn't new – / but a deep practice very old she's watching me" (66). Long Soldier sounds and paces out, through her page arrangements, the inscriptions of colonial trauma at the root of motherhood, family relations, tribal membership, and daily interactions with the settler culture. Even or especially when the culture's gesture is well-intentioned, it points to injury and raises basic, existential questions: Where does one stand? "[T]his location. Where I must be firmly positioned to receive an apology the spot from which to answer" (71). Identity politics, which paint the "Native" person into a representative position, standing for that which the settler subject negates, are betrayed by language itself, as the speaker is "reminded of the linguistic impossibility of identity, as if any of us can be identical ever" (75). How does the poet "language a collision arrived at through separation?" (70).

As with Spahr's *That Winter the Wolf Came* and Collis's *Once in Blockadia*, Long Soldier's *Whereas* is drawn to a site of resistance configured by the seemingly irresistible flow of a commodity we now know destroys not only social and labor relations but the cross-species relations sustaining life itself on planet Earth, a resistance convened by the "cloud-nets" of indeterminate digital networks, opening onto an alternate temporality with unexpected social possibilities. The DAPL protests (known by the internet hashtag, #NoDAPL) began in early 2016 in reaction to the approved construction of Energy Transfer Partners' DAPL in the northern United States. Those gathered at the camp dubbed themselves Water Protectors. While the poem "Direct Action Principles" places *Whereas* at the site of resistance at Standing Rock, Long Soldier has disavowed any intent to speak for the Standing Rock community.[9] Her book's interrogation of "American Indian emptiness" puts *Whereas* at odds with some of the representational politics of the DAPL protests. Nevertheless, the poem "38," which sits at the center of the book, was circulated widely on social media at the height of the protests. The poem brings the composition of sentences as poetic form to the documented but little known fact of President Abraham Lincoln's sentencing of thirty-eight Dakota men to hanging after the Dakota War of 1862, the largest government-sanctioned mass execution in US history, occurring the same week that President Lincoln signed the Emancipation Proclamation. Noting that "[e]verything is in the language we use," the speaker recounts events leading up to the hanging and, in an all too familiar reiteration of colonial violence, the subsequent dissolution (theft) of remaining Dakota territory in Minnesota: "Homeless, the Dakota people of Mnisota [*sic*] were relocated (forced) onto reservations in South Dakota and Nebraska" (51–52). The dispossessions the Anthropocene visits upon the Romantic poet, who can no longer go home with Wordsworth, is nothing new to Indigenous peoples dispossessed of their ecology (*oikos*) through several hundred years of colonial aggression.

The next three sentences describe an annual 325-mile, 18-day memorial horse ride from Lower Brule, South Dakota to Mankato, Minnesota (site of the hanging) by a group called the Dakota 38 + 2 Riders, concluding on December 26, the day of the hanging. "The memorial for the Dakota 38," a sentence reads, "is not an object inscribed with words, but an *act*" – recalling Collis's "Underneath the poetry / Not just description but the act" (52, *Once in Blockadia* 14). This sentence opens up ground for Long Soldier to present an episode that nails this poem to the opening lines of the book: "Now / make room in the mouth / for grassesgrassesgrasses" (5). A trader named Andrew Myrick famously refused to provide credit to starving Dakota people with the words, "If they are hungry, let them eat grass." He was one of the first to be executed by the Dakota in the Sioux Uprising, and when his body was found, "his mouth was stuffed with grass." "I am inclined," the speaker states, "to call this act by the Dakota warriors a poem" (Long Soldier 53). If an act can be a memorial, an act can be a poem. Behind this assertion lurks the history of oral and intermedial poetry practiced across the Americas as documented and exemplified for contemporary readers in, for example, the work of Cecilia Vicuña.[10] The act as poem also arguably includes the nonhuman agency of grasses in its making, in symbiosis with the bison, both sustaining and sustained by prairie grasses, a mutualism well established by ecologists (Owen and Wiegert). Settler destruction of the bison was arguably a first step in the eradication of the tallgrass prairie as well as of the human cultures (and languages) that depended on the buffalo. Some scholars hypothesize an earlier date than the twentieth century for the Anthropocene, based on global atmospheric registration (a spike in atmospheric oxygen, from resurgent forests in the wake of abandoned landscape management) of the genocide of 40 million Indigenous Americans. The violent act inscribes aesthetics within a site of resistance to unspeakable violence inflicted on peoples excluded from the social contract of settler cultures, a violence with planetary effects – all of which, in Long Soldier's poem, is confronted within the frame or constraint of the sentence: "Here, the sentence will be respected" (49). To "make room in the mouth / for grassesgrassesgrasses" is to align the "linguistic impossibility of identity" with the multiplicity of orders resistant to logocentric segmentation (words, sentences, clauses, and resolutions) (75).

The title sequence of Long Soldier's book explores how, within the qualifying structure of the "whereas statement" with its semicolons, "Together we reach a full stop" (77). Yet the poem at its center, "38," locates the book in a "mouth stuffed with grass," another kind of full stop. The use of the singular, "grass," in conjunction with the reversal of the poem's speech act (the act of a poem become the poem of an act), more forcibly enacts the poem's intervention in and on American poetry, specifically on Walt Whitman's poetry of "grass" in his "Song of Myself" and its assertion of settler nativism: "I lean and loafe at my ease observing a spear of summer grass. // My tongue, every atom of my blood, form'd from this soil, this air, / Born here of parents born here from parents the same, and their parents the same … " (188). Making room in her poetry for grasses (in all of Whitman's *Leaves of Grass* the word "grass" never appears in the plural), Long Soldier "language[s] a collision arrived at through separation" (70). Her poetry both asserts the unrepaired, and possibly unrepairable, roots of the Anthropocene, legible in its purporting to speak for a universal Anthropos – "the root of reparation is repair … The root, gone," ends one section of "Whereas" – and acknowledges the uncommon solidarities called up for the "biotariat," a form of collective awareness the human mind cannot "scale up" to unaided, as it emerges into the light of the Anthropocene (Long Soldier 84). Membership is claimed not by a new form of "consciousness" but by standing, riding, walking, and sometimes rioting together at sites of memory, healing, and resistance, along the ecotone of tar sands, pipeline, port, gas pump, cell phone, waste sink. (The degree to which poets respond to a streak of successful labor actions and talk of a "Green New Deal" in mainstream politics, as of this writing, remains to be determined: Labor organizing is bound to join the list of actions by which membership is claimed in the biotariat.) For the Lakota writer, the act of writing itself entails uncommon, and uncomfortable, solidarity with the (English) language of the settler: an impossible response that must begin by refusing the position the language makes available.

Whether it be a loss of the future, of the revolutionary poet's aspiration to come before; a loss of the past, of the subaltern poet's right to come after; a loss of the present, of the Romantic poet's ability to belong; or loss of an elsewhere, of the Native poet's ground for reclaiming sovereignty, the Anthropocene is marked for these poets by losses warping time and space into unexpected configurations of concept and affect. In responding by placing their work at active terminals of the Anthropocene, these poets both confront the loss, and the claims the Anthropocene might have on their poetics, and expose how differently we are in the Anthropocene. Doing so offers such differences as sites for uncommon forms of solidarity, and for ethical models, powerful yet indeterminate as clouds and blockade chants, of what is yet to come.

Notes

1. The Anthropocene has not been universally embraced, even or especially not by geologists, who in being challenged to identify a stratigraphic unit-in-formation are asked to map "a unit conceptually rather than conceptualiz[e] a mappable stratigraphic unit" (Whitney J. Autin and John M. Holbrook, qtd. in Solnick 7). Just as the Anthropocene takes the humanists out of their depths, it has plunged geologists into unknown strata. The pressures behind the project are more political than scientific, though its contours are existential insofar as that which is being mapped threatens the species mapping, especially if it isn't mapped quickly enough – we have to map it to stop it. Wait until the Anthropocene is empirically legible and there won't be human geologists around to make use of it. In this sense, the Anthropocene mirrors climate change as only perceptible through simulations and models, since any given individual weather event can only be statistically linked to rising parts per million of carbon dioxide in the atmosphere. (Its scale-confounding dimensions make climate change the exemplary "hyperobject," in Timothy Morton's memorable coinage [*Hyperobjects* 1–3].) From an

environmental justice perspective, the Anthropocene has been critiqued for the way its anthro- and speciesism erases the combined and uneven distributions of world-ecology: As Rob Nixon puts it, "we are all in it, but we are not all in it in the same way" (qtd. in Solnick 7). Andreas Malm and others have proposed "Capitalocene" to more precisely name the world-ecological system that has turned the atmosphere into a sink for capitalists' relentless accumulation (Moore xi). Again, these differences are mirrored in the climate change negotiations, where nations of the global economic South rightly object to sharing equally the costs of the affluence of the North. Anna Tsing has proposed "Plantationocene," which focuses attention on the human and environmental costs of the colonial project of capitalism: It helps to historicize changes in a landscape no longer so easily comprehended by a nature vs. culture binary, while also keeping the human dimensions visible (Haraway 162). Donna Haraway has pointed to the arrogance built into the term Anthropocene, which seems to overlook the fact that "from the start the greatest planetary terraformers (and reformers) of all have been and still are bacteria and their kin, also in inter/intra-action of myriad kinds (including with people and their practices, technological and otherwise)" (159). There is a cognitive dissonance inherent to the term insofar as it names a kind of mastery precisely where control is being lost. Haraway proposes "Chthulucene," to name "the dynamic ongoing sym-chthonic forces and powers of which people are a part, within which ongoingness is at stake" (160). Paul J. Crutzen himself, the originator of the term, may well have intended the connotation of mastery, having at first suggested that only geoengineering on a planetary scale could stabilize warming (Solnick 16). Never mind the unintended consequences: The stakes for the human species are too high not to play them.

2. Ecocritics such as Timothy Clark and Derek Woods have focused on scale variants and scale effects, which mean that "the observation and the operation of systems are subject to different constraints at different scales due to real discontinuities" (Woods 133). Such discontinuities prevent a smooth scaling up or down (as with the cartographic scale of Google Maps) and can introduce contradiction or failure; the mind, as Lynn Keller puts it, "is itself like the nonscaling phenomena in nature that [climate change] call[s] to our attention" (Keller 38). If so, such "derangements of scale" may be fatal to the political and cultural ambitions of literary criticism, predicated on an ability to scale the (human) imagination to the problems it confronts (Clark 150–151). Keller herself prefers to characterize such effects as "scalar dissonance," with both cognitive and affective dimensions, dimensions she sees poetry particularly well-suited to exploring (Keller 38). Kathryn Yusoff has suggested historicizing the Anthropocene concept (or a "billion black Anthropocenes") in the shadow of the chattel slavery that made possible the mineral extraction out of which geology itself was born (Yusoff 2). For David Farrier "the peculiarly wrought (and fraught) intimacies of the Anthropocene" that our "enfolding in deep time" exposes us to "ask us to accept the ethical proximity between the most fleeting act in our present and planet-shaping effects that will play out over millennia." These "warping effects" lead to strange forms of intimacy, entanglement, and what he calls swerves of kin-making, the poetic pursuit of which models an "Anthropocenic perspective" (Farrier 2–8). There is a sense of having to think everything at once, bound to be aggravated in the "Great Acceleration" (Clark 152; Solnick 5).

3. See, for instance, Byrd (110–111).
4. "Soon it will be necessary to start a behavior of moaning outdoors when pumping gas" (Hillman 37).
5. See Mitchell.
6. While Alberta's tar sands contain the world's third largest proven oil reserve, producing a barrel of oil from this bituminous source emits three times more carbon dioxide than conventional production (Leahy n. pag.; Nikoforuk 129). Tar sands exploitation, if pursued unhindered, according to scientist James Hansen, would mean "game over" for a livable climate, thus making such oil pipelines and shipping terminals critical points for the Anthropocene (Hansen).
7. "Wake up in the morning **smash the petro state** get out of bed **smash the petro state** lover still asleep **smash the petro state** jump on the bus **smash the petro state** everyone's got phones **smash the petro state** on Facebook and Twitter **smash the petro state** moving through the city **smash the petro state**" (*Once in Blockadia* 56).
8. In 2019, Wong was sentenced to twenty-eight days in jail for her 2018 peaceful direct action at Trans Mountain's Westridge Marine Terminal in Burnaby, BC (Campbell n. pag.).
9. See Long Soldier, "There's the death sentence working alongside the literary sentence."
10. See especially Vicuña's *Precarios*, ephemeral installations using found materials both manmade and natural.

Works Cited

Bernes, Jasper, Joshua Clover, and Juliana Spahr. "Self-abolition of the Poet (Part 3)." *Jacket2*, January 23, 2014, www.jacket2.org/commentary/self-abolition-poet-part-3/

Brannen, Peter. "The Anthropocene Is a Joke." *The Guardian*, August 13, 2019, www.theatlantic.com/science/archive/2019/08/arrogance-anthropocene/595795/

Byrd, Don. *Charles Olson's Maximus*. University of Illinois Press, 1980.

Campbell, Chris. "This Poet Is Tied for Longest Jail Sentence Yet for a Burnaby Pipeline Protest." *Burnaby Now*, August 22, 2019, www.burnabynow.com/news/this-poet-is-tied-for-longest-jail-sentence-yet-for-a-burnaby-pipeline-protest-1.23923285/

Chakrabarty, Dipesh. "The Climate of History: Four Theses." *Critical Inquiry* vol. 35, Winter 2009, pp. 197–222.

Clark, Timothy. "Scale." *Telemorphosis: Theory in the Era of Climate Change*, Vol. 1, edited by Tom Cohen. Open Humanities Press, 2012, pp. 148–166.

Clarke, Killian and Korhan Koçak. "Eight Years after Egypt's Revolution, Here's What We've Learned about Social Media and Protest." *Washington Post*, January 25, 2019, www.washingtonpost.com/news/monkey-cage/wp/2019/01/25/eight-years-after-egypts-revolution-heres-what-weve-learned-about-social-media-and-protest/

Clover, Joshua and Juliana Spahr. "Gender Abolition and Ecotone War." *Anthropocene Feminisms*, edited by Richard Grusin. University of Minnesota Press, 2017, pp. 147–68.

Collis, Stephen. *Once in Blockadia*. Talon Books, 2016.

"On Embedded Poetry." *Jacket2*, August 7, 2015, www.jacket2.org/article/embedded-poetry/

Davison, Nicola. "The Anthropocene Epoch: Have We Entered a New Phase of Planetary History?" *The Guardian*, May 30, 2019, www.theguardian.com/environment/2019/may/30/anthropocene-epoch-have-we-entered-a-new-phase-of-planetary-history/

Donovan, Thom. *Occupy Poetics*. Essay Press, 2015. www.essaypress.org/ep-33/

Farrier, David. *Anthropocene Poetics: Deep Time, Sacrifice Zones, and Extinction*. University of Minnesota Press, 2019.

"Global Climate Change: Evidence." NASA Global Climate Change and Global Warming: Vital Signs of the Planet. Jet Propulsion Laboratory / National Aeronautics and Space Administration, July 20, 2020, https://climate.nasa.gov/vital-signs/global-temperature/

Grusin, Richard, editor. *Anthropocene Feminism*. University of Minnesota Press, 2017.

Hansen, James. "Game Over for the Climate." *The New York Times*, May 9, 2012, www.nytimes.com/2012/05/10/opinion/game-over-for-the-climate.html

Haraway, Donna. "Anthropocene, Capitalocene, Plantationocene, Chthulucene: Making Kin." *Environmental Humanities* vol. 6, 2015, pp. 159–165.

Hillman, Brenda. *Seasonal Works with Letters on Fire*. Wesleyan University Press, 2013.

IPCC (Intergovernmental Panel on Climate Change). *Summary for Policymakers. Global Warming of 1.5 °C. An IPCC Special Report on the impacts of global warming of 1.5 °C above pre-industrial levels and related global greenhouse gas emission pathways, in the context of strengthening the global response to the threat of climate change, sustainable development, and efforts to eradicate poverty*, edited by V. Masson-Delmotte et al. World Meteorological Organization, 2018, www.ipcc.ch/site/assets/uploads/sites/2/2019/05/SR15_SPM_version_report_LR.pdf

Keller, Lynn. *Recomposing Ecopoetics: North American Poetry of the Self-Conscious Anthropocene*. University of Virginia Press, 2017.

Klein, Naomi. *This Changes Everything: Capitalism vs The Climate*. Simon & Schuster, 2014.

Leahy, Stephen. "This Is the World's Most Destructive Oil Operation – and It's Growing." *National Geographic*, April 11, 2019, www.nationalgeographic.com/environment/2019/04/alberta-canadas-tar-sands-is-growing-but-indigenous-people-fight-back/

Long Soldier, Layli. *Whereas*. Minneapolis: Graywolf Press, 2017.

"There's the Death Sentence Working Alongside the Literary Sentence. Layli Long Soldier, interviewed by Kaveh Akbar." *Divedapper*, October 9, 2017, www.divedapper.com/interview/layli-long-soldier/

Mitchell, Timothy. *Carbon Democracy: Political Power in the Age of Oil*. Verso, 2011.

Moore, Jason W., editor. *Anthropocene or Capitalocene? Nature, History, and the Crisis of Capitalism*. PM Press, 2016.

Morton, Timothy. *Hyperobjects: Philosophy and Ecology after the End of the World*. University of Minnesota Press, 2013.

Nikiforuk, Andrew. *Tar Sands: Dirty Oil and the Future of a Continent*. Greystone Books, 2010.

Olson, Charles. *The Maximus Poems*, edited by George F. Butterick. University of California Press, 1983.

OUP (Oxford University Press). "Turnt." *Lexico*, n.d., www.lexico.com/definition/turnt/

Owen, Denis F. and Richard G. Wiegert. "Mutualism between Grasses and Grazers: An Evolutionary Hypothesis." *Oikos* vol. 36, no. 3, March 1981, pp. 376–378.

Ritchie, Hannah. "Where in the world do people emit the most CO_2?" *Our World in Data*, October 4, 2019, www.ourworldindata.org/per-capita-co2

Smith, Danez. *Don't Call Us Dead*. London: Chatto & Windus, 2017.

"Tonight, in Oakland." *Poetry Foundation* with *PoetryNow*, 2015, www.poetryfoundation.org/poems/58027/tonight-in-oakland/

Solnick, Sam. *Poetry and the Anthropocene: Ecology, Biology and Technology in Contemporary British and Irish Poetry*. Routledge, 2017.

Spahr, Juliana. *That Winter the Wolf Came*. Commune Editions, 2015.

Staples, Heidi Lynn and Amy King, editors. *Big Energy Poets: Ecopoetry Thinks Climate Change*. BlazeVOX, 2017.

Vicuña, Cecilia. *Cloud-Net*. Art in General, 1999.

Wallace-Wells, David. *The Uninhabitable Earth: Life after Warming*. Penguin, 2019.

Whitman, Walt. *Poetry and Prose*, edited by Justin Kaplan. Library of America, 1996.

Wong, Rita. *Undercurrent*. Nightwood Editions, 2015.

Woods, Derek. "Scale Critique for the Anthropocene." *Minnesota Review* no. 83, 2014 (New Series), pp. 133–142.

Wordsworth, William. *The Poems: Volume One*, edited by John O'Hayden. Penguin, 1977.

Yusoff, Kathryn. *A Billion Black Anthropocenes or None*. University of Minnesota Press, 2018.

JAVON JOHNSON AND
ANTHONY BLACKSHER

Give Me Poems and Give Me Death: On the End of Slam(?)

The date June 2, 2018, marked the twentieth anniversary of Da Poetry Lounge (DPL), a slam and spoken-word poetry venue in Hollywood, California that was created by Dante Basco, Shihan Van Clief, Devin "Poetri" Smith, and Gimel Hooper. For this anniversary, DPL family members past and present came home, so to speak, and shared our own origin narratives because "Such storytelling matters"; it is how we make sense of our lives, identities, relationships to one another, and, in this case, how many of us began to claim "poet" as an identity, as well as how our lives relate to DPL.[1] Given that a great many spoken-word venues fold within two to three years due to poor attendance, leadership disputes, financial troubles, organizational issues, or any number of other problems, twenty years of storytelling, life-sharing, and poetic world-making is an enormous achievement. It also offers a resounding yes to the question: Can poetry matter?

In recent literary history, that question is most familiar from Dana Gioia's "Can Poetry Matter?," first published in 1991 as an essay for the *Atlantic* and taken up a year later in a full-length monograph of the same title. Gioia argues that while poetry subcultures have grown, along with the amount of poetry produced from them, the art form has paradoxically become increasingly irrelevant to the general population. "Not long ago," Gioia argues, "'only poets read poetry' was meant as damning criticism. Now it is a proven market strategy" (2). For Gioia, "Over the past half century, as American Poetry's specialist audience has steadily expanded, its general readership has declined" (2). In order to circumvent this solipsistic structure of poets reading poems to audiences full of fellow poets who have all been trained in similar poetry programs, Gioia suggests a move away from traditional poetic readings to more dynamic engagements with poetry, including poets reciting other poets' work, mixing poetry reading with other art forms, writing prose about poetry, focusing on performance, and recognizing that poetry is an aural medium and not something relegated strictly to the page (19–20). In other words, he makes a call for all the things slam and spoken-word poets have cut their creative teeth on, what DPL poets have been doing effectively in front of weekly audiences upwards of 300 of poets and non-poets alike.

We begin this chapter by discussing DPL because it is an incredibly important spoken-word space, especially for us Southern California poets, and provides us the best location from which to think through how the context and practice of spoken word have evolved since 2000. The emergence of HBO's *Russell Simmons presents Def Poetry Jam* in 2002, the multimedia company Button Poetry in 2011, the many slam and spoken-word poets who have become well published and entered the academy to earn degrees, awards, faculty positions, and significant literary grants – these have all altered the art form and its surrounding communities. In what follows, we trace the movement of slam and spoken-word poetry from a subjugated and lesser art form to an established and valid one, while suggesting that these institutionalizing forces and desires can be caught up in anti-Blackness.[2]

Despite never having seen a slam in person, the noted literary critic Harold Bloom has notoriously called poetry slams "the death of art" (Johnson 1). Bloom's troubling statement, which is unable to recognize anyone other than the great white male literati as valid and valuable, as well as the fact that a number of early slam and spoken-word poets were denied access to academia via publishing, grants, and graduate programs demonstrate that traditional institutions initially relegated the slam to the status of an unsophisticated low art. As depicted in the critically successful documentary *SlamNation* (1998), then executive editor of St. Martin's Press, Jim Fitzgerald, dismisses Jessica Care Moore's manuscript by offering slam as "neat" yet "on the decline." He diminishes Moore's rising popularity, explaining, "Jessica's appearance on the cover of the New York Times was probably an attempt by the New York Times to say 'we're hip and we're doing the youth thing.'" In other words, publishing houses and the university, as Gioia mentions, acted as poetic gate-keepers and, we argue, pushed the new art and artists to the margins or jettisoned it and them all together. The rejection forced some slam and spoken-word poets to build workshops, classes, curricula, and publishing houses. Others have sought to legitimize themselves and the art form by publishing in reputable spaces, earning degrees, and winning grants and awards. Still others have tried some sort of mix of the previous two. These cultural tensions around the legitimacy and institutionalization of slam and spoken word are deeply tied to these poetry communities' relationship with race, and particularly Blackness.

The Changing Slam

On the heels of *SlamNation* and the award-winning 1998 film *Slam* starring Saul Williams and Sonja John, *Def Poetry Jam* premiered on HBO in

February 2002. Interestingly enough, it was initially slated to film in September 2001 and air in December of that same year. However, due to the flight restrictions immediately following 9/11, as well as the heightened security alert, both the production and the series debut were pushed back a few months. Given that moment's particular brand of Islamophobia that, according to Carmen Aguilera-Carnerero and Abdul Halik Azeez, "reached a peak in the aftermath of the 9/11 attacks and the War on Terror," it is surprising that the xenophobic George W. Bush era that ushered in the Patriot Act also gave birth to a series that featured loud, outspoken, and highly critical poets, including Suhier Hammad's careful exploration of a just barely post-9/11 New York, "First Writing Since" (24). Indeed, Hammad and the larger series are shinning testaments of the ways in which the poetic voice functions.

If it is true that, as George Lakoff writes in the *Huffington Post*, "From 9/11 on, the American people have been subject to conservative intimidation by framing" thanks in part to how conservatives used the attacks to their rhetorical advantage, *Def Poetry Jam*'s popularity signals the fraught nature of the term "the American people" (n. pag.). The spoken-word poets featured on the show often provided what series-opening poet Stephen Coleman called "poem[s] that attack[ed] the status quo," as audiences cheered them on. *Def Poetry Jam* answered Coleman's call for poems "about revolution / About fists raised high / And hips twisting in a rumble like a rumba / ... the footsteps of Che/ And ... about the day the CIA killed Lumumba" (n. pag.). However, in the series' run from 2002 to 2007, producers Russell Simmons and Stan Lathan gave us such a carefully curated set of poems that, at times, it felt like we were only getting a poem. While the show made space for marginalized groups and rather progressive viewpoints, each episode offsets the effects of radical counter-politics through humorous or otherwise safe poetry that relies on a repackaging of American multiculturalism through hip-hop.

While Simmons's describes *Def Poetry Jam* as representing the voice of America, nearly two-thirds of the performances on the series were by Black performers. The featured celebrities and established literary poets skewed heavily toward Black artists, actors, and writers. Visually, the representation of community theater relied on a *mise-en-scène* similar to that of *Def Comedy Jam* a decade prior. *Def Poetry Jam*, a highly produced and stylized televisual marker of contemporary spoken-word and slam success, centered the young Black poetic voice in way that popularized a particular defiant Black aesthetic and had the general cultural consciousness assuming that slam was indeed a Black thing.

With *Def Poetry Jam* having become the benchmark of success, the height of a slam poet's career, the 2000s were marked by a series of slam and spoken-word poets who no longer wanted to sound like their scene's local heroes or even like national slam champions but instead like those poets who frequented the show. While a range of styles and modes can and does exist in the poetry slam, Def Poetry established the gold standard for slam and contemporary spoken word's poetic voice, ultimately helping to construct what might be considered a slam poetry form or style. As Shihan, a *Def Poetry Jam* talent producer, a series regular, tour member, and slam poetry veteran, said to us in a 2019 interview, "The show definitely established certain slam styles that poets around the nation began to follow."[3]

In a rhetorical analysis of *Def Poetry Jam*, Felicia R. Walker and Viece Kuykendall identify five defining features of poetry on the series: rhythm, soundin' out, repetition, call and response, and mythication. Linking these features to an Afrocentric oral tradition, they note how "the elements are also prevalent in the poets of other cultures and ethnicities. Asians, Hispanics, White, and Jewish poets showed their ability to relate to those of all culture through poetry" (244). While we are not arguing these elements as unique or exclusive to the Black oral tradition, when these poetic devices are set alongside the visual representation of Black community theater and the prevalence of Black performers, Def Poetry recodifies a wide range of poetic and performance styles into variations of the Black poetic tradition. For poets trying to earn a living, or at least a reputation as a spoken-word or performance poet, employing those elements most familiar with Def Poetry, along with a dynamic use of the body, became commonplace.

While the second wave of slam poets unlocked the market-economy for the "full-time" spoken-word and performance poet (Aptowicz 245), an appearance on *Def Poetry Jam* fast-tracked one's notoriety and earning potential for performances, especially with gigs at college campuses. It might seem somewhat contradictory that *Def Poetry Jam* was a driving force behind the institutionalization of slam and spoken word while showcasing outspoken and defiant poetics. However, in this current stage of capitalism where activists have agents, Andy Warhol was recently featured on a Burger King commercial, and Black History Month is used to sell products, defiance of institutions is readily consumed by the very institutions that many artists and activists challenge.[4] Borrowing from hip-hop scholar Regina Bradley's conception of the messy organic intellectual, *Def Poetry Jam* reflects Russell Simmons's ability to create a platform for artists to address the conditions of aggrieved communities and potentially affect substantive change, while simultaneously profiting from those conditions, communities, and any ensuing change.

In a 2014 essay, Susan B. Anthony Somers-Willett, who wrote the first academic book on slam, speaks directly to *Def Poetry Jam*'s commercialization of slam, stating, "one also must remember that these are highly constructed expressions selected to serve the Def Jam enterprise ... In the HBO series, the lineup of poets and the studio audience are constructed ... to deliver a particular kind of countercultural narrative" ("From Slam" 18). While we take issue with the line she draws from "slam to jam" or "between counter-public and commercial culture" (Somers-Willett, "From Slam" 17, 18), we find Somers-Willett's discussion of Def Poetry as a commercially produced engagement useful in that she opens up space for us to think about how "the Def Poetry enterprise ... seems to capitalize on the counterdiscourses its poets circulate while simultaneously profiting off of its relationship to more dominant systems" ("From Slam" 18).

Somers-Willett also claims that race was central to the show's selection process, stating that "One poet auditioning for the cable series reported being told by the production staff that poets would be selected on the bases of ethnicity first, gender second, and on the quality of their poetry third" ("From Slam" 16). This claim is significant in her argument that spoken-word, slam, and performance poetry relies and subsequently rewards performances of identity. However, her criticism of the centrality of race in *Def Poetry Jam* obscures the fact that open-mic list managers and organizers of poetry readings also rely on categories of identity to create an experience for their audiences. In comparison to local open-mics and readings, the nationally televised audience of HBO raises the stakes for Def Poetry. Consequently, the show's reliance on an American multiculturalism grounded in hip-hop, that foregrounded the representation of Black performers, along with the overrepresentation of certain poetic devices, leads to an impression that *Def Poetry Jam* was making slam a Black thing.

At the end of the popular HBO show in 2007, some slam poets began to push back against what many saw as a *Def Poetry Jam* style of poetry and performance, ultimately opting for a still and quiet style. This style dramatically deemphasizes those poetic devices associated with the lyricism of rappers, namely soundin' out, repetition, and call and response. The rhythm of this poetry is dramatically slower. This mythication relies more on imagery and complex metaphors rather than the "righteousness of the cause" (Walker and Kuykendall 238). In a stark visual contrast to the Def Poets who would stride across the small stage and stretch their bodies toward their audience, this quiet style of poetry is marked by the subtle and controlled body movements of the hands, arms, neck, and head, with little to no movement below the waist. As one poet said years ago, "Def Poetry was all loud, based less on writing and more on performance."[5] While on some level the move was a natural progression of art, we argue, it was also a move grounded in establishing slam and contemporary spoken word as a more legitimate poetic form – a movement arguably based in anti-Blackness.

Few poetry slam teams effectively employed this style more than the 2009 and 2010 Soap Boxing team from St. Paul/Minneapolis, which included performers Khary (6 is 9) Jackson, Michael Mlekoday, Kyle Myhre, Sierra DeMulder, and Jenn Parks in 2009, and Jackson, DeMulder, Myhre, Sam Cook, and Shane Hawley in 2010 (Rubrecht n. pag.; Gustafson n. pag.). Boris "Bluz" Rogers, a multiple slam champion with Slam Charlotte, said of the team in a brief 2019 interview with the authors, "Their group dynamic was different. You didn't know what to expect from that team. Yeah, 6 is 9 talked to the Black experience but not Blackly if I can say that. And they understood the game. They knew their group pieces had to be innovative and they knew they had to write."[6] While both Bluz and 6 is 9 are Black men, Bluz's remark invites us to compare the styles of the two artists, which we can do by reading his performance of his poem "Joseph" against 6 is 9's performance of his piece "Carolina." Bluz's performance offers the biblical figure of Joseph as the penultimate stepfather through a poem marked by alliteration, faster rhythm, the repetition of sound, and the repetition of sacrifice. In contrast, 6 is 9's performance of "Carolina" relies on the dialect and imagery of antebellum plantations to tell an emotionally riveting story of a slave risking his life to reunite with his wife. Bluz's phrase "not Blackly" should not be read as a claim that there is a singular way to sound Black but rather as reflecting an awareness of the Black poetics made popular by *Def Poetry Jam*, from which 6 is 9 and others from the Minneapolis/St. Paul scene departed.

During the first decade of the 2000s, the domination of the poetry slam by Black voices became so pronounced that Somers-Willett's *The Cultural Politics of Poetry Slam* grapples with the question of whether the Black voice registers as more authentic in the slam. She suggests that "the slam may serve as a rare opportunity for liberal, white, middle-class audience to legitimately support poets of color who critique white positions of privilege. Rewarding these poets may be a way of showing support for antiracist attitudes, confirming members of the slam audience's own positions as liberal, rebellious, hip, and against the status quo" (*Cultural Politics* 79). If, as Somers-Willett suggests, white slam audiences' celebration of the perceived authenticity of the Black voice stems from a desire for interracial dialogue – or from the desire to assuage white guilt – then the rise of the quiet style of poetry epitomized by the Twin Cities scene can be seen as relying on a related, though different, politics of race. By positioning themselves in opposition to the aesthetics – and, implicitly, the Blackness – of Def Poetry, poets employing this quiet style arguably appealed to a white, liberal, middle-class aspiration toward a post-racial society, symbolized above all in the late 2000s by the election of a Black man as president of the United States.

Our analysis is not meant as a criticism of the many outstanding poems written by folks out of the St. Paul/Minneapolis scene in this period, which contributed to their back-to-back national titles in 2009 and 2010. However, we argue that anti-Blackness, and frustration with Black success and pervasive Black sound, was a factor in the national trend toward a more still, quiet, and formal mode of poetry. We suggest that racism and classism opened up space for these so-called quiet poems – operating in implicit opposition to loud Black ones – that began their rise in the St. Paul/Minneapolis scene and elsewhere in the mid-to-late 2000s. The discourse that dominated slam and spoken-word poetry communities in this period centered on the supposed need to stop yelling (code for angry Blacks), focus less on performing (code for Black poets who are too embodied), and focus more on formal training and reading of, as many poets quipped, "real poetry" (code for traditional form and printed text). In other words, there was a demand to move back to what Dana Gioia's "Can Poetry Matter?" identifies as a self-congratulatory and problematic poetic subculture of "real" poetry, made by and for "real" poets who can best appreciate it. Yet such formalized training is often still the province of historically white academic institutions, which have traditionally focused on white writers to the exclusion and detriment of writers of color.

In 2011, Sam Cook and Sierra DeMulder, two members of the Soap Boxing poetry slam team, created the online platform Button Poetry. Button Poetry has since grown into a wildly popular multimedia platform known for producing viral poetry videos such as Neil Hilborn's "OCD," Sabrina Benaim's "Explaining My Depression to My Mother," Patrick Roche's "21," and Lily Myers "Shrinking Women," all of which have more than 5 million views on YouTube; Hilborn's "OCD," with some 14 million views, is one of the most popular YouTube poetry videos of all time. At the outset, Button Poetry was an audio production team. Their first recording, *Button Poetry Volume One: Minnesota Edition*, features members of the Soap Boxing teams, including DeMulder, Cook, Hawley, Hieu Minh Nguyen, Kait Rokowski, and Button's assistant director Dylan Garity. Following a partnership with the producers of Poetry Observed, an NYC-based collective of filmmakers, Button Poetry switched its focus from audio production to filming and sharing spoken-word performances filmed at poetry slams and curated poetry readings throughout the Twin Cities. In 2012, Button launched its Tumblr and YouTube channel, rebranding itself as a producer, distributor, and promoter of performance poetry. In his essay "Video Killed the Poetry Star," author and poet Ken Arkind reflects, "They were not the first to post performances of slam poets online but they are easily the biggest. At this point, it wouldn't be a stretch to call them the largest distributor of slam and spoken word poetry content in the world."

Now expanded also to house a publishing press, Button Poetry has published well-known books by Hanif Abdurraqib, Danez Smith, Rudy Francisco, and Andrea Gibson. However, as Javon Johnson notes in *Killing Poetry*, some "poets think the fact that the company responsible for popularizing performance poetry in the digital age is headed by two white men is inherently problematic" (104). Some slam and spoken-word poets felt that Button was curating a particular aesthetic that was counter to *Def Poetry Jam*'s stylized Blackness, and that they were concerned with, as one poet who preferred to remain anonymous said, "certain types of Black poems" not gaining traction on their incredibly popular YouTube channel. Former National Poetry Slam champion Shihan Van Clief added, "Oh, for sure, that's what happened. Even their initial thing of 'We're creating a platform for our friends,' which was all white at the time, proves their rise was opposite of Def Poetry's."[7] While the emergence of Button Poetry helped birth discussions centering on poetic form, technique, and quality in the national slam and spoken-word scene, such terms can often be grounded in exclusionary logics that sustain racism and classism. St. Paul/Minneapolis's emphasis on the quiet style, highlighted by the poems their slam teams often performed, can be seen as advancing the ideal of the disembodied performer who, through the rejection of theatrics, focuses on the "real" art of poetry – that is, writing.

What Barbara Christian says of the Black Arts Movement in her classic essay "A Race for Theory" can be riffed on and employed here: "It is true that the ... [slam and contemporary spoken-word world] resulted in a necessary and important critique of ... the white-established literary world. However, in attempting to take over power, it ... became much like its opponent, monolithic and downright repressive" (74). We argue that a number of factors, including the success of the St. Paul/Minneapolis teams and of Button Poetry; the anti-Black turn to "real" poetry and writing; and the large number of slam and spoken-word poets who have now entered the world of academic creative writing in various capacities, have pushed the national slam and spoken-word scene toward the very things slam initially rejected: elitism and prescriptive theories on form, technique, and quality in poetry.

Locating Michel Foucault's notion of "subjugated knowledges," which "include all the local, regional, vernacular, naïve knowledges at the bottom of the hierarchy," opposite "the dominant ways of knowing in the academy," performance studies scholar Dwight Conquergood argues that "[s]ubjugated knowledges have been erased because they are illegible; they exist, by and large, as active bodies of meaning, outside of books, eluding the forces of inscription that would make them legible, and thereby legitimate" (33). In many ways, the current anti-Black and anti-theatrical trend in slam and spoken word is an attempt to rescue the art from its subjugated and under-appreciated status, thereby making it legible and legitimate to academic and/ or high art critics that established it as subjugated and lesser. Also, as Christian has already warned, "Rather than wanting to change the whole model, many of us want to be at the center," foregoing the very radicality of slam and contemporary spoken word and thus erasing ourselves (77).

In the summer of 2018, the voting body of Poetry Slam Incorporated (PSI) elected to cease all major tournaments for the forthcoming 2019 season (National Poetry Slam, Individual World Poetry Slam, and Women of World Poetry Slam), with the promise of a revote in 2019 to decide the fate of 2020 and beyond. However, the growing sentiment is that PSI will likely not produce another major slam for the foreseeable future. Without PSI's tournaments, slam teams and individual poets have turned to regional competitions such as the Rustbelt Midwest Regional Poetry Slam, the Southern Fried Poetry Slam, the Ink Slam in Los Angeles, and the Texas Grand Slam Poetry Festival. Others have begun to create new individual and/or team slams.

We have heard a number of reasons for the fall of PSI, including financial problems, claims that it was taking advantage of volunteer labor, and, as always, inner turmoil and politics. We are intentionally vague here, as we are not entirely sure about the particular legal issues at play; however, the general discourse in the community centered on how PSI failed to properly respect Black women, many of whom have generously labored in paid and unpaid positions. This discourse permeated the networks of slam communities nationwide and spilled onto the 2018 National Poetry Slam stage in the form of protest and performance. The quixotic attempt to institutionalize a theater firmly planted in countercultural values and the voices of marginalized communities may have existed only in so far as it exploited the labor and creativity of women, poets of color, and especially the work of Black women. PSI's failures may teach us that legitimacy, be it connected to liberal or conservative spaces, requires some level of exploitation that's caught up in anti-Blackness and heteropatriarchy.

PSI's rise and fall, which feels less like an ending and more like an opportunity to pivot, reimagine, and rebuild, forces us to think about how outsider art forms with revolutionary potential might establish themselves without becoming a part of the very establishment that never valued their aesthetic. Further, this current slam moment opens up space for slammers, those who like the slam, and other artists to seriously contend with the politics of legitimacy and establishment. In his poem "Rifle," a piece about working toward a healthy masculinity, slam champion Rudy Francisco tells us of Mexican artist Pedro Reyes, who repurposed government-confiscated weapons and turned them into instruments. Ending with the idea that, although he grew up as violent as the weapons, perhaps he, too, can be repurposed, he teaches us that "The difference between a garden and a graveyard / is only what you choose to put into the ground" (n. pag.). In the twenty-first-century, those of us who love slam and spoken word must decide what we are going to put into the ground.

Notes

1. See Kristin Langellier and Eric Peterson's *Storytelling in Daily Life*. A book that is as much about method as it is theory, the authors explore storytelling as a communicative practice to better understand how we make use of stories in our daily lives to both confirm and resist dominant narratives.
2. Capitalizing the B in Black is a political move, one that, like Black lives, fully recognizes that grammar matters. With similar logics to the *Columbia Journalism Review*, "We capitalize *Black*, and not *white*, when referring to groups in racial, ethnic, or cultural terms." We understand that "For many people, *Black* reflects a shared sense of identity and community" that persists despite the onslaught of brutal white supremacy. In this way, white, for us "carries a different set of meanings; capitalizing the word in this context risks following the lead of white supremacists."
3. Ron "Shihan" Van Clief, interview by Javon Johnson, January 3, 2019.
4. During the 2019 NFL Superbowl, the fast-food chain giant Burger King aired a commercial in which Andy Warhol simply ate their signature Whopper burger in a nondescript room with the tagline, "Eat like Andy."
5. Unnamed poet in discussion with the author, August 2013.
6. Boris "Bluz" Rogers, interview by Javon Johnson, January 3, 2019.
7. Ron "Shihan" Van Clief, interview by Javon Johnson, January 3, 2019.

Works Cited

Aguilera-Carnerero, Carmen, and Abdul Halik Azeez. "'Islamonausea, Not Islamophobia': The Many Faces of Cyber Hate Speech." *Journal of Arab & Muslim Media Research* vol. 9, no. 1, 2016, pp. 21–40.

Aptowicz, Cristin O'Keefe. *Words in Your Face: A Guided Tour through Twenty Years of the New York City Poetry Slam*. Soft Skull Press, 2017.

Arkind, Ken. "Video Killed the Poetry Star." *The Pantograph Punch*, August 3, 2016, www.pantograph-punch.com/post/video-killed-the-poetry-star

Benaim, Sabrina. 2014. "Explaining My Depression to My Mother." Uploaded by Button Poetry, www.youtube.com/watch?v=aqu4ezLQEUA

Christian, Barbara. "The Race for Theory." *Cultural Critique*, no. 6, 1987, pp. 51–63.

Coleman, Stephen. "I Wanna Hear a Poem." *Russell Simmons' Presents Def Poetry Jam*, HBO, 2002.

Conquergood, Dwight. "Performance Studies: Interventions and Radical Research." *Cultural Struggles Performance, Ethnography, Praxis*, edited by Dwight Conquergood and E. Patrick Johnson. The University of Michigan Press, 2016.

Devlin, Paul, director. *SlamNation: The Sport of Spoken Word-Educators Edition*. DevlinPix, 1998.

Díaz, Junot. "MFA vs. POC." *The New Yorker*, June 18, 2017, www.newyorker.com /books/page-turner/mfa-vs-poc

Francisco, Rudy. "Rifle." Uploaded by Button Poetry, 2016. www.youtube.com /watch?v=ZvLmkQIg-FI

Gioia, Dana. *Can Poetry Matter?: Essays on Poetry and American Culture*. Graywolf Press, 2002.

Gustafson, Amy Carlson. "What Rhymes with Victory?" *Pioneer Press*, July 31, 2010, www.twincities.com/author/amy-carlson-gustafson/page/97/

Hammad, Suheir. "Fist Writing Since." *Russell Simmons' Presents Def Poetry Jam*, HBO, 2002.

Hilborn, Neil. "OCD." Uploaded by Button Poetry, 2013. www.youtube.com /watch?v=vnKZ4pdSU-s&t=4s

Johnson, Javon. *Killing Poetry: Blackness and the Making of Slam and Spoken Word Communities*. Rutgers University Press, 2017.

Lakoff, George. "The Use of 9/11 to Consolidate Conservative Power: Intimidation via Framing." *The Huffington Post*, November 10, 2011, www.huffingtonpost.com /george-lakoff/the-use-of-911-to-consoli_b_955954.html

Langellier, Kristin, and Eric E. Peterson. *Storytelling in Daily Life: Performing Narrative*. Temple University Press, 2004.

Levin, Marc, director. *Slam*. Trimark Pictures, 1998.

Myers, Lily. "Shrinking Women." Uploaded by Button Poetry, 2013. www.youtube .com/watch?v=zQucWXWXp3k

Peterson, James P. *Hip-Hop Headphones: A Scholar's Critical Playlist*. Bloomsbury Publishing, 2016.

Roche, Patrick. "21." Uploaded by Button Poetry, 2014. www.youtube.com/watch? v=6LnMhy8kDiQ

"Russell Simmons' Presents Def Poetry Jam on Broadway (promotional video)." Fox Associates, 2002.

Somers-Willett, Susan B. A. "From Slam to *Def Poetry Jam*: Spoken Word Poetry and Its Counterpublics." *Liminalities* vol. 10, no. 3/4, 2014, pp. 1–23.

   Cultural Politics of Slam Poetry: Race, Identity, and the Performance of Popular Verse in America. The University of Michigan Press, 2010.

Walker, Felicia R., and Viece Kuykendall. "Manifestations of Nommo in Def Poetry." *Journal of Black Studies* vol 36, no. 2, 2005, pp. 229–247.

Ward, Rubrecht. "St. Paul's Soapboxing Poetry Slam Team Wins Nationals," *City Pages*, August 10, 2009, www.citypages.com/music/st-pauls-soapboxing-poetry-slam-team-wins-nationals-6645865

12

CHRISTOPHER NEALON

Anti-capitalist Poetry

This chapter will take stock of the emergence of an emphatically anti-capitalist poetry in the decade since the global financial crash of 2008. As a range of scholars and commentators have noted, the aftermath of the 2008 crisis was marked by a retrenchment of capitalist accumulation rather than by serious reform – not to speak of revolutionary change. Efforts at repair coming from the president and the Federal Reserve were primarily focused on maintaining liquidity for banks and for the financial classes, and the FBI, the Department of Homeland Security, and local police forces across the United States worked in tandem to monitor and dissipate the energy of the Occupy movement that sprang up in the wake of the crash.[1]

Meanwhile, many observers have argued that the emergency measures taken to stave off the effects of the crash on the financial sector cannot cover over the looming possibility that capitalism has reached a terminal period of "secular stagnation," that is, a long-term decline in profitability that cannot be counteracted by even the most frantic measures. Describing the aftermath of the crash in his 2015 volume *Postcapitalism*, the economic journalist Paul Mason writes,

> the long-term prospects for capitalism are bleak. According to the OECD [the Organisation for Economic Co-operation and Development], growth in the developed world will be 'weak' for the next fifty years. Inequality will rise by 40 per cent. Even in the developing countries, the current dynamism will be exhausted by 2060 ... for the developed world the best of capitalism is behind us, and for the rest it will be over in our lifetime.
>
> What started in 2008 as an economic crisis morphed into a social crisis, leading to mass unrest; and now, as revolutions turn into civil wars, creating military tension between nuclear superpowers, it has become a crisis of the global order. (x)

In a brief prediction about the short- to middle-term future, Mason briefly summarizes what he sees as the two most likely scenarios for a terminally stagnant capitalist order. The second, more chilling scenario, sounds quite a bit like the world of 2019:

> There are, on the face of it, only two ways it can end. In the first scenario, the global elite clings on, imposing the cost of crisis on to workers, pensioners and the poor over the next ten or twenty years. The global order – as enforced by the IMF [International Monetary Fund], World Bank and World Trade Organization – survives, but in a weakened form. The cost of saving globalization is borne by the ordinary people of the developed world. But growth stagnates.
>
> In the second scenario, the consensus breaks. Parties of the hard right and left come to power as ordinary people refuse to pay the price of austerity. Instead, states then try to impose the costs of the crisis on each other. Globalization falls apart, the global institutions become powerless and in the process the conflicts that have burned these past twenty years – drug wars, post-Soviet nationalism, jihadism, uncontrolled migration and resistance to it – light a fire at the centre of the system. In this scenario, lip-service to international law evaporates; torture, censorship, arbitrary detention and mass surveillance become the regular tools of statecraft.
> (Mason x)

These chilling developments (Mason's speculations have become developments) have led to an un-ignorable shift in the poetry of the last decade. Writing in *The New York Times* at the end of 2018, US Poet Laureate Tracy K. Smith highlighted a variety of poetry that had broken past what she had experienced, in her MFA program in the 1990s, as a quiet injunction against political poems. Although she does not mention the financial crisis – she dates the beginnings of the shift she sees to the attack on the World Trade Center in 2001 and the Iraq War – one of her central examples is a poem by Evie Shockley called "semiautomatic," which pointedly rewrites typical phrases about money by replacing the word "money" with the phrase "black boys": "you act like we're swimming in black boys. / you can't keep black boys in your pocket. / if you had a million black boys, what would you do with them? / do you think we're made of black boys?" (1). For Smith, Shockley's poem is exemplary of a turn away from private, meditative poetry to a lyric speech that is public and willing to be controversial, to tackle rifts in the social body – here, of course, the rift opened up by the decade's horrible increase in police violence against black people. Yet Shockley's poem also forms part of an explosion of writing that explores the links between violence and commodity production; and one of the striking things about this recent poetry is that it also explores links among kinds of violence – racial, sexual, economic – and kinds of depredation – colonial, environmental – that liberal political language has tended to grasp in parallel rather than as part of a totality.

Consider the poem "Black Mass" by Jasmine Gibson, for instance, which takes up similar questions to Shockley's poem, while also coordinating the anguish of racial violence with on-the-ground relations between bosses and workers, with sexuality, and with geopolitics. It begins like this: "On Twitter stating you are 'in general anti-millenial' / Which is code for anti-black /brown power / Because we all know white people are disappearing from imaginations / Just ask the Balkans / They're still waiting on becoming white" (73). The casually bravura, leap-making thought in the opening stanza ranges across the rest of the poem (twelve stanzas in total) to develop a remarkably undeceived, disabused tone, piercing progressive myths and threatening to dissolve the ground under the poet's feet – an abyssal possibility she welcomes. Anything less than a deep transmogrification, a conjuring, a "Black Mass," will fail to address the anti-blackness and the pain the poem describes. Intimacy does not clear the bar: "people, like our white exes, / do funny things like show up to / marches for black women when they actually hate black women" (Gibson 73). Neither do cheap celebrations of black culture, stories of progress, or class-blind angles of vision on race: "I'm not tryna assimilate or congratulate you for loving Beyoncé / Booker T already wanted that, manifested it / we're reaping it still unfree / Only black bougie jawns can eat up / All of us can get rich or die trying" (Gibson 74).

The last four stanzas name the sources of the deep hurt that demands a dark, healing conjuration but not before specifying what stands in its way: "some stupid promissory note that may never deliver / it goes to my liver . . . // get used to it / it's just a uterus shedding its lining // I was told I could taste anything I liked / But to spit out whatever could nourish me / So I walked around emaciated and clouded with hunger / Everyone wants the world back again" (Gibson 74–75). The poem's close coordination of line and sentence is one index of its intellectual confidence and political clarity: It needs no line breaks to startle or surprise the reader. Instead, the sentence-like lines make links between the endless delay of full payment that marks the wage relation ("some stupid promissory note that may never deliver") and the open-ended trudge of a racialized suffering that may never end ("get used to it") while preparing for a leap into its final, startlingly universal claim ("Everyone wants the world back again"). The deftness of "Black Mass" is not only formal but generic: It dips into an African American literary tradition of thinking racial blackness in relation to sensory darkness, and it pivots nimbly, in its last stanzas, toward the minor poetic tradition of the nocturne: Indeed the lines "I was told I could taste anything I liked / But to spit out whatever could nourish me" read like a dystopian rewrite of the famous opening line of John Ashbery's 1975 poem, "As One Put Drunk Into the Packet-Boat," which begins "I tried each thing, only some were immortal and free" and concludes not with a black mass but with gratitude for darkness: "The summer demands and takes away too much, / But night, the reserved, the reticent, gives more than it takes" (427). The distance between the two nocturnal gestures is sobering.

The poetic force of unguarded line-like sentences also suffuses Daniel Borzutzky's 2016 volume *The Performance of Becoming Human*, which won the National Book Award for poetry in 2016. Based in Chicago, Borzutzky is the son of Chilean immigrants, and the poems in *The Performance* repeatedly coordinate contemporary police violence against black people with the practices of torture developed under the Chilean dictator Augusto Pinochet in the 1970s. The poems signal unambiguously that the basis for the parallel is the global reach of capitalist accumulation, which not only links distant populations but makes the social abstraction of capital – so hard to localize, so hard to "see" – horribly concrete in policed and tortured bodies. In making these kinds of links, Borzutzky's volume reads like a poetic expansion of the argument Naomi Klein made in her groundbreaking 2007 book *The Shock Doctrine*, which begins its story of neoliberal "disaster capitalism" (6) in Pinochet's Chile, where the CIA-backed regime perfected techniques of torture and traumatization that later proved applicable to whole nations. A long poem called "The Privatized Waters of Dawn," for instance, begins with the line "The appraisers from the Chicago Police Department prod my body in the bathtub" (Borzutzky 51) and that scene of violated intimacy quickly unfolds into a disassociated account of torture ("They don't smoke their cigarettes / They just jam them into my arm" [Borzuztky 52]). The speaker drifts away from the bathtub and settles by his window, where he witnesses another scene of police intimidation: ". . . from my window I watched the police pull a young man out of a black sedan . . . / They made him do twenty pushups / Why do I have to do twenty pushups, he asked / Because you're a decrepit, public body, the police officer said, and you do not own yourself anymore" (Borzutzky 53).

The speaker moves away from the window and returns to the interior of his apartment, where he is tormented by questions and taunts from a voice that is clearly expert in the cruelties of interrogation ("They say: Poet your favorite poet from now on is my boot" [Borzutzky 55]). The poem ends not only with the erasure of the world ("They take away the horizon / They take away the sky and the streets" [Borzutzky 55]) but with the emphatic devaluation of the speaker's flesh: "And as usual I watch from the bathtub until someone comes to conduct the daily appraisal of my body / I cost much less than my historical value and the bank has no choice but to deny the loan I need in order to buy myself back" (Borzutzky 56). Like the "stupid promissory note" that endlessly delays both racial liberation and the wage in

Gibson's "Black Mass," the denied loan here is the pivot on which the world is lost. Both poems draw on forms of poetic surprise that owe nothing to enjambment and everything to spatial and temporal shifts of attention, as well as to a pointed, agonized insistence on the corporeal effects of finance.

The poems in Allison Cobb's 2016 volume *After We All Died* share that insistence. As the title of Cobb's book suggests, the poems are focused on the prospect of mass extinction and on the dawning terrors of climate change; and they share with Gibson's and Borzutzky's poems a willingness to let go of matter itself, in order to see how it de- and re-composes under conditions of crisis that are specifically identified as capitalist. Yet the transformations of the body Cobb imagines are more perpetual and low-grade, even if they are linked to epochal shifts and historical traumas. She writes about nuclear radiation (she was born in Los Alamos, New Mexico, where the atomic bomb was developed), as well about the penetration of the body by plastic and industrial chemicals; and she experiences herself as a failed barrier against the material flows that serve as carriers for the flow of capital. *After We All Died* is full of apologies and the dynamics of apology: The opening poem is a prose blazon called "I forgive you," which repeats the title phrase ("I forgive you sacroiliac ... I forgive you coiled intestines ... " [Cobb 1]) until it becomes a kind of mantra for both an aging body and a body that has not successfully held off toxicity. There is a poem called "Sorry," which redeploys with dark humor the figure of the albatross in Coleridge's Rime of the Ancient Mariner, whose rotting carcass becomes an excruciating emblem of mass extinction (Cobb 22–24); and another poem called "You were born" twists itself around the question of privileged complicity with the destruction of the earth's resources under capitalism: "one poison is how we know we kind of want that / melancholy that lets we who are wealthy in the West / relax into our sadness about the end / of all the stuff we destroyed without knowing or trying ... " (Cobb 99).

This problem of complicity reaches a kind of climax in "Poem of force," which draws its title from Simone Weil's renowned 1939 essay about *The Iliad*. In that essay, Weil famously argued that, in Homer's poem full of heroes, the real protagonist is not a person or a god but force, violence itself. Cobb leverages Weil's insight into a poem that places racist police violence alongside the sexual violation of otherwise "privileged" white women; finds these categorical comparisons unsatisfying, since they end up feeling like a ranking of oppressions; and places them both, finally, against the backdrop of a terrible, worldwide momentum: "Can you hear / the global engine gunning, getting / louder? Once it's out and hot and / loaded up, it's just too hard to stop" (75). Though Cobb's volume is full of sentence-like lines like those in Gibson's and Borzutzky's work, line breaks are a formal touchstone for the poems in *After All We Died*, where they recall not Homer so much as Ovid: Their tiny surprises and twists are a running corollary to the book's topoi of metamorphosis, in which chemicals and plastic inhabit the body's cavities and tissues, changing its character and its destiny alike. Though the book's generic polestar is elegy, as its title makes clear, its attention to the transformations driving both death and natality give its poetics of apology a hint of something beyond sheepish guilt: When Cobb writes, "This is our death. We share it, we who come after the future," the lines call up Bertolt Brecht's great poem "An die Nachgeborenen" ("To Those Who Follow in Our Wake"), whose own closing lines apologize to those who will be born in future generations for having become hard, violent, and militant in the face of rising fascism: "But you, when at last the time comes / That man can aid his fellow man, / Should think upon us / With leniency" (n. pag.).

In a different vein, a no-apologies militant skepticism organizes Wendy Trevino's extraordinary 2018 volume, *Cruel Fiction*. The book's title recalls Lauren Berlant's widely read 2011 collection of critical essays, *Cruel Optimism*, which describes the "cruelty" of the process by which people commit themselves to capitalist versions of a "good life." The poems in Trevino's book range from sentence-based list poems to sonnet sequences to short journal-like entries on politics and solitary literary reading and small-group revolutionary reading groups, but the various forms all share a clarity about the loss of "fictions," including beloved ones, that has the miraculous feel of being resolute and effortless at the same time. This clarity drives a series of remarkable acts of literary revaluation, the centerpiece of which is the thirty-poem sequence "Brazilian Is Not a Race," which is written in prose so flat and disabused that it takes a while to recognize that the poems are essentially sonnets. "Brazilian Is Not a Race" thinks through the collisions of race and class from a revolutionary vantage, centering its attention on contemporary Oakland, California, and on the Texas–Mexico border of Trevino's youth. The thirty poems begin with a sonnet that takes off from the title of the sequence and which foregrounds what will be Trevino's signature practice of conjoining literary deflation and revolutionary clarity. In "Brazilian Is Not a Race," Trevino alludes to Elizabeth Bishop's notoriously ignorant and condescending attempts to serve as literary patron to Clarice Lispector, which included racializing her "Brazilian-ness" in colonial terms – as primitive, parochial.[2] The irony for Trevino is that, in Brazil, the European-born Lispector would have functioned as "white." Redesignating her that way, Trevino instantly notes that she doesn't mean that whiteness is better – "that passage sounded / Anti-black" – but that she's committed (as the sequence will brilliantly demonstrate) to thinking race and nation in a dialectical relation to class. This project, as a poetic matter, means endlessly sorting through one's aesthetic education, not to make it more "pure," more perfectly revolutionary, but less toxic. The poet knows young writers will probably always fall in love with writing that carries attitudes inimical to them, and that that's okay, but that so is telling the literary past to fuck off, as it were. It's never easy – "Why destroying what / Destroys you is more difficult than you/ Expect every time" (Trevino 30) – but it's nothing to apologize for.

The ironies of how race and nation obscure class formation and capital accumulation are not only a literary matter for Trevino. In another sonnet, she describes these twists playing out in a political group for "people of color," where the elasticity of that phrase is taken to its limit; of one woman who "introduced herself & explained / Her father was white & her mother was / From Guatemala," it is later revealed that "her / Mother's family owned a plantation in / Guatemala. Otherwise they were Basque" (Trevino 103). Inasmuch as "people of color," in the United States, has become a category of liberal politics – and, indeed, a category rather than a concept – it becomes, for Trevino, the occasion for the obscuring of property relations and the history of colonialism, including the history of the roles of local elites' relation to empire. The last line of the poem, however, invites a certain rueful laughter, and indeed the volume's ironies of literary revaluation produce a host of pleasures, often tangled with the pleasures of small-group reading and comradeship. In a short, playful poem titled only by its first line – "Santander Bank was smashed into!" – Trevino affectionately rewrites Frank O'Hara's poem that begins "Lana Turner has collapsed!," transforming O'Hara's funny admission of the way mass culture worms itself into our hearts ("Oh Lana Turner we love you get up" [64]) into a riff on the joyous minoritarian bond among those who look at mass culture and mass media through the lens of revolutionary skepticism: "the party melted into the riot melted into the party / like fluid road blocks & gangs & temporary / autonomous zones & everyone & I / & we all stopped reading" (19). Against depoliticized mass media lamentations over property destruction in times of rioting, Trevino sees the smashed bank window as an opening onto political possibilities of revel and revolution. The last line and a half of the poem rewrites the end of another O'Hara classic, "The Day Lady Died," in which the poet, learning of the death of Billie Holiday, recalls hearing her perform: "thinking of / leaning on the john door in the 5 SPOT / while she whispered a song along the keyboard / to Mal Waldron and everyone and I stopped breathing" (Trevino 21). If Trevino's revaluation of Bishop as literary taste-maker is liberatingly negative, here revaluation works another way, taking O'Hara's wistful, admiring analogy between the held breath of aesthetic amazement and the end of life and playfully turning it into a celebration of another "stoppage," the end of "mere" reading at the beginning of anti-capitalist action.

"Santander Bank was smashed into!" is a fantasia, but *Cruel Fiction* includes reflections on actual, on-the-ground struggle, not least in the volume's long opening poem, "128–131," which names the number of the cell in Santa Rita jail in Dublin, California, where Trevino was placed along with dozens of other women after Occupy Oakland's attempt to take over an empty building led to mass arrests on January 28, 2012. "128–131" is a list poem and a counting poem: It consists almost entirely of the poet's enumeration of what she saw while awaiting release. It is a deliberately, even ruthlessly simple poem, and at first it feels "anti-poetic." But lists are an ancient poetic form, of course, and numbers and counting are part of poetry's deep tissue – so the poem becomes a performance of continuous de- and re-valuation of "poetry." It narrates police cruelty ("I heard 1 pig say, 'This isn't about the constitution … If I don't like your face … '") and inmate humor ("I heard 1 woman admit she was waiting to be released to take a 'victory poop.'") and accrues into a picture of how social relation springs up among strangers whose only connection is having taken part in revolutionary action. The politics on the inside of Santa Rita are all over the map, as are the degrees of revolutionary consciousness: Along with the police officer who calls herself a member of the "99%," there is a protestor who works in the Financial District in San Francisco; the "Oakland to Greece" chant militantly links the struggles in Oakland to the politics of resisting police violence in Greece, but Trevino also notes one prisoner naively suggesting starting a website to replace the encampments the Oakland Police Department has dismantled. The poet's cool accounting of it all is a triumph of steadiness, but it is also, if we read "128–131" along certain formal lines, a game on the meaning of numbers in poetry and politics: They ground facts and provide data and steady memory, but they can also dissolve into mere recitation, and they can obscure the texture of relationships (as in the way the figure of the "99%" reflects numerical incomes but not actual class agon). As a remarkable addition to the history of prison literature, meanwhile, "128–131" makes clear the overlap (we can see it in Borzutzky and in Cobb) between anti-capitalist poetry and poetry describing the police.

The anonymous prisoner in Trevino's poem who likens Santa Rita jail to Dante's *Inferno* points to one last facet of recent anti-capitalist poetry I'd like to mention. The communist, Christian poems of David Brazil tap into millenarian and apocalyptic literary and religious traditions in order to name an ache for a just world that has always had an ambiguous relationship to Marxist materialism. This Marxist anti-idealism, which insists on "objective interests" as the sole ground for militancy, has firm roots in a century and a half of liberal betrayals of radical struggle, dating to the European revolutions of 1848; but the question of what makes people revolutionary remains stubbornly resistant to purely materialist answers (since, of course, not all working-class or oppressed people develop revolutionary consciousness, and revolutionary intellectuals, in particular, have a whole range of class origins); and of course there are Marxist thinkers – not least figures like Walter Benjamin – who have tried to tap into millenarian energies in order to force open ways of thinking past capitalist relations. So Brazil's radical Christianity – Oakland-based, queer, feminist, antiracist, and anticolonial – exists both inside and outside Marxist anti-capitalism. In the poem "Prole Song," from his 2016 volume *Holy Ghost*, Brazil writes a prayer for the end of capital that is styled like an old-fashioned want ad in a print newspaper. It is a witty, open-hearted poem, spoken by a time-pressed ("chrono / choked") worker (the proletarian "prole" of the title) seeking what he needs in an outmoded, demotic form (the want ad) who can't spend too much money on it (the abbreviations "&," and "w/" are cheaper) but whose desires are quite extravagant: moral transparency ("glass architecture"), the spiritual dedication of Buddhist community ("sangha"), and a new "epoch" altogether. The polite "please" that follows these requests opens onto apocalypse ("Please / communicate direct w / / ground zero at the / end of time") and urges the end of both race and capitalist money before coming back in for a landing on a modest "shake hands w / / everyone" that carries, even so, the after-echo of the end-time revolutionary militancy the poem has let us briefly glimpse. Poems across *Holy Ghost* and elsewhere in Brazil's work make clear that his "everyone" is as riven and implausible a collective subject as Gibson's "everyone" is in her "Black Mass" – but it's no coincidence that her diabolical, heavy-metal inversion of the sacred, like Brazil's ironic miniaturization of it, carries an anti-capitalist desire that cannot help but touch the universal. The emergence of that universality – everyone senses the disaster – and the impossibility of it – not everyone will work to end it – these can't be captured by conceptualizing a tension between "the individual and society," that liberal ur-dilemma, so much as between those who can no longer bear to assume the endless continuation of life under capital, and all those who gladly, or willing, or resignedly do so.

So what does it mean to read these poems together, as part of something – a tendency, a set of stances – that makes most sense to read in relation to the catastrophe of contemporary capitalism? What they share is elusive but intermittently clear. It's not just that the poems here all emerge from a small-press world that remains, even in the case of Borzutzky's National Book Award–winning volume, on the other side of a gulf between so-called independent publishing and the remaining poetry publishing handled by larger, capitalist houses. Nor is it just that many poems from this milieu were first published in comparatively ephemeral journals. It's not even that the majority of the poets in this chapter work outside the academy, which is almost unheard of in "mainstream" poetry today (Borzutzky's Wikipedia page lists him working at a community college).

That's part of it; but it's also that the poets here are willing to imagine their poetry as subcultural, as not for everyone – without, meanwhile, putting up particularly heavy coterie barriers to unexpected readers. This expresses itself, I think, in the range of de- and re-valuations of poetry here, in its various anti-literary gestures, in its ferocity and its accounts of bodily abjection. Most of the poets here work on the West Coast, or have passed through West Coast poetry worlds; and there is a matter of tone, or rhetorical address: More prestigious or prestigiously published poetry, much of which is still centered on the East Coast, tends to existentialize its grief into melancholy when it addresses climate change or the predations of finance, for instance, rather than take grief as grounds for the reevaluation, the loneliness, and the camaraderie to which militancy leads.

Rhetorical stance, small-press ecosystem, conditions of (un)employment or relation to old literary geographies – there is no one thing that marks these poems off categorically as "anti- capitalist." That's not surprising – such lines are always difficult to draw; and capital, in any case, is like poetry in that it is always transforming, as well, producing new antagonisms in old forms, even if it is unlike poetry in that it also always keeps track of its potential enemies. Or perhaps that's not an unlikeness, after all. It wouldn't be the worst way to think of the cotemporary tendency I've tracked in this wonderful writing: poetry with enemies.

Notes

1. The crash produced a huge outpouring of investigative journalism and scholarship that either assumes or notes the primacy of preserving liquidity for the financial classes. For one of the most comprehensive of these accounts, which benefits from a decade of hindsight and documentation, see Tooze. For a brief account of the uncovering of the practices of surveillance around Occupy, see Wolf.
2. For a brief account of Bishop's relation to Lispector, see Pechman.

Works Cited

Ashbery, John. *Collected Poems 1956–1987*. Library of America, 2008.
Berlant, Lauren. *Cruel Optimism*. Duke University Press, 2011.
Borzutzky, Daniel. *The Performance of Becoming Human*. Brooklyn Arts Press, 2016.

Brazil, David. *Holy Ghost*. City Lights Books, 2016.

Brecht, Bertolt. "Brecht's 'To Those Who Follow in Our Wake.'" Translated by Scott Horton. *Harper's Magazine*, January 15, 2008, https://harpers.org/blog/2008/01/brecht-to-those-who-follow-in-our-wake/

Cobb, Allison. *After We All Died*. Ahsahta Press, 2016.

Gibson, Jasmine. *Don't Let Them See Me Like This*. Nightboat Books, 2018.

Klein, Naomi. *The Shock Doctrine: The Rise of Disaster Capitalism*. Picador, 2007.

Mason, Paul. *Postcapitalism: A Guide to Our Future*. Farrar, Straus and Giroux, 2015.

O'Hara, Frank. *Lunch Poems*. City Light Books, 2014.

Pechman, Alexandra. "It's Complicated: Clarice Lispector and Elizabeth Bishop's Fraught Relationship." *Poetry Foundation*, September 29, 2015. www.poetryfoundation.org/articles/70270/its-complicated-56d24a0b3a371

Smith, Tracy K. "Political Poetry Is Hot Again. The Poet Laureate Explores Why, and How." *The New York Times*, Sunday Book Review, December 10, 2018, p. 1.

Tooze, Adam. *Crashed: How a Decade of Financial Crises Changed the World*. Viking, 2018.

Trevino, Wendy. *Cruel Fiction*. Commune Editions, 2018.

Weil, Simone. "*The Iliad*, or the Poem of Force." *Chicago Review* vol. 18, no. 2, 1965, pp. 5–30.

Wolf, Naomi. "Revealed: How the FBI Coordinated the Crackdown on Occupy." *The Guardian*, December 29, 2012, www.theguardian.com/commentisfree/2012/dec/29/fbi-coordinated-crackdown-occupy

13

STEPHEN VOYCE

Of Poetry and Permanent War in the Twenty-First-Century

The world is a battlefield.
  – Anonymous, Joint Special Operations Command (qtd. in Scahill 4)

The poets are reading
        Machiavelli when they should be
                reading Clausewitz.
      – Joshua Clover, *Red Epic* (54)

Since 2001, the United States has engaged in an opaque and borderless war both global in scale and endless in scope. Two full-scale wars in Iraq and Afghanistan, further military operations in Libya, Pakistan, Yemen, Somalia, Syria, and elsewhere, along with an unprecedented expansion of the US military's footprint have cost by some estimates a million lives and fueled the largest refugee crisis since World War II.[1] This most recent phase of US imperial adventurism includes the systemic use of torture, extrajudicial assassination, and indefinite detention. Moreover, in the wake of the September 11 attacks, the US government had secretly developed and implemented the most elaborate surveillance apparatus in world history, affording unprecedented powers to the nation's sixteen major intelligence agencies. While political commentators tend to separate domestic and foreign policy, law enforcement and the military have become increasingly intertwined with one another; this includes the militarization of police and the use of counterinsurgency doctrine (both of which have much longer histories than is typically understood), the use of private military contractors both at home and abroad, domestic spying programs disproportionately fixated on people of color and left protest groups, along with the formation of the Department of Homeland Security, whose mandate has radically expanded beyond the scope of its initial charge. In a telling shift in military nomenclature, what was once dubbed the "global war on terror" is now more commonly referred to as "national security policy," whereby war is normalized and rendered permanent.

A host of theorists and military historians now write of "unending war," "perpetual war," the "forever war," the "long war."[2] According to *Washington Post* journalist Greg Jaffe, senior Pentagon officials now speak openly of "infinite war" (n. pag.) and this shortly before the term appeared in the subtitle of a Marvel film.[3] Still others speak in spatial terms of an ever-expanding "everywhere war" (Gregory "Everywhere War" 239), "multi-sited war" (Sassen 37), and "reconnaissance wars of the planetary frontier-land" (Bauman 81). Yet on this account the war planners are hardly cryptic. By 2006, former Secretary of Defense Donald Rumsfeld had delivered a lecture aptly titled "The Long War" to the National Press Club on the eve of the release of the *Quadrennial Defense Review* (*QDR*). The *QDR* charts the US military's national security agenda for the next twenty years. Its central section, "Fighting the Long War," lays out the Defense Department's plan for "long-duration unconventional warfare, counterterrorism, counter-insurgency, and military support for stabilization and reconstruction efforts." Rumsfeld's revisionist account sought to both placate and ready the nation for a decades-long conflict defined not by the total wars of the twentieth century but rather by a "globally mobile," "rapid strike" form of unconventional warfare, "[m]aintaining a long-term, low-visibility presence in many areas of the world where U.S. forces do not traditionally operate" (*QDR* v, 4, 23). In what is perhaps the most telling statistic of American empire today: The historically unprecedented expansion of the US military's footprint now includes 800 installations garrisoned in more than 130 countries on earth, along with more than 420 military bases located in the continental United States, Guam, and Puerto Rico.[4]

That war has also become *boundaryless* is, for the gifted geographer Derek Gregory, best understood by "the replacement of the concept of the battle-*field* in U.S. military doctrine by the multi-scalar, multi-dimensional 'battle-*space*'" ("The Everywhere War" 239). The coordinates of war have no front or back, no absolute territorial ground; Carl von Clausewitz's "theater of war" now comes to denote a totalizing, planetary sphere of action as such;[5] and just as it expands outward in space, it folds inward to saturate all aspects of everyday life – often in ways that remain imperceptible to those who actively participate in it. This includes more obviously the militarization of police and the prison system, cyberspace, telecommunications, academic research, and public infrastructure but also clothing, marriage, entertainment, and language. In *Globalization and Militarism: Feminists Make the Link* (2007), Cynthia Enloe defines *militarization* as the adoption of military values both inside and outside the space of active battle, "a belief in hierarchy, obedience, and the use of force" that extends military solutions to every other facet of social and political life (4). Indeed, she observes, "most of the people in the world who are militarized are not themselves in uniform"; often "militarization can look less like conventional aggressiveness and more like deferential passivity" (Enloe 4–5).[6] Hence permanent war's ontological properties are spatial ("everywhere"), temporal ("endless"), and ubiquitous ("saturation").

No credible history of the twenty-first-century can ignore these events, which means that no history of twenty-first-century aesthetics should ignore them either. The central purpose of this study is to account for a poetry of war resistance that directly engages the clandestine activities of the national security state. How do poets help us to see anew a highly mediated form of warfare that nonetheless conceals itself in the black ops, redacted docs, dark money, and classified landscapes comprising the secretive theaters of "low-visibility" twenty-first-century violence? War writing has come from numerous camps of American verse over the past seventeen years; I will argue, however, its most sustained treatment appears in three overlapping communities: Middle Eastern American poetries, documentary poetics (or "docpo"), and left communist circles. Philip Metres's *Sand Opera* (2015), Solmaz Sharif's *Look* (2016), Juliana Spahr's *This Connection of Everyone with Lungs* (2005), Sinan Antoon's *The Baghdad Blues* (2007), and Khaled Mattawa's *Tocqueville* (2010) are exemplary, as are works by Lawrence Joseph, Craig Santos Perez, Ara Shirinyan, Etel Adnan, Joshua Clover, Hilary Plum, Hayan Charara, Allison Cobb, Samuel Hazo, Anne Boyer, CAConrad, Judith Goldman, and Jena Osman, among others.

It should be said from the outset that nowhere are the limits of studying a national literature more apparent than when one addresses themes of war. This is a chapter about twenty-first-century warfare from the perspective of poets whose nation-state is the century's chief instigator of global conflict. I offer a modest attempt to characterize the work of *American* poets representing wars perpetrated by the US government and its allies. Farid Matuk recalls that, just as the Syrian civil war had commenced, "white U.S. writer friends, on learning I was working on a new manuscript of poems, started asking, '[a]re you writing about Syria?'" (n. pag.). Matuk, who was born in Peru to a Syrian mother and presently lives in Arizona, offers this instructive response: "for those sincerely interested in artistic experiences of conflict, positioning really should matter. Given a choice between my book and, say, *Adrenaline* (2017) by Ghayath Almadhoun, it is absolutely Almadhoun we should be reading – since he is a Palestinian refugee born and raised in Syria whose *positioning* has situated his imagination in relation to particular acts of witness" (n. pag., emphasis added). Evoking Adrienne Rich's "Blood,

Bread, and Poetry: The Location of the Poet," Matuk insists we not make the erroneous demand that American poets of a particular racial or ethnic group speak on behalf of those who live in socio-politically distinct locales to which they have wide and varying degrees of affinity. To this end, the purpose of American protest poetry today should not be to speak on behalf of the victims of empire but rather to expose and challenge by way of illumination the machinations of US imperial violence.

Permanent War Economy: A Primer

In 2008, the Bush administration sanctioned the $700 billion-dollar bailout of the US banking sector in response to the subprime mortgage crisis. Officially known as the Emergency Economic Stabilization Act of 2008, several commentators noted that this upward redistribution of wealth amounted to "socialism for the rich."[7] For a very small group of historians and journalists who study national security, however, this number was significant for a different reason: $700 billion is the approximate annual budget of the Department of Defense. (As we shall see, the actual overall war expenditure is much higher, but this is the stated number.) Few scholars working in the humanities fully understand the economics of national security or militarism's infiltration into virtually every facet of social life, making it an understudied yet central focus for the critique of political economy and its relation to a US popular cultural imaginary that largely celebrates its protracted expansion. Notably, the term *permanent war* – now commonplace in the vocabulary of journalists and critics – was first defined by Seymour Melman in *Permanent War Economy* (1974) during the height of the cold war.[8] His study carefully tracks the consequences of the United States' excessive post–World War II war budget (what he calls "military Keynesianism"), calculating that it would inevitably deplete spending on public infrastructure, affordable housing, health, and education – a prediction that is bearing out today.

To this end, a rudimentary breakdown of present-day defense spending is instructive. The Pentagon ("Base") Budget constitutes the foundational operations expenditure, including peacetime training, intelligence, weapons acquisition, and the extensive civilian workforce and infrastructural resources required to run a military. Its cost as of 2016 exceeded $525 billion. What many fail to recognize, however, is that this amount excludes the cost of active wars. The invasions of Afghanistan and Iraq are largely paid for by way of the Overseas Contingency Operations (OCO) account, which fluctuates by fiscal year and has reached as high as $180 billion during eighteen consecutive years of war. For the current period

October 1, 2019, through September 30, 2020, Congress is set to allocate a combined $730 billion in base and OCO funding. Yet the economic costs of war are frequently buried in additional government agencies, chief among them the Department of Energy's nuclear arsenal ($24.8 billion), the State Department's International Affairs Budget ($51 billion), the Department of Homeland Security ($69.2 billion), and the Department of Veterans Affairs ($216 billion). Moreover, as William Hartung and others point out, the share of interest on the national debt directly attributable to defense spending now totals $156 billion annually; no military venture in American history has depended so exclusively on borrowed funds.[9] Compile these numbers and *the real annual cost of national security exceeds $1 trillion dollars.*

The historians who address militarism in economic terms – among them Seymour Melman, Cynthia Enloe, Chalmers Johnson, William Hartung, and Alfred McCoy – argue, as Tom Engelhardt does, that a proper critique of American empire must begin from the premise "that Washington is a war capital, that the United States is a war state, that it garrisons much of the planet, and that the norm for us is to be at war somewhere at any moment" (n. pag.). Yet what is perhaps most notable is not simply the scale of the war economy but that it largely operates unnoticed by the general public. In their 2017 study of coalition airstrikes in Iraq, Azmat Khan and Anand Gopal register a similar complaint: Despite the expanded media with which to document conflict, "this may be the least transparent war in recent American history" (n. pag.).

The poet, critic, and anti-war activist Philip Metres avers that "it is not difficult to understand why few poems directly address such abstract phenomena as weapons sales, nuclear stockpiles, or U.S.-funded military regimes" (*Behind the Lines* 11). He reminds us of Richard Wilbur's cautionary advice for poets and prophets alike: "Spare us all word of the weapons, their force and range, / The long numbers that rocket the mind; / Our slow, unreckoning hearts will be left behind, / Unable to fear what is too strange" (182). Despite some striking exceptions (among them Adrienne Rich, Carolyn Forché, Denise Levertov, Joy Harjo, and June Jordan), Metres laments that poetry during the American Century generally "displays a quiescence when it comes to the militarism of American culture" (*Behind the Lines* 12). What might a poetics look like that addresses it directly? While protracted engagement with American militarism stateside is still arguably missing in action, the striking outliers of our era are emerging – Metres among them.

"16 Seconds"

Poets Against the War (2003) was arguably the most visible collection of American protest verse published in response to the invasion of Iraq. Its editor Sam Hamill, along with several other poets, had been invited to the White House by then First Lady Laura Bush for a symposium on "Poetry and the American Voice," which was to commemorate the work of Walt Whitman, Langston Hughes, and Emily Dickinson. After learning that Hamill planned to protest the "shock and awe" campaign against Baghdad, the event was initially postponed and later cancelled. Hamill instead solicited work for his website[10] and later published a selection of these poems in book form. At the time Hamill observed, "one of the great questions poets face today is just how we carry our tradition into a world of 'pre-emptive war'" (xx). The speaker of Hayan Charara's "Usage" likewise declares: "The doctrine / of preemption ultimately negated its need" (78). Hamill and Charara immediately understood that the mandate to wage perpetual war had constituted the formative logic of the Bush administration's national security strategy from the outset. The centerpiece of the "Bush Doctrine" stressed the right of unilateral preemption against perceived future threats: "[t]o forestall or prevent such hostile acts by our adversaries, the United States will, if necessary, act preemptively in exercising our inherent right of self-defense" (The White House 18). This right was further codified in the Authorization for Use of Military Force (AUMF), which grants unprecedented authority to the office of the president to engage in military actions against those who perpetrated the September 11 attacks, along with any "associated forces" deemed to have "planned, authorized, committed or aided" the attacks ("Authorization" n. pag.).

By the time neoconservatives like Rumsfeld realized the conflict would extend well into the fledgling century, poets had already begun to register a rhetorical shift in the war on terror. Samuel Hazo, writing just before the publication of Rumsfeld's 2006 *QDR Report*, and whose work appeared in Hamill's volume, captures this tendency in "For Which it Stands": the "President / proclaims we will be at war forever – / not war for peace but war / upon war" (176).[11] In Lawrence Joseph's "Rubaiyat" (so named for the Persian verse form made famous by the medieval author Omar Khayyam), the speaker inquires, "[w]hat? War / as a living text? ... Cyber war and permanent / war, Third Wave War, neocortical war, / Sixth Generation War, Fourth Epoch / War, pure war and war of computers ..." (44). Joseph's immediate reference is the military historian Chris Hables Gray, whose *Postmodern War: The New Politics of Conflict* (1997) features an extraordinary list of no less than fifty competing terms that variously describe a computer-driven "Revolution in Military Affairs" (RMA), among them hypermodern war, hyperreal war, information war, and netwar. Increasingly, this has involved strategies to combat nonstate actors, marked in part by highly advanced weapon systems (or so-called smart weapons) and biometric surveillance, all linked to a telecommunications system used both to wage war and to propagandize the efficacy of its calculated violence. "As a weapon, as a myth, as a metaphor, as a force multiplier, as an edge, as a trope, as a factor, and as an asset," Gray argues, "information (and its handmaidens – computers to process it, multimedia to spread it, systems to represent it) has become the central sign of postmodernity" (21–22). Elsewhere in "Rubaiyat," we see "... a pulled up / satellite image of a major / military target, a 3-D journey / into a landscape of hills and valleys ... / all of it from real-world data" (Joseph 41). For Joseph and others, a poetics of witness must negotiate a labyrinthine network of screens and video feeds akin to an act of reverse engineering, whereby one must navigate through a litany of hypermediated environments back to the source of its surveilling gaze. It is partly for this reason the drone has emerged as the consummate symbol of our era. Notably, every poet mentioned in this chapter has written about them.

Solmaz Sharif's remarkable volume *Look* (2016) offers an exemplary case study. The text imitates the clausal structure of a legal document. That is, the term *whereas* comprises the first word in what is called a *recital*, a repeated phrase that introduces a statute, contract, or proclamation. In the case of a legislative bill, *whereas* is synonymous with *because*; where it pertains to a poem, one calls this rhetorical device *anaphora*: "Whereas it could take as long as 16 seconds between / the trigger pulled in Las Vegas and the Hellfire missile / landing in Mazar-e-Sharif, after which they will ask / *Did we hit a child? No. A dog.* they will answer themselves" (Sharif 3). While Sharif alludes to a city in the northern Balkh province of Afghanistan, the dialogue bears an uncanny resemblance to the transcript of a drone chat log published by the *Los Angeles Times* in 2011, revealing an attack on a civilian convoy in the remote southern Daikundi province 200 miles southwest of Kabul (Cloud n. pag.). *Look* repurposes jargon culled from the US Defense Department's *Dictionary of Military and Associated Terms*[12] (appearing in small caps) in a series of texts that examine the global scope of US war and the weaponization of language. Military officials update the dictionary frequently, as unclassified terms are added and subtracted based on factors such as military usage and the presence of the term in standard English. "For example," Sharif explains, "the term 'drone' appeared in the 2007 version, but no longer appears in the 2015 version. It is likely 'drone' was removed from the dictionary since understanding of the term has fully entered English vernacular; in other words, the military is no longer a *supplement* to the English language, but the English language itself" (95). Hence the term's disappearance marks the drone's ubiquity in the American cultural imaginary.

The volume's titular list poem instructs, "[i]t matters what you call a thing" (Sharif 3). The term "Look" in military-speak refers to "a period during which a mine circuit is receptive to an influence" and so in this context the lag time between the trigger pull and a bomb's detonation. Sharif demands her reader track this "16 second" interval. Reverse engineer the drone strike from the sixteenth second, at which point the missile reaches its destination, and what one sees is an expansive public–private enterprise to manage and maintain the remote internment of tribal populations in remote regions of Afghanistan, Pakistan, and elsewhere. Video footage is often fed directly to military officials located in the vicinity of targets and nearby operation centers, along with intelligence analysts stationed throughout the United States. Derek Gregory reports that currently 192 personnel are needed to support a single Predator or Reaper combat air mission over a twenty-four-hour period ("Drone Geographies" 7). Integral to this vast infrastructure is a band of private military contractors that produce and maintain UAVs, surveillance data, software capabilities, and the payloads they deliver. Meanwhile, the authorization process for assassinating high-value targets (colloquially known as the "Kill Chain") involves a complicated bureaucracy passing through, for example, the Joint Special Operations Command (JSOC) taskforce tracking a target, regional command (e.g. Centcom, Africom), the Joint Chief of Staff, the Secretary of Defense, and then on to a circle of top advisors to the president known as the Principals Committee of the National Security Council.[13]

The crucial point, however, is that we are neither meant to see this process nor the ethnically diverse populations of rural Afghanistan and the Federally Administered Tribal Areas – their languages, kinship systems, political councils, and wedding ceremonies. What instead we encounter is a system of covert operations, "black budgets," and classified geographies whose purpose is to redact whole populations from consideration.

Like Sharif's incisive critique of military jargon, Juliana Spahr's *This Connection of Everyone with Lungs* captures the militarization of intimate daily life. "Poem Written from November 30, 2002, to March 27, 2003," for example, takes the form of an aubade: "Beloveds, my desire is to hunker down and lie low, lie with yous in beds and bowers, ... [b]ut the military-industrial complex enters our bed at night" (Spahr 63, 72). Indeed, "every word we say is caught – every word, whether it is ironic or not, whether it is articulate or not ... every moment of beauty occupied" (Spahr 67). The verse continues in the form of a blazon: "In bed, when I stroke the down on your cheeks, I stroke also the carrier battle group ships, the guided missile cruisers, and the guided missile destroyers. / When I reach for your waists, I reach for bombers, cargo, helicopters, and special operations" (Spahr 74–75). Spahr employs traditional poetic forms designed to capture the private sphere of the lovers' embrace in order to examine "levels of complicity so intense and various" that the instruments of global violence saturate "our dream[s]" (63).

In response to Eisenhower's oft-quoted 1961 farewell address, critics have sought to trace the military's pervasive reach beyond the armaments industry. One speaks of a "military-industrial-academic complex," a "military-industrial-entertainment complex," and a "military-industrial-think tank complex." More recently, critics have examined emergent derivations of these structures: the "security-industrial complex," the "homeland security complex," the "surveillance-industrial complex," and the "prison-industrial complex."[14] Each term attempts to capture the militarization of civilian life that Enloe so succinctly defines. Yet, for Spahr, "the three legged-stool of political piece, military piece, and development piece" (18) upon which the nation sits moves beyond government-corporate assemblages and into affective-aesthetic ones: "Some say that the most beautiful thing upon the black earth is an army of AS90 self-propelled guns, other infantry, still others ships" (45–46). The aestheticization of war is hardly new; it forms the kernel of our oldest poems after all. What is striking, however, about Spahr's representation of global violence is its very absence of spatiotemporal distinctions between wartime and peacetime, battlespace and homefront, soldiers and civilians. Following Enloe, Spahr depicts and critiques a form of warfare that increasingly looks like something altogether different than conventional battle. Hence, she intimates that the twenty-first-century will require a poetics of witness that follows militarism's restructuring of forms of life as such.

The works of Charara, Lawrence, Sharif, Spahr – along with others such as Judith Goldman's *agon* (2017), Moez Surani's عملية *Operación Opération Operation* 行 动 *Операция* (2017), Dionne Brand's *Inventory* (2006), and Craig Santos Perez's *from unincorporated territory* series (2008) – demonstrate that, while the weaponization of language and everyday life sometimes involves explicit provocation, more often than not its preferred metaphors are deliberately mundane, intended to obscure, sanitize, redirect, and conceal. In the Canadian poet Moez Surani's book-length inventory of more than 4,000 code names of military operations conducted by UN member states, two images frequently recur: morning dawn and cleanliness. For example, Morning Light, June Dawns, Sunrise, Total Cleansing, Cleansweep, and Clean & Beautiful. In what amounts to an unwitting homage to F. T. Marinetti's glorification of war as "the only hygiene of the world" (51), such terms reveal that what undergirds acts of mass violence is an aesthetics of purity and renewal.

STEPHEN VOYCE

Infinite Enemy

In *Precarious Life* (2004), Judith Butler observes: "[t]he infinite paranoia that imagines the war against terrorism as a war without end will be one that justifies itself endlessly in relation to the spectral infinity of its enemy" (34). This is the structural logic of the "war on terror": a self/other dichotomy by which the State justifies perpetual violence on accord of the "unreality" of another whose ontological status is rendered "interminably spectral." The practice of indefinite detention of so-called enemy combatants is Butler's central example, a label designed in the wake of 9/11 to circumvent international laws governing the rights of prisoners of war. Yet it is precisely what she calls the "infinity" of the enemy that informs both the juridical frameworks that enable perpetual war and the operational frameworks that set it into motion. Just as the AUMF had entitled the executive branch to initiate military force preemptively, the irregular and asymmetric nature of twenty-first-century warfare outlined in the *QDR Report* ultimately justifies action "against new and *elusive* foes" by virtue of their very illegibility, and thus the enemy's interchangeability (vi, emphasis added).

The justification for war in Iraq outlined in the Bush Doctrine, one should not forget, capitalized upon Western perceptions that homogenize deeply complex sectarian and ethnic differences throughout the Greater Middle East. The perpetrators of the Afghanistan and Iraq wars exploited deep-seated racial anxieties and Islamophobia to justify economic control of the region. "Like the Western maps of the Middle East," the speaker of Metres's "Mappemonde" wryly declares, "the names of nations" appear "beneath the names of oil companies" (*Ode* 8). In Metres's *Sand Opera*, the bifurcated hemispheres in maps of conquest are found written on the human body: "[i]n the sudden wake, how to see the difference between 'or' & 'and' – on which matters of matter and spirit hang. If the eye. If a body a body none/theless loved by anons & disappeared" (83). The body in question is that of Mohamed Farag Ahmad Bashmilah, a Yemeni citizen detained in Jordan in 2003 and rendered to a black site in Bagram, Afghanistan, where he was repeatedly tortured over a period of eighteen months. He would provide meticulous diagrams of his cell, interrogation room, and prison block, which Metres dutifully reproduces on transparent paper overlaying passages from Bashmilah's testimony: "[w]henever I saw / a fly in my cell / I was filled / with joy / though I wished for it / to slip under the door / so it would not be / imprisoned itself" (*Sand Opera* 66–67). The speaker of Khaled Mattawa's "Tocqueville" declares that fear "makes all kinds of violence legitimate, or a desire to kill that rationalizes itself as fear of violence. In the end, it doesn't matter which. And then you take that energy outward, and like a searchlight, you beam it on whatever target you want … And you tell them that's the enemy" (28). Metres and Mattawa demonstrate that, in the figure of the alleged terrorist, the enemy combatant, the other, one finds an empty signifier, a body on which to project whatever fantasy of the enemy serves its purpose.

Again, on what Butler calls the "unreality" of the other (33), the war planners are occasionally candid. In a 2004 piece for *The New York Times Magazine*, Ron Suskind attributes the following anonymous quote to a high-ranking Bush administration official: "[w]e're an empire now, and when we act, we create our own reality" (n. pag.). The unnamed source continues, "[a]nd while you are studying that reality – judiciously, as you will – we'll act again, creating other new realities, which you can study too, and that's how things will sort out. We're history's actors … and you, all of you, will be left to just study what we do" (qtd. in Suskind n. pag.). Suskind later revealed that his source was Bush's senior advisor Karl Rove (though he denies having said it). For poets, journalists, and scholars alike, Rove's comments are an understandable source of anxiety with regards to what a poetry of active resistance – let alone investigative prose – can realistically achieve. After all, "no lyric," Seamus Heaney surmised, "has ever stopped a tank" (107). On the efficacy of poetry, consider the left communist collective and founders of Commune Editions (CE), who argue that we should abandon the desire for a text *to act* by itself. Instead, CE's members, who consist of Juliana Spahr, Joshua Clover, and Jasper Bernes, describe the poem as a companion to anti-capitalist struggle, as the beloved riot dogs of Athens accompanied activists in the streets (Spahr, Clover, and Bernes 184). Dogs inspire loyalty, they bark when there is trouble, and their behavior is occasionally unpredictable. Yet the metaphor's chief function is more understated. It reflects their rejection of what the group calls poetic "substitutionism": "[a]ll three of us," they remark in an interview, "have slightly different ways of approaching questions about the political effectivity of poetry, but we more or less agree that the real action is in the streets and poetry isn't a substitute for that kind of contestation" (Spahr, Clover, and Bernes 184). Hence, "the metaphor is a way of describing our own modesty with regard to political effects but also our sense that we imagine the press [and our poetry] as a part of something larger, something that can be truly transformative" (Spahr, Clover, and Bernes 184). To say that the poem alone cannot generate revolutionary change need not be interpreted as a declaration of nihilistic entrapment. Instead, one might adopt a view of poetic writing that is intimately allied to other forms of contestation.

As it pertains to a poetics of war resistance, this will require a challenge to conventional war narratives. Metres identifies four pernicious elements that haunt the history of war writing from *The Iliad* to late-twentieth-century writing and film: a highly limited attention to the male soldier on the battle-front, a captivated gaze upon the spectacle of violence, the reinforcement of gender and racial stereotypes, and the absence of dissenting voices. This "narrow focus," Metres contends, "naturalizes war, distracts from its causes, and turns away before its final devastation" (*Behind the Lines* 3). The task of war resistance writing today finds a deft starting point in Bashmilah's blue-print of a black site. A twenty-first-century poetics of witness, as Metres, Joseph, Spahr, Sharif, and others conceive it, should decenter the privileged position of the soldier, illuminate the disproportionate consequences of war for the civilian populations who will bear the worst of its effects, and render transparent the economic and political machinery of national security.

Notes

1. Brown University's Cost of War Project's most recent report on total casualties conservatively estimates that at least 480,000 people have been directly killed in these conflicts, more than 244,000 of them civilians. Additionally, indirect deaths caused by disease and loss of critical infrastructure likely brings the total above 1 million. Note, importantly, the study confines itself to Afghanistan, Iraq, and Pakistan only. See Crawford.
2. See, for example, Duffield; Schwartz; Amin; Filkins; and Singh. A number of prominent journalists have since adopted and popularized the term "permanent war," among them Tom Engelhardt, Jeremy Scahill, William Hartung, Nick Turse, and Cora Currier in publications such as *TomDispatch*, *The Nation*, and *The Intercept*.
3. Marvel Studios premiered *Avengers: Infinite War* (directed by Joe Russo and Anthony Russo) less than a month after Jaffe reported this story.
4. See Johnson pp. 109–110 and Vine.
5. The Defense Department's *Dictionary of Military and Associated Terms* provides the following entry for "theater of war": "[d]efined by the President, Secretary of Defense, or the geographic combatant commander as the area of air, land, and water that is, or may become, directly involved in the conduct of major operations and campaigns involving combat." See *DOD Dictionary*, 220.
6. Virilio similarly describes what he calls "pure war" (Virilio and Lotringer 7).
7. Critics as diverse as Slavoj Zizek, Nouriel Roubini, and Bernie Sanders evoked this phrase in the immediate aftermath of the 2008 Economic Crisis, though variations on it date to the work of Martin Luther King Jr. and Gore Vidal, among others, who in turn may have first encountered the phrase in Harrington (58).
8. The socialist economist Ed Sard (who went by the aliases Frank Demby, Walter S. Oakes and T. N. Vance) first coined the term "permanent arms economy" in 1951, after which Melman adapted and expanded the concept. See Vance; Melman.
9. See Hartung and Smithberger. For additional resources, consult the Costs of War Project, Watson Institute International & Public Affairs, Brown University.

10. See www.poetsagainstthewar.org.
11. The penultimate line of the poem likely alludes to Harry Elmer Barnes's edited collection, *Perpetual War for Perpetual Peace* (1953), a phrase suggested to him by the historian Charles Austin Beard.
12. Sharif uses the October 2007 edition, which contains more than 5,900 entries.
13. See Currier.
14. See Eisenhower. For an excellent overview of the term's many adaptations, see Turse.

Works Cited

Amin, Samir. *The Liberal Virus: Permanent War and the Americanization of the World*. Monthly Review Press, 2004.

Authorization for Use of Military Force. Pub. L. 107–40. 115 Stat. 224. September 18, 2001, www.congress.gov/107/plaws/publ40/PLAW-107publ40.pdf

Bauman, Zygmant. "Reconnaissance Wars of the Planetary Frontierland." *Theory, Culture, & Society* vol. 19, no. 4, 2002, pp. 81–90.

Brecht, Bertolt. *War Primer*, translated and edited by John Willet. Verso, 2017.

Butler, Judith. *Precarious Life: The Powers of Mourning and Violence*. Verso, 2004.

Charara, Hayan. "Usage." *Inclined to Speak: An Anthology of Contemporary Arab American Poetry*, edited by Hayan Charara. The University of Arkansas Press, 2008, pp. 76–83.

Cloud, David S. "Anatomy of an Afghan War Tragedy," *Los Angeles Times*, April 10, 2011, www.latimes.com/world/la-fg-afghanistan-drone-20110410-story.html

Clover, Joshua. *Red Epic*. Commune Editions, 2015.

Crawford, Neta C. "Human Cost of the Post-9/11 Wars: Lethality and the Need for Transparency." *Costs of War*. Watson Institute of International and Public Affairs, Brown University, November 2018, https://watson.brown.edu/costsof war/papers/2018/human-cost-post-911-wars-lethality-and-need-transparency

Currier, Cora. "The Kill Chain: The Lethal Bureaucracy Behind Obama's Drone War." *The Intercept*, October 15, 2015, https://theintercept.com/drone-papers/the-kill-chain/

Department of Defense Dictionary of Military and Associated Terms, U.S. Department of Defense, June 2019, www.jcs.mil/Portals/36/Documents/Doctrine/pubs/dictionary.pdf

Duffield, Mark. *Development, Security and Unending War: Governing the World of Peoples*. Polity Press, 2007.

Eisenhower, Dwight D. "Farewell Radio and Television Address to the American People." *Public Papers of the Presidents of the United States: Dwight D. Eisenhower 1960–1961*. Government Printing Office, pp. 1035–1040.

Englehardt, Tom. "War Is Peace." *TomDispatch*, September 17, 2009, www.tom dispatch.com/post/175129/tom_engelhardt_war_is_peace

Enloe, Cynthia. *Globalization and Militarism: Feminists Make the Link*. Rowman & Littlefield, 2007.

Filkins, Dexter. *The Forever War*. Vintage Books, 2009.

Gray, Chris Hables. *Postmodern War: The New Politics of Conflict*. Guilford Press, 1997.

Gregory, Derek. "Drone Geographies." *Radical Philosophy* vol. 183, January–February 2014, pp. 7–20.

"The Everywhere War." *The Geographical Journal* vol. 177, no. 3, 2011, pp. 238–250.

Hamill, Sam. "Introduction." *Poets Against the War*. Thunder Mouth, 2003, pp. xvii–xxi.

Hammad, Suheir. "First Writing Since." *Inclined to Speak: An Anthology of Contemporary Arab American Poetry*, edited by Hayan Charara. The University of Arkansas Press, 2008, pp. 112–126.

Harrington, Michael. *The Other America: Poverty in the United States*. Macmillan, 1962.

Hartung, William D. and Mandy Smithberger. "America's Defense Budget Is Bigger Than You Think." *The Nation*, May 7, 2019, www.thenation.com/article/arch ive/tom-dispatch-america-defense-budget-bigger-than-you-think/

Hazo, Samuel. "For Which It Stands." *And the Time Is: Poems, 1958–2013*. Syracuse University Press, 2014, pp. 176–177.

Heaney, Seamus. *The Government of the Tongue: Selected Prose, 1978–1987*. Faber & Faber, 1988.

Jaffe, Greg. "For Trump and His Generals, 'Victory' Has Different Meanings." *The Washington Post*, April 5, 2018, www.washingtonpost.com/world/ national-security/for-trumpand-his-generals-victory-has-different-meanings /2018/04/05/8d74eab0-381d-11e8-9c0a-85d477d9a226_story.html?utm_ term=.2508c17f703d

Johnson, Chalmers. *Dismantling the Empire: America's Last Great Hope*. Metropolitan Books, 2010.

Joseph, Lawrence. "Rubaiyat." *Into It: Poems*. Farrar, Straus and Giroux, 2005, pp. 41–45.

Kaczynski, Andrew. "Michael Flynn in August: Islamism a 'Vicious Cancer' in Body of All Muslims that 'Has to Be Excised.'" *CNN*, November 22, 2016, www .cnn.com/2016/11/22/politics/kfile-michael-flynn-august-speech/index.html

Khan, Azmat and Anand Gopal. "The Uncounted." *The New York Times*, November 16, 2017, www.nytimes.com/interactive/2017/11/16/magazine/ uncounted-civilian-casualties-iraq-airstrikes.html

Marinetti, F. T. "The Founding and Manifesto of Futurism." 1909. *Futurism: An Anthology*, edited by Lawrence Rainey, Christine Poggi, and Laura Wittman. Yale University Press, 2009, pp. 49–53.

Mattawa, Khaled. *Tocqueville*. New Issues Poetry & Prose, 2010.

Matuk, Farid. "A Real American." *Dispatches from the Land of Erasure: Arab American Poetry and the Work of Liberation*, special issue of *Boston Review*, May 10, 2018, http://bostonreview.net/poetry/farid-matuk-real-american

Melman, Seymour. *Permanent War Economy: American Capitalism in Decline*. Simon & Schuster, 1974.

Metres, Philip. *Behind the Lines: War Resistance Poetry on the American Homefront since 1941*. University of Iowa Press, 2007.

Sand Opera. Alice James Books, 2015.

Ode to Oil. Kattywompus Press, 2011.

Miller, Greg. "Brennan Speech Is First Obama Acknowledgement of Use of Armed Drones." *The Washington Post*, April 30, 2012, www.washingtonpost.com

/world/national-security/brennan-speech-is-first-obama-acknowledgement-of-use-of-armed-drones

Quadrennial Defense Review Report, Department of Defense. February 6, 2006, https://history.defense.gov/Portals/70/Documents/quadrennial/QDR2006.pdf?ver=2014-06-25-111017-150

Sassen, Saskia. "When the City Itself Becomes a Technology of War." *Theory, Culture & Society* vol. 27, no. 6, 2010, pp. 33–50.

Scahill, Jeremy. *Dirty Wars: The World Is a Battlefield.* Nation Books, 2013.

Schwartz, Michael. *War Without End: The Iraq War in Context.* Haymarket Books, 2008.

Sharif, Solmaz. "Look." *Look: Poems.* Graywolf Press, 2016, pp. 3–5.

Singh, Nikhil Pal. *Race and America's Long War.* University of California Press, 2017.

Spahr, Juliana. *This Connection of Everyone with Lungs.* University of California Press, 2005.

Spahr, Juliana, Joshua Clover, and Jasper Bernes. "Poetry and Other Antagonisms: An Interview with Commune Editions." Interview with Stephen Voyce. *The Iowa Review* vol. 47, no. 1, Spring 2017, pp. 176–187.

Surani, Moez. عمليّة *Operación Opération Operation* 行 动 *Операция.* BookThug, 2017.

Suskind, Ron. "Faith, Certainty, and the Presidency of George W. Bush." *The New York Times,* October 17, 2004, www.nytimes.com/2004/10/17/magazine/faith-certainty-and-the-presidency-of-george-w-bush.html

Turse, Nick. *The Complex: How the Military Invades Our Everyday Lives.* Henry Holt & Co., 2008.

Vance, T. N. "The Permanent Arms Economy." *New International* vol. 17, 1951, pp. 1–6.

Vine, David. *Base Nation: How U.S. Military Bases Abroad Harm American and the World.* Metropolitan Books, 2015.

Virilio, Paul, and Sylvère Lotringer. *Pure War: New Edition,* translated by Mark Polizzotti and Brian O'Keeffe, 2nd ed. Semiotext(e)/Foreign Agents, 2008.

The White House. "The National Security Strategy of the United States of America," 2006, https://georgewbush-whitehouse.archives.gov/nsc/nss/2006/

Wilbur, Richard. *New and Collected Poems.* Harcourt Brace & Company, 1988.

14

KIMBERLY QUIOGUE ANDREWS

Poetry in the Program Era

No general survey of poetry in the twenty-first-century would be complete without some kind of assessment regarding its relationship to academic institutions. This state of affairs was also true in the last century: In *The Cambridge Companion to American Poetry since 1945* and *The Cambridge Companion to Modern American Poetry*, one can find not one but three separate chapters on poetry in and around the university.[1] The question, then, becomes: What, if anything, is different now that we are well into the 2000s – an era of perpetual war and a global economic downturn from which we have yet to recover but also an era of perhaps unprecedented richness and diversity of poetic production? An era in which creative writing MFA and PhD programs are an established and durable part of the academic landscape?

As it turns out, some of the discussions have remained much the same, because they have always been with us. Evaluative debates about the quality of poetry produced within academic contexts continue apace, in substance not fundamentally different from Matthew Arnold's tackling of a corollary problem in "The Literary Influence of Academies" in 1888.[2] An uptick in the number of polemics about whether or not creative writing is "good" or "bad" for literature as a category is a predictable byproduct of the ubiquity of the creative writing program; in what remains one of the only full-length studies of its influence upon the literary landscape, Mark McGurl describes a "literary journalism" full of a "suspicion ... that there may be something inherently wrong" with the program and, thus, its products (24). The situation has not changed appreciably since his writing: Indeed, *The Program Era* (2009) might have made it worse, occasioning in 2010–2011 a collection of essays published by *n+1* eventually grouped under the heading "MFA vs NYC." The handwringing contained therein stands testament to the fact that we still want to know what we ought to think about writers who go through these programs, as if there were any one way to think about them.[3]

McGurl, ironically, had offered his work as a corrective to this tendency, doing so by way of a type of historicized aestheticism: *The Program Era* devotes considerable time to the notion of "autopoiesis," linking it in the case of the postwar novel and short story to questions of individualization as expressed through methods of perspective-creation. The reflexive point of view, in other words, allows for an "autobiographical drama of self-authorization" that validates the author in a professional context (McGurl 49). In the case of poetry – a genre tackled by neither *n+1* nor McGurl – such autopoietic gestures cannot reasonably be pinned to the development of creative writing programs, as reflexive autobiography in poetry has been a standard way of doing things since at least the Romantic period. Indeed, one of the more surprising effects of the academicization of creative writing on the genre of poetry has been a type of inversion of its effect on fiction. It is doubtless true that a certain strain of "confessional" poetry attended the germination and rise of poetry programs, and that the appeal of creative writing still rests on the purported freedom that it gives students to "express themselves" in a literary way. Yet the real solidification of poetry's academic situatedness – not ameliorated, as in fiction, by the possibility of other, larger sources of patronage – has also given rise to poetry that chooses to interrogate the notion both of that freedom and of personal expression itself, not in spite but precisely *because* of the ways in which the professionalization of creativity has created a mythology of those concepts.

This poetics of interrogation has a non-program, but tellingly academic, prehistory: that of the Language school of writing. As Alan Golding has detailed, the central ideological tenets of poets such as Charles Bernstein, Lyn Hejinian, and Bruce Andrews lined up quite well with developments in literary and semiotic theory that took hold in the academy in the latter part of the twentieth century (144–170). These poets, while perhaps not consciously taking aim at established departments of creative writing, did provide a bracing alternative to the type of autobiographical lyric that proliferated there and that continues to be a target of critique, as I'll discuss briefly in this chapter. In our current moment, it would not be entirely accurate to view these two (very loosely defined) types of poetry as competing for space at the academic table: Indeed, given the fact that programs of creative writing are no longer upstart ventures, one might say that there is enough space in the room, now, for two (or more) tables.

It remains the case, however, that the institutionalization of Language and Language-adjacent poetry puts a particularly fine point on the vexed relationship between the production of literary writing and the insides and outsides of the academic culture industry. Charles Bernstein, in fact, *has* consciously taken aim at the discipline of creative writing, but from the position – once curious, now relatively widespread – of an avant-garde poet who has found a comfortable survival mechanism in higher education.

He often engages that survival mechanism directly. In "A Defence of Poetry," a poem whose title he takes from Shelley and that is dedicated to the scholar Brian McHale, Bernstein gives us misshapen theses on poetics: "My problem with deploying a term liek / nonelen / in these cases it acutually similar to / your / cirtique of the term ideopigical / unamlsing as a too-broad unanuajce / interprestive proacdeure" (*All the Whiskey in Heaven* 213). Bernstein is responding to an essay by McHale entitled "Making (Non)sense out of Postmodern Poetry," and the blunt object of his misspelling (look! Nonsense! *Or is it*) exists in a strained relationship to the words' conformation to a type of agreed-upon method of academic discourse. In this case, Bernstein is acknowledging the intellectual contribution of his interlocutor while voicing a reservation about that contribution in a specific instance. This way of "speaking," as it were, is the kind of thing that one learns in graduate school or, in the case of Bernstein, through a long relationship with the university that involved at one point the founding and chairing of the Poetics Program at SUNY Buffalo, one of the preeminent drivers of experimental poetic production in America.

This relationship, for Bernstein, has produced not only the knowing, nose-thumbing poetry just quoted but also much more serious, decidedly not-misspelled defenses of the possibility inherent within the academic humanities. In *Attack of the Difficult Poems* (2011), a collection of essays and poem-essays and poems geared toward assessing the state of challenging poetry in the twenty-first-century, Bernstein updates an essay first published in 1997 in a special issue of *Daedalus* dedicated to the examination of the academic profession. In the later version, he praises the ability of the university to be profoundly multivalent: "the academic profession is not a unified body but composite of many dissimilar individuals and groups pursuing projects ranging from the valiantly idiosyncratic to the proscriptively conventional" (Bernstein, *Attack of the Difficult Poems* 11). While the essay does contain the kinds of knee-jerk critiques often leveled at and within the academic humanities – that it promotes "lifeless prose, bloated ... with compulsory repetitive explanation," that its "austere probity" is insufficient to effect change, that he submitted an essay to *PMLA* and was rejected – we also find a sincere and stirring belief that, at its best, the literary academy could realize a "grand democratic vista" that looks forward toward "what it is possible to do" in art and letters (*Attack of the Difficult Poems* 16–19, 8). Bernstein's, in other words, are not bad faith critiques: He is genuinely interested in making the project of tertiary education the best thing that it can be in the face of what he sees as an unprecedented attack from the forces of the corporate marketplace. For an avowed experimentalist to be so committed speaks volumes about the ways in which the literary academy has come to imagine itself – politically, culturally, stylistically – in recent years.

There is, of course, a flip side: Bernstein is also the coiner of the term "Official Verse Culture," which he uses as a thinly veiled stand-in for the economies of poetic circulation propped up by the proliferation of academic creative writing programs.[4] Although he remains sanguine regarding the possibilities for creativity within the academy, Bernstein's definition of "Official Verse Culture" is in many ways representative of a pervasive sentiment about institutionalized creativity writ large: "American Official Verse Culture," Bernstein writes, "operates on the premise that innovation and originality are not criteria of aesthetic value" (*Attack of the Difficult Poems* 33). The mass production of writers within a system of proliferating programs in creative writing would seem to feed right into such a culture – after all, what can mass production produce besides products for the masses?

The problem here is that there is virtually no mass market for poetry.[5] Thus, the "professionalization" of poetry writing within graduate programs in the United States is met with an oddly hermetic kind of suspicion: There's the general feeling, expressed with clipped precision by Marjorie Perloff, that due to the expansion of these programs, "the sheer number of poets now plying their craft inevitably ensures moderation and safety." She goes on: "the national demand for a certain kind of prize-winning, 'well-crafted' poem – a poem that *The New Yorker* would see fit to print and that would help its author get one of the 'good jobs' advertised by the Association of Writers & Writing Programs – has produced an extraordinary uniformity" ("Poetry on the Brink"). Perloff, here, combines an aesthetic concern with an economic one: Poetry is boring, she claims, because you have to be boring in order to get a job teaching others to produce boring poetry. So while there may be no "mass culture" for poetry, it somehow manages to have enough devoted adherents to have a definable center against which advocates of more "innovative" work can push. This center is the place from which the creative writing ideological apparatus reproduces itself, and from Perloff's point of view, it's a disaster.

This dim view of the program era and its products is widely shared.[6] Perloff goes on to describe that "well-crafted poem" as the type of poem that "you will read in *American Poetry Review* or similar publications," and that usually contains the following:

1) irregular lines of free verse, with little or no emphasis on the construction of the line itself or on what the Russian Formalists called "the word as such"; 2) prose syntax with lots of prepositional and parenthetical phrases,

laced with graphic imagery or even extravagant metaphor (the sign of "poeticity"); 3) the expression of a profound thought or small epiphany, usually based on a particular memory, designating the lyric speaker as a particularly sensitive person who really *feels* the pain. (n. pag.)

This is a particularly ungenerous way of reading contemporary poetry, and in Perloff's case, it also contains traces of a more insidious suspicion of the first-person subject as it has become particularized (and politicized) along lines of sociocultural identity.[7] I would argue that there are more interesting and more usefully generative ways of critiquing the notion of the "lyric speaker." In particular, I want to suggest that many of these ways have come from within recent poetry itself, as poets interested in such complications have turned to the interpretive frameworks of literary study to do their work – and in the process, they have put real pressure on creative writing's relative autonomy from that study.

That autonomy is at least partially the result of a disciplinary reliance on the cultivation of "voice" that is particularly useful to higher education's focus on professionalized self-building. This focus, for its part, is the result of the so-called progressive educational reforms of the early and mid-twentieth century – reforms that cemented the university as a producer of trained *individuals* who could market themselves successfully into the workforce.[8] Thus it is that an activity that many of its own practitioners say "cannot be taught" winds up, in a way so successful as to occasion the founding of whole departments and schools, being taught: While the notion persists that proper and true self-expression, as intimacy, can only be brought forth through an Iowa-esque "nurturing of talent," self-expression is also necessary for an educational enterprise in which "creativity" becomes "a value beloved by American artists and scientists and corporate types alike – by everyone, really" (McGurl 21). For what is creativity in late capitalism, in essence, if not a series of personal quirks that can somehow be monetized? For poets, the money is more or less out of the question – but as holders of deeply rooted symbolic capital, it is their self-expression, perhaps, from which all other kinds of creative self-expression follow.

Consider Robert Lowell, who did manage to monetize his family's dark idiosyncrasies after the publication of *Life Studies* (1959), proclaiming that poetry writing "isn't a craft, that is, something for which you learn the skills and go on turning out. It must come from some deep impulse, deep inspiration" (Seidel n. pag.). The job of the creative writer in the academy, in such a view, is not to transmit sets of abilities but rather to model being struck by the muse. Lowell's anti-craft pedagogy is a particularly good example of what Kelly Ritter and Stephanie Vanderslice have called "teaching lore." Yet whether or not you agree with it, it remains true that it is in some ways much more expedient – not to mention more philosophically consistent, in this instance – to teach students how to write narratives about personal turmoil ("Mother! Mother! / as a gemlike undergraduate, / part criminal and yet a Phi Bete, / I used to barge home late" [Lowell 84]) than it is to strenuously inquire after the cultural frameworks, assumptions, and allowances of such narratives.

Lowell's remarkable ability to capture the swinging polarities of his public and private selves is, of course, anything but easy. His work reflects not only a tremendous amount of skill but also an articulate honesty about his own historical positionality; if those detractors of the "McPoem" (as Donald Hall [n. pag.] has called it) have Lowell to blame for anything, it might be for being too good at his job.[9] His exacting type of clarity, in which a defiant skunk can carry the weight of crushing self-hatred, requires not an unfettered display of emotional life but rather a form of control over that life that invests its energy in imagistic specificity. Insofar as the writing of poetry *can* be taught, the goal of metaphoric precision is one that responds well to the kinds of scrutiny that a poem will receive in a workshop: group-oriented scrutiny, that is, that often revolves around questions of exactitude. Is the imagery "sharp" enough? Is the situation "clear"? Are the emotional stakes appropriate to the subject matter? These are the kinds of microscope lenses under which Lowell's poetry shines. Such lines of questioning, then, become the primary form of interpretive labor practiced by poets within the semi-autonomous institutional space of creative writing programs.

This form of independence performs a role both as itself and as its opposite: On the one hand, the insularity of the program and the ensuing (perceived) homogeneity of its products is the feature against which poets like Bernstein and Hall and critics like Perloff and Ritter and Vanderslice bristle. On the other, this very autonomy functions as a signal of the program's total absorption within the academic institution, when said institution is seen as the reproducer of a dominant cultural mode. This is a lose-lose situation: Creative writing as a practice or vocation is chastised for losing its autonomy in favor of academicity, and then for being too autonomous within that academic space. If the forms of labor performed in the semi-detached creative writing program stand in for institutionalization gone "wrong," however, there remains a powerful sense that there is such a thing as institutionalization gone *right*: that there must be some way for poetry writing to exist as a discipline that does not succumb to, or at the very least acknowledges, the program's "fiction of autonomy."[10]

Over the last twenty years, the recognition of that fiction has resulted in a flurry of renegotiations of the poetic subject-position in relation to systems and structures of knowledge production. As the university has become the foremost patron of the poetic arts, poets seeking an alternative to the types of personal narrative developed in and propagated by departments of creative writing have had to find that alternative *within* that larger structure of patronage. The result is not so much a difference in kind from Language poetry so much as a difference in degree: Now that such poetry, alongside the literary theory that paralleled it, has diffused more broadly into the literary humanities, the humanities' own ways of scrutinizing and historicizing texts have become methodologies for poetic production as well. Folding an explicitly hermeneutic practice or process into the poetry itself creates a reflexivity that imagines the speaking subject as an actively, discursively *analytical* subject – one that sees in these analytical methodologies not a way to stifle creative possibility but rather to expand it.

One example of a poet at the forefront of such methodological cooptation is Myung Mi Kim, who is often seen as a kind of "second-generation" Language poet but whose career trajectory – an MA from Johns Hopkins University, an MFA from the University of Iowa, and professorships at San Francisco State University and, eventually, SUNY Buffalo – reflects the newer ideal for creative writers in the academy. Over the course of this rather staid-looking professional arc, Kim has produced increasingly innovative work that stands as testament to the heterogeneity that such seeming staidness can foster. Her five books span the turn of the twenty-first-century, and each deals fundamentally with Kim's identity as a Korean American (she immigrated to the United States with her parents at the age of nine). They are all expressly political, and they all, despite that focus on identity, generally avoid the narrative disclosure of authorial-personal detail. Yet her 2002 book *Commons*, I'd argue, stems most obviously from the compilation of a long-standing poetic project and a dedicated "reading project" (Keller 343), as Kim herself has put it. In *Commons*, in other words (its own), "those which are of foreign origin" merge with "those which are of forgotten sources" (*Commons* 4). In this meshing, questions of knowledge production and archival memory draw out a version of the personal that contains, in addition to the wavering alienation of cross-cultural identity, a sense of the work required to fully articulate that identity. That work, for Kim, involves a careful study of multiple strains of history, and *Commons* collects this work in a testament to the tenuous whole contained within the empirical fragment.

The work of *Commons* thus reads as study – specifically, as a poeticized form of archival historicism, which has enjoyed a return to prominence in academic literary criticism over the past few decades. This return (which has taken many forms, from sociologically inflected cultural criticism to new forays into the materiality of books and book production) stems in part from the recognition that individual literary works are not fully legible when kept separate from their historical contexts. In the archive, these contexts must often be woven together from bits and pieces of material evidence, often tantalizing but rarely complete in and of themselves. With its detached and fragmentary style, Kim's work reads as both the pieces and the weaving. It is in this way reminiscent of that of the poet Susan Howe, but it is not simply this chestnut of postmodern poetics that makes Kim a logical-seeming successor to Howe at Buffalo.[11] Howe's most "archival" books of poetry, such as *The Midnight* (2003) and *Pierce-Arrow* (1999), are more explicit in their academic settings, but *Commons* shares with them a commitment to building an authority of identity out of that identity's placement within (and near disappearance into) a Foucauldian version of material history.[12]

In *The Archaeology of Knowledge* (1969), Foucault insists upon a broad but compelling definition of the archive as the abstract, disciplinary, and terminological function that renders statements intelligible as belonging to this or that generalized field of knowledge. There exists a *"historical a priori,"* in his account, that is "not a condition of validity for judgements, but a condition of reality for statements" (Foucault 126, emphasis original). That enunciations can be pitted against one another at all is thus a function of the archive. That we can think of ourselves as being in any sense delimited or connected – and how we register the difference between the two – is also a function of the archive. Kim puts it thusly toward the very beginning of *Commons*, setting the tone from the start: "the transition from the stability and absoluteness of the world's contents / to their dissolution into motions and relations" (*Commons* 13). The lines don't form a sentence; instead, they leave "the transition" as an object of definition or scrutiny to stand on its own, without a controlling verb to tell us what its function might be. There is the distinct sense, however, that its function might be to dictate how the book is read. The book itself, in other words, details the dissolution of historical stability into "motions and relations" – a move that does not negate historicity so much as change its essential character.

The clutter of texts, quotation fragments, and fictions that follow give one the sense that the book is almost more curation than creation. In several sections entitled "Vocalise," Kim reprints bits of material from her reading project involving anatomy and dissection, particularly that of the female body. These selections range from the notes of fourteenth-century anatomist Mondino di Lucci to an anonymous account of the death of a girl from massive internal injury after the bombing of Hiroshima. They are arranged in chronological order, which is a kind of stability, but they are surrounded by text that contains a much more inscrutable principle of organization, even as it often shares the anatomists' dry tone: "In southwest and south-central Kansas the worst condition is plants stunted or killed off by extremely dry soil. Adding to farmers' woes are infestations of green bugs and brown wheat mites" (Kim, *Commons* 42). The destruction of bodies by war and natural disaster, and of female bodies by science, are brought together in *Commons* under the auspices of an ecological retelling (broadly conceived) of the history of violence and imperialism, and about the perils of viewing history as a series of discrete events. The fractured nature of Kim's poetic compilations is meant to undermine "the central organizing myth of comprehensive knowledge" (*Commons* 44) even as it attempts, in its "desire for the encyclopedic" (*Commons* 107), to read through to the sources of her identity as Korean, displaced, linguistically liminal, female.

The concept of the self as an immutable part of "the world's contents" is in many ways the primary subject of Kim's poetic renegotiation, though it is couched in abstract terms that thwart conventional expectations of "identity writing." There's no sense at all, really, of autobiographical narrative in *Commons* – what shows up is a much more generalized sense of "Koreanness," as well as the precarity of that identification in the face of the conditionality of all statements, poetic or historical. This is a feature of the majority of her poetry, but *Commons* has a relentless, multi-sourced feel to it that distinguishes it from her earlier work and signals a different, if still related, set of concerns about the link between personal experience and the experience of history. Experience, transmitted through statement, becomes subject to the disciplinary-archival conditions of all historical statements: "This is the leveling of the ground" (*Commons* 7) Kim writes, in reference both to writing and to war. Because of its overt engagement with "documentation," *Commons* shifts the frame of the personal in a subtle but significant way, such that it includes the intimate anxiety surrounding the work of writing itself: "Mapping needles. Minerals and gems. Furs and lumber. Alterations through the loss or transposition of even a single syllable" (Kim, *Commons* 4). The imperative to "get it right," as it were, comes up against the very unclear category of "right" itself. Whose history? Whose politics? Written by whom, for whom?

In a sense, *Commons* rewrites and reframes Kim's first book, *Under Flag* (1991). War dominates both works thematically, but while *Under Flag* relies on a more face-value or semi-transparent version of experiential memory, *Commons* interrogates the concept of historical transparency itself. It is telling that one of the more popular poems from *Under Flag* is "Into Such Assembly," a poem that very directly details the alienating process of immigrating to the United States. The lines "Over there, we had a slateblue house with a flat roof where / I made many snowmen, over there" jostles against the stanza that follows it: "No, 'th,' 'th,' put your tongue against the roof of your mouth, / lean slightly against the back of the top teeth" it begins, continuing this way for a couple more lines before ending with the poignant "look in the mirror, / that's better" (Kim, *Under Flag* 30). The poem conveys the vaguely humiliating ritual of learning to speak English (and the implication that one is a "better" person after having done so) via an appeal to the *ethos* of experience and personal narrative. The experiences conveyed in *Commons* are very different, and are raw in a different way: The jumble of voices that vie for attention throughout the book give testament not only to themselves but also to the authorial presence collecting, collating, and occasionally creating them whole cloth. This procedural focus shifts our attention to a slightly different facet of Kim's identity, one that is a compilation of reading and research: one that is, in her own words, an active agent in the "perpetually incomplete task of tracking what enters into the field of perception" (Kim, *Commons* 107).

Kim's work in *Commons* thus relies less on experience of identity than it does on the experience of *encounter*.[13] It is a slight but important distinction. The self, in this reformulation, is just as much a historian as the subject of history, a position that parallels the kind of creator/critic persona favored by institutions such as Buffalo. When the more traditionally personal enters into the work, it serves not as a window into truth so much as an occasion to turn the work back outwards towards the wide community of statements that make up any given archive. An entire page in *Commons* contains nothing but the following: "[when my father died and left me nothing] // [this is how I speak]" (37). Kim's father died suddenly when she was a teenager; while this is normally the kind of subject matter that carries deep confessional *pathos*, Kim uses it to reiterate the inextricability of the personal from the sociopolitical. The following couple of pages contain a reference to "sister, brothers, and mother" but situate them firmly within the collective trauma of refugee flight, using documentary-style quotations ("'left their homes after two solid days of attacks' / 'they had stayed to take care of their cow'") to de-individuate the narrative. It turns, then and characteristically, to quotes pulled from Leonardo da Vinci's *Notebooks*. In a move that is really only thinkable from the perspective of academic poetic experiment, *Commons* contains its own thesis statement: "*COMMONS* elides multiple sites: reading and text making, discourses and disciplines, documents and documenting. Fluctuating. Proceeding by fragment, by increment. [. . .] The meaning of becoming a historical subject" (107). It cannot be described much better than that, and it is abundantly clear that the process of "becoming a historical subject," for Kim, involves the "discourses and disciplines" tasked with keeping, revising, and rewriting the history books.

As we enter into the second decade of the twenty-first-century, innovative poetry that favors a discursive, research-forward approach to capturing or recovering a sense of historical-political collectivity has become increasingly prominent: In 2006, for example, Nathaniel Mackey's *Splay Anthem*, an extremely challenging poetic meditation on (among other things) jazz and Dogon creation mythologies, won the National Book Award; in 2014, Claudia Rankine's *Citizen*, a book of prose poems written in the second person and containing long meditations on Serena Williams and Zinedine Zidane, rocketed to national prominence, becoming a finalist for the National Book Critics Circle Award in both poetry *and* criticism. Although it eventually won in poetry, the dual nomination (a first for the organization) is telling: The book was read as not only a portrayal but also an analysis of its subject matter. This heightened reflexivity (Mackey, for his part, wrote the scholarly preface to his own book of poems) demonstrates the degree to which the *condition* of experimentality in the twenty-first-century has increasingly come to rely on discursive structures and methodological frameworks utilized just across the hall from, but typically not in, the creative writing workshop.

That said, both Mackey and Rankine have had careers in creative writing not unlike Kim's. They have had hundreds of students; some of those students have gone and will go on to teach others, bringing with them a sense that MFA programs ought to have a "philosopher, an eco-poetics person, and a political analyst on staff with the poets" (Rankine "Interview"). It's worth noting, too, that these experiments in writing into and around identity have been written both in the face and also because of one of the academy's most striking paradoxes: Traditionally and still often hostile to incursions by marginalized populations, the disciplinary landscape of the university has nevertheless expanded to encompass the study of precisely those populations – one thinks here of Women's, Gender, and Sexuality Studies, African American Studies, and Indigenous Studies departments and programs across the country, among others. Here, perhaps, is the most important difference between these experimental writers of the twenty-first-century and their more homogeneous predecessors and Conceptual contemporaries: Rather than denying the importance of personal narrative altogether, poets like Myung Mi Kim seek to reconfigure the personal in service of the more broadly intellectual: the lyric speaker, in other words, as an active analyst both of "lyric" and of "speaker."[14] It's no accident that Claudia Rankine's two most recent books, deeply cutting-edge in both their form and their treatment of race, are subtitled "An American Lyric." The point is not to move beyond having a body or a voice – indeed, for these writers, American history has been the history of being denied these facets of humanity. The point, instead, is to theorize that having in the moment of lyric making.

All of this work has been done on institutional time, because the institution is where many of the advances in the aforementioned theorizing get made. It thus makes less and less sense to think of academic creative writing as a monolith – there is no single "poetry in the program era." As Evan Kindley has noted, however, there is a bittersweet edge to this fact: Almost all of the eggs of poetry and poetry criticism have been put into the basket of the university, and "if the university ultimately prove[s] the most receptive audience, it may not be so forever" (257). The ongoing and manufactured "crisis in the humanities" only exacerbates this feeling, and there is, too, the fact that if the university is almost singlehandedly propping up poetic production both traditional and avant-garde, it's because there is no other structure currently equipped to do so. Yet it remains worthwhile to consider the multitudes that "academic poetry" – a term that "as an insult," as Oren Izenberg has put it, "has always had more punch than precision" (187) – can currently contain. When the avant-garde stays in school, we do not simply get a watered-down experimentalism. Instead, at the crossroads of programs in creative writing and those in literature, history, philosophy, and the other humanities, we have what we might call an academic avant-garde: one frontier of many, perhaps, but one that is indispensable to our understanding of the ongoing conversation between poetry and the university.

Notes

1. See Kindley; Izenberg; Lazer.
2. Arnold's prescient and often very funny dissection of the merits of English vs. French literature finds French literature (particularly poetry) lacking in the "genius" he ascribes to the English poetic tradition but concedes that the tendency of the French to form academies dedicated to the passing on of intellectual skill and tradition concentrates "the mental aptitudes and demands which an open mind and a flexible intelligence naturally engender" (Arnold 56).
3. See Harbach; Jamison.
4. Andrew Epstein's concise summary of the relationship between Language poetry and the academy describes this culture, fittingly, as an "amorphous blob" consisting of "the academic creative writing establishment and its presses, prizes, and professors" (46). He notes that, in the 1980s, poets such as Bernstein "still prided themselves on their marginal status," but by the end of the decade, their transition into the academy (both as workers in the system and as objects of analytical work) was well underway (48).
5. See Hank Lazer's sober(ing) treatment of this subject. Timothy Yu has recently examined this claim in light of "Instagram poetry"; he argues that such

poetry – which does have mass-market appeal – exists in an almost entirely separate economy from poetry produced outside the social media platform (Yu, "Instagram Poetry and Our Poetry Worlds").

6. See Hall, as well as Myers; Ritter and Vanderslice.

7. See Hong.

8. For an outline of this history that takes modernist poetry (specifically Wallace Stevens) as its focus, see Filreis.

9. Indeed, Hall invokes Lowell multiple times over his long invective against "Hamburger University" and its creative issue.

10. I take this phrase from the title of Goldstone's book on modernity and autonomy; he describes the phrase as "granting the problematic status of ideas of autonomy" while "steer[ing] clear of treating those ideas as mere deceptions or delusions" (Goldstone 8).

11. Howe taught at Buffalo for many years. Timothy Yu has also noted similarities between Kim and Howe in a wide-ranging overview of very recent Asian American poetry, which builds on his previous work in Asian American poetry and the avant-garde ("Asian American Poetry in the First Decade of the 2000s").

12. Indeed, the "personal narrative" in these books of Howe's is in fact the story of the author-in-archive: She details her struggles in gaining access to Emily Dickinson's papers in Harvard's Houghton Library and the inhospitable conditions in the microfiche room at Yale University. See also Izenberg.

13. This is a term that Kim uses herself when talking about her more documentary impulses: As she tells Lynn Keller, she is less interested in the "document as artifact" (a statement that distinguishes her sharply from Howe) and much more interested in the way in which "documents evoke the possibility of encounter" (Keller 345).

14. I refer here to writers, such as Kenneth Goldsmith and Christian Bök, of what is loosely defined as Conceptual poetry. Goldsmith in particular has been a champion of what he has termed "uncreative writing" – writing that champions the impersonal, automatic, or even plagiaristic.

Works Cited

Arnold, Matthew. *Essays in Criticism.* Macmillan and Co., 1906.

Bernstein, Charles. *All the Whiskey in Heaven: Selected Poems.* 1st ed, Farrar, Straus and Giroux, 2010.

Attack of the Difficult Poems: Essays and Inventions. University of Chicago Press, 2011.

Epstein, Andrew. "Verse vs. Verse." *Lingua Franca,* September 2000, pp. 45–54.

Filreis, Alan. "Wallace Stevens and the Strength of the Harvard Reaction." *The New England Quarterly* vol. 58, no. 1, March 1985, pp. 27–45.

Foucault, Michel. *The Archaeology of Knowledge,* translated by A. M. Sheridan Smith. Pantheon Books, 1972.

Golding, Alan C. *From Outlaw to Classic: Canons in American Poetry.* University of Wisconsin Press, 1995.

Goldstone, Andrew. *Fictions of Autonomy: Modernism from Wilde to de Man.* Oxford University Press, 2013.

Hall, Donald. "Poetry and Ambition." *Poets.org*, March 9, 2005, www.poets.org /poetsorg/text/poetry-and-ambition

Harbach, Chad, editor. *MFA vs NYC: The Two Cultures of American Fiction*. n+1, 2014.

Hong, Cathy Park. "Delusions of Whiteness in the Avant-Garde." *Lana Turner* no. 7, 2014, https://arcade.stanford.edu/content/delusions-whiteness-avant-garde

Izenberg, Oren. "Poems In and Out of School: Allen Grossman and Susan Howe." *The Cambridge Companion to American Poetry since 1945*, edited by Jennifer Ashton. Cambridge University Press, 2013, pp. 187–201.

Jamison, Leslie. "'MFA vs NYC' Is Most Useful as an Explanation of How Writers Get Paid." *The New Republic*, February 2014, www.newrepublic.com/article/ 116778/mfa-vs-nyc-most-useful-explanation-how-writers-get-paid

Keller, Lynn. "An Interview with Myung Mi Kim." *Contemporary Literature* vol. 49, no. 3, October 2008, pp. 335–356.

Kim, Myung Mi. *Commons*. University of California Press, 2002.
  Under Flag. Kelsey St. Press, 1998.

Kindley, Evan. "Poet-Critics and Bureaucratic Administration." *The Cambridge Companion to Modern American Poetry*, edited by Walter Kalaidjian. Cambridge University Press, 2015, pp. 248–57.

Lazer, Hank. "American Poetry and Its Institutions." *The Cambridge Companion to American Poetry since 1945*, edited by Jennifer Ashton. Cambridge University Press, 2013, pp. 158–72.

Lowell, Robert. *Life Studies and for the Union Dead*. Farrar, Straus and Giroux, 2007.

Mackey, Nathaniel. *Splay Anthem*. New Directions Book, 2006.

McGurl, Mark. *The Program Era: Postwar Fiction and the Rise of Creative Writing*. Harvard University Press, 2009.

McHale, Brian. "Making (Non)Sense out of Postmodern Poetry." *Language, Text and Context: Essays in Stylistics*, edited by Michael J. Toolan. Routledge, 1992, pp. 6–35.

Myers, D. G. *The Elephants Teach: Creative Writing since 1880*. Prentice Hall, 1996.

Perloff, Marjorie. "Poetry on the Brink." *Boston Review*, June 2012, www.bostonre view.net/BR37.3/marjorie_perloff_poetry_lyric_reinvention.php

Rankine, Claudia. *Citizen*. Graywolf Press, 2014.
  "Interview with Claudia Rankine." *Jubilat* no. 12, 2006, http://poems.com/spe cial_features/prose/essay_rankine.php

Ritter, Kelly, and Stephanie Vanderslice. "Teaching Lore: Creative Writers and the University." *Profession*, 2005, pp. 102–112.

Seidel, Frederick. "Robert Lowell, The Art of Poetry No. 3." *Paris Review* no. 25, Winter–Spring 1961, www.theparisreview.org/interviews/4664/the-art-of-poetry-no-3-robert-lowell

Yu, Timothy. "Asian American Poetry in the First Decade of the 2000s." *Contemporary Literature* vol. 52, no. 4, 2011, pp. 818–851.
  "Instagram Poetry and Our Poetry Worlds." *Poetry Foundation*, April 15, 2019, www.poetryfoundation.org/harriet/2019/04/instagram-poetry-and-our-poetry-worlds

15

DOROTHY WANG

The Future of Poetry Studies

Poetry studies[1] as we have been practicing it for almost a century in the Anglo-American context is no longer viable in the twenty-first-century – unless we commit such mental and psychic acts of delusion that we in English Departments become the academic equivalents of those who wish to make America great again – states of psychosis, which, as we know from our political sphere, can be frighteningly durable.

It just seemed yesterday that we were speaking in English literary studies of having arrived at being "post-race," with some arguing that racial identity was elective (kind of like an after-school activity). Then there was the fist-pumping for having achieved the enlightened state of being "beyond identity."[2]

In 2014 and 2015, in the middle of our first black president's second term, various unpleasantries ruptured the normally smooth and corporate functioning of Poetry, Inc. – or at least Avant-Garde Poetry, Inc. ("experimental" and "avant-garde" themselves being not unvexed or uncontested terms, of course). Perhaps most visible in the poetry world was the intense pushback, mostly by poets of color, to Kenneth Goldsmith's performance of reading Michael Brown's autopsy report as "poetry" at Brown University in mid-March 2015. Goldsmith's re-rend(er)ing of the autopsy to end on Michael Brown's penis occurred the same weekend as the second convening of the first national conference on race and creative writing, founded by the poet Prageeta Sharma, at the University of Montana.[3]

Yet things had already been percolating in the poetry world and the world at large before that weekend: The Black Lives Matter movement, founded in 2013 in response to multiple murders of black men and women on the streets by police, had gathered force and was focusing a light on the anti-black practices of law enforcement and the state, holdovers from the days of slavery. The first Thinking Its Presence conference on race and creative writing, as mentioned above, had taken place in April 2014, four months after my book by the same name had been published. And, last but not least, there were the brilliant social media interventions of the anonymous Mongrel Coalition Against Gringpo, which enraged, as if on cue, good liberals in the academy and in the poetry world on both ends of the aesthetic spectrum.

In other words, people of color and the issue of race had become the counter-friction to the whirring cogs of high-profile professional careers, mostly at elite institutions; their efforts exposed the machinic elements of racism at work among even the hippest-of-the-hip wordsmiths and cosmopolitans.

I think it is safe to surmise that the keepers of the Poundian-Objectivist-New York School-Language-Conceptual tradition were completely blind-sided: The last place they thought a serious challenge would come from was from those brown folks on the sidelines, with their overly sincere and not-so-good "identity" poems. Up until that point the LangPo-ConPo monopoly franchise had seemed secure and had entrenched itself institutionally, with the Language Poets at the University of Pennsylvania and the University of California–Berkeley and their anointed successors, the Conceptual Poets, at Princeton, the University of Pennsylvania, and the Museum of Modern Art. Between them, they pretty much had a lock on what was considered "avant-garde" American poetry.

Likewise, what was considered Modern or Postmodern seemed fairly clear, the latter still hewing to High Modernist forms, such as the fracturing of syntax. For example, various Electronic Poets use Beckett's work as source texts, processing it through various "electronic" formats but leaving the fundamental literary and cultural assumptions intact.

What I argued in my book now seems shockingly self-evident: It is possible to pay close attention to formal properties of a poem *and* take into account the historical and sociopolitical contexts of a poem and the large role ideologies and institutional structures and practices play, both in the production and in the reception of poems.

We have been told forever and ever that form and content are not separable. Yet poetry scholars continued – and continue – to read poetry by minority writers primarily as ethnographic reportage or, in the rare case of the work of pet experimental poets, as the exceptional exception. While many avant-garde poets can deftly address language's imbrication with capitalism and hold forth on issues of class (and, at times, gender), the issue of race and – horrors – racism has too often been deflected by such coded (or not so coded) putdowns as "identity politics," "autobiographical writing," or "expressivity."

In December 2013, *The Lyric Theory Reader* came out from Johns Hopkins University Press, coedited by Virginia Jackson and Yopie Prins, the leaders of the "New Lyric Studies." Not a single entry was written by a US minority scholar and not a single entry or even passage touched on the issue of race and the lyric. Though there are five essays included in the section on "The Lyric and Sexual Difference," there is no section on "The Lyric and Racial Difference." In this respect, the "New Lyric Studies" seemed a lot like the old lyric studies, and "historical poetics" did not seem all that historical.

A little over three years later, in March 2017, a special issue of the *Journal of Literary Theory* devoted to "Theories of the Lyric" also omitted any discussion of race. No one bothered to consider that core concepts under-girding our idea of the lyric, such as the notion of the poetic speaker, are deeply racially inflected. After all, whose interiority was for centuries deemed worthy of expressing? Why are the musings of a speaker in a poem written by a white straight middle-aged gentleman farmer in Vermont automatically read as universalizable, while those of a speaker in a poem by an Asian American female poet from Oregon are inevitably read, even by well-trained poetry critics, as if they were transcriptions from her diary? (And this problem goes beyond what Jonathan Culler pinpoints as the general tendency to read lyric as dramatic monologue.)

In announcing the presidential theme for the 2018 MLA convention, "#States of Insecurity," Diana Taylor, the incoming president of the association of around 20,000 members – the largest organization of humanities scholars in the world – wrote: "This theme invites reflection on how our intellectual, artistic, and pedagogical work in the humanities offers strategies for navigating the crises of our time: political volatility, fluctuating financial markets, fear-mongering media, and increasingly hateful acts and rhetoric that contribute to a general sense of malaise" (n. pag.). She then goes on to say: "We can begin by reexamining our own epistemologies, disciplines, technologies, and organizational and governing structures."

For the most part I agree with Taylor, though for many BIPOC and academics of color the danger is not simply a "general sense of malaise" but something much more threatening. Who is the "our" here? Who is the "we"?

Let me say that there are ways to engage with the crucial issue of race and poetics and there are ways to *seem* to engage with race and poetic/literary studies.

In 2016, Caroline Levine's book *Forms* – described by her publisher as "a radically new way of thinking about form and context in literature, politics, and beyond" – won the MLA's top prize for best book of literary criticism for the year. Levine has been seen as a primary leader of the "New Formalism," which is usually characterized as bringing formalism and politics together for the first time. Levine begins her book with a passage from *Jane Eyre* to illustrate how contemporary critics would tend to interpret it:

Traditional formalist analysis – close reading – meant interpreting all of the formal techniques of a text as contributing to an overarching artistic whole. A contemporary critic, informed by several decades of historical approaches, would want instead to take stock of the social and political conditions that surrounded the work's production, and she would work to connect the novel's forms to its social world. She would seek to show how literary techniques reinforced or undermined specific institutions and political relationships, such as imperial power, global capital, or racism [note the "or" here] ... But would our critic be right to distinguish between the *formal* and the *social*?

(1, emphases original)

Like Jonathan Culler, Simon Jarvis, and those touting Surface Reading (such as Stephen Best and Sharon Marcus), Levine has become skeptical of "historicism" – meaning primarily New Historicism and Jamesonian Marxist analysis.

Levine is right to point out the binarizing of the formal and the social, but I want to ask (as I did with the Taylor quote), "Who is the assumed 'We' here in the phrase 'our critic'?"

I pointedly ask because there has been a long and substantial tradition of black intellectuals and cultural critics and practitioners who have thought hard and at great length about the inseparability of the formal and the social in the "real world": Stuart Hall, C. L. R. James, Aimé Césaire, Amiri Baraka, Édouard Glissant, and, more recently, Fred Moten and the Afropessimists, among others. Many of these thinkers did not or do not work inside English departments. By occluding an entire tradition of black thought that has engaged with the problem of form and larger sociopolitical structures, such as those of colonialism and white supremacist racial hierarchies, the "New Formalism" betrays the telling and endemic provinciality of Anglo-American literary studies.

One major conceptual problem within poetry and literary studies today is hardly news, and has been pointed out by not only Levine but the proponents of deconstruction for decades: the tendency to binarize concepts and categories. None of these oppositions seem surprising to us: the mainstream versus the "avant-garde"; formalist analysis versus cultural-studies approaches; theory versus empiricism; race versus class; the cool theorizing of postcolonial studies versus the slightly embarrassing political protestations of ethnic studies.

Poetry studies today also suffers from an inability to engage with concrete materialities and structures of power so as to fully look at the topic of race and colonialism and its relationship to the cultural artifacts that are produced and received in the habitus and ether of these ideologies – a relationship that is not only contextual but inheres in the very *forms* of the works. English poetry was used not only as an example but as an active cudgel of Britain's vaunted inherent and natural might and superiority. Colonialist arguments, explicit and implied, for the moral, ethical, imaginative, intellectual, and racial superiority of white Englishmen were often made on the basis of the achievements of its Great Poets. Most poetry scholars do not like to think of poetry in relation to violence and power. It feels like a violation of the special "imaginative" and "private" nature of poetry.

What I am asking we do more of is not the surface historicizing of New Historicists or the often abstract theorizing of Jamesonians – those whom Levine and others are reacting against – but the kind of difficult and necessary work that is deep, not surface, the type of historicizing that is often seen as too depressing and "heavy" (for example, slogging through archives to follow the money trail – as Noam Chomsky so often reminds us is the key to what is actually happening – as Eunsong Kim has so brilliantly done in her essay on the creation of the Archive for New Poetry at the University of California San Diego).

Yet painstaking work at the level of the concrete and the material can and should be coupled with risk-taking leaps in the realm of the imagination: thinking new possibilities for what American and English-language poetry might be, not simply what we have been bequeathed by centuries of British colonialism and white supremacist ideology and race science.

In the United States, these Enlightenment beliefs about biological and poetic capacities began from the first days of the republic: Thomas Jefferson in his *Notes on the State of Virginia* lays out his "scientific" case why black bodies such as Phyllis Wheatley's lacked the biological capacity to write poetry:

> Love is the peculiar oestrum of the poet. Their [black people's] love is ardent, but it kindles the senses only, not the imagination. Religion indeed has produced a Phyllis Whately [*sic*]; but it could not produce a poet ... The improvement of the blacks in body and mind, in the first instance of their mixture with the whites, has been observed by every one, and proves that their inferiority is not the effect merely of their condition of life.   (266–267)

Jefferson, of course, would know firsthand about this mixing.

The question of who has the capacity to write poetry haunts literary studies to this day, and the link between pseudo-scientific discourse and literary methodology has been largely obfuscated even up to the present moment.

John Guillory's research on the history of close reading draws out the influence of the ideas of the English neurophysiologist Sir Charles Sherrington (1857–1952) on the thinking of I. A. Richards in the formulation of his Practical Criticism. In a 2010 piece in the publication of the Associated Departments of English, Guillory writes,

> In his two great works of the 1920s, *Principles of Literary Criticism* and *Practical Criticism*, Richards constructed a psychology of reading on the foundation of the stimulus-response model emerging in Russia by Ivan Pavlov, in the United States by John Watson, and in Britain by Charles Sherrington, author of *The Integrative Action of the Nervous System*, the work that strongly influenced Richards in *Principles of Literary Criticism*. This scientific or perhaps quasi-scientific origin of close reading is often forgotten in current accounts of our disciplinary practices. (12)

He then goes on to make the connection to literary study:

> Richards understood his task in teaching Cambridge undergraduates as the training of their literary judgment, which he hoped to put on a surer, scientific footing. The faculty of judgment is what he meant by the term "literary criticism" in the *Principles of Literary Criticism*. But judgment, he argued, depended on an underlying cognitive potentiality, which is the focusing of attention in reading. (Guillory 12)[4]

What Guillory does not mention is that Sherrington was, in fact, a member of the Eugenics Society in Britain – not surprising, as eugenics was considered a reputable and respected science at the time.[5] As Columbia University professor emeritus of history Nancy Stepan writes in her 1982 book *The Idea of Race in Science: Great Britain 1800–1960*, many major British thinkers of the era were members of the Eugenics Society, including not just Sherrington but John Maynard Keynes, Havelock Ellis, and Arthur Balfour, who, of course, was a loyal servant of British colonialism and the author of the Balfour Declaration (119).

Why is it so difficult for even the most brilliant literary critics to see, first, the "horizontal" links between poems or poetic methods and their immediate sociopolitical and ideological contexts of production and reception and, second, the "vertical" links across historical time so that a contemporary poem can be read in relation to transhistorical ideologies and material practices, such as colonialism and race-science-inflected classificatory systems and hierarchies – long since naturalized – that undergird current methodologies and institutional structures?

Is it not self-evident that the elite status of English as a field – coming slowly to an end in the twenty-first-century – was a byproduct of the power and prestige of the British Empire?

The inability to think the micro (formal elements) and the macro (colonialism, eugenics) together could be, one might argue, a problem of the periodization of the discipline. Yet poetry critics have no problem ranging across millennia in speaking of the lyric – from the ancient Greek writings of Sappho to the twenty-first-century poems of Louise Glück.

Let me emphasize that what I am speaking about is not simply contextual and thematic but formal and structural – about how even the most foundational and seemingly neutral or "objective" elements of poems and of critical methodologies carry within them ideologies and assumptions that are unmarked and made to seem "natural." The link to power, violence, and war does not hold only for poetic products that are obviously marked as "political" but also for those poems read as "nonpolitical" – as delicate, nuanced, and, yes, "beautiful."

Take, for example, the poetic issue of tone. This is crucial to notions of the poetic speaker on both sides of the aesthetic spectrum: For traditionalists, it is linked to "voice"; for those hewing to the experimental side of things, it is a key rhetorical aspect tied to the deployment of language. Indeed, so many avant-gardists love the work of John Ashbery precisely because his tone is so often read as ironic and mediated, not simplemindedly sincere. Likewise, their affection for Frank O'Hara, whose poems radiate an urbane cosmopolitanism and a performatively throwaway-while-still-affecting tone. Yet one might ask, "Who has the privilege to be endlessly ironic?" "Why is sincerity in a poem seen as incredibly gauche?" Some poets must constantly regulate not only their stanzas, lines, and meter but also the rhetoric of the speakers in their poems and the tone of these speakers, so as to conform to the dictates of a dominant white culture and the logic of racial hierarchy.[6] And, it goes without saying that poets of color must also self-regulate in their lived lives – and I mean not just the slave Phyllis Wheatley but also the young black poet sitting in an all-white writing workshop or in her other English classes or walking down the street.

What is the link between the politics of the self/speaker and the politics of (poetic) regulation? What does it mean to strike the "right" or "proper" tone in a poem and in person? Preferably not too angry ("too black") or uncontrolled ("lacking in rigor"). Are emotional distance and an endlessly distanced and ironic pose in poetry the byproducts of colonial imperatives? Is an imperious tone tied to the imperium?[7]

Poetry scholars have largely failed to ask these important questions about both aesthetics and politics. Even internet hackers working on behalf of the Russian state to disrupt US electoral politics understand something that critics of American poetry seem – or choose – not to: that race is a core aspect of our society and conditions all social interactions, the flow of capital, our ideas of beauty, our ideas of imaginative and cognitive capacities, and so on. In response to the ruptures into the status quo of poetry studies brought about by a few unruly unmodel minorities in recent years, some poetry scholars have resorted to palliative responses, while others continue doing business as usual.

There are a number of typical moves that scholars still make to evade deeper structural and concrete material change in our thinking about poetics and race and about how our institutions and fields deploy their power in the service of racialized assumptions. One of these is tokenism: The inclusion of one or two black or brown bodies in a special journal issue, conference, or event, or the inclusion of one work by a minority writer or artist in a volume so as to foreclose the charge of racism is not new, of course, but it seems to have stepped up in recent years. Caroline Levine writes a chapter on the TV show *The Wire*, set in black Baltimore, in *Forms: Whole, Rhythm, Hierarchy Network* (2015), and Jonathan Culler includes snippets of Jay-Z's lyrics in his section on rhyme in *Theory of the Lyric* (2015). Yet neither engages more deeply with the long tradition of black critical thought or speak in their work of the historical circumstances that produced that work. Can one talk about hip-hop without discussing structural racism and centuries of rhetorical strategies used by black people as a means of sheer survival?

Another technique is the old colonial standby of divide and conquer, which involves making a sharp distinction between "good" POC mascots and angry "difficult" ones.[8] In his sympathetic piece on Kenneth Goldsmith in the October 5, 2015, issue of *The New Yorker*, staff writer Alec Wilkinson blatantly deployed what he implicitly characterizes as loyal black and brown poets against stridently angry Asian American poets and critics who criticized Goldsmith and the whiteness of the poetry avant-garde. Wilkinson's article also reduces the critique by Asian American scholars and poets of racism within the poetry world to either the petty *ressentiment* of individual poets against Goldsmith for his career success or the aggregated resentments of individual poets of color who were just "pissed off."[9] To have identified how Goldsmith's actions were an unacknowledged function of his white privilege and unmarked racial entitlement would have implicated Goldsmith – and Wilkinson himself. In short, Wilkinson deflects the focus to individuals – whether to the good intentions or the hurt feelings of well-meaning whites or to the actions of individual "good" or "bad" POC – rather than the larger edifices and ideologies structured by racial privilege and racism.

Let me be clear: I am not interested in whether individual persons are "racist" or not. My point is about something much larger: ideologies and structures as they intersect with our aesthetic practices – that is, reading and writing – and, most importantly, what we knowingly and unknowingly impart to our students about what poetry is and what the limits and possibilities of poems, including their poems, are. How do these imbedded racialized aesthetic and colonial ideologies limit the poetic means by which young poets of color might fully realize themselves and become poetic and political beings through language? What avenues of intellectual and meta-physical exploration, what means of creating new worlds through the forms of poetry are abrogated for them as they imbibe the explicit and implicit "universal" and objective" poetic concepts saturated with racial assumptions that are promulgated in an English poetry class or in a writing workshop?

In the poetic "tradition" we are usually taught, the perceptive feeling and thinking poetic speaker is almost always white, often male, and usually straight. He possesses the "freedom of the imagination." He is sensitive. His white interiority is rich and complex and contradictory and fine-grained. What gets conveyed to a young poet of color when almost every poem she reads is about the feelings and thoughts of white poetic speakers – their broken hearts, their erotic desires, their descriptions of starlings and wood thrushes and pine trees, or (as in Goldsmith's *Soliloquy*) the transcription of every word they utter in a week?

Let us think of the privileged links among the perceptual, perceptivity, the perceiver, and perceptiveness when it comes to poetry and the question of the gaze and the wider visual field in the world and on the white page. Let us not forget the aural too: Which rhythms, accents, tones are counted as proper, poetic? And whose?

What kind of violence is done to the potential a young person (white or of-color) might have – and only fleetingly or briefly possessed – to fully realize who they can be as poets and thinkers when what they are taught in poetics sends the unspoken message that the white poetic speaker, the white perceiving intellect is central – modernist, postmodernist – while the poetry of writers of color is only an ethnic sidebar, whose presence functions primarily as a means to inoculate white gatekeepers from the charge of racism?

How do our poetic techniques do violence as well? What constitutes "rigor"? "Craft"? Should a poet have the right to "borrow" the autopsy report of a murdered black body in the name of poetry? Like Goldsmith, Wilkinson the journalist sampled the words of people of color – in this case, Asian American critics and poets – stripping them from their contexts. Is this sort of extractive violence structurally akin to the extractive violence of British colonialism?

I am not saying that every poetry scholar should be a political activist, but one cannot be a responsible textual scholar if one pretends that literary analysis is a "neutral" activity and that the foundational concepts of our field are exempt from history. The technique of description is not a neutral exercise because the gaze of the (white) poet is not a neutral gaze.

It is intellectually dishonest and, yes, sloppy to willfully blind oneself to the social and political contexts, systems, structures, and histories that poetries come out of and are received. No wonder young scholars of color who study poetry (and often write it, too) have turned away from literary studies and English departments and have moved toward fields such as critical race studies (especially black studies), indigenous studies, American studies, performance studies, and gender and sexuality studies. The work of scholars and writers such as Christina Sharpe, Denise Ferreira da Silva, Sara Ahmed, Jared Sexton, M. NourbeSe Philip, Bhanu Kapil speak to them more than do the writings of traditional poetry scholars.

One might ask then, "Who cares what poetry scholars in the academy do then?" I myself do not want to turn my back on poetry studies, though I completely understand why so many younger scholars of color find good reason to, given the dismal current state of affairs. There are personal reasons for my attachment to literary studies but also, more importantly, realpolitik ones: What happens in English departments in the United States has a significant effect on not only US students but students around the world. I have seen firsthand the power *The Norton Anthology of Poetry* has on English professors and students in Palestinian universities and the mesmerizing hold the pronouncements of English professors at Harvard and other elite institutions have on English professors in China and Japan.

We are a superpower not only in the political world realm but in the literary one as well, and while the public image of Conceptual Poetry may have taken a hit in the United States, it still stands as the representative example of the American poetic avant-garde abroad, especially in the contemporary art world and especially in Europe.

I see at least six tasks worthy of taking on as poetry scholars and critics in the era of both Trump and Black Lives Matter and beyond:

1. Doing archival work (without fetishizing the archive) to uncover and recover forgotten BIPOC poets, working-class poets, women poets so as to reconceive/reframe/recontextualize literary history and to undo the whitewashing of English poetry history. The Lost & Found project at The CUNY Graduate Center, under the direction of Ammiel Alcalay, is a real spot of brightness in doing this kind of valuable work.
2. Decentering white poets and poetry scholars as the sole or primary objects of focus in poetics.[10]
3. Looking to alternative poetic and formal models of poetics and poetic thinking, such as Glissant's "poetics of relation" or Moten's idea of fugitivity. We need to focus on texts by a broader range of poets – including

non-English-language poets and those poets writing in English outside the United States and the UK – so that nonwhite poets are seen not just as examples of "difference" but also as creators of core concepts of poetics. Experimental minority poets can and do expand our ideas about English-language poetry and poetics.

4. Questioning supposedly "neutral," "objective," and "universal" concepts and assumptions of poetics.

5. Doing concrete acts, not making vague abstract and generalizing gestures, in one's scholarship and in one's life in a department, an institution, a professional organization. A white critic who gets cred for writing on race and African American poets cannot stand by silently when scholars of color are attacked for speaking out about race/racism, even if the white scholar would prefer to avoid "conflict." Silence is not neutrality but an active position one has chosen. Silence allows the status quo to remain, violence to continue, damage to be done. As Diana Taylor writes: "The academy cannot be separate from the political, economic, and ideological turmoil of our time: #States of Insecurity calls on academia to uphold its commitment to critical and historical reflection, inquiry, and intervention" ("2018 Presidential Theme"). Intervention, however, often entails taking concrete and uncomfortable action – not smooth armchair theorizing – for example, naming names (to do so seems uncollegial, unseemly).

6. Taking seriously the work that poems themselves do: as means of theorizing, as presenting possible alternative ways to think and interpret.

Despite the somewhat skeptical cast of this chapter, I am actually optimistic about what young poet-scholars, who are now just undergrads, grad students, and untenured professors, will bring about in the coming years. I am confident that in a few decades those in poetry studies will look back and think, "How did we ever think that we could do close readings of poems without also at least acknowledging the institutional and socio-historical contexts of the work?"

There is an urgent need to decolonize and desegregate poetry studies and literary studies in general – this would be beneficial to white students and white professors as well as students and professors of color. A *radical* revolution of aesthetics and politics is needed, a wholesale overturning and rethinking of English-language poetry and poetics from the foundations up, taking into account the ongoing and long-lasting effects of colonialism and racial capitalism and the racial ideologies they have produced (which of course, cannot be thought separately from class and gender). We do not need more ameliorative and tokenizing "diversity" practices. The myths of multiculturalism, "color-blindness," the "post-race," and the discourse of "diversity" have acted as smokescreens and impediments to intellectually honest and historically accountable scholarship on English-language poetics and poetry.

I end with a quote from Édouard Glissant's *Poetics of Relation*, in which he makes a crucial distinction between two modes of thinking, knowing, relating:

> [T]hought of the Other is sterile without the other of Thought.
>
> Thought of the Other is the moral generosity disposing me to accept the principle of alterity, to conceive of the world as not simple and straightforward, with only one truth – mine. But thought of the Other can dwell within me without making me alter course, without "prizing me open," without changing me within myself. An ethical principle, it is enough that I not violate it.
>
> The other of Thought is precisely this altering. Then I have to act. That is the moment I change my thought, without renouncing its contribution. I change, and I exchange. This is an aesthetics of turbulence whose corresponding ethics is not provided in advance.
>
> If, thus, we allow that an aesthetics is an art of conceiving, imagining, and acting, the other of Thought is the aesthetics implemented by me and by you to join the dynamics to which we are to contribute. This is the part fallen to me in an aesthetics of chaos, the work I am to undertake, the road I am to travel. Thought of the Other is occasionally presupposed by dominant populations, but with an utterly sovereign power, or proposed until it hurts by those under them, who set themselves free. The other of Thought is always set in motion by its confluences as a whole, in which each is changed by and changes the other.
>
> (Glissant 154–155)

Notes

1. By this term I make a distinction between work on poetry and poetics done by scholars in the academy and discussions about poetry and poetics in the "poetry world" – done mainly by poets and increasingly on online platforms, especially social media. While I am of the opinion that the walls between the two worlds should be broken down and am acutely aware that what happens in academic poetry studies lags far behind the discussions online, poetry scholarship still produces significant effects – even if not immediate or visible – for students of poetry, reviewers, practicing poets, literary critics, teachers at all levels, and others, as I discuss later in the chapter. I am aware that the discussions of race and poetry have been more "woke" in nonacademic settings though it remains to be seen whether those discussions – and the awarding of poetry prizes to a few poets of color in recent years – will shift the structures of power within English departments, MFA programs, and the literary world.

2. Though this chapter was written before the George Floyd protests, the facility and speed with which heads of corporations and universities were able to reel out their

"anti-anti-blackness" messaging – even as these same institutions continue to damage and destroy black, indigenous, and POC (BIPOC) bodies – demonstrate how neoliberal racial capitalism is endlessly adaptive to new challenges so as to insure its stranglehold on the world.

3. A few days earlier, on March 9, "Race and the Poetic Avant-Garde," a forum co-curated by Stefania Heim and me, went live on the *Boston Review*'s online site.

4. In the idea of "underlying cognitive potentiality," one can hear echoes of Jefferson's "quasi-scientific" judgment that black bodies lack the cognitive-imaginative apparatus to appreciate, much less write, poetry.

5. When I raised this connection to eugenics in the Q&A after a talk Guillory gave at Williams College in 2017, Guillory said he was unaware of it and did not seem in the least interested in the link (his talk was entitled "I.A. Richards and the Neurophysiology of Reading").

6. Thanks to Emily Vasiliauskas for planting the seeds of this thought.

7. I am indebted to David Lloyd for this idea.

8. For example, a major poetry scholar marshaled her Asian American dissertation student to denounce the work of another Asian American poetry scholar.

9. Tan Lin, one of the poets mentioned in the article, objected to his treatment by Wilkinson. In a letter to the editor, he wrote, "My comments about racism were not grounded in feelings of individual exclusion, as Wilkinson seems to suggest. Goldsmith's work needs to be evaluated by taking into account the complex role of race in contemporary poetry, and its context within national conversations about race. Many African-American poets objected to Goldsmith's performance, and their voices are almost entirely absent from Wilkinson's piece. The African-American poetry community merited more serious engagement than it got in the article. Just as troubling, the piece comments on a broad social problem having to do with racial inequality and reduces it to an individual grudge by a person of color" (n. pag.).

10. I must note that no BIPOC scholar of poetry has ever won the MLA's major book awards: the James Russell Lowell Prize or the first book prize.

Works Cited

Culler, Jonathan. *Theory of the Lyric*. Harvard University Press, 2015.

Glissant, Édouard. *Poetics of Relation*, translated by Betsy Wing. The University of Michigan Press, 1997.

Guillory, John. "Close Reading: Prologue and Epilogue." *ADE Bulletin* no. 149, 2010, pp. 8–14.

Hillebrandt, Claudia et al., editors. *Journal of Literary Theory* vol. 11, no. 1, March 2017.

Jackson, Virginia, and Yopie Prins, editors. *The Lyric Theory Reader: A Critical Anthology*. Johns Hopkins University Press, 2014.

Jefferson, Thomas. *Thomas Jefferson: Writings: Autobiography / Notes on the State of Virginia / Public and Private Papers / Addresses / Lectures*, edited by Merrill D. Paterson. Library of America, 1984.

Kim, Eunsong. "Appraising Newness: Whiteness, Neoliberalism, and the Building of the Archive for New Poetry." *Journal of Critical Library and Information Studies* vol. 1, no. 2, 2017, pp. 1–40.

Levine, Caroline. *Forms: Whole, Rhythm, Hierarchy, Network*. Princeton University Press, 2015.

Stepan, Nancy. *The Idea of Race in Science: Great Britain 1800–1960*. Macmillan Press, 1982.

Tan, Lin. "Mail." *The New Yorker*, October 12, 2015, www.newyorker.com/maga zine/2015/10/19/the-mail-from-the-october-19–2015-issue

Taylor, Diana. "2018 Presidential Theme: #States of Insecurity." *Modern Language Association*, 2018, www.mla.org/Convention/Convention-History/Past-Conventions/2018-Convention/2018-Presidential-Theme

Wilkinson, Alec. "Something Borrowed." *The New Yorker*, September 28, 2015, www.newyorker.com/magazine/2015/10/05/something-borrowed-wilkinson

FURTHER READING

TIMOTHY YU AND CAROLINE HENSLEY

Anthologies

Ager, Deborah Ager and M. E. Silverman, editors. *The Bloomsbury Anthology of Contemporary Jewish American Poetry*. Bloomsbury, 2013.

Animashaun, Abayomi, editor. *Others Will Enter the Gates: Immigrant Poets on Poetry, Influences, and Writing in America*. Black Lawrence Press, 2015.

Banerjee, Neelanjana, Summi Kaipa, and Pireeni Sundaralingam, editors. *Indivisible: An Anthology of Contemporary South Asian American Poetry*. University of Arkansas Press, 2010.

Bergvall, Caroline, Laynie Browne, Teresa Carmody, and Vanessa Place, editors. *I'll Drown My Book: Conceptual Writing by Women*. Les Figues, 2012.

Brown, Stacey Lynn and Oliver de la Paz, editors. *A Face to Meet the Faces: An Anthology of Contemporary Persona Poetry*. The University of Akron Press, 2012.

Chang, Victoria, editor. *Asian American Poetry: The Next Generation*. University of Illinois Press, 2004.

Dworkin, Craig and Kenneth Goldsmith, editors. *Against Expression: An Anthology of Conceptual Writing*. Northwestern University Press, 2011.

Fisher-Wirth, Ann and Laura-Gray Street, editors. *The Ecopoetry Anthology*. Trinity University Press, 2013.

Fuhrman, C. Marie and Dean Rader, editors. *Native Voices: Indigenous American Poetry, Craft and Conversations*. Tupelo Press, 2019.

Gardner, Drew, Nada Gordon, Sharon Mesmer, K. Silem Mohammad, and Gary Sullivan, editors. *Flarf: An Anthology of Flarf*. Edge, 2017.

Glenum, Lara and Arielle Greenberg, editors. *Gurlesque: The New Grrly, Grotesque, Burlesque Poetics*. Saturnalia, 2010.

González, Kevin A. and Lauren Shapiro, editors. *The New Census: An Anthology of Contemporary American Poetry*. Rescue Press, 2013.

Gould Axelrod, Steven, Camille Roman, and Thomas Travisano, editors. *The New Anthology of American Poetry. Vol. 3, Postmodernisms 1950–Present*. Rutgers University Press, 2012.

Hazelton, Rebecca and Alan Michael Parker, editors. *The Manifesto Project*. University of Akron Press, 2017.

Johnson, Dennis Loy and Valerie Merians, editors. *Poetry After 9/11: An Anthology of New York Poets*. Melville House, 2011.

Katz, Vincent, editor. *Readings in Contemporary Poetry: An Anthology of Poems Read at Dia, 2010–2016*. Dia Art Foundation, 2017.

Keniston, Ann and Jeffrey Gray, editors. *The New American Poetry of Engagement: A 21st Century Anthology*. McFarland & Co., 2012.

Nielsen, Aldon Lynn, and Lauri Ramey, editors. *What I Say: Innovative Poetry by Black Writers in America*. University of Alabama Press, 2015.

Rankine, Claudia, and Lisa Sewell, editors. *Eleven More American Women Poets in the 21st Century: Poetics Across North America*. Wesleyan University Press, 2012.

Rankine, Claudia, and Juliana Spahr, editors. *American Women Poets in the 21st Century: Where Lyric Meets Language*. Wesleyan University Press, 2002.

Ridker, Andrew, editor. *Privacy Policy: The Anthology of Surveillance Poetics*. Black Ocean, 2014.

Rosen, Kenneth, editor. *Voices of the Rainbow: Contemporary Poetry by Native Americans*. Skyhorse Publishing, 2012.

Rowell, Charles Henry, editor. *Angles of Ascent: A Norton Anthology of Contemporary African American Poetry*. W.W. Norton & Co., 2013.

Smith, Tracy K., editor. *American Journal: Fifty Poems for Our Time*. Graywolf Press, in association with the Library of Congress, 2018.

Taylor, Shelly and Abraham Smith, editors. *Hick Poetics: An Anthology of Contemporary Rural American Poetry*. Lost Roads Press, 2015.

General

Aldama, Frederick Luis. *Formal Matters in Contemporary Latino Poetry*. Palgrave Macmillan, 2013.

Bendixen, Alfred and Stephanie Burt, editors. *The Cambridge History of American Poetry*. Cambridge University Press, 2015.

Bernes, Jasper. *The Work of Art in the Age of Deindustrialization*. Stanford University Press, 2017.

Bernstein, Charles. *Attack of the Difficult Poems: Essays and Inventions*. University of Chicago Press, 2011.

Bruns, Gerald L. *What Are Poets For?: An Anthropology of Contemporary Poetry and Poetics*. University of Iowa Press, 2012.

Burt, Stephanie. *The Poem Is You*. Harvard University Press, 2016.

Caplan, David. *Rhyme's Challenge: Hip Hop, Poetry, and Contemporary Rhyming Culture*. Oxford University Press, 2014.

Dewey, Anne and Libbie Rifkin, editors. *Among Friends: Engendering the Social Site of Poetry*. University of Iowa Press, 2013.

Dowdy, Michael. *Broken Souths: Latina/o Poetic Responses to Neoliberalism and Globalization*. University of Arizona Press, 2013.

Epstein, Andrew. *Attention Equals Life: The Pursuit of the Everyday in Contemporary Poetry and Culture*. Oxford University Press, 2016.

Fink, Thomas and Judith Halden-Sullivan, editors. *Reading the Difficulties: Dialogues with Contemporary American Innovative Poetry*. University of Alabama Press, 2014.

Finkelstein, Norman. *On Mount Vision: Forms of the Sacred in Contemporary American Poetry*. University of Iowa Press, 2010.

Frost, Elisabeth A. *The Feminist Avant-Garde in American Poetry*. University of Iowa Press, 2005.

Gander, Forrest. *Redstart: An Ecological Poetics*. University of Iowa Press, 2012.

Gray, Jeffrey and Ann Keniston, editors. *The News from Poems: Essays on the 21st-Century American Poetry of Engagement*. University of Michigan Press, 2016.

Howard, W. Scott and Broc Rossell, editors. *Poetics and Praxis "after" Objectivism*. University of Iowa Press, 2018.

Hume, Angela and Gillian Osborne, editors. *Ecopoetics: Essays in the Field*. University of Iowa Press, 2018.

Hunter, Walt. *Forms of a World: Contemporary Poetry and the Making of Globalization*. Fordham University Press, 2019.

Jeon, Joseph Jonghyun. *Racial Things, Racial Forms: Objecthood in Avant-Garde Asian American Poetry*. University of Iowa Press, 2012.

Johnson, Javon. *Killing Poetry: Blackness and the Making of Slam and Spoken Word Communities*. Rutgers University Press, 2017.

Jones, Meta DuEwa. *The Muse Is Music: Jazz Poetry from the Harlem Renaissance to Spoken Word*. University of Illinois Press, 2011.

Keller, Lynn. *Thinking Poetry: Readings in Contemporary Women's Exploratory Poetics*. University of Iowa Press, 2010.

Keniston, Ann. *Ghostly Figures: Memory and Belatedness in Postwar American Poetry*. University of Iowa Press, 2015.

Kinnahan, Linda A. *Lyric Interventions: Feminism, Experimental Poetry, and Contemporary Discourse*. University of Iowa Press, 2005.

Kirsch, Adam. *The Modern Element: Essays on Contemporary Poetry*. W.W. Norton & Company, 2008.

Milne, Heather. *Poetry Matters: Neoliberalism, Affect, and the Posthuman in Twenty-First-Century North American Feminist Poetics*. University of Iowa Press, 2018.

Mitchell, Angelyn and Danille K. Taylor, editors. *The Cambridge Companion to African American Women's Literature*. Cambridge University Press, 2009.

Moten, Fred. *In the Break: The Aesthetics of the Black Radical Tradition*. University of Minnesota Press, 2003.

Nealon, Christopher. *The Matter of Capital: Poetry and Crisis in the American Century*. Harvard University Press, 2011.

Nolan, Sarah. *Unnatural Ecopoetics: Unlikely Spaces in Contemporary Poetry*. University of Nevada Press, 2017.

Orr, David. *You, Too, Could Write a Poem: Selected Reviews and Essays, 2000–2015*. Penguin Books, 2017.

Perloff, Marjorie. *Unoriginal Genius: Poetry by Other Means in the New Century*. University of Chicago Press, 2010.

Phelps, Jennifer and Elizabeth Robinson, editors. *Quo Anima: Innovation and Spirituality in Contemporary Women's Poetry*. The University of Akron Press, 2019.

Ramey, Lauri. *A History of African American Poetry*. Cambridge University Press, 2019.

Reed, Anthony. *Freedom Time: The Poetics and Politics of Black Experimental Writing*. Johns Hopkins University Press, 2016.

Retallack, Joan and Juliana Spahr, editors. *Poetry and Pedagogy: The Challenge of the Contemporary*. Springer, 2016.

Richardson, Mark, editor. *The Cambridge Companion to American Poets*. Cambridge University Press, 2015.

Ronda, Margaret. *Remainders: American Poetry at Nature's End*. Stanford University Press, 2018.

Scigaj, Leonard M. *Sustainable Poetry: Four American Ecopoets*. University Press of Kentucky, 2015.

Shockley, Evie. *Renegade Poetics: Black Aesthetics and Formal Innovation in African American Poetry*. University of Iowa Press, 2011.

Skillman, Nikki. *The Lyric in the Age of the Brain*. Harvard University Press, 2016.

Spiegelman, Willard. *The Didactic Muse: Scenes of Instruction in Contemporary American Poetry*. Princeton University Press, 2014.

Vincent, John. *Queer Lyrics: Difficulty and Closure in American Poetry*. Springer, 2016.

Wang, Dorothy J. *Thinking Its Presence: Form, Race, and Subjectivity in Contemporary Asian American Poetry*. Stanford University Press, 2014.

Yu, Timothy. *Race and the Avant-Garde: Experimental and Asian American Poetry since 1965*. Stanford University Press, 2009.

Articles/Chapters/Interviews

Altieri, Charles. "What Theory Can Learn from New Directions in Contemporary American Poetry." *New Literary History* vol. 43, no. 1, Winter 2012, pp. 65–87.

"The Place of Rhetoric in Contemporary American Poetics: Jennifer Moxley and Juliana Spahr." *Chicago Review* vol. 56, no. 2/3, Autumn 2011, pp. 127–145.

Ashton, Jennifer. "Labor and the Lyric: The Politics of Self-Expression in Contemporary American Poetry." *American Literary History* vol. 25, no. 1, Spring 2013, pp. 217–230.

Avant, A. H. Jerriod, Joshua Bennett, Rickey Laurentiis et al. "Coming to the Clearing: Contemporary Black Poets in Conversation." *Callaloo* vol. 39, no. 2, 2016, pp. 277–289.

Davidson, Michael, editor. "American Poetry, 2000–2009." *Contemporary Literature* vol. 52, no. 4, 2011, pp. 597–915.

Gray, Jeffrey. "Precocious Testimony: Poetry and the Uncommemorable." *Literature after 9/11*, edited by Ann Keniston and Jeanne Follansbee Quinn. Routledge, 2013, pp. 270–293.

Hong, Cathy Park. "Delusions of Whiteness in the Avant-Garde." *Lana Turner Journal of Poetry and Opinion* vol. 7, 2014.

Hume, Angela. "Imagining Ecopoetics: An Interview with Robert Hass, Brenda Hillman, Evelyn Reilly, and Jonathan Skinner." *ISLE: Interdisciplinary Studies in Literature and Environment* vol. 19, no. 4, Autumn 2012, pp. 751–766.

Hume, Angela and Samia Rahimtoola. "Introduction: Queering Ecopoetics." *ISLE: Interdisciplinary Studies in Literature and Environment* vol. 25, no. 1, Winter 2018, pp. 134–149.

Shivani, Anis. "Is This the Best American Poetry?" *The Midwest Quarterly* vol. 51, no. 1, 2009, pp. 92–110.

Index

Index

Cambridge Companions to ...

AUTHORS

Edward Albee edited by Stephen J. Bottoms

Margaret Atwood edited by Coral Ann Howells

W. H. Auden edited by Stan Smith

Jane Austen edited by Edward Copeland and Juliet McMaster (second edition)

Balzac edited by Owen Heathcote and Andrew Watts

Beckett edited by John Pilling

Bede edited by Scott DeGregorio

Aphra Behn edited by Derek Hughes and Janet Todd

Saul Bellow edited by Victoria Aarons

Walter Benjamin edited by David S. Ferris

William Blake edited by Morris Eaves

James Baldwin edited by Michele Elam

Boccaccio edited by Guyda Armstrong, Rhiannon Daniels, and Stephen J. Milner

Jorge Luis Borges edited by Edwin Williamson

Brecht edited by Peter Thomson and Glendyr Sacks (second edition)

The Brontës edited by Heather Glen

Bunyan edited by Anne Dunan-Page

Frances Burney edited by Peter Sabor

Byron edited by Drummond Bone

Albert Camus edited by Edward J. Hughes

Willa Cather edited by Marilee Lindemann

Cervantes edited by Anthony J. Cascardi

Chaucer edited by Piero Boitani and Jill Mann (second edition)

Chekhov edited by Vera Gottlieb and Paul Allain

Kate Chopin edited by Janet Beer

Caryl Churchill edited by Elaine Aston and Elin Diamond

Cicero edited by Catherine Steel

J. M. Coetzee edited by Jarad Zimbler

Coleridge edited by Lucy Newlyn

Wilkie Collins edited by Jenny Bourne Taylor

Joseph Conrad edited by J. H. Stape

H. D. edited by Nephie J. Christodoulides and Polina Mackay

Dante edited by Rachel Jacoff (second edition)

Daniel Defoe edited by John Richetti

Don DeLillo edited by John N. Duvall

Charles Dickens edited by John O. Jordan

Emily Dickinson edited by Wendy Martin

John Donne edited by Achsah Guibbory

Dostoevskii edited by W. J. Leatherbarrow

Theodore Dreiser edited by Leonard Cassuto and Claire Virginia Eby

John Dryden edited by Steven N. Zwicker

W. E. B. Du Bois edited by Shamoon Zamir

George Eliot edited by George Levine and Nancy Henry (second edition)

T. S. Eliot edited by A. David Moody

Ralph Ellison edited by Ross Posnock

Ralph Waldo Emerson edited by Joel Porte and Saundra Morris

William Faulkner edited by Philip M. Weinstein

Henry Fielding edited by Claude Rawson

F. Scott Fitzgerald edited by Ruth Prigozy

Flaubert edited by Timothy Unwin

E. M. Forster edited by David Bradshaw

Benjamin Franklin edited by Carla Mulford

Brian Friel edited by Anthony Roche

Robert Frost edited by Robert Faggen

Gabriel García Márquez edited by Philip Swanson

Elizabeth Gaskell edited by Jill L. Matus

Edward Gibbon edited by Karen O'Brien and Brian Young

Goethe edited by Lesley Sharpe

Günter Grass edited by Stuart Taberner

Thomas Hardy edited by Dale Kramer

David Hare edited by Richard Boon

Nathaniel Hawthorne edited by Richard Millington

Seamus Heaney edited by Bernard O'Donoghue

Ernest Hemingway edited by Scott Donaldson

Homer edited by Robert Fowler

Horace edited by Stephen Harrison

Ted Hughes edited by Terry Gifford

Ibsen edited by James McFarlane

Henry James edited by Jonathan Freedman

Samuel Johnson edited by Greg Clingham

Ben Jonson edited by Richard Harp and Stanley Stewart

James Joyce edited by Derek Attridge (second edition)

TOPICS

9 781108 741958